Twenty-First-Century Feminist Classrooms

COMPARATIVE FEMINIST STUDIES SERIES
Chandra Talpade Mohanty, Series Editor

PUBLISHED BY PALGRAVE MACMILLAN:

Sexuality, Obscenity, Community:
Women, Muslims, and the Hindu Public in Colonial India
by Charu Gupta

Twenty-First-Century Feminist Classrooms

Pedagogies of Identity and Difference

Edited by
Amie A. Macdonald
and Susan Sánchez-Casal

For Chandra

Twenty-First-Century Feminist Classrooms
Copyright © Amie Macdonald and Susan Sánchez-Casal, 2002.
All rights reserved. No part of this book may be used or reproduced in any manner whatsoever without written permission except in the case of brief quotations embodied in critical articles or reviews.

First published 2002 by
PALGRAVE MACMILLAN™
175 Fifth Avenue, New York, N.Y. 10010 and
Houndmills, Basingstoke, Hampshire, England RG21 6XS.
Companies and representatives throughout the world.

PALGRAVE MACMILLAN is the global academic imprint of the PALGRAVE MACMILLAN division of St. Martin's Press, LLC and of Palgrave Macmillan Ltd. Macmillan® is a registered trademark in the United States, United Kingdom and other countries. Palgrave is a registered trademark in the European Union and other countries.

ISBN 0–312–29533–2 hardback
ISBN 0–312–29534–0 paperback

Library of Congress Cataloging-in-Publication Data
Twenty-first-century feminist classrooms: pedagogies of identities and difference / [edited by] Sánchez-Casal, Susan, and Amie A. Macdonald.
    p.   cm. – (Comparative feminist studies)
    Includes bibliographical references and index.
    ISBN 0–312–29534–0 (alk. paper)—ISBN 0–312–29533–2
    1. Feminism and education.   2. Multicultural education.   I. Sánchez-Casal, Susan.   II. Macdonald, Amie.   III. Series.

LC197.T94   2002
370.11'5—dc21

                                                                    2002020725

A catalogue record for this book is available from the British Library.

Design by Letra Libre, Inc.

First edition: September 2002
10 9 8 7 6 5 4 3 2 1

Printed in the United States of America

CONTENTS

Acknowledgments

We are very grateful to Chandra Talpade Mohanty, not only for encouraging us to take on this project, but also for her brilliant intellectual companionship throughout the process of bringing the book to press. Chandra's friendship and our shared homespace continue to support and inspire us in every way.

We thank all of our antiracist feminist friends and colleagues who are always willing to think through difficult theoretical and political issues with us. We want to give special thanks to Margo Okazawa-Rey for her pedagogical mentoring, to Gwyneth Kirk for her abiding interest in the project, and to Tamara R. Williams for her insightful and enthusiastic comments on earlier drafts of our work. We are deeply appreciative to Satya P. Mohanty for his generosity of spirit in giving us his challenging and rigorous commentary on our introductory essay. We also want to acknowledge Ilia O. Edwards-Vargas and thank her for many stimulating conversations about pedagogical theory and practice. We recognize and thank our colleagues in the Women's Studies Program, Thematic Studies Program, and Philosophy Department at John Jay College and the Departments of Spanish and Women's Studies at Hamilton College for feminist intellectual sustenance and for opening an academic space to teach our radical courses. Amie extends special thanks to the philosophers Enrique Chávez-Arvizo, MaryAnn McClure, and John Pittman, for their interest in and enduring support for the project. Susan thanks Nancy Rabinowitz for her initiative and leadership in constructing feminist institutional "spaces" that nurture antiracist, feminist teachers and scholars at Hamilton College.

We have benefited enormously from audience comments and questions at panels where selections of this work were presented, including those sponsored by the Radical Philosophy Association Meetings at San Francisco State University in 1999, the Dean of Graduate Studies at John Jay College in 2000, the Women's Studies Program at John Jay College in 2000, the Kirkland Project for the Study of Gender, Culture, and Society at Hamilton College in 2001, and the Peace Studies Regional Conference at Hamilton College in 2001.

For generous research funding, we acknowledge and thank the Office of the Dean of Faculty at Hamilton College and the Professional Staff Congress of the City University of New York.

We want to express our gratitude to Elenitsa Weld of Hamilton College, for her diligent editorial assistance and preparation of several drafts of the manuscript. We are indebted to Kristi Long, Roee Raz, and Meg Weaver at Palgrave Macmillan for their commitment to the book.

For his innovative and relentless technical support, we extend our thanks and appreciation to Craig Kollegger.

To our contributors and to our students we give our deepest gratitude, for sharing with us the project of reaching for innovation in antiracist feminist teaching and learning.

Amie thanks her husband Gur Melamede for his passionate enthusiasm for the project and for his spectacular dedication to their family; both have been crucial to the completion of this book. Amie is grateful to her son Ishai and to the Macdonald and Melamede families, for everything they are.

Susan thanks her husband Craig Kollegger for working hard to keep the home fires burning and for his willingness to listen to endless brainstorming and problem-solving during the production of this volume. Susan gives special thanks to her sons Ryan, Colin, and Max Fernando, and to the entire Sánchez family, for their colorful love and support.

Finally, Amie and Susan thank each other for our shared dedication to depth, honesty, and love as devoted friends of heart and mind.

INTRODUCTION

FEMINIST REFLECTIONS ON
THE PEDAGOGICAL RELEVANCE
OF IDENTITY

Susan Sánchez-Casal and Amie A. Macdonald

We are proposing a new paradigm for feminist educators by reevaluating the significance and application of identity theory in feminist pedagogy. Specifically, we formulate a new theoretical approach that actively deploys a post-positivist realist[1] position on identity and experience in the feminist classroom. Up until now, feminist pedagogy has utilized identity categories mainly as explanatory claims about how oppression works in the world, but not as a way of revolutionizing the methodologies of feminist teaching. We propose that by mobilizing the theoretical and pedagogical application of realist identity theory feminist educators can activate the explanatory power of identity—specifically the way that identity categories refer outward to and produce knowledge about our shared social world. Moreover, our approach provides a coherent theoretical framework for the classroom that avoids the essentialist tendency to overlook the dual status of cultural identities as both real and constructed. At the theoretical level, feminist educators have taken seriously the constructed nature of social identities; still much of feminist teaching continues to operate on the unspoken essentialist assumption that identities are stable, homogeneous and deterministic. We assert that feminist educators can organize teaching practices that democratize and enhance the production of liberatory knowledge by engaging the realist view that identities are politically and epistemically significant, while also being variable, nonessential and radically historical (Moya 2000).

Theorists from a wide range of disciplines have debated the relevance of identity to literary criticism, history, cultural studies and so on. But until now no one has theorized feminist pedagogy through a realist formulation of the epistemic status of identity. Postpositivist realist theory asserts that identity and experience are mutually constitutive, that one's social location will to a large extent determine the experiences one has, and that in turn, one's cultural identity will affect how one makes sense of those experiences. By understanding experience as theory-mediated, realist theory asserts that cultural identities can be *more* or *less* epistemically reliable depending on the theoretical bias through which experience is interpreted. For example, when a person takes on the cultural identity *woman,* her experience as a *woman* is mediated by various—and potentially contradictory—theories; consequently, her identity as a *woman* does not automatically produce accurate knowledge about gender oppression in a self-evident way. We (Amie and Susan) have both taught extensively about sexual violence to women in private colleges, public universities, community centers, women's centers, multicultural student associations, and faculty groups. On each of these occasions we have encountered women who readily embrace the analysis of male sexual violence as a manifestation of systematic sexist oppression; but we have also encountered many women—some of whom are themselves survivors of sexual assault—who reject feminist analyses of sexual violence and who reproduce sexist ideologies that assign blame to women who are sexually violated. Thus, identifying as a *woman* can be *more* or *less* epistemically valid, depending on how accurately that identity explains the consequences of women's social locations, i.e., that sexist oppression targets women on the basis of gender as potential victims of sexual assault. This example demonstrates the accuracy of the realist claim that identity can both enhance and obstruct our ability to know, thereby highlighting the indeterminate relationship among experience, identity and knowledge.

In feminist classrooms where teachers encourage students to activate their ability to know through experience, the pursuit of truth is immediately politicized by the various and often competing assertions that students advance about their identities and our shared social world. Thus feminist educators need a pedagogical strategy that can manage the proliferation of experience-based knowledge claims and avoid the anti-democratic tendency to see experiential claims to know (especially to know about oppression) as sacrosanct. Our pedagogical theory addresses these political complexities by foregrounding the epistemic role of experience and identity, while at the same time providing us with the means to examine and contest untheorized assertions about an individual's or a social group's lived experiences. Furthermore, we believe that a realist feminist pedagogy will democratize the classroom by drawing upon the full range of student and faculty subject positions in the production of knowledge.

Rethinking feminist pedagogy through the lens of realist identity theory thereby generates an entirely new epistemic framework for the feminist classroom, one that suggests a fundamental restructuring of authority. As we see it, much of the discussion on authority in the feminist classroom is characterized by an implicit binarism that locates two subjects in the classroom: teacher and student. But by reframing the discussion of epistemic authority through realist theory we are able to break open the dyad of teacher/student by placing it in dynamic and continuous dialogue with a third term, *difference*. We propose that feminist educators ground our analyses in the conceptual triad of <teacher/student/difference>, an approach that highlights how multiply-situated cultural identities can be engaged by feminist teachers in order to shift epistemic authority in the classroom. Given that " . . . feminist and antiracist pedagogies place a high value on subjective experience as a route to understanding our lives and the lives of others and emphasize the legitimacy of knowledge that arises from socially marginalized positions" (Bell, Morrow, Tastsoglou 23), we see our introduction of this conceptual triad as building upon the theoretical trajectory of both realist and antiracist feminisms.

Our theory assumes that feminist teachers can advocate experiential and identity-based epistemologies as the foundation for producing objective knowledge in the classroom. Postpositivist realism demonstrates how theory-mediated objectivity—the only kind of objectivity possible for us—is fully attainable within a rich epistemic framework that fundamentally accepts the function of experience and identity in the creation of knowledge and assessment of truth.[2] Retheorizing difference as the subject of the feminist classroom transfers epistemic authority from the deterministic binarism of teacher/student to shifting communities of knowers that may include both faculty and students. These knowledge-making communities—what we call *communities of meaning*—cultivate a diversity of socially embedded truth claims out of which epistemic wholeness develops. We therefore recommend that feminists continue to ground our teaching on the claim that there are real social, political, and epistemic consequences of identity, but that we reject essentialist feminist and liberation theories that understand identity to be fully determinate of what and how we know. This model is crucial for feminist pedagogies: first, because it does not force us to give up on the ability to know, on the ability to make evaluations, take positions, identify causes and outcomes (of oppression, violence, colonialism, for example); second, because it takes seriously the role of experience and identity in the collective production and assessment of knowledge; third, because in so doing it does not absolutely anchor our ability to know in our identities, nor does it make the postmodernist claim that all identity categories are ontologically and hence epistemically unreliable.[3]

Critique of Essentialism in Pedagogy

As feminist educators we reject essentialist identity theories because of their failure to account for the uncertain epistemic effects of social identities; nonetheless, we believe that in practice many feminist teachers continue to operate on deterministic assumptions about identity and its relationship to knowledge production. Because essentialism posits a direct correspondence between identity and knowledge-making, this theory supports the view that only marginalized people can produce liberatory knowledge about oppression. Consequently, essentialism illegitimately fixes authority in the classroom by ignoring the fact that "marginalized" students may also produce inaccurate knowledge about the social world and their relationship to it. Moreover, feminist teachers who rely on essentialist assumptions about the epistemic status of identity give students from "dominant" social locations only one epistemic choice: to accept or reject the knowledge produced by those who are socially marginalized. Perhaps even more importantly, this theoretical standpoint prevents feminist teachers from thoroughly investigating our own implication in the 'isms' that constitute our social world, since it allows us to proceed from the false notion that our political identities as feminists guarantee that the knowledge we produce in the classroom is automatically "progressive."

Like many feminist scholars we write directly from the experience of disenchantment: frustration and dissatisfaction with both student resistance in our classrooms as well as with the limits and failures of our own teaching methods.[4] While we know that the Women's Studies, Race and Ethnic Studies classrooms (or any classroom that centers on what Melanie Kaye/Kantrowitz refers to as "Liberation Studies") will always be marked by conflict, dissonance, and a lack of resolution, we believe that essentialist frameworks prevent us from accurately identifying the multiple origins of student resistance. Moreover, essentialist tendencies in feminist teaching may exacerbate student resistance itself while at the same time robbing us of the pedagogical resources necessary to engage it productively and creatively as a salient aspect—and not an aberration—of the feminist classroom.

After years of negotiating tense classroom dynamics on our feet, attributing what feels like the "stuckness" of our courses to the refusal of "dominant" students[5] to "take risks," to "give up or unlearn privilege," and to "question themselves and their assumptions," we have come to believe that what goes wrong in our classrooms has as much to do with the inadequacy of feminist pedagogies as with the problematic attitudes and responses of our students. Classroom discussions of racism, violence against women, homohatred, and so on, commonly produce a standoff between what many of us term the "progressive" students who understand and embrace antiracist, feminist analyses of reality and "dominant" students who cling to conservative positions—for example, assumptions that racism doesn't exist anymore, that racism has nothing to do with white people, that rapists are strangers jumping out of bushes, or that gay and lesbian people wouldn't experience discrimination if they simply wouldn't "flaunt" their sexuality. We don't mean to dispute the myriad ways that real social contradictions divide a classroom along the lines of race, class, gender, and sexuality, and help to create both ideological polarities and unequal power relations among students. We also do not mean to suggest that the "right" pedagogical methods can talk students out of their deeply held and often problematical belief systems. One of the ethical challenges of the antiracist feminist classroom is precisely the absence of a comforting boundary between students and the object of study; the feminist classroom collapses the difference between learning about the world "out there" and investigating how students' lives are implicated in that world—how the world "out there" also operates in the classroom and turns students themselves into objects of study. Our critique of essentialism in feminist pedagogy thus enables us to reevaluate the origins and uses of student resistance by recoding these conflictive moments as central to the process of feminist teaching.

We therefore advance the claim that by anchoring feminist antiracist pedagogy in realist identity theory, educators can engage students' inaccurate evaluations of power relations as a productive and necessary step in feminist teaching and learning. In this way feminist teachers can construct a learning community that effectively challenges reactionary thinking in "dominant" students without prematurely reducing these students to mere embodiments of reactionary politics. At the same time our theoretical groundwork provides a way for "marginalized" students to speak and learn about oppression without falsely imbuing them with uncontested epistemic authority and the unchallenged power to speak "for" their "people."

The feminist pedagogical principles that guide our classroom strategies—decentering the authority of the professor, developing and foregrounding subjugated knowledges, legitimizing personal identity and experience as the foundation of authentic and liberatory knowledges (especially marginalized identities and experiences), discussion-based classes, emphasis on student voice—have enormous power to democratize knowledge production in the classroom, but only if we engage them through a progressive theoretical standpoint on the epistemic salience of cultural identity. Reframing our teaching through realist identity theory will not solve all of the problems in the feminist classroom, but it will provide a coherent context for developing pedagogies that account for the complex networks of privilege and oppression that structure all of our identities. By foregrounding the indeterminacy of the relationship between experience and knowledge, and by providing a theoretical means for teachers and students to both assert and contest explanatory claims about social groups and the world, the feminist classroom can construct and deconstruct epistemic authority according to shifting curricular and political contexts.

Difference as the Theoretical Subject of the Feminist Classroom

In 1981 *This Bridge Called My Back: Writings by Radical Women of Color* (Moraga and Anzaldúa) cast a critical eye on the white solipsism, homophobia, classism and cultural imperialism of the feminist movement by criticizing and negating prevailing feminist understandings of difference.[6] By retheorizing the relationships among experience, identity and epistemic authority, these critical perspectives in turn generated groundbreaking social theories focused on interaction among women of color and between oppressed women and society. Subsequently Third Wave feminists re-engaged the brilliant analyses formulated in *This Bridge* and sustained this revolutionary theoretical movement by producing comprehensive criticisms of identity politics. From a visionary and self-critical standpoint, many Third Wave feminists have argued that personal identity is complex and heterogeneous, and thus that dominance and subjugation can exist simultaneously in individuals and social groups (Gloria Anzaldúa, María Lugones, Cherríe Moraga, Chandra Talpade Mohanty, Bernice Johnson Reagon, Paula Moya, and others). These theories of identity open an expansive new paradigm for feminist pedagogy, one that simultaneously reaffirms the epistemic status of cultural identity while it challenges the wholesale validity of experience—including the experience of oppression—in the production of knowledge.

The question for feminist educators, then, becomes: How do we transform our teaching in order to engage the dramatic shifts in the theory and practice of antiracist feminist identity politics? In 1989 Elizabeth Ellsworth addressed this question by redefining the task of the feminist teacher from one of " . . . building democratic dialogue between free and equal individuals," to that of " . . . building coalition among the multiple, shifting, intersecting, and sometimes contradictory groups carrying unequal weights of legitimacy within the culture and the classroom"(109). Ellsworth's main focus in this essay is critiquing the "repressive myths" of critical pedagogy as decontextualized, abstract, and universalist principles that reproduce relations of domination in the classroom. She is particularly interested in scrutinizing the failure of critical pedagogy to decentralize the teacher's authority and to produce democratic dialogue among diverse students. Ellsworth's insightful analysis broke the silence among feminist teachers about the shortcomings of critical pedagogical tactics commonly applied in our classrooms, and even more significantly, it opened a space for feminists to reevaluate the epistemic and political impact of identity and difference. Ellsworth's analysis therefore enables us to think deeply about the relevance of identity to feminist pedagogy. However, because Ellsworth continues to theorize these issues from within the binary of teacher/student, she does not offer a new analytical framework that coheres with the advances in feminist and realist identity theory.

Our theory attempts to surpass this binary and advance feminist pedagogy by proposing that *difference* be the theoretical subject of the antiracist feminist classroom. Naming *difference* as the theoretical subject of the classroom provides a contextual frame that allows the multiple identities—and thus the authority—of teacher and student to shift according to changing circumstances and contexts in or outside the classroom.[7] In this model, the teacher moves between centered and decentered positions, not because she renounces all authoritative postures as dominating and coercive, but because she acts upon a revolutionized concept of experience and identity; this conceptual foundation enables the teacher to cultivate the ground for contesting and/or qualifying claims to know, while upholding cultural identity as a crucial factor in the production of knowledge.

By focusing classroom production through the theoretical triad of <teacher/student/difference> we suggest that neither teachers nor students are the most authentic knowers in the classroom, nor is either constituency automatically most equipped to guide the production of liberatory knowledge.[8] Our theoretical repositioning moves feminist pedagogy forward into a conceptual space where we can produce objectivity in the classroom through a sustained focus on difference. For even Ellsworth's pragmatic analysis of critical and feminist pedagogies ultimately retreats to a postmodernist "pedagogy of the unknowable," where it is impossible for us to make objective explanatory claims about our shared social world. The political and epistemic power of our theory is that it does not shy away from the claim that we can produce objective knowledge about social groups and the world; where other theorists see the proliferation of difference as an obstruction to our ability to know, our theory is instead based upon the supposition that it is only from within the examination of difference that we can reach for theory-mediated objectivity.[9] This theory is ontologically compelling since we develop our epistemology from the reality of human difference, the complexity of cultural identities, and the contingency of identity upon experience.

We offer an example to show how the cultivation of difference in the classroom according to the tenets of realist identity theory will help to facilitate political coalition across differences as it makes possible the production of theory-mediated objective knowledge. Susan's course "The Latina Experience" examines the literary and cultural production of Latina writers whose social difference casts them to the margins of both "dominant" society and Latino communities. The course is grounded in a theoretical framework that assumes the epistemic and political relevance of cultural identities and that foregrounds an analysis of difference as it intersects both individuals and social groups. During a discussion of Cherríe Moraga's essay "A Long Line of Vendidas" (1983), the class began to debate the significance of color in Latino/a social experience and identity construction. In response to Moraga's claim that she began to identify with her brownness only after she came out as a lesbian, a dark-skinned Dominican student—we will call him Nelson—argued that we could use Moraga's analysis to conclude that light-skinned Latinos/as "aren't Latino the same way that dark-skinned Latinos are, since they don't experience racism." Nelson's argument rested on the theory that since light-skinned Latinos/as are not targeted by anti-Latino racist oppression, they therefore lack vital experiences that constitute Latinoness in the United States.

Susan—who makes explicit in the classroom the social, epistemic, and political consequences of her own status as a light-skinned Latina—said nothing, waiting for the class to respond. After a moment of silence, a light-skinned Dominican—whom we will call David—contested Nelson's claim by saying "well Nelson, but there are Dominicans who are darker than you even; does that make them more Dominican than you? As Latinos we all have different experiences; are you arguing that some of those experiences make us *more* or *less* Latino? What criteria will we use to judge who is most Latino?" While Nelson's point about the difference in experience between light- and dark-skinned Latinos/as is valid—although his contention that light-skinned Latinos/as do not experience anti-Latino racism is overstated—his conclusion that the difference makes one group more fully Latino/a was now openly in dispute; at this point the class collective was able to examine both Nelson's and David's theories about color and cultural identity.

David disputed Nelson's theoretical assumption that identities can be reduced to social liabilities—that identities are mostly ways of talking about oppression, i.e., the bad things that happen to people because of how difference is socially constructed. Motivated by David's argument, a third student—a non-Spanish speaking Latina woman—pointed to the ways that authentic Latino/a identity is often linked to one's cultural abilities: she argued that Latino/as who don't speak Spanish often find their claim to Latino/a identity in dispute by those who do. She also pointed out that if we accepted Nelson's theory, we would have to conclude that Latina women have more claim than Latino men to authentic cultural identity, since Latinas experience oppression on the basis of gender as well as race and class. Engaging Moraga's realist theory of oppression and coalition,[10] David argued that by ranking oppressions and/or cultural affinities and using the tally to determine who can authentically claim an ethnic identity, we not only produce less accurate knowledge about ourselves and the world but we also preclude the possibility of cultural and political coalitions across differences. Thus David's and the class's critiques are contingent upon their ability to theorize their own identities and discern the inadequacy of Nelson's theory about the relationship of social location, experience and authentic Latino identity. By examining their peers' articulated theories about the relationship of color, racism and Latino/a identity, the entire class participates in the production of objective knowledge about race, racism and the diversity within cultural identity groups.

This example demonstrates the epistemic power of a pedagogical framework that centers identity and difference in the classroom. Repositioning feminist pedagogy in the conceptual frame of postpositivist realism offers us a sound theoretical base from which to historicize and interpret the partiality and interestedness of knowledge claims that surface in the feminist classroom. Chandra Talpade Mohanty emphasizes the importance of historicizing difference when she argues that " . . . a particular problematic effect of certain pedagogical codifications of difference is the conceptualization of race and gender in terms of personal or individual experience. . . . Thus, while "experience" is an enabling focus in the classroom, unless it is explicitly understood as historical, contingent, and the result of interpretation, it can coagulate into frozen, binary, psychologistic positions" (51, 52). By taking seriously the implications for pedagogy of the multiply-situated and historical nature of identities, feminist teachers can authorize the marginal experiences of our students without either exotifying their subject positions or excluding and/or silencing "dominant" students. Doing so thereby democratizes knowledge production by supporting the creation of collective communities of meaning where both students and teachers can investigate the partiality and objectivity of their experience-based assertions.

If we agree that the authority of individual experience is always relative to course content and its historical referent, and that it is always subject to critique, the feminist teacher can work to embody this theory in the classroom by modeling for students the historical contingency of her experience and its epistemic and political relevance. In this way, teachers whose privileged social locations implicate them in the very structures of hegemonic power that the feminist classroom aims to critique, may, in Leslie Roman's language, go "beyond the usual confessions (e.g., 'I am a white, middle-class, heterosexual feminist') that function as little more than disclaimers of privilege" (1993, 78). Rather than uncritically asserting her epistemic authority, the teacher—through her own example—demonstrates the need to highlight the causal and relational connection between location, experience and identity in the process of feminist knowledge production. At the same time, by surfacing how her social location may both enhance and obstruct her claims to know, the feminist teacher urges students to consider the productive instability of the link between experience and epistemology. This awareness is crucial to the political project of the feminist classroom because it underscores the possibility of claiming transformational identities—identities that directly reflect the politicized context in which we mediate our experiences, evaluate our positionalities, and make political choices.

Michiko Hase provides a compelling example of this innovative pedagogy in her essay "Student Resistance and Nationalism in the Classroom: Reflections on Globalizing the Curriculum"(Chapter 3). By foregrounding her national identity (Japanese) and national difference from her mostly North American students, Hase centers *nation* as a category of subject position. Moreover, Hase models critical analysis of her own national identity and nationalism by holding Japan, Japanese citizens, and herself accountable for the deplorable sexual violence committed against Korean women during World War II; she thereby motivates her students to consider how their subject positions as North Americans both enhance and obstruct their ability to learn and know about non-U.S. women. As a Japanese feminist, Hase's identity helps her to explain oppression in her own country on the basis of gender. By denouncing Japanese sexual violence during World War II, she repositions herself within a transnational feminist identity that allows her to formulate a critique of Japanese exploitation of Korean women.

By foregrounding the contradictions in gendered and nationalized identities, Hase productively restructures knowledge-making in her classroom. Specifically, she exposes the contradiction in U.S. students' enduring preoccupation with the horror of female genital mutilation, and their concurrent refusal to address the violent effects of global racism—especially that perpetrated by the United States—on the bodies of third-world women. When Hase joins her critique of the sexual exploitation of Korean women with her critique of Japan's imperial domination, she communicates to her students that their interpretations of third-world women's oppression must also be read through hegemonic national and global contexts. This pedagogy highlights how a teacher's performance of identity and its inherent complexity—in this case, Hase's willingness to critique the global politics of Japan in spite of her explicitly stated discomfort with being viewed as an oppressor—exemplifies the collective nature of feminist knowledge production through difference. Hase demonstrates how to democratize epistemic authority and create new classroom methods by historicizing, rather than essentializing, our consciousness of difference.

Communities of Meaning

A feminist pedagogy based on a realist theory of identity necessarily brings forth accompanying transitions in the epistemology of the feminist classroom. When we assert that experiences, and thus identities, shape what and how we know, but maintain that identities (even oppressed identities) do not automatically yield epistemic privilege, we need to generate an account of how students will bring their experiences and identities to bear upon the creation of feminist knowledge. This process is crucial for democratizing the classroom since it assumes that all members of the learning community— "dominant," "marginalized," "progressive," and "conservative"—share equal responsibility for producing liberatory knowledges. Historicizing the awareness of difference facilitates a learning community in which students and teachers "find a commonality in the experience of difference without compromising its distinctive realities and effects" (Gentile 7). We recognize that the call to deepen the awareness of differences might be construed as a divisive or separatist strategy, one that might seem to hinder the creation of progressive political coalitions across social, cultural and national differences. But what we are suggesting rests on the assumption that cross-cultural coalitions are not precluded by a heightened awareness of difference; in fact, we believe that political coalitions aimed at dismantling oppressions can be most effective when differences are charted out and contextualized in the construction of diverse and shifting *communities of meaning* in the classroom. *Communities of meaning* are defined by a complex of factors including social location, cultural identity, epistemic standpoint, and political convictions. Thus, *communities of meaning* are also *communities of knowing*, places where people discover some commonality of experience through which they struggle for objective knowledge.

Theories about how to get students into the center of inquiry become more strategic and sharp in a classroom structured around the relational play of difference, because rather than thinking about sidelining the teacher while moving all students into the center, we now invest different *communities of meaning* with authority at different times. Therefore, we suggest that students and teachers in feminist classrooms see themselves as members of various and shifting *communities of meaning*, epistemic communities that are defined not simply by identity markers (such as race, class, gender, sexuality, religion, or nation), but instead are defined by shared experiences, ways of understanding the world, and political choices. This recommendation makes good epistemic sense, since feminist, post-colonial, queer, and racial identity theories all point to the fact that there is no such thing as "the black experience," "the gay experience," "women's experience," and so on. Indeed, in many cases people who join together in a *community of meaning* will share certain identity markers. However, when membership in the community is (1) self-defined, and (2) experience-dependent, we avoid the theoretically untenable practice of presuming that all—here we may insert any identity term such as [Arab] or [working-class] or [immigrant] or [female] or [Jewish], and so on—people have a common experience from which to evaluate assertions, analyze theories and social identities, and create objective knowledge. For example, although the "Latino community" shares a common experience of racial and economic oppression, this racial/ethnic group is deeply divided along lines of gender, sexuality, color, class, language, religion, national ancestry and political orientation; all of these differences in location generate distinct experiences from which Latinos/as forge identities, decide what is true about themselves and the world, what is right and wrong, which political battles are worth fighting for, and so on. Given that there is no easy alliance among Latinos/as in a radical classroom, an epistemic structure based on *communities of meaning* may provide Latino/a students and faculty with better options for articulating the complexity of Latino/a identities, for producing emancipatory knowledges, and for organizing progressive political action in cross-cultural coalitions.

These shifting *communities of meaning* are both invested and divested of epistemic authority, depending upon the content under study in any course. So, for example, when teaching about reproductive rights and the politics of choice, various *communities of meaning* will crystallize in a classroom: religious students who oppose abortion under any circumstances, students who have experienced pregnancy—and may or may not believe in or have had an abortion—, politically defined pro-choice students, politically defined anti-choice students, and so on. The teacher can affiliate with any particular community—or form one of her own—based upon her subject position. In so doing she models for students a way to join together in feminist collective struggle for knowledge based on identity and experience. The epistemic salience of this pedagogy is that it cultivates a variety of *communities of meaning* from which a diversity of socially embedded knowledge claims can emerge.

Admittedly, when we cultivate difference in the classroom we confront an ethical and political dilemma: How do we create a pedagogy that does not trivialize students' performance of difference, even when we construct that difference as antithetical to antiracist feminist political goals? How do we deepen the awareness of *privileged difference* that may be directly at odds with the goals of feminist analyses? Amie addresses this challenge in "Feminist Pedagogy and the Appeal to Epistemic Privilege" (Chapter 4): A Jamaican woman student—we'll call her Deborah—in her class who has volunteered to present the assigned reading for the day—doris davenport's "The Pathology of Racism: A Conversation with Third World Wimmin"—begins her presentation by saying that: "Homosexuality is immoral and violates the law of God. All homosexuals are disgusting, and against God and my religion. I'm Jamaican, and I don't believe in homosexuality" (115). Without question, such remarks are cruel and vicious. However, in a feminist classroom that prompts students to engage and evaluate all forms of identity and difference, contentious claims like these provide the conditions for collective, progressive knowledge-making. In fact, we argue that the construction of theory-mediated objectivity requires that we cultivate both privileged and subjugated differences, identities, and experiences.[11] By examining the relationship between students' stated beliefs and their justifications for those beliefs, we can contest pernicious worldviews without suppressing students' performance of difference. Deborah, for example, articulates a socially embedded knowledge claim that is pervasive but typically silenced in U.S. feminist classrooms. By surfacing this commonly held yet unspoken "knowledge," the feminist teacher encourages individuals from other *communities of meaning*—especially those to which epistemic authority shifts in the context of homohatred—the opportunity to critique heterosexism and homohatred. Epistemically authoritative communities in this case might include lesbian and gay students of all races, as well as heterosexual students who define themselves as allies of gay and lesbian people and/or who may have the experience of being discriminated against for the unorthodox ways in which they perform their own sexualities. And the entire class—as a conglomeration of *communities of meaning*—engages in the project of generating the theory-mediated objectivity that grows out of epistemic diversity.

When we guide students to understand more about the network of moral and political assumptions that inform their cultural identities, different *communities of meaning* can themselves effectively contest hegemonic knowledges. Deborah's assertions are complicated, since she occupies both dominant and marginalized subject positions in the classroom and in the world. As a ruling-class, Jamaican, Black, Catholic woman attending a private and predominantly white liberal arts college, Deborah's insidious attempt to justify her homohatred by the appeal to an oppressed national identity is an expression of both privileged and subjugated difference. In effect, Deborah is operating on an essentialist theory of identity by claiming that (1) her cultural identity (race, gender, class, nationality, and religion) "determines" her judgment of lesbian and gay people, and (2) that her cultural identity cannot be evaluated, theorized or contested.

Undoubtedly, the most effective opposition to Deborah's claims will come from other *communities of meaning* whose members share certain aspects of Deborah's cultural identity but who oppose her homohatred. We want to be very clear that effective challengers do not need to be Jamaican, Black, or female; other Catholics or non-Americans, for example, have the epistemic opportunity to formulate powerful refutations of Deborah's perspectives. By debunking Deborah's essentialism, and highlighting the theory-mediated quality of experience and identity, we can concretize the realist claim that some cultural identities are more epistemically reliable than others. By "epistemically reliable" we mean that some cultural identities—Deborah's for example—distort the relationship between identity and knowledge by assuming that a one-to-one correspondence exists between "who someone is" and "what she knows" (in this case, Deborah assumes that her cultural identity as a Jamaican Catholic *produces and justifies* her belief that "homosexuality is disgusting. . . ."). Members of other *communities of meaning* can now expose the error in her claim that Jamaican cultural and national identity automatically generates a fixed worldview. As this example shows, the pursuit of truth in the classroom is dependent upon teaching students to understand the function of experience and identity in meaning-making, while providing them the tools to distinguish and contest the theories that mediate experience. This collective epistemic framework delineated by shifting *communities of meaning*—becomes the arbiter of truth in the feminist classroom.

Concluding Remarks

We have argued that feminists fully reinvigorate the role of identity in pedagogy, and do so specifically from the standpoint of postpositivist realism. We are fully aware however, that the struggle to democratize university education cannot be detached from its institutional context. In other words, the success of a revolutionized antiracist feminist pedagogy is contingent upon the creation of equally transformed curricular policies *at the institutional level.* Audre Lorde's radical critique of the colonizing effects of institutional practices of inclusion and exclusion continues to be valid in the twenty-first century academy. Lorde's analysis of how academic hierarchies consolidate power in dominant identity groups reveals how institutional agendas tokenize, marginalize and appropriate radical curricula and radical teachers. These hegemonic practices provide the illusion of institutional transformation while exhausting the resources of "minority," feminist and progressive faculty in organizing "special" courses on cultural diversity, race and gender studies, queer theory, and so on. Yet, as Lorde argued so convincingly over 20 years ago, these institutional strategies are actually the "tools of racist patriarchy . . ." that ensure " . . . that only the most narrow perimeters of change are possible and allowable" (111).

Therefore, in order to contribute meaningfully to the struggle for deep structural transformation of the academy, we must continue to petition our institutions to change the current practice of marginalizing insurgent courses and to instead organize diversity courses in what we call "Diversity Curriculum Clusters": themed groupings of courses in a variety of disciplines that situate antiracist, feminist curricula sequentially. Contra the current practice of encouraging students to take a lone course on "diversity" to satisfy a college-wide requirement, we recommend that radical courses be mapped out and offered in sequences that include appropriate interdisciplinary prerequisite courses. This curricular program would allow students to become self-reflexive about the progressive cognitive and affective stages they will confront in courses that analyze the social construction of racial, gender, class and sexual identities.[12]

It is a mistake to assume that students with "dominant" cultural identities who enroll in "Introduction to Women's Studies" or "Introduction to U.S. Latino Studies" are cognitively prepared to confront not only radical analyses of history and difference, but also radical critiques of how their own raced, gendered, classed, and sexed identities are intricately bound with relational structures of power. It is also a mistake to assume that lesbian and gay students, students of color, working class students, and women of all social locations, by virtue of their oppressed social locations, will automatically be prepared to engage the political and ethical views of the feminist classroom and to authentically locate themselves in the analytical spaces that it opens. We are not suggesting that by implementing these clusters feminist teachers would suddenly be free of the conflictive, tense dynamics of radical classroom practice or of the substantive challenges that students sometimes pose to feminist knowledge production. What we are arguing is that in order to have a reasonable shot at reaching our intellectual and political objectives in the feminist classroom, we need to continue working to transform the structural relationship of feminist education and institutional curricular policy.

Overview of Chapters

The contributors to *Twenty-First-Century Feminist Classrooms* bring together diverse and challenging theoretical perspectives on the experiences of feminist educators as we work to redefine pedagogies for communicating the claims of both insurgent disciplines—Women's Studies, African-American Studies, Latino Studies, Ethnic Studies, Queer Theory, etc.—and radicalized versions of traditional areas of study—History, Sociology, Foreign Languages, Literature, Philosophy. Each chapter opens a space for engaged feminist criticism and self-criticism that seeks to reinvigorate pedagogical practices grounded in multicultural feminist identities. By generating supportive critiques of current feminist pedagogies, the authors of the anthology articulate new methods for understanding and centralizing the function of experience and identity in the classroom; thus many contributors investigate how particular pedagogical epistemologies are complicated or constrained by complex expressions of identity and difference in the classroom and within institutional hierarchies.

Many essays in the volume make explicit the kinds of unspoken knowledges that operate in the radical classroom, and investigate how educators can begin to formulate new pedagogical theories and practices that authentically link the intellectual and political objectives of feminist movement. Our contributors ask: as teachers introducing subject material, what are the explicit and implicit instructions we give to our students regarding feminist analysis of ideas, histories, and political realities? In what ways do we both assert and decry the claims of identity politics and epistemic privilege? And what are the consequences of these practices for the freedom struggle in the feminist classroom? While exploring the legacy of feminist pedagogies aimed at dismantling histories and practices of domination, the authors at the same time provide a critique of the pedagogical theories, assumptions and practices that they believe to be undertheorized and/or counterproductive, as a means of outlining new strategies and methods for the feminist classroom of the twenty-first century.

I. Cultural Identity and Student Resistance

As a feminist of color who operates within the private white institution, Betty Sasaki investigates the connections between the institutional erasure of whiteness and the resistance of students in the classroom to antiracist pedagogies. Additionally, in "Toward a Pedagogy of Coalition," Sasaki scrutinizes how the imperatives of pluralist multiculturalism work to constrain the performance of minority identities by constructing specious images of racial/ethnic Otherness.

Sasaki engages these questions by closely examining the history of the pluralist "family metaphor" at the small liberal arts college where she teaches. Sasaki's essay generates a powerful critique of the mechanisms by which diversity and multiculturalism are dehistoricized and aimed at generating stagnant consensus among different campus constituencies. Additionally, Sasaki develops a brilliant analysis of the ways that her own heterogeneous racial/ethnic identity exceeds the borders of white perspectives on Otherness, resulting in public constructions of her identity as an inauthentic version of a "real" Asian American. Sasaki argues that the perturbing "wholeness" of her identity is perceived as threatening to the mythical constructions of a harmonious cultural pluralism, since her difference and sameness are narrowly and perniciously accommodated only in service of quelling racial disharmonies and reestablishing an exclusive sense of community conformity. Finally, Sasaki argues for the creation of a pedagogy of coalition that is both epistemological and political, one that takes as its foundation a historical notion of multiculturalism that exposes, and thereby deepens—rather than resolves—difference.

In her chapter "Unleashing the Demons of History: White Resistance in the U.S. Latino Studies Classroom," Susan Sánchez-Casal explores the questions of experience, identity, and difference by focusing on white resistance in the U.S. Latino Studies classroom. Sánchez-Casal argues that decontextualized multicultural narratives in the educational system (from elementary school through the university) miseducate students about the historical struggles of peoples of color in the United States, to such an extent that the content and focus of antiracist courses in the academy are often construed as "propaganda." Sánchez-Casal draws pertinent connections between the epistemic basis of white resistance and what anthropolitical linguist Ana Celia Zentella refers to as the *chiquitafication* ("making small") of Latino history. Sánchez-Casal elaborates on how she organizes the metaphors of chiquitafication, the border and the wound as central to both the way she constructs U.S. Latino curriculum and the way she develops general methodological practices of radical pedagogy.

Michiko Hase explores how the construction of feminist knowledge in the classroom can be significantly and problematically shaped by differences in linguistic codes, skin complexion, and by students' perception of the professor's relative racial, cultural or national proximity. Hase's chapter "Student Resistance and Nationalism in the Classroom: Some Reflections on Globalizing the Curriculum" outlines powerfully the terrain of nationalist resistance in her classroom by detailing how students construct her identity as a non-American woman of color. Her pedagogy is shaped by her interest in exploring Japanese women's identities as both oppressor and oppressed, and thus Hase concretizes the relationship between multicultural feminist identities and shifting authority in the feminist classroom. Hase asserts that by foregrounding the construction of her national identity, she enables students to think critically about their own national identities and to resituate themselves productively in relation to antiracist, global curriculum. Throughout, Hase provides a candid self-criticism of her own pedagogical methods and offers specific recommendations for democratizing the global feminist classroom.

II. The Epistemology of Experience

In "Feminist Pedagogy and the Appeal to Epistemic Privilege" Amie Macdonald engages questions of the epistemic status of experience and its use in the classroom by criticizing the ways that we currently engage personal experience in feminist classrooms and by proposing that feminist educators create new pedagogies aimed at a collective struggle for a feminist standpoint. While she explicitly defends the continued practice of making students' experiences central in feminist education, she sets out to scrutinize this feminist strategy in order to confront the ways that students and professors either appeal to an oppressed identity in order to substantiate an argument, or (just as commonly) appeal to their lack of experience of an oppressed identity in order to justify their "inability" to analyze an argument. From this vantage point, Macdonald aims to reinvigorate a feminist pedagogy of experiential learning. Macdonald demonstrates how feminist educators have misinterpreted classic feminist standpoint theory (especially Nancy C. M. Hartsock), and details through many classroom examples how exactly the appeal to epistemic privilege disenfranchises both experiential and non-experiential knowers. Throughout the essay, Macdonald offers criticism of her own responses to classroom appeals to epistemic privilege. She concludes that a feminist pedagogy that takes learners' experiences as central to the classroom enterprise, and operates on a realist conception of personal identity, will necessarily push us toward a collective struggle for knowledge in the feminist classroom.

Tamara Williams's and Erin McKenna's essay "Negotiating Subject Positions in a Service-Learning Context: Toward a Feminist Critique of Experiential Learning" critiques the experiential basis of the service-learning classroom for its tendency to reproduce dominant ways of representing the white self and its Others, and for its failure to theorize the extreme emotional responses that it elicits in students whose experiences in relation to the "at risk" communities being "served" constructs them as Other in the classroom. This chapter provides a detailed discussion of two students in service-learning courses—Pilar, who is forced to confront her own immigrant history and construction as racial/ethnic Other in a course of predominantly white students that requires her to work for a Latino empowerment agency; and Tanya, who must face the death by AIDS of her closest friend while she works for an AIDS hospice as part of fulfilling course requirements. Williams and McKenna explore the transformative benefits of service learning—especially the ways that privileging experience radically alters foundational assumptions about the constitution of texts, knowledge, and authority. At the same time, they argue that because service learning underscores the role of experience by asserting its function as text, it is imperative that we answer serious questions about the pedagogy of service learning, including: Do we grade the quality of the student's service, or the degree of their transformational experience? How should feminist educators evaluate students who have no personal experience with the service component versus those who are forced to confront critically painful memories and experiences because of the service in which they engage? Is feminist service learning about the students themselves, or about the course material? In each of these cases, Williams and McKenna target the issue of representation: as feminists, they are troubled by the potential of service learning to reinforce racist, sexist, and classist views. For this reason, Williams and McKenna aim to develop a feminist pedagogy of service learning that takes into account the epistemic rationale for learning through experience.

Eva María Valle raises pertinent questions about diversity and multiculturalism from the perspective of a Latina feminist teaching at a frontline multi-ethnic public university (University of California, Dominguez Hills). Working from a critique of Paulo Freire's concept of *concientización,* Valle's essay "Antiracist Pedagogy and Concientización: A Latina Professor's Struggle" rewrites her own personal/professional history as explicitly structural and reflective of prevailing power relations. In the process, Valle also offers a supportive critique of Gloria Anzaldúa's notion of *mestiza consciousness,* arguing that Anzaldúa fails to foreground structural inequalities—the real area for collective political action—by focusing too heavily on individual strategies to combat discrimination and racism. Valle analyzes the effects of tokenization on faculty and students of color, and argues that an antiracist pedagogy of *concientización* offers the greatest hope for authentic transformation of racist and elitist hierarchies in academia.

Nancy Sorkin Rabinowitz describes an innovative and experientially based pedagogy for feminist, queer-theory classrooms in her essay "Queer Theory and Feminist Pedagogy." In the process she addresses pedagogical challenges specific to the queer-theory classroom: the oppressive nature of homophobia and heterosexism, the ways that small and active queer student constituencies influence one another, and the decision—especially for professors—to identify or conceal their own sexual identity. Rabinowitz discusses in detail the pedagogical, personal, and professional consequences of teaching "what you are not," and in so doing raises important criticisms of the foundational claims of identity politics in feminist teaching. Rabinowitz also considers the difference between "Gay and Lesbian Studies" and "Queer Studies," concluding that while the former is situated within the limiting structures of feminist identity politics, Queer Studies offers us an expansive intellectual perspective that forces us to reflect on heteronormativity and broader questions of experience and difference. In this respect, Rabinowitz offers yet another innovative strategy for moving past outdated identity politics and towards a feminist pedagogy of liberation.

III. Contextualizing Difference

Like Michiko Hase, Allison Dorsey explores how the construction of feminist knowledge in the classroom can be significantly and problematically shaped by differences in linguistic codes, skin complexion, and by students' perception of the professor's relative racial, cultural, or national proximity. In her essay "'white girls'" and 'Strong Black Women': Reflections on a Decade of Teaching Black History at PWIs," Dorsey examines these categories of analysis by defining difference in two distinct student constituencies in her Black history courses: self identified "just white girls" and "strong Black women." Through her insightful elucidation of these student-types, Dorsey challenges fundamental theories, assumptions and strategies of feminist pedagogy—the link between local and global community action; the "decentering" of authority; the possibility of productive dialogue in classroom conditions of social inequality; the possibility of creating "safe spaces" in the classroom; the productive link between the personal and the political. In each case, Dorsey demonstrates the ways in which these recommendations of feminist pedagogy can inadvertently contribute to reactionary, racist, and sexist outcomes in the classroom. For example, Dorsey argues that centralizing students' experiences leads many of her students to self-identify as either "strong Black women" (a stereotype that undermines the potential of black women's sisterhood by inordinately valorizing the experience of oppression) or as "just white girls" (an escape strategy that conveniently allows white students to avoid grappling with the historical and political functions of whiteness). Furthermore, Dorsey demonstrates that the feminist pedagogical recommendation to link the personal to the political contributes to what she calls the intellectualized "black mammy" image. Ultimately, Dorsey recommends that we seek a feminist pedagogy that helps students of history to empathize with those who have experienced injustice—a goal that we can achieve by helping students to see their multiply situated and sometimes contradictory identities as historical agents.

In "Teaching (About) Genocide" Bat-Ami Bar On reflects on years of teaching from a feminist perspective about extreme cases of violence. Through a detailed exploration of student responses to Hannah Arendt, Bar On concludes that her reliance on critical and feminist pedagogies—particularly the expectation that students will engage in collective knowledge production and ideology critique—placed far too much responsibility on the students and on course materials. Adopting a revealing standpoint of self-criticism, Bar On argues that her students' "narratives of boredom and prevention" highlight the limitations of critical and feminist pedagogies. A comprehensive analysis of this student response forms the basis of Bar On's essay. Reviewing Santer's work on narrative fetishism and related literature on secondary trauma, Bar On concludes that her genocide courses are failing precisely because while they do in some sense shake students out of naïve ignorance, they are simultaneously traumatizing students. She explains that we cannot hope to activate the feminist goal of collective knowledge production in our classrooms—especially in regard to genocide—unless we address the fundamental truths about students' cognitive and emotional reactions to extreme violence. Bar On therefore asks us to consider theories of trauma as we reformulate basic tenets of feminist pedagogy in classrooms that focus on histories of extreme violence.

Teaching from an explicit and relatively unfamiliar perspective on identity and difference requires that we think in detail about the relationship between our curriculum and our methods for effectively teaching it. Margaret Hunter's essay "Decentering the White and Male Standpoint in Race and Ethnicity Courses" offers explicit pedagogical strategies and perspectives for antiracist feminist theory and practice in the classroom, by examining how racial epistemologies and the unspoken knowledge systems of women of color must be organically foregrounded in knowledge production. Hunter organizes her argument by offering clear perspectives on how to decenter the implicit white, male standpoint in race and ethnicity courses, how to put race and gender into inextricable dialogue, and how to create student-centered learning that is aimed at surfacing subjugated knowledges. Specifically, Hunter offers a compelling case for the view that feminist teachers can and should access the unique knowledge bases and epistemologies of students of color, and organize feminist pedagogy according to these epistemic frameworks.

In the essay "Representation, Entitlement, and Voyeurism: Teaching Across Difference" Melanie Kaye/Kantrowitz offers a brilliant historical defense of the most current version of her course called "Gender, Race, Class, and Nation." Tracing the recent history of Women's Studies, she suggests that feminists are at a critical juncture in the evolution of our discipline. Kaye/Kantrowitz recommends that we forgo the gridlock of identity politics (e.g., courses on this or that group of women, pedagogies and epistemologies based on this or that social identity), and instead transform our discipline by making its central focus a transnational perspective on all kinds of structural subordination. Calling this new discipline "Liberation Studies," Kaye/Kantrowitz details the theoretical justification for linking together Women's Studies with Ethnic Studies, Jewish Studies, Queer Studies, Postcolonial Studies, and so on. It is within this discussion that Kaye/Kantrowitz explains her choices in pedagogy and subject matter for such a course, at every turn showing how these choices are reflective of a global perspective on structural subordination and liberation. For these reasons, we have chosen Kaye/Kantrowitz's essay to conclude the volume, for she offers an expansive and creative vision of a feminist pedagogy and curriculum defined by revolutionized concepts of experience, identity, epistemology, and curriculum.

Notes

1. In 1993 Satya P. Mohanty introduced the theory of postpositivist realism in his groundbreaking essay "The Epistemic Status of Cultural Identity: On *Beloved* and the Post-Colonial Condition." Since then three important

books have been published elaborating the realist theory of identity. See S. P. Mohanty 1997, Moya and Hames-García 2000, and Moya 2002. Realist theories of identity are also the subject of an ongoing multidisciplinary research project (*The Future of Minority Studies*) and a forthcoming volume that includes theorists from English, Comparative Literature, Philosophy, Women's Studies, Sociology, History, Anthropology, Ethnic Studies, African American Studies, Puerto Rican Studies, Latino Studies, Psychology, Native American Studies, and so on.

2. We are operating on the epistemic view that pure objective knowledge about anything is neither possible nor desirable. However, we are unwilling to retreat to any kind of relativist standpoint that ultimately claims "we cannot know." Therefore, postpositivist realism offers more than a powerful description of identity; it also provides a compelling account of how experience is central to the creation of theory-mediated objectivity. See S. P. Mohanty, Moya, Alcoff, Harding, Macdonald, Hames-García.

3. For a discussion of postmodernist critiques of identity see Butler, Brown, Jenkins, deLauretis, Nicholson.

4. Student resistance in feminist classrooms has been theorized from different perspectives and has been the subject of many insightful studies: see Roman, Deay and Stitzel, Mayberry and Rose, Tatum, Felman.

5. Although we critique the wholesale classification of students as "dominant" and "marginalized," we do in many instances rely on these terms in order to speak generally about differences in students' social locations and their consequences in the classroom. We do not mean for the reader to understand our usage as a negation of feminist theories about the multiplicity and contradictions of identity. Additionally, we use the term "dominant" students rather than "privileged" to emphasize not only that dominant students have social privilege but also to signify the way that privilege is manifested in relation to power and authority in the classroom.

6. We especially want to highlight the creation of feminist identity theory produced in the "Combahee River Collective: Black Feminist Statement," first published in 1979 and reprinted in *This Bridge*. The Combahee River Collective (CRC) critiqued the racism of the feminist movement, the sexism of the Black Liberation movement, and the prevalence of heterosexism in all areas of social life. This political collective of Black lesbians articulated the theory of identity politics (i.e., that identity is relevant to politics) by claiming that those who share a common social location, experience and identity are most aptly suited to form successful political coalitions. But, as Linda Martín Alcoff (2000) points out, the CRC's theory of identity points up the realist nature of identities and thus avoids the pitfalls of essentialism.

7. These shifting circumstances might include course materials, interventions by either teacher or students or groups of students, classroom confrontations, classroom or homework activities, related campus events, institutional policies, national and international events, and so on.

8. For enriching discussions about the construction of authority in the classroom see: hooks 1994, Ellsworth, Roman, Chandra Talpade Mohanty, Maher, Davis, Tompkins, Luke and Gore, and Srivastava.

9. Opponents of standpoint theory (whether those standpoints are based on gender, race, class, sexuality, nationality and so on) have rightly argued that a proliferation of the epistemic status of identity standpoints can leave us unable to assert any objectively true claims about our shared social world (Said, Searle). Although we understand this concern, we are convinced that a postpositivist realist theory of identity—and especially of the epistemic status of cultural identity—can both grapple with the ontological realities of human difference and retain the prospect of creating objective knowledge.

10. For a rigorous discussion of the realist basis of Moraga's theories of oppression and identity, see Paula M. L. Moya, "Postmodernism, 'Realism,' and the Politics of Identity: Cherríe Moraga and Chicana Feminism."

11. For an extensive discussion of "privileged difference" and its uses in the classroom, see Amie Macdonald's chapter in this volume, "Feminist Pedagogy and the Appeal to Epistemic Privilege." Macdonald argues that "the exclusion of white people, men, straight people, and rich folks from the process of creating feminist knowledge about social domination may be somewhat desirable, at least metaphorically, given that it is not the responsibility of the oppressed to educate their oppressors. However, such a strategy brings with it a curious outcome: people who cannot be experiential knowers are made utterly unaccountable for the creation and consideration of feminist knowledge. The utility of this disenfranchisement is dubious, for it makes students (and professors) who have lived experience of oppression primarily responsible for directing and defining the production of feminist knowledge, and it seems to say that people without oppressed identities are not responsible for constructing and justifying knowledge about difference, exploitation, and liberation" (122).

12. Beverly Daniel Tatum highlights the significance of teaching students to recognize how their affective and psychological bases may impede or enhance learning in classrooms that provide openly political frameworks for social analyses. She argues that we can work toward dismantling student resistance to oppression-related content by teaching students to evaluate their negative responses to course material and classroom dynamics according to the progressive stages outlined in Racial Identity Development Theory. By making students self-reflexive about why they are feeling the way they are feeling, by theorizing their emotional responses and seeing them as part of a progression of cognitive stages that can eventually lead to a positive reinscription of racial identity (both for white students and for students of color), feminist educators can not only reduce resistance but enhance learning. Tatum elaborates:

The emotional responses that students have to talking and learning about racism are quite predictable and related to their own racial identity development. Unfortunately, students typically do not know this; thus they consider their own guilt, shame, embarrassment, or anger an uncomfortable experience that they alone are having. Informing students at the beginning of the semester that these feelings may be part of the learning process is ethically necessary (in the sense of informed consent), and helps to normalize the students' experience. Knowing in advance that a desire to withdraw from classroom discussion or not to complete assignments is a common response helps students to remain engaged when they reach that point (19).

Tatum's analysis of the pedagogical importance in antiracist feminist classrooms of racial identity development theory supports our contention that diversity courses must be taught in clusters that adequately prepare students cognitively for the psychological and emotional effects of radical curriculum and pedagogy. While Tatum focuses these pedagogical strategies specifically on courses about race and racism, the pedagogical and analytical principles she outlines can also be used to organize courses that focus on gender, sexuality, and class (or any and all conjunctions of these social categories).

Works Cited

Alarcón, Norma. "Conjugating Subjects in the Age of Multiculturalism." *Mapping Multiculturalism*. Ed. Avery Gordon and Christopher Newfield. Minneapolis: University of Minnesota Press, 1996, 127–148.

———. "The Theoretical Subjects of *This Bridge Called My Back*," *Making Face Making Soul/Haciendo Caras: Creative and Critical Perspectives by Feminists of Color*. Ed. Gloria Anzaldúa. San Francisco: Aunt Lute Foundation Books, 1990, 356–370.

Alcoff, Linda Martín. "Cultural Feminism Versus Post-Structuralism: The Identity Crisis in Feminist Theory." *Signs* 13 (Spring 1988): 405–437.

———. "Who's Afraid of Identity Politics?" *Reclaiming Identity.* Ed. Paula M. L. Moya and Michael Hames-García. Berkeley: University of California Press, 2000, 312–344.

———. "Latina/o Identity Politics." *The Good Citizen.* Eds. David Batstone and Eduardo Mendieta. New York: Routledge, 1999, 93–112.

Anzaldúa, Gloria. *Borderlands/La Frontera: The New Mestiza.* San Francisco: Spinster/Aunt Lute, 1987.

———. *Making Face Making Soul/Haciendo Caras: Creative and Critical Perspectives by Feminists of Color.* San Francisco: Aunt Lute Foundation Books, 1990.

Aronowitz, Stanley. "Postmodernism and Politics." *Social Text* 18 (Winter 1987/88): 99–115.

Bell, Sandra, Marina Morrow and Evangelia Tastsoglou. "Teaching in Environments of Resistance: Toward a Critical, Feminist, and Antiracist Pedagogy." *Meeting the Challenge: Innovative Feminist Pedagogies in Action.* Ed. Maralee Mayberry and Ellen Cronan Rose. New York: Routledge, 1999, 23–46.

Brown, Wendy. *State of Injury: Power and Freedom in Late Modernity.* Princeton: Princeton University Press, 1995.

Bunch, Charlotte and Sandra Pollack, eds. *Learning Our Way: Essays in Feminist Education.* Trumansburg, New York: The Crossing Press, 1983.

Butler, Judith. *Gender Trouble: Feminism and the Subversion of Identity.* New York: Routledge, 1990.

Collins, Patricia Hill. *Black Feminist Thought.* New York: Routledge, 1991.

Combahee River Collective. "The Combahee River Collective: A Black Feminist Statement." *Capitalist Patriarchy and the Case for Socialist Feminism.* Ed. Zillah R. Eisenstein. New York: Monthly Review Press, 1979, 362–372.

Cohee, Gail E., Elisabeth Daumer, Theresa D. Kemp, Paula M. Krebs, Sue Lafky, and Sandra Runzo, eds. *The Feminist Teacher Anthology: Pedagogies and Classroom Strategies.* New York: Teachers College Press, Columbia University, 1998.

Culley, Margo and Catherine Portuges. *Gendered Subjects: The Dynamics of Feminist Teaching.* Boston: Routledge and Kegan Paul, 1985.

davenport, doris. "The Pathology of Racism: A Conversation with Third World Wimmin." *This Bridge Called My Back: Writings by Radical Women of Color.* Ed. Cherríe Moraga and Gloria Anzaldúa. New York: Kitchen Table: Women of Color Press, 1983, 85–90.

Davis, Angela. *Women, Race and Class.* New York: Vintage Books, 1981.

———. "Gender, Class, and Multiculturalism: Rethinking 'Race' Politics." *Mapping Multiculturalism.* Ed. Avery Gordon and Christopher Newfield. Minneapolis: University of Minnesota Press, 1996, 40–48.

Deay, Ardeth and Judith Stitzel. "Reshaping the Introductory Women's Studies Course: Dealing Up Front with Anger, Resistance, and Reality." *The Feminist Teacher Anthology: Pedagogies and Classroom Strategies.* Ed. Gail E. Cohee, Elisabeth Daumer, Theresa D. Kemp, Paula M. Krebs, Sue Lafky, Sandra Runzo. New York: Teachers College Press, Columbia University, 1998, 87–97.

de Castell, Suzanne and Mary Bryson, eds. *Racial in<ter>ventions: Identity, Politics and Difference/s in Educational Praxis.* Albany: State University of New York Press, 1997.

de Lauretis, Teresa. "Fem/Les Scramble." *Cross Purposes: Lesbians, Feminists and the Limits of Alliance.* Ed. Dana Heller. Bloomington: Indiana University Press, 1997, 42–48.

Delgado, Richard and Jean Stefancic, eds. *Critical White Studies: Looking Behind the Mirror.* Philadelphia: Temple University Press, 1997.

de Sousa, Ronald. "The Rationality of Emotions." *Explaining Emotions.* Ed. Amelie O. Rorty. Berkeley: University of California Press, 1980, 127–51.

D'Souza, Dinesh. *Illiberal Education: The Politics of Race and Sex on Campus.* New York: Free Press, 1991.

Ellsworth, Elizabeth. "Why Doesn't This Feel Empowering? Working Through the Repressive Myths of Critical Pedagogy." *Feminisms and Critical Pedagogy.* Ed. Carmen Luke and Jennifer Gore. New York: Routledge, 1992, 90–119.

Felman, Shoshana. "Psychoanalysis and Education: Teaching Terminable and Interminable." *Yale French Studies* 63 (1982): 21–44.

Freire, Paulo. *Pedagogy of the Oppressed.* New York: Herder, 1972.

Gabriel, Susan L. and Isaiah Smithson, eds. *Gender in the Classroom: Power and Pedagogy.* Chicago: University of Illinois Press, 1990.

Gentile, Mary. *Film Feminisms: Theory and Practice.* Westport, CT: Greenwood Press, 1985.

Gilligan, Carol. *In a Different Voice: Psychological Theory and Women's Development.* Cambridge, Massachussetts: Harvard University Press, 1982.

Giroux, Henry. "Radical Pedagogy and the Politics of Student Voice." *Interchange* 17 (1986): 48–69.

———. "Literacy and the Pedagogy of Voice and Political Empowerment." *Educational Theory* 38 (1988): 61–75.

——— and Peter MacLaren. "Teacher Education and the Politics of Engagement: The Case for Democratic Schooling." *Harvard Educational Review* 56. 3 (1986): 213–238.

Gore, Jennifer. *The Struggle for Pedagogies.* New York: Routledge, 1992.

Harding, Sandra. *Whose Science? Whose Knowledge? Thinking from Women's Lives.* Ithaca: Cornell University Press, 1991.

———. "Rethinking Standpoint Epistemology: What is Strong Objectivity?" *Feminist Epistemologies.* Ed. Linda Martín Alcoff and Elizabeth Potter. New York: Routledge, 1993, 49–82.

Hames-García, Michael R. "'Who Are Our Own People?'" Challenges for a Theory of Social Identity." *Reclaiming Identity: Realist Theory and the Predicament of Postmodernism.* Berkeley: University of California Press, 2000, 102–29.

Hase, Michiko. "Student Resistance and Nationalism in the Classroom: Reflections on Globalizing the Curriculum." *Twenty-First-Century Feminist Classrooms: Pedagogies of Identity and Difference.* Ed. Amie A. Macdonald and Susan Sánchez-Casal. New York: Palgrave Macmillan, 2002, 87–107.

hooks, bell. *Teaching to Transgress: Education as the Practice of Freedom.* New York: Routledge, 1994.

———. *Ain't I a Woman: Black Women and Feminism.* Boston: South End Press, 1981.

———. *Feminist Theory: From Margin to Center.* Boston: South End Press, 1984.

Jenkins, Keith. "Introduction: On Being Open About Our Closures." *The Postmodern History Reader.* Ed. Keith Jenkins. London: Routledge, 1997, 1–34.

Kaye/Kantrowitz, Melanie. *The Issue is Power: Essays on Women, Jews, Violence and Resistance.* San Francisco: Aunt Lute, 1992.

Kimball, Roger. *Tenured Radicals: How Politics Has Corrupted Higher Education.* New York: Harper and Row, 1990.

Lorde, Audre. *Sister Outsider: Essays & Speeches.* Freedom, CA: Crossing Press, 1984.

Lowe, Lisa. *Immigrant Acts: On Asian American Cultural Politics.* Durham: Duke University Press, 1996.

Luke, Carmen and Jennifer Gore. *Feminisms and Critical Pedagogy.* New York: Routledge, 1992.

Lugones, María C. "Playfulness, 'World'-Traveling, and Loving Perception." *Making Face Making Soul/Haciendo Caras: Creative and Critical Perspectives by Feminists of Color.* Ed. Gloria Anzaldúa. San Francisco: Aunt Lute Foundation Books, 1990, 390–402.

Macdonald, Amie A. "Racial Authenticity and White Separatism: The Future of Racial Program Housing on College Campuses." *Reclaiming Identity: Realist The-*

ory and the Predicament of Postmodernism. Ed. Paula M. L. Moya and Michael Hames-García. Berkeley: University of California Press, 2000, 205–225.

McIntosh, Peggy. "White Privilege and Male Privilege: A Personal Account of Coming to See Correspondences through Work in Women's Studies." *Critical White Studies: Looking Behind the Mirror.* Ed. Richard Delgado and Jean Stefancic Philadelphia: Temple University Press, 1997, 291–299.

Maher, Frances and Mary Kay Thompson Tetreault. *The Feminist Classroom: An Inside Look at How Professors and Students are Transforming Higher Education for a Diverse Society.* New York: Basic Books, 1994.

Mayberry, Maralee and Ellen Cronan Rose. *Meeting the Challenge: Innovative Feminist Pedagogies in Action.* New York: Routledge, 1999.

Mendieta, Eduardo, and David Batstone, eds. *The Good Citizen.* New York: Routledge, 1999.

Mendieta, Eduardo. "Becoming Citizens, Becoming Hispanics." *The Good Citizen.* Ed. David Batstone and Eduardo Mendieta. New York: Routledge, 1999, 113–131.

Mohanty, Chandra. "On Race and Voice: Challenges for Liberal Education in the 1990s." *Beyond a Dream Deferred: Multicultural Education and the Politics of Excellence.* Ed. Becky W. Thompson and Sangeeta Tyagi. Minneapolis: University of Minnesota Press, 1993, 41–65.

Mohanty, Satya P. "The Epistemic Status of Cultural Identity: On *Beloved* and the Post-colonial Condition." *Reclaiming Identity: Realist Theory and the Predicament of Postmodernism.* Ed. Paula M. L. Moya and Michael Hames-García. Berkeley: University of California Press, 2000, 29–66.

———. "Radical Teaching, Radical Theory: The Ambiguous Politics of Meaning." *Theory in the Classroom.* Ed. Cary Nelson. Urbana: University of Illinois Press, 1986, 149–176.

———. *Literary Theory and the Claims of History: Postmodernism, Objectivity, Multicultural Politics.* Ithaca: Cornell University Press, 1997.

Moraga, Cherríe and Gloria Anzaldúa. *This Bridge Called My Back: Writings by Radical Women of Color.* New York: Kitchen Table: Women of Color Press, 1983.

Moraga, Cherríe. *Loving in the War Years: Lo que nunca pasó por sus labios.* Boston: South End Press, 1983.

Moraga, Cherríe. "A Long Line of Vendidas." *Loving in the War Years: Lo que nunca pasó por sus labios.* 2nd edition. Boston: South End Press, 2000, 82–133.

Morgan, K. P. "The Perils and Paradoxes of Feminist Pedagogy." *Resources for Feminist Research* 16. 3 (1987): 49–52.

Moya, Paula M. L. and Michael Hames-Garcia. *Reclaiming Identity: Realist Theory and the Predicament of Postmodernism.* Berkeley: University of California Press, 2000.

Moya, Paula M. L. "Introduction: Reclaiming Identity." *Reclaiming Identity: Realist Theory and the Predicament of Postmodernism.* Berkeley: University of California Press, 2000, 1–26.

———. *Learning from Experience: Minority Identities, Multicultural Struggles.* Berkeley: University of California Press, 2002.

———. "Postmodernism, 'Realism,' and the Politics of Identity: Cherríe Moraga and Chicana Feminism." *Reclaiming Identity: Realist Theory and the Predicament of Postmodernism.* Ed. Paula M. L. Moya and Michael Hames-García. Berkeley: University of California Press, 2000, 67–101.

Narayan, Uma. "Working Together Across Difference: Some Considerations on Emotions and Political Practice." *Hypatia* 3 (Summer, 1988): 31–47.

Nicholson, Linda, ed. *Feminism/Postmodernism.* New York: Routledge, 1990.

Nussbaum, Martha. *Love's Knowledge.* New York: Oxford University Press, 1990.

Paglia, Camille. *Sexual Persona: Art and Decadence from Negertiti to Emily Dickinson.* New Haven: Yale University Press, 1990.

Patai, Daphne and Noretta Koertge. *Professing Feminism: Cautionary Tales From the Strange World of Women's Studies.* New York: Basic Books, 1994.

————. *Heterophobia: Sexual Harassment and the Future of Feminism.* Lanham, Maryland: Rowman & Littlefield Publishers, 1998.

Reagon, Bernice Johnson. "Coalition Politics: Turning the Century." *Home Girls: A Black Feminist Anthology.* Ed. Barbara Smith. New York: Kitchen Table/Women of Color Press, 1983, 356–368.

Roman, Leslie G. and Linda Eyre. *Dangerous Territories: Struggles for Difference and Equality in Education.* New York: Routledge, 1997.

Roman, Leslie. "White is a Color! White Defensiveness, Postmodernism and Anti-racist Pedagogy." *Race, Identity and Representation in Education.* Ed. Cameron McCarthy and Warren Crichlow. New York: Routledge, 1993, 71–88.

Said, Edward. "The Politics of Knowledge." *Raritan* 11 (1) (Summer 1991): 17–31.

Sandoval, Chela. "US Third World Feminism: The Theory and Method of Oppositional Consciousness in the Post Modern World." *Genders* 10 (1991): 1–24.

Scheman, Naomi. "Anger and the Politics of Naming." *Women and Language in Literature and Society.* Ed. Sally McConnell-Ginet, Ruth Borker, and Nelly Furman. New York: Praeger, 1980, 174–187.

Schniedewind, N. and Frances Maher, eds. Special Feature: Feminist Pedagogy. *Women's Studies Quarterly.* 15.3/4 (1987).

Searle, John. "Postmodernism and the Western Rationalistic Tradition." *Campus Wars.* Ed. John Arthur and Amy Shapiro. Boulder, CO: Westview Press, 1995, 28–48.

Shor, Ira and Paulo Freire. "What is the 'Dialogical Method' of Teaching?" *Journal of Education* 169 (1987): 11–31.

Simon, Roger. "Empowerment as a Pedagogy of Possibility." *Language Arts* 64 (1987): 370–382.

Srivastava, Aruna. "Anti-Racism Inside and Outside the Classroom." *Dangerous Territories: Struggles for Difference and Equality in Education.* Ed. Leslie G. Roman and Linda Eyre. New York: Routledge, 1997, 113–126.

Tatum, Beverly Daniel. "Talking About Race, Learning About Racism: The Application of Racial Identity Development Theory in the Classroom." *Harvard Educational Review* 62.1 (1992): 1–24.

Tompkins, Jane. "Pedagogy of the Distressed." *College English* 52. 6 (1990): 653–660.

Trinh T. Minh-ha. *Woman, Native, Other.* Bloomington: Indiana University Press, 1989.

Weedon, Chris. *Feminist Practice and Poststructuralist Theory.* New York: Basil Blackwell, 1987.

PART I

CULTURAL IDENTITY AND STUDENT RESISTANCE

CHAPTER ONE

TOWARD A PEDAGOGY OF COALITION

Betty Sasaki

*Academic thinkers mediate the cultural politics of difference and have it
end up recodified as "multiculturalism."*

—Norma Alarcón

*[I]t may be through contradiction that we begin to address the systematic
inequalities built into cultural institutions, economies, and geographies,
and through conflict that we call attention to the process through which
these inequalities are obscured by pluralist multiculturalism.*

—Lisa Lowe

In the very recent history of the academic institution where I have taught for
the greater part of the last decade, a group of students of color and their
white allies took over the president's office to protest institutional racism.
The official response from the president, delivered at a Campus Community
Committee meeting, was a written document, which addressed the students'
demands primarily by reframing them within the college's "history" of successes in the area of diversity. Both before and after the occupation of the
president's office, student protestors organized informal forums, open to the
entire community, to discuss institutional racism. These meetings were
packed with students, whose competing identities, interests, needs, and desires came roiling to the surface in the form of often heated and contentious
debate. The fact that no administrator, let alone the president, attended any

of these discussions constitutes a disavowal of both the pervasive presence of racism on campus, and the experiences and knowledges that informed the students' actions and efforts toward social change. At the same time, it raises serious questions, many of which have been raised by the editors of this anthology, about the place, or lack thereof, for critical and dissenting voices within the educational institution.

The broad objective of this essay, then, is to formulate both a theoretical and practical response to some of those questions: What kinds of unspoken knowledge operate in the multicultural classroom? How have these conditions [of unspoken knowledge] been created and sustained? How can we begin to formulate new pedagogies that authentically promote freedom for all constituencies? What these questions point to is the complexity, confusion, and contradictions inherent to the multicultural enterprise that, despite its good intentions, often ends up neutralizing difference by way of appropriating it in the name of equality and inclusion. When considered from the more specific context of a small, liberal arts college committed to diversifying its historically majority white, upper-middle-class constituency, the "multi" in multiculturalism is often understood in relation to the One Culture. As a result, the prefix meaning, which denotes the many, ends up being redefined as something closer to "all others." Defined against the dominant culture, the many (multi) cultures are conflated, producing the illusion of a monolithic Second Culture that bespeaks a concept of "alter-culturalism" (as opposed to multiculturalism), a concept that, despite its aims and claims to the contrary, ends up maintaining the very binaries (center-margin; oppressor-oppressed, and so on) that it purportedly seeks to subvert. To keep the center intact, the margin must be policed with a vigilance that is masked beneath a discourse of consensus—a discourse that is all too easily and unproblematically conflated with the values of a just and democratic society.

As a biracial (Japanese-German American) woman who teaches Spanish at a private, liberal arts college in New England, I want first to problematize some of the more confusing and homogenizing narratives of multiculturalism, whose tendencies toward a kind of harmonious pluralism often silence, or exclude the possibility for oppositional narratives that challenge and disrupt the multicultural family metaphor. It is not my objective to resolve these contradictions but rather to argue that it is precisely at the site of these contradictions where the most productive and potentially transformative connections can be made between the multiple subjects that constitute the community. Such connections do not, as Cornel West rightly insists, "signal a homogenous unity or a monolithic totality but rather a contingent, fragile coalition building in an effort to pursue common radical libertarian and democratic goals that overlap" (30–31).

The question of how we as educators move from the paradigm of consensus to a more complex notion of coalition is at the center of my discussion on pedagogical praxis. Such a praxis entails the cultivation of conflict, not only among members of the classroom community, but within individual members of that community. From a critical pedagogical point of view, it means helping them understand and acknowledge that they occupy many, often contradictory subject positions, which may not be easily reconciled. Indeed, I would hazard that, from my own experience as a teacher, the pressure to resolve one's contradictions constitutes one of the conditions that creates and sustains a kind of "unspoken knowledge," one that can take the form of self-censorship in order to maintain a kind of self-consensus—an illusory sense of wholeness that replicates what I term an institutional discourse of consensus. By making explicit the ways in which such a discourse can mask the material, social, and historical differences, we can begin to entertain the possibility of building coalition with these multiple, at times, divergent positions and experiences as a first step toward apprehending the importance and the necessity of building coalition in the larger community.

Consensus and Ideal Community

In this section, I want to examine the ideal of community that, despite its good intentions, arises from what Iris Marion Young identifies as "the same desire for social wholeness and identification that underlies racism and ethnic chauvinism, on the one hand, and political sectarianism, on the other" ("The Ideal Community" 234). A part of that desire is informed by a notion of consensus that, as I shall argue, forecloses the possibility for coalition precisely because it insists upon a seamless correspondence both within and between the constituents of the ideal community.[1] In other words, what I shall call the discourse of consensus becomes the means by which to fulfill the desire for social wholeness while obscuring the more insidious project of creating the ideal citizen subject. As part of that project, such a discourse takes on a totalizing function that ends up eliding or denying difference. The problem arises, however, when the desire for wholeness collides with the reality of fragmentation and ambivalence brought on by diversifying an historically homogenous community.

Within the context of small, closed communities characteristic of private, liberal arts colleges publicly committed to diversifying both its curricular and civic "subjects," the discourse of consensus often couches itself in a liberal-pluralist version of multiculturalism, one which "develops a patronizing etiquette of tolerance and inclusiveness, a paternalistic exhortation to be nice to minorities" (Stam 190). It is along those same paternalistic lines that the family metaphor emerges, insisting with mantra-like relentlessness that we are all members of the same tribe. The analogy begs extension because it assumes that what we all share is not merely the same values, goals, and desires, but much more disturbingly, the same genealogy, the same family history. While the latter assumption may seem ludicrous, and it would most likely be denied by administrators and institutionally-identified campus citizens, it points to another troubling mechanism of the discourse of consensus that, alongside its totalization of social life, also dehistoricizes any understanding of social change.[2]

In the case of my institution, which as a typical private, liberal arts college I have no reason to believe is exceptional, there is no acknowledgement let alone discussion of the college's past exclusionary practices, whether it be with regard to women, minorities, or the working class. From the standpoint of the ideal of community built around the multicultural family metaphor, this truncation of history is not surprising; it maintains the illusory narrative that we have arrived, that collective wholeness has been achieved, that we have been triumphantly reunited with all our brothers and sisters to live happily ever after as we sit around the home fires sharing our stories. Indeed, it is a seductive scenario precisely because it promises the plenitude of authentic relationship by setting up inclusiveness as equality, and equality as sameness.[3] This convoluted, syllogistic formula is the result of the totalizing and detemporalizing effects of the discourse of consensus, which denies the material and historical contingencies that necessarily inform any concept of community as a social formation always in progress. The discourse of consensus is one that, in Stuart Hall's words, forgets that "it comes from a place, out of a specific history, out of a specific set of power relations. It speaks within a tradition" (185). When that tradition goes unrecognized, or is strategically cut-and-pasted into the college viewbooks, the historical picture is unproductively distorted and becomes a series of discrete images or imaginaries—a gallery of framed anecdotes that come to represent a utopian present informed by a nostalgicized, but not explicitly acknowledged past. In the brief historical overview presented in the college catalogue, the highlights and hallmarks are underscored, and we learn that the college, founded in 1813, became in 1871 "the first previously all-male college in New England to admit women" (5). A few sentences later, we jump to the present, where "Colby's 1,700 students—evenly divided between men and women—come from virtually every state and more than 43 foreign countries" (5). By this historical account, we are to infer that, as the concluding paragraph proudly asserts, "Colby stands for diversity" (5). We have in the space of a few lines stepped into the multicultural marketplace where, by this promotional soundbyte, the institution's history of exclusionary practices is unsurprisingly omitted. At the same time, also unsurprisingly, the college's viewbook and alumni magazine churn out photos of students and faculty of color at such a voluminous and unedited rate that one administrator recently remarked to me in private that "anyone would think every other student on campus was a student of color."

The discrepancy between a disacknowledged/understated past and an overdetermined present, between what is repressed and what goes to press, between private and public discourse is symptomatic of a dehistoricized multiculturalism—one that, ironically, in its aim toward inclusion operates on a series of exclusions, and in its desire for wholeness relies upon a discourse divorced from the material, social, and political contingencies, differences, and positions that necessarily inform the increasingly diverse constituencies of its community. In a sense, then, in order to let in "difference" and still maintain unity, it is necessary to keep out knowledge, or, at the very least, to carefully define what constitutes legitimate knowledge. It is this contradictory dimension, one that arises out of difference, that the institution, in an attempt to sustain a cohesive "self"-image, suppresses or denies in the stories or "histories" that it constructs about itself and its members. The success of that project depends upon the participation of institutional members whose individual "selves" are most often and successfully invoked by a rallying cry from the institution to come together around issues that threaten the cohesiveness of the community. In other words, the Western notion of a unified and coherent self informs the institutional "self"-definition of community,[4] one constructed by a discourse of consensus, which in turn becomes normalized through the pervasive reiteration of the family metaphor.

The family, or even the dysfunctional family, as a signifying trope within the epistemological frame of multicultural pluralism, is fundamental to generating and maintaining consensus. It immediately implies that all members of the community are in direct relation to one another, and privileges the notion of the nuclear, autonomous, self-made social unit. What gets erased in the process are the differences of race, class, and gender, along with the historically inscribed power differential among these categories.

A pedagogy of coalition does not simply invert this dynamic, replacing one set of "legitimate" knowledges for another. Instead, it addresses the ways in which knowledges are dynamically produced in the multiple, intersecting, and often competing narratives of the personal, political, and social. It means reframing the dominant notion of difference as something purely outside oneself to include an interrogation of one's own subjectivity. Thus, a pedagogical project of coalition begins by identifying and historicizing how narratives such as the one informing the consensus model of ideal community are legitimated, normalized, and internalized. By challenging the seamlessness of those narratives as one and the same, students can begin to question what many start out believing to be the seamlessness of their own subjectivity. This is uncharted territory for many of the students I teach, both white and nonwhite, because the discourse of consensus not only establishes but reaffirms the incontestability of what they know about the world and about themselves.

I have found in my own classroom experience that a framework of inquiry initially grounded in a larger historical narrative allows students to depersonalize their experiences so that when conflict arises, both between students and within students, they can begin to consider the dynamic of opposition outside the moral realm. The aim, then, is not to avoid conflict in the classroom, but rather to expand the ground of opposition from the purely personal and moral domains toward questions of how we come to know what we know, and how we value or devalue that knowledge. In the process, we forge a critical space in which our students can both recognize and examine the multiplicity of their own subjectivity ("I am a woman and a person of color," or "I am Latino and gay"), which a discourse of consensus systematically works to suppress by reducing "difference" to contradiction. This is, I believe, a crucial point of departure for a liberatory pedagogy, for it reconceptualizes difference by letting buried knowledges into a public discussion that challenges and critiques the consensus narrative of the ideal citizen subject.

I turn now to a series of anecdotal texts that both exemplify the totalizing mechanisms of consensus discourse and clarify some of the institutional challenges to the development of a pedagogy of coalition. Following that, I want to suggest ways in which we as educators might intervene in that discourse from a pedagogical perspective aimed at "teaching to transgress." (hooks, *Teaching to Transgress*).

Now You See Me, Now You Don't

People play different roles under different conditions; their identities emerge through complex interactions with others as well as through constant internal dialogue and negotiation.

—George Lipsitz

The paradigm of a coherent, institutional identity promoted by a consensus-based ideal of community presents serious challenges to the development of alternative, liberatory pedagogies. As the discussion above suggests, the foreclosure of any critical inquiry into the college's own history can perpetuate the reproduction of its liberalist ideology, creating a tightly closed community where historically dominant cultural values, practices, and knowledges remain at the center. Both the pedagogical and material repercussions of this self-replicating system are manifest in institutional policies concerning re-cruitment and retention, for such policies most directly ensure ideological homogeneity. Thus is born the "Colby-type," a term I have heard invoked in student admissions meetings, search committees, and promotional reviews.

To the extent that many of us exceed that type, a politics and pedagogy of coalition become crucial to our survival. Without it, we run the risk of re-producing an equally homogenous system that, to paraphrase Gloria An-zaldúa, leaves us on opposite sides of the river throwing rocks at one another. It is precisely this kind of divisiveness that consensus discourse promotes, challenging radical educators with the question of how to transform the com-mon ground of consensus into the uncommon ground of coalition. Uncom-mon because coalition work is both oppositional and relational at the same time. This is the paradox that makes coalition so difficult. As Bernice Reagon so rightly asserts, "Coalition work is not done in your home" (359). It is both dangerous and painful because, as my own experience continues to teach me, it requires a constant and simultaneous engagement with both myself and others, many of whom I would rather keep out of my "home." A theory of coalitional pedagogy is thus informed by the practical necessity of leaving "home." By that, I mean that along with exposing the structural, institutional mechanisms that keep us out, we must also "expose" ourselves. This is no easy task because it goes against everything I have learned to survive as a woman of color in an academic community and discourse that inscribe me as "other" by disavowing that inscription. In effect, it is this paradoxical location that makes coalition such a difficult but imperative proposition.

In the anecdotal texts I discuss below, I analyze my own experiences in order to elucidate the complexity of negotiating this seeming double bind. My goal here is not prescriptive; instead, I hope to clarify how such experi-ences have influenced my theoretical thinking around a pedagogy of coali-tion as a practice grounded in the acknowledgement and critical examination of the paradoxical and contradictory. My critical approach to these textualized experiences is informed by several feminists across disci-plines and social locations, whose work on identity formation provides a conceptual foundation and language for my own theoretical reflections.

Shortly after I arrived at Colby College in 1991, I was tempted to hang a sign around my neck that read: "My name is Betty Sasaki and I am a Span-ish teacher." Except for my colleagues in the Spanish Department who had hired me, each person I met invariably assumed that I was the new person in East Asian Studies. Each time I would respond, "No, I'm the new person in Spanish." And each time, with varying degrees of embarrassment or con-fusion, they would laugh and say something like, "Oh, isn't that funny—you're Japanese but you teach Spanish." Or, doing a double-take to peer more closely at my face, "Oh, are you part Hispanic?"

In the nine years I have been at the college, I have compiled a collection of such anecdotes because they are telling examples of both the anxiety and the ambivalence generated around my difference. Such anecdotes are all the more problematic to the extent not only that they expose the pervasive presence of ethnic stereotyping, but also that they point out the ways in which the process of "other identification" is informed by an understanding of difference as both an excess and a lack. On the one hand, from an institutional perspective, I and "others" like me constitute a victory in the college's struggle to diversify—a worthy struggle to say the least, but one that often operates on the assumption that diversity necessarily and "naturally" equals inclusiveness. Consequently, my status as an Asian American becomes a missing piece in the not quite complete family portrait that the college community would like to have of itself. Within the frame of this picture, my place among the family is already determined, indeed, is already overdetermined, by the good intentions and hopeful expectations of those who are more than willing to make room for their newly adopted member. On the other hand, however, my multiple positions as a biracial woman of color, with German as well as Asian heritage, who, in addition, teaches Spanish, become excessive when they don't quite fit familiar categories of otherness. As my initial anecdote suggests, my failure to meet the expectations of my colleagues gives rise to their anxiety because the different aspects of my identity seem to overflow the boundaries of the picture frame. Because I am suddenly neither easily quantifiable nor easily knowable, I often experience a subtle tightening of that welcoming embrace, which lends a dimension of confinement to the well-intentioned gesture of inclusion. As a result, I become, in the eyes of my predominantly white beholders, a curious oddity (an Asian who teaches Spanish) or an inauthentic version of what a "real" Asian American should be. This particular paradox reveals the way in which, because of my visible and invisible differences, I am seen as what Ruth Frankenberg calls a "memorable sign"—one that from a white perspective is "simultaneously over- and under-visible" ("When We Are Capable" 6).

The seesaw phenomenon of being positioned at the extremes of either hypervisibility or invisibility raises both a series of questions and a range of contradictions as to the benefits and limitations of diversity campaigns that are neatly and idealistically framed within the tenets of affirmative action. As a feminist and a woman of color, I strongly support affirmative action because I believe that structural changes such as hiring practices are necessary to counterbalance the legacy of institutional inequality. Yet, as the above example suggests, recruitment efforts in the name of diversity often amount to little more than superficial changes that do more to spice up "the dull dish that is white mainstream culture" (hooks, *Black Looks* 14) than complicate or deepen an understanding of difference. Indeed, as the fallout from the student protest against institutional racism shows, when attempts to diversify begin to gain political momentum, and various constituencies voice their distinct needs, those differences are deemed threatening to the happy family imaginary. And it is precisely at these critical junctures when the discourse of consensus is most strongly invoked as a means of containing and appropriating the contestatory voices that demand change and accountability. Along with the college president who publicly announced his paternal disappointment, insisting that the sit-in was unnecessary because he "has always maintained a open-door policy," written documents rapidly emerged in which long sections were devoted to a truncated historical account of everything the college has done in the name of diversity.[5]

A coalitional response to such discursive maneuvering is to identify and reframe it publicly as a community concern. Thus the student protestors organized extracurricular discussions on institutional racism, they set up information tables outside the student union, and they attended subsequent "campus community" meetings despite, or, more accurately, because the president presided at these meetings. With both persistence and courage they left the safety of their "home" to forge a contestory coalitional space that was both oppositional and relational. As a result, they forged an uneasy and provisional alliance with the administration, which has led to the formation of a standing committee on institutional racism as well as a proposal for a new diversity requirement specifically focused on systems of oppression within the United States. That such reforms might result in another institutional co-optation of diversity is the ongoing challenge of educators committed to a pedagogy of coalition. As alluded to above, the difficulty of coalition is that it is largely provisional, and most likely, uncomfortable. In order to critically intervene in such co-optation, a pedagogical project of coalition must promote "the active creation of oppositional analytic and cultural spaces" (Mohanty 148). At the same time, however, we must bear in mind that, despite the common goal of equality and justice, community members continue to occupy diverse locations within the institution, locations that both arise from and give rise to asymmetrical relationships of power. In the anecdote that follows, I analyze one such dynamic in order to highlight the ways in which asymmetrical locations are elided by the subtle invocation of consensus discourse. At the same time, drawing from theoretical discussions around identity formation by feminists of color, I examine this experience for the strategies of resistance it presents, strategies that, directly and indirectly, inform my later discussion of coalition strategies in the classroom.

During my second year at the college, I was approached by an administrator who, concerned by the rise in racial tension due to the Rodney King incident, asked me a question that, since then, has been addressed to me frequently: "How can we better accommodate our minority students?" Before

I could formulate a response, he posed another, which seemed to answer the first: "Do you find that the Asian American students are seeking you out?" Momentarily overwhelmed by the nature and velocity of his inquiry, I stared blankly at his expectant face, a blankness that prompted him to further explanation: "Since you are one of the few Asian American faculty members on campus, I was hoping that the Asian American students would perceive you as a role model, someone they could approach and talk to about their problems and experiences here."

I struggled for a response that would neither offend nor betray how offended I was. I was offended not by the explicit concern for the well-being of minority students, but rather by the implicit question, which remained buried and unacknowledged: How can we institutional leaders feel better about these discontented minority students whose voices of dissent pose a destabilizing threat to the whole? (Indeed, what happens when the kodachrome, multicolored images from the viewbook step off the page and begin to speak?) Where a crack appears in the desired seamlessness of community, a body is needed to repair it. The irony inherent in this particular instance is worth noting to the extent that it exposes the invisible contradictions, the cracks, so to speak, which consensus discourse anxiously attempts to deny. The interpellated other, therefore, is identified as both the cause and the cure for what ails the collective body, both the source of its fracturing and the glue that will hold together the disparate pieces. Having read the visible signs of my difference, the administrator had already assigned me the role I was to play in the college's multicultural family romance. In my discomfort, I felt both that I wanted disappear, and that I was disappearing, or being "disappeared." "I teach Spanish," I reminded him, "so I see a lot of students: white, Hispanic, African and Asian American, if they are in my classes. Since I have only been here a year, many students of color don't know me, nor do I know them." Now, it was the administrator's turn to stare blankly at me—a blankness that I read with mounting anxiety as the awkward silence between us expanded like a balloon ready to burst. He had not expected this response, which made me suddenly unfamiliar to him. He was looking at me, yes, but I could tell that he did not see me.

Who is it the administrator did not see? And who is it that he saw before I answered the question? Both questions posit identity in terms of seeing, and it is precisely this emphasis on the visible that needs to be problematized as it functions within an institutional community that operates on consensus largely through the invocation of the family metaphor. While there is, on the part of the administrator, an acknowledgement of the political dimensions of community unrest and discomfort, those dimensions are undermined to the extent that they remain within the realm of the private, informal conversation. The informality of the encounter creates a space of intimacy, or pseudo-intimacy, outside the public, official discourse of the institution. Within that space, the administrator assumes a familiar and familial relationship to me—one that allows him to see me simultaneously as different and same. Different to the extent that I am an Asian American woman with a racially visible affiliation to "another" culture; same to the extent that I am, nonetheless, a "family member" enjoined to mediate in a family problem. Ironically, the gesture of inclusion, of inviting me to participate in solving the institution's problems, is preceded by, or results from, identifying me as excluded, as marginal, and different.[6] It is, however, precisely the fallacy of intimacy that masks the initial racialized identification by creating the illusion that the administrator and I share equal positions because we might share equal concern. The further paradox is that my standing as a "good" citizen of the community depends upon my willingness both "to be" what he expects me to be and to place my "difference" and my "sameness" in the service of bridging political dissonance and reestablishing community harmony. The place of pseudo-intimacy becomes, then, to borrow Homi Bhabha's term, "a place of splitting" (44)—one in which the invitation to a wholeness of identity carries with it the implicit requirement that I disconnect from myself, or, more specifically, to speak from only one position as the totality of my subjectivity.

This interaction has been particularly instructive in my thinking around coalitional pedagogy because it delineates explicitly the pervasive deployment of consensus discourse in the formation of ideal citizen subjects. Its success depends upon my internalization of that narrative, my acceptance of the value assigned to my difference. As stated earlier, because a pedagogy of coalition aims to engage critical discussion of difference outside the purely moral and personal/private domain, it challenges the institutional narrative of good citizenship. One's standing as a member of coalitional community is determined not only by the risks we take in claiming our difference, but more importantly, by the ways in which we negotiate those claims in relationship to the differences of others. In a coalitional community, my differences may not be erased but that does not mean they are uncontested. The irony and the challenge of coalition building is that to be a good citizen does not mean that we get to feel good.

I would like to consider now the question of who it is the administrator did not see at the end of our conversation. By who I don't mean to imply that there is some essential or authentic self that went unseen or unacknowledged by the administrator. On the contrary, my "disappearance" was the result of my response, which defamiliarized me, or, at least, the administrator's version/vision of me. Because my response fails to mirror his assumptions about who I am, as an Asian and as a "kinswoman," I disrupt his gaze and interrupt the "cultural fiction" of family in which I have been cast.

Consequently, the administrator did not see me because he did not see himself reflected in me: an operation of failed identification, which resulted in his disengagement. Suddenly neither same nor other, I am momentarily undefinable and invisible, too much and too little. My "disappearing act," which ironically occurs when I attempt to identify myself from the specific institutional location as an untenured professor of Spanish, destabilizes the essentialist notion that my visible racial markers are a sign of some authentic Asian identity. At the same time, it brings to light the often-unproblematized premise that, in interactions such as these, my interlocutors' whiteness constitutes the normative measure of my difference. The double vision and viewing in this type of identity negotiation points out that racial identity is, as Frankenberg observes, "relational, made through the claiming and imposition of sameness and otherness" ("When We Are Capable" 4). To claim the disappearing act as mine is, in this context, to posit identity formation as a process that is "dynamic, temporally expansive, centrally concerned with self-revision" (Butler 443).

The emphasis on relationality and self-revision underscores the potential for agency and counters the common misunderstanding that often equates contestation and resistance with "a culture of complaint" and victimhood. The relational dimension of identity formation operates both externally, in interactions between people and groups, and internally, in interactions between the multiple locations and varied aspects of one's own subjectivity. Such a reformulation of identity is a crucial step in the formation of a theoretical model for coalitional pedagogy. By providing an alternative conceptual model in which to examine difference as both an external and internal operation of identity formation, it disrupts the consensus model, which insists upon an integrated, nonconflicted sense of wholeness not only among constituents of a community, but also within individual members of that community. As Iris Marion Young so forcefully argues:

> The dissolution of cultural imperialism . . . requires a cultural revolution which also entails a revolution in subjectivity. Rather than seeking a wholeness of the self, we who are the subjects of this plural and complex society should affirm the otherness within ourselves, acknowledging that as subjects we are heterogeneous and multiple in our affiliations and desires. (*Justice and the Politics of Difference* 125)

To the extent that Young's affirmation of a kind of auto-otherness expands and complicates notions of identity by reproblematizing oppositional narratives and voices as more than a simple polarization between competing groups, it provides a useful conceptual tool for a working theory of coalitional pedagogy. The construction of identity as dialogical (not just oppositional) opens the possibility for alternative critical spaces and relationships. At the same time, the reconfiguration of identity as an ongoing process of becoming that is both interrelational and intrarelational resists the closure, the promised wholeness, of discretely defined epistemological, ontological, and experiential knowledges that inform who we are. This refusal to closure is neither an abrogation or giving up of historical and cultural specificity for a kind of pluralistic totalization of a transcendent selfhood, nor is it a reductive claim to an essentialist totality. Instead, to conceive of the self as a "subject-in-process"[7] is to open the borders between those separate spheres of knowledge as a way of deterritorializing our very understanding of subjectivity as both product and producer of history. As a result, there is more room to move, or, as María Lugones terms it, to travel both in and between these "worlds" because "we are not fixed in particular constructions of ourselves" (400).

My response to the administrator deflects his unconscious yet troubling attempt to interpellate me into the weakened family narrative, not because I disavow my racial and ethnic identity, but rather because I acknowledge it as hybrid, heterogeneous, and multiple.[8] The question of seeing, of how visible differences are read from the standpoint of consensus is thus further complicated by the question of speaking. Given my gender, my biraciality, my heterosexuality, my working-class background, my institutional status as an untenured faculty member, my occupational status as a teacher of Spanish, from where did I speak? As I engage the administrator at the various locations he occupies (i.e., power broker in the institutional hierarchy, male, white, and so on), I also engage my own multiple positions. It is the multiple engagement of locations, and my movement among them, which provides the ground from which I speak, and that ground is not populated only by the singular "Asian" woman, the one-dimensional "other," whom the administrator "sees."[9] Such a strategy allows for resistance against the simple reduction of multiple social, political, occupational, and psychological locations to a single category of identity because it rejects the implicit terms of the relational contract, which require me to see the administrator as equally one-dimensional: in this case, as a fellow family member. The refusal to collude, therefore, is neither a simple withdrawal from relationship, nor a mere inversion of the power dynamic, but rather a renegotiation of the relational contract that requires an acknowledgement not of our "familial" sameness, nor only of our social differences, but of what I call our mutual alterity.

Derived, in part, from Lugones's concept of "world-travelling," mutual alterity suggests a two-way operation. In other words, to the extent that I "travel" into the "world" of the administrator and his construction of me in it, my presence there, when it does not correspond to his expectations, compels him to experience a discontinuity in his own sense of self. It is precisely by way of this operation that the dominant, normative gaze is decentered, producing the discomfort of a potentially productive self-consciousness. By that, I mean that the contradictory messages and double-binds are momentarily left between us, not as unresolvable, but as unresolved. And, it is precisely in this space of the unreconciled that an opening for change can occur, not only, I would argue, with regard to institutional "identifications" of difference, but also in relation to the process of self-identity. As Norma Alarcón so convincingly asserts:

> [a] bi- or multiethnicized, raced, and gendered subject-in-process may be called upon to take up diverse subject positions that cannot be unified without double binds and contradictions. . . . The paradoxes and contradictions between the subject positions move the subject to recognize, reorganize, reconstruct, and exploit difference through political resistance and cultural productions in order to reflect the subject-in-process." (138)

These experiences have been crucial to my formulation of a pedagogy of coalition. In the next section, I focus on classroom experiences with the following questions in mind. How does a theory of coalitional pedagogy work in the classroom, where my positionality is different? How do the relational complexities of identity formation discussed above operate in and inform a pedagogical practice of coalition?

Coalition in The Classroom

In a small, private liberal arts college in rural New England whose student body is predominantly white and upper-middle class, the most difficult part of this pedagogical project of coalition arises in student resistance and/or inability to conceptualize difference outside the paradigm of visibility. Within the powerful framework of consensus, diversity becomes either transparent (invisible) or purely cosmetic (hypervisible). For white students this often means that they are blinded by their own whiteness, which remains unmarked and fosters the illusion of wholeness. For students of color, this often means they are limited by the imposition of a purely racialized identity, which as my own experience shows, is institutionally constructed as their only choice. The challenge we face is breaking open that either/or formulation, and by so doing, creating a third-space or borderland where, I believe, we have the greatest opportunity to hear both the unspoken and unspeakable knowledges that all too often don't make their way into classroom discussion. A pedagogical project of coalition is one that works simultaneously on two levels: externally, with the aim of critiquing the institutional, cultural, and social hierarchies in which we are located, and internally, with the aim of interrogating how those locations inform who we are as both multiple and contradictory subjects. It involves helping students mediate these two levels of critical inquiry so that connections can be made along the lines of difference rather than sameness.[10] Contrary to the consensus model, a coalitional approach acknowledges the points of resistance that arise when students are faced with contradictions that they often find threatening to "who they are." For both students of color and white students, anxiety arises from a limited view of their own multiple positioning not merely as students in a classroom, or citizens of a community, but as subjects in history. I turn now to a classroom experience, which in many ways addresses some of the issues I've raised.

In a discussion on race with my students (all of them white), I recount the same anecdotes discussed above and then ask them if they think these anecdotes are examples of racism. In the silence that follows I watch as each of them averts his or her gaze from me, as if, by calling attention to my racial identity, I have suddenly become a light too bright to look at directly. Sensing a mixture of discomfort and pensiveness, I wonder if I have gone too far, if I have abused my authority as professor by using my racial and ethnic subject position to turn myself into the object of discussion. "No," I hear a voice say, snapping me out of my thoughts. It is a student, responding to my initial questions. "I don't think those are racist examples," he continues, "because they were not intended to be hurtful. They were not motivated by hatred." I see a couple of heads nod in tacit agreement, but, before I can respond, another student speaks. "I disagree," she says. "Maybe they didn't mean to be racist, but their comments indicate their ignorance about another culture." "But," another student counters, "most people in New England don't have much contact with other races or cultures. That's not something they can control; it's not their fault they live where they do." As the discussion moves away from the specificity of my experience to the more general realm of racism, I notice how my students become more comfortable, vocal, and articulate. Despite disagreements as to the definition, they have found common ground—all of them are opposed to racism. Yet, between that moral binary—racism is bad, antiracism is good—there are, I believe, a host of other positions, attitudes, experiences, and knowledges that are discretely bounded outside their conscious sense of a whole self. How do we access what lies outside of consciousness? How do we bring to consciousness "the languages and knowledges that [students] have inherited and which unconsciously exert control over their thinking and behavior" (McLaren "Multiculturalism" 206)? What are the risks that we and our students take by exploring that question? And, how do we create an environment in which such risk-taking is possible?

Feminist pedagogies over the last 20 years have provided partial answers to these questions by transforming the politics of the classroom. While the initial aim of these efforts was to create "safe" classroom environments for women students, these efforts have been extended to include the voices of other groups that have been historically marginalized and silenced. The results of these efforts, however, have been as mixed as the different constituencies that currently inhabit many classrooms. As history shows, (and as my previous encounter with the administrator supports), the democratizing and liberatory aims of such strategies are easily recodified within institutional discourses and practices that obscure the continued operations of hierarchy, power, and inequality. The result can be a kind of "staged openness" in the classroom, where the power dynamic between students and teachers is often superficially mediated by inverting the authoritative center from teacher to students. A problematic aspect of the "non-authoritarian classroom"[11] is that, while it aims to address unequal relationships of power by encouraging student participation in the construction of knowledge, it often lacks a theoretical frame and a critical language through which to examine the "knowledges" produced. Many educators, despite their good intentions, are not prepared to critically engage the many differences they confront, not only among an increasingly diverse student body, but also, I would venture, among the multiple positions they occupy in the classroom, the institution, and society at large.[12]

A truly transformative feminist pedagogy must strategically and actively engage the multiple relationships of power that come into play in any classroom. It must move critically beyond mere gestures of equality and inclusiveness by examining the historical, cultural, and political differences both within and among members of a given community that, when they remain unrecognized, render such well-meaning gestures meaningless. It means developing strategies that encourage both students and educators to reconceptualize their differences by acknowledging and naming themselves as positioned subjects. At the same time, it is imperative to analyze how these various locations within academic, institutional, and social structures shift in ways that afford or deny them varying degrees of privilege and power.

In this particular classroom context, for example, where a discussion on race takes place among 15 white students and one female professor of color, the unspoken and the unspeakable become highly nuanced and potentially charged because the relationships of power and authority are multiple. There is, on the one hand, the teacher-student relationship, in which, from an occupational standpoint, I ostensibly hold the position of greater authority. On the other hand, however, from a social perspective that is replicated in the institutional structure, I, as a woman and person of color, occupy an inferior position. The pressure not to name these relational distinctions is great, for it runs counter to the myth of equality and sameness, indeed, against the very values of democracy that the liberal arts institution claims to stand for. In an institutional and pedagogical culture that privileges student voices and experiences, there is a dangerous tendency to overlook the multiplicity of hierarchical relationships that come into play. Practically and pedagogically speaking, this tendency results in an often-uncritical support for creating "safe" classroom environments in which mutual respect and trust become the cornerstone for honest and open discussion. While most educators would certainly agree on principle with the goals of respect, trust, and honesty, the question arises as to what we are keeping both students and ourselves safe from. The pseudo-intimacy invoked by the administrator in our interaction comes to mind, and underscores the ways in which the familiar and familial relationship can become both reinscribed and reproduced in the classroom. Safety, in this sense, becomes the code word for the absence of conflict, a tacit and seductive invitation to collude with the unspoken ideological machinery of the institutional family.

Returning for a moment to my anecdote, the common ground of my white students' opposition to racism, while admirable, is also "safe"—not just for them, but for me. To stay here is tempting precisely because it unites us and reaffirms our sense of wholeness; the differences that initiated the discussion are suddenly gone. We are momentarily secure in our common knowledge about the evils of racism, and the specificity of both my anecdotes and their responses disappears. This disappearance of difference, if left unchallenged and unexamined, can easily be mistaken for a resolution of difference when, in fact, it is the consequence of my students' resistance, albeit unconscious, to acknowledging whiteness as a social position they occupy. Thus, I return to their comments with the conscious and strategic goal of refocusing the discussion not on the personal dimensions of my experience, but on the unconscious assumptions underlying some of my students' responses to it. From a pedagogical perspective, I am well aware of the potential for such a move either to shut the discussion down or elicit a defensive reaction. I believe, however, that a truly liberatory classroom "involve[s] the shifting relations of power as students engage with ideas they may find threatening" (Elshtain 110). I begin by taking up the assertion held by about half the class that racism is an act or comment motivated by a conscious hatred of the other. In other words, one's conscious intentions inform the meaning of what one says, creating a false syllogism of sorts, that goes something like this:

a. If the visible differences of the racialized other bring on a comment offensive to that "other"
b. but the speaker does not intend to be offensive
c. then the initial visible difference is neutralized in the discourse of intentionality, which completely sidesteps the issues of racialized perceptions.

In this formula, I point out, the perceived "other" is magically disappeared, though paradoxically, it was her hypervisibility that brought on the comment in the first place.

The second premise, held by the other half of the students, posits racism as the product of one's ignorance about those differences from one's own experience. As one of my students asserts, "Knowledge will eradicate racism." While I appreciate her optimism and forthrightness, I add, "Knowledge about what or whom?" From this perspective, I explain, the racial markers of the other are "seen" as another type of sign—one whose meaning is fixed and, therefore, "learnable" or "translatable" into the language of the perceiver's experience. Rather than erasing the hypervisibility of difference, one ends up appropriating that difference to fill in the gaps of his or her own worldview. In this formula, the perceived other is still objectified as a knowable and quantifiable fact. It is one thing, and an important one, to learn about another's culture, race, gender, class, or sexuality. "But," I ask my students, "what do you know about your own? What does it mean to be white?"[13]

It is at this point, when I pose this question, that the animated discussion falters, and I watch my students avert their eyes from me once again. From where I sit at the front of the room, I know they look away not only because they see me as "other," but also, and perhaps more importantly, because I see them as "other." By asking them to look at their own whiteness, I am asking them to see themselves, for a moment, through my eyes, rather than in my eyes, and so I have denied them the reassuring reflection of themselves they expect from their teacher (specifically their female teacher of color). That mirror cracked, I sense that their view of both me and themselves has shifted out of focus as their apparently seamless, unified, and coherent picture of who they are, or who they believed they were, is momentarily filled with the fault lines and fractures of their own alterity.

From both a theoretical and practical perspective, this moment of profound discomfort is also a moment of profound pedagogical potential. It constitutes an opening into the borderlands of subjectivity because it moves, albeit incrementally, some part of what was previously unconscious into the disquieting realm of self-consciousness. Paradoxically, perhaps, it transforms knowledge by transforming what was once familiar (and familial) into something unfamiliar. The challenge is how to proceed without falling into the potentially depoliticized and ahistorical void of personal experience. To decolonize pedagogical practices, as Chandra Talpade Mohanty asserts, "requires that teachers and students develop a critical analysis of how experience itself is named, constructed, and legitimated in the academy" (155). As my students and I gaze at each other in uneasy silence, I wonder if I have merely inverted a paradigm by interpellating my students into a counternarrative opposed to consensus discourse. Perhaps. Yet, I think the value of the exercise remains to the extent that it calls attention to their whiteness and thereby calls upon them to question the irreducibility of their own sense of identity. That, I believe, is a starting point, not a destination, for a more explicit analysis of their own subjectivity as it is produced in relation to knowledge and power.

From the back of the room, a student asks, "What do you mean?" Her tone is both tentative and defensive, and I am simultaneously perturbed and pleased. Perturbed because it seems clear to me that she, along with most of her peers, has not encountered this discussion in other contexts. Pleased because, despite her resistance, she is willing to risk the question, she is willing to respond. To take that risk may well be motivated by a sense that she has something to lose, but the awareness of potential loss may provide an inroad to naming what we have, and where our historical, social, and material investments have been made. Those investments inform the "multiple interests" to which McLaren refers, and as such, they are grounded in a variety of locations, histories, and knowledges. By acknowledging those differences explicitly, we interrupt the discourse of consensus, and move a step closer to a model of coalition.

At the moment when my students experience their "otherness," they enter the terrain of their own alterity. As they become conscious of their whiteness, their view of themselves changes. That shift in consciousness is uncomfortable because it threatens the epistemological and ontological ground they have always assumed to be not just their world, but the world. The discomfort they feel, therefore, is not only internal, in relation to the way they see themselves, but also external, in relation to the way they see me, the classroom, and the world beyond it. This is a moment, similar to my interaction with the administrator, of mutual alterity. It is here that the family model, previously understood as "the natural order of things," can be demystified and examined critically because it provides an opening and extends an invitation to each of us to leave "home." What we forge may leave either or all of us feeling dissatisfied, but I would argue that, from a coalitional perspective, that dissatisfaction may well be the place we must occupy—at least for the moment.

This shift in students' awareness happens in a single moment, and the real challenge for a transformative, critical pedagogy is charting ways in which to make this new knowledge more conscious, explicit, and critical. My student's question contains both a request to return to the familiar, affirming dynamic of the family and an imperative to move further into the more unfamiliar, less affirming relationship of coalition. As I confront her question, I am equally aware that the defensive tone of her question signals that, in the disquieting borderland of her own identity, she is ready to take this discussion as a personal indictment. Having experienced this type of personalization before (and not only with white students and colleagues), I recognize that this is a moment of both potential divisiveness and alliance. The question here is how to cultivate the potential for alliance without falling back into the consensus model. In terms of formulating an effective pedagogical strategy, it also concerns an awareness of the particular power I hold at this juncture, both as their teacher and the "author" of the narratives under discussion. My pedagogical inclination, informed by what I believe to be the limitations of personal narrative when it is not historicized, is to depersonalize the issue by historicizing it. Thus, in response to her question, I propose that we attempt to answer it collectively. Breaking them into groups, the assignment I give them is double: first, to research and narrate a "history" of the college, and second, to develop a family genealogy that takes as its starting point the year the college was founded. Clearly, my goal is to highlight the ways in which the personal, historical, social, and cultural are, indeed, inter-related, but not synonymous. Moreover, such an assignment invariably produces different versions of the institution's history, depending upon how each student group interprets and includes (or omits) what students deem to be important, "historical" information. How these decisions are informed by students' multiple locations is clarified, in part, by their personal genealogies and the extent to which they parallel or diverge from that institutional history.

For the students of this class, an important aspect of this project included historicizing their whiteness as an inseparable but specific part of who they understood themselves to be. But, the same project can be equally challenging and productive to more multicultural classroom constituencies. It allows students of color to speak from "the authority of experience" without restricting them to that standpoint alone.[14] Moreover, it encourages them to historicize and theorize their own experiences so that when they march on the president's office, for example, they speak from the ground in which their social, political, institutional, and personal locations are co-aligned.[15] This intrasubjective coalition of multiple subject positions, for both students of color and white students, is, I believe, a fundamental element of forging alliances between different groups. To claim that one is not racist does not mean that one is antiracist, just as disclaiming oneself as a sexist by no means qualifies one as a feminist. The simple denial of what we consider to be morally reprehensible can reduce the issue of collective and historical accountability to a question of blame that keeps us locked out of relationship to ourselves and each other. A pedagogy of coalition, therefore, is a collective endeavor to bring to the surface the unconscious and buried knowledges that will ultimately complicate and question, destabilize and open up for critique the normative ways of seeing ourselves and others. The ground from which we speak is forged not through maintaining consensus, but by making alliances, however uneasy they might be, both internally within ourselves and, externally, with others. In this way, the central question becomes one "not just about having a voice, but the sort of voice one comes to have as the result of one's location both as an individual and as part of a collective" (Mohanty 162).

Conclusion

As we enter the new millennium, I believe that the impact of economic and political globalization on conceptions of national borders and identities will increasingly complicate the formation of citizen subjects. In much the same way that discriminatory immigration policies reflect an increasing anxiety about holding the center intact, so do recruitment policies and normative pedagogical practices. Thus it is urgent that we develop alternative pedagogical practices committed to the creation of a citizenry able to critically engage in public thought and social action. The hidden cracks in consensus discourse like the "fractures of identity in struggle" (Spivak 180) are always there—faultlines that stretch like borders between territories of knowledge. As educators in the twenty-first century, I believe we have both a political and ethical imperative to encourage ourselves, each other, and our students to live on those borders in order to understand that notions of self, community, and culture are grounded in processes of struggle and resistance rather than coherence and consensus. By that, I am not advocating a postmodernist privileging of the fragmented and fragmentary. I agree with Peter McLaren's call for a type of provisional totalizing:

> Without a shared vision (however contingent and provisional) of democratic community, we risk endorsing struggles in which the politics of difference collapses into new forms of separatism. . . . We need to retain some kind of moral, ethical, and political ground—albeit a provisional one—from which to negotiate multiple interests. (207).

As I have discussed in this essay, however, before multiple interests can be negotiated, those interests must be acknowledged. Because the discourse of consensus is largely rooted in a legacy of moral certitude that has shaped the historical narratives around the colonizing practices of the United States, including the colonization of its citizen subjects, a truly liberatory pedagogy of coalition is a project of decolonization. As its point of departure, it works to transform the classroom into a space where the "openings" I have referred to not only let difference in but also let knowledge out. I believe that the analyses of my own experiences attest to the difficulty of forging coalition because it requires us to reimagine ourselves as incomplete, as works-in-progress, as multiple and contradictory subjects. Rather than deny those contradictions, a pedagogy of coalition moves toward them in order to examine the intersections and conflicts between structural and subjective narratives as a step toward transforming the contradictory subject into a coalitional subject— one whose critical awareness of her multiple "selves" allows her to stay engaged with both herself and the world so that the actions she takes and the decisions she makes are consciously responsive rather than unconsciously reactive. Thus the ground of coalition may be uncommon, but it is not impossible. As we teach students to live, think, and be at the crossroads of knowing and not knowing, of confronting and negotiating the contradictions of their own lives, and of embracing the possibility that their own beliefs can and should be subject to critical analysis, we practice and continue to develop a pedagogy of coalition.

Notes

1. Problematizing the presuppositions and implications upon which many radical theorists and activists define an ideal community, Iris Marion Young notes that "[t]he ideal of community presumes subjects who are present to themselves and presumes subjects can understand one another as they understand themselves" ("The Ideal of Community," 234).

2. Young specifies the mechanisms by which these processes operate: "The ideal community . . . totalizes and detemporalizes its conception of social life by setting up an opposition between authentic and inauthentic social relations. It also detemporalizes its understanding of social change by positing the desired society as complete negation of existing society" ("The Ideal of Community" 234).

3. The conflation of inclusiveness, equality, and sameness are institutionally promoted through countless early indoctrination and bonding rituals that occur each year before classes begin. Such rituals are specifically aimed at first-year students in the form of small group camping trips, myriad orientation workshops especially aimed at students of color, and "unofficially" sanctioned dorm parties.

4. The notion of a rational, agentive, unitary concept of selfhood stems, in part, from the European tradition of transcendental philosophy. "Beginning with Descartes, modern philosophy is particularly preoccupied with the unity of consciousness and its immediate presence to itself" (Young, "The Ideal. . . ." 235). In their historicization of the Western autobiographical subject, Watson and Smith trace that unified subject to the Enlightenment, where they note that "the Enlightenment 'self' . . . becomes 'Man,' putatively a marker of the universal human subject whose essence remains outside the vagaries of history, effectually what Spivak has termed the 'straight white Christian man of property,' whose identity is deeply embedded in a specific history of privilege" (De/Colonizing the Subject xvii).

5. It is worth noting that in his official written response to the student protest and the Task Force that came out of that protest, the president addressed the demand for an increase in minority student and faculty recruitment by citing numbers: "The current student body (Fall 1998) is approximately 10 percent ALANA, a total of 182: 40 African Americans, 46 Latino/Latina, 6 Native Americans, and 90 Asian Americans. In addition, there are 81 international students. . . . [O]ur current numbers (for faculty of color) are: 4 African American, 6 Latino/Latina, and 13 Asian or Asian Americans, for a total of 23 faculty of color" ("Response to the April 14 Report of the Task Force and the Two April Memoranda on Racial Concerns at Colby" 4–5). What the report omits is the brief review of the college's diversity goals and progress, included in a report by the Trustee Commission on Multicultural and Special Interest Housing, and conducted in 1994 in response to student of color demands for a Multicultural House: "A trustee planning exercise in 1990 set a goal for the entering class of 1995 to have at least 20 percent representation from the nation's three most populous ethnic groups-African American, Hispanic, and Asian American. Although the class that entered in the fall of 1994—one year short of the goal time frame—had the largest minority group representation in Colby history (10 percent), the College is still well short of the goal" (3).

When these two documents are read together, there emerges a much more problematic perspective on the College's "commitment to diversity." The bald use of numbers in itself reifies and commodifies so-called community members of color. But, even more disturbing is the institution's blatant refusal to acknowledge its failure not merely to recruit and retain more students of color, but, more importantly, to address the reasons why. Instead, the president simply omits the 1994 chapter of the college's history and attempts to avoid the obvious implications of accountability that it holds for the newest 1999 chapter. This type of historical "revision," deployed as a means of maintaining the illusion of family cohesion, erases the history of oppositional struggle for change, and denies difference.

6. Young identifies this type of experience as the result of "cultural imperialism," which "consists in a group's being visible at the same time that it is marked out and stereotyped" (*Justice and the Politics of Difference* 123).

7. In her discussion of critical modes of consciousness necessary to counter the structural and discursive overdetermination of the subject, Alarcón proposes the concept of "the subject-in-process who constructs provisional identities, or Sandoval's tactical subjectivity, which subsume a network of signifying practices and structural experiences imbricated in the historical and imaginary shifting national borders of Mexico and the United States for Chicanas, for example" (137). See also Anzaldúa, Lugones, Moraga, and Sandoval.

8. See Lowe's discussion of the importance of heterogeneity, hybridity, and multiplicity in the formation of Asian American cultural identity.

9. The formation of a ground from which the subaltern speaks, which Hall has located in the arena of race and ethnicity, has been complicated by U.S.

third-world feminists. Specifically, my notion of speaking among multiple locations is derived, in part, from Sandoval's concept of "differential consciousness," which "permits the practitioner to . . . self-consciously break and reform ties to ideology, activities which are imperative for the psychological and political practices that permit the achievement of coalition across differences" (15). Alarcón elucidates the powerful effects of this mode of consciousness as "moving us toward and/or finding the relationality between the inside . . . and the outside as the cross-cultural, intersubjective site; that is, [Sandoval] poses the challenge of resistance to oppositional hegemonies through a *différance* that works inside and outside on multiple planes—a factor that works itself out through a "speaking subject" conscious that she can be constituted by discourse and yet not be completely determined by it" (137).

10. Forging connections along lines of difference rather than sameness finds resonance in McLaren's call for a "dialogic pedagogy in which subjects see others as subjects and not as objects. When this happens, students are more likely to participate in history rather than become its victims" ("White Terror" 55).

11. Elshtain, "The Social Relations of the Classroom," 110.

12. There is an increasingly substantial body of scholarship on critical and radical pedagogy that addresses the importance of location consciousness for both students and teachers. Maher and Tetreault call for "pedagogies of positionality, . . . approaches to teaching in which [the] complex dynamics of difference and inequality could be named and examined" (141). Building on this concept, Sleeter develops a pedagogical strategy of "repositioning perspective," grounded in the recognition that "one is situated in an unequal context, and one's perspective grows partially out of one's situation" (417). As a pedagogical response to the "the multiple misuses of pedagogy in terms of race/class/gender," Haymes suggests that educators need to "[confront] their own racial formation as well as that of their students" (107). For a number of excellent essays that discuss this issue, see *Between Borders: Pedagogy and the Politics of Cultural Studies*, eds. Henry Giroux and Peter McLaren; *Multicultural Education, Critical Pedagogy, and the Politics of Difference*, eds. Christine Sleeter and Peter McLaren.

13. I want to clarify that heuristic studies about whiteness are most often distinct from notions of White Studies programs that have been proposed largely by the conservative, academic right. Drawing on critical scholarship about the impact of whiteness on pedagogical practices, my discussion of whiteness in this essay intends, in part, to contribute to that body of critical work, which challenges us to make transparent the axes of power and privilege that an unmarked whiteness obscures.

14. I agree with hooks, who compellingly complicates the "authority of experience" as "the passion of experience," whose complexity "can rarely be voiced and named from a distance. It is a privileged location, even as it is not the only or even always most important location from which one can know" (*Teaching to Trangress* 91).

15. Gallegos underscores the crucial role, especially for students of color, to theorize their experiences as a means of disrupting dominant discourses that attempt to contain them.

Works Cited

Alarcón, Norma. "Conjugating Subjects in the Age of Multiculturalism." Gordon and Newfield 127–148.

Anzaldúa, Gloria. *Borderlands/La Frontera: The New Mestiza*. San Francisco: Spinsters/Aunt Lute, 1987.

———. *Making Face/Haciendo Cara: Creative and Critical Perspectives by Feminists of Color*. San Francisco: Aunt Lute Books, 1990.

Appiah, Kwame Anthony, and Henry Louis Gates, Jr., eds. *Identities*. Chicago: University of Chicago Press, 1995.

Bhabha, Homi. *The Location of Culture*. New York: Routledge, 1994.

Butler, Judith. "Collected and Fractured: Response to Identities." Appiah and Gates 439–447.

Colby College Catalogue. 1998.

Cotter, William. "Response to the April 14 Report of the Task Force and the Two April Memoranda on Racial Concerns at Colby." 30 April 1999.

Elshtain, J. B. "The Social Relations of the Classroom: A Moral and Political Perspective." *Telos* 97(1976): 110.

"Final Report of the Colby College Trustee Commission on Multicultural and Special Interest Housing." March 1994.

Frankenberg, Ruth. "When We Are Capable of Stopping, We Begin to See: Being White, Seeing Whiteness." Thompson and Tyagi 3–17.

———. *White Women, Race Matters: The Social Construction of Whiteness*. Minneapolis: University of Minnesota Press, 1993.

Gallegos, Bernardo. "Memory, Location, and Theory in Postcolonial Education." First Annual Colby Education Conference. Colby College. 1 May 1999.

Giroux, Henry. *A Pedagogy and Politics of Hope: Theory, Culture, and Schooling*. Boulder: Westview Press, 1997.

Giroux, Henry A., and Peter McLaren, eds. *Between Borders: Pedagogy and the Politics of Cultural Studies*. New York: Routeldge, 1994.

Gordon, Avery, and Christopher Newfield, eds. *Mapping Multiculturalism*. Minneapolis: University of Minnesota Press, 1996.

Hall, Stuart. "The Local and the Global: Globalization and Ethnicity." McClintock et al.173–187.

Haymes, Stephen. "White Culture and the Politics of Radical Difference: Implications For Multiculturalism." Sleeter and McLaren 105–127.

hooks, bell. *Black Looks: Race and Representation*. Boston: South End Press, 1992.

———. *Teaching to Transgress: Education and the Practice of Freedom*. New York: Routledge, 1994.

Kincheloe, Joe L., et al. *White Reign: Deploying Whiteness in America*. New York: St. Martin's Press, 1998.

Lipsitz, George. *The Possessive Investment in Whiteness: How White People Profit From Identity Politics*. Philadelphia: Temple University Press, 1998.

Lowe, Lisa. "Imagining Los Angeles in the Production of Multiculturalism." Gordon and Newfield 413–434.

————. *Immigrant Acts: On Asian American Cultural Politics*. Durham: Duke University Press, 1996.

Lugones, María. "Playfulness, 'World'-Traveling, and Loving Perception." Anzaldúa, *Making Face/Haciendo Caras* 390–402.

Maher, Frances, and Mary Kay Thompson Tetreault. "They Got the Paradigm and Painted It White: Whiteness and Pedagogies of Positionality." Kincheloe et al. 137–158.

McClintock, Anne, Aamir Mufti, and Ella Shohat, eds. *Dangerous Liaisons: Gender, Nation, and Post Colonial Perspectives*. Minneapolis: University of Minnesota Press, 1997.

McLaren, Peter. "Multiculturalism and the Post-Modern Critique: Toward a Pedagogy of Resistance and Transformation." Giroux and McLaren 192–222.

————. "White Terror and Oppositional Agency: Towards a Critical Multiculturalism." Sleeter and McLaren 33–70.

Mohanty, Chandra Talpade. "On Race and Voice: Challenges for Liberal Education in the 1990's." Giroux and McLaren 145–166.

Moraga, Cherríe and Gloria Anzaldúa, eds. *This Bridge Called My Back: Writings by Radical Women of Color*. New York: Kitchen Table Press, 1981.

Reagon, Bernice Johnson. "Coalition Politics: Turning the Century." Smith, Barbara 356–368.

Sandoval, Chela. "US Third World Feminism: The Theory and Method of Oppositional Consciousness in the Post Modern World." *Genders* 10 (1991): 1–24.

Sleeter, Christine. "Reflections on My Use of Multicultural and Critical Pedagogy When Students Are White." Sleeter and McLaren 415–437.

Sleeter, Christine E., and Peter McLaren, eds. *Multicultural Education, Critical Pedagogy, and the Politics of Difference*. New York: State University of New York Press, 1995.

Smith, Barbara, ed. *Home Girls: A Black Feminist Anthology*. New York: Kitchen Table: Women of Color Press, 1983.

Smith, Sidonie, and Julia Watson, eds. Introduction. *De/Colonizing the Subject: The Politics of Gender and Autobiographical Practices*. Minneapolis: University of Minnesota Press, 1992, xiii–xxxi.

Spivak, Gayatri Chakravorty. "Acting Bits/Identity Talk." Appiah and Gates 147–180.

Stam, Robert. "Multiculturalism and the Neoconservatives." McClintock et al. 188–203.

Thompson, Becky and Sangeeta Tyagi, eds. *Names We Call Home: Autobiography and Racial Identity*. New York: Routledge, 1996.

Weiss, Penny A. and Marilyn Friedman, eds. *Feminism and Community*. Philadelphia: Temple University Press, 1995.

West, Cornel. *Keeping Faith: Philosophy and Race in America.* New York: Routledge, 1993.

Young, Iris Marion. "The Ideal Community and the Politics of Difference." Weiss and Friedman 233–257.

———. *Justice and the Politics of Difference.* Princeton: Princeton University Press, 1990.

CHAPTER TWO

UNLEASHING THE DEMONS OF HISTORY

White Resistance in the U.S. Latino Studies Classroom

Susan Sánchez-Casal

An insurgent multiculturalism takes as its starting point the question of what it means for educators and cultural workers to treat schools and other public sites as border institutions in which teachers, students and others engage in daily acts of cultural translation and negotiation. For it is within such institutions that students and teachers are offered the opportunity to become border crossers. . . .

—Henry Giroux,
"Insurgent Multiculturalism and the Promise of Pedagogy"

*The border is all we share/*La frontera es lo único que compartimos

—Guillermo Gómez-Peña, *"The Multicultural Paradigm"*

Antiracist pedagogy is an intellectual and political practice aimed at decolonizing racially exclusive institutional curricula and teaching practices in college and university classrooms. As such, it represents a radical incursion into the hegemonic knowledge bases and belief systems of racially privileged North American students whose previous educational and social experience has positioned them in the epistemically disadvantaged position of the "power-illiterate" (Kincheloe and Steinberg). White, middle- and upper-class students who have been taught to understand their social advantages as "natural," and "merit-based" most often reject the central assumption in antiracist work, namely that U.S. society is marked by relations of domination in which some groups are targeted for oppression on the basis of race, class, gender, sexuality and others are conferred unearned advantages. Thus, at private liberal arts colleges where the student population is predominantly white and ruling-class, the U.S. Latino studies classroom becomes a space that generates white defensiveness and white resistance in an overtly politicized, counterhegemonic context. Theorizing and understanding white resistance is fundamental to the task of antiracist pedagogy, since this phenomenon (1) reflects the intellectual and ideological effects of the histories of domination that the course seeks to deconstruct, and (2) calls for a pedagogy whose methodology is attentive and responsive to the workings of white power and unexamined white identity in the classroom.

My goal in this chapter is to map the dynamic relationship of radical curriculum and antiracist methodology in the U.S. Latino Studies classroom. I am particularly interested in drawing pertinent connections between the epistemic basis of white resistance and what anthropolitical linguist Ana Celia Zentella refers to as the *chiquitafication* of Latino history. Zentella's metaphor theorizes how the historically racist and anti-Latino lens of the dominant white imagination "makes small" (from the Spanish verb "achicar" and the adjective "chiquita/o"), trivializes, and distorts Latino histories. Specifically, I will elaborate on how I organize the metaphors of *chiquitafication,* the *border* and the *wound* as central to both the way I construct U.S. Latino curriculum and also to the way I develop general methodological practices of radical pedagogy.

The Epistemic Basis of White Defensiveness

[. . .]*given the tendency of multicultural discourse to celebrate diversity without adequately analyzing power differentials among groups positioned by racial categorizations and inequalities, the phrase "people of color" still implies that white culture is the hidden norm against which all other racially subordinate groups' so-called "differences" are measured.*

—Leslie Roman, *"White is a Color!"*

When a very perturbed white woman student in my recent "Introduction to U.S. Latino Literatures" course complained that the authors of an important essay on the pedagogy of whiteness[1] were not qualified to make truth claims about the material effects of race because their essay was "poorly written," I could see students in the class begin to line up on different sides of a sharply edged border. I could feel myself lining up with them. As I stood in front of the class, I was on the verge of letting loose my anger and frustration. But I channeled my emotions into a useful pedagogical strategy aimed at shifting the focus from me to the class and producing "dialogue" among students: I asked the student who made the claim to clarify her criteria for judging an essay "well" or "poorly written," and then I asked the rest of the class if they felt inclined to either support or challenge the student's critique of this important course reading. Of the 25 students in this class, 18 were white (14 women, 4 men), 5 Latino/a (2 women, 3 men), and 2 African American (1 woman, 1 man). Compared to other classes I teach where the ratio might be 23 white students and 2 students of color, this was an incredibly diverse constituency. The dialogue that we entered into featured a chorus of several white students who used the opportunity to voice complaints about the "white-bashing" that they thought was going on in the course; most white students remained silent as did all of the Latino/a students and the African American woman. The "voice" of the lone student of color who entered into dialogue—a politicized, articulate African American man who was typically outspoken—was angry and confrontational. Ronnell[2] spoke last and launched a pointed critique at the student who claimed the text was "poorly-written" as well as at those who had surfaced their impressions that the class was tromping on white people. I paraphrase his concluding remarks to his peers:

> I think y'all just can't take it when you find yourselves put under the microscope. . . . People of color have been objectified and scrutinized since kingdom come, but for white students this is something that only happens in classes like this one.

I agreed with Ronnell's analysis and I was as angry and frustrated as he was, but was this encounter what antiracist feminists have in mind when we talk about "dialogue" and "student voice"? What about all the silences? How many different strategies were at work behind all those closed mouths? I was most perturbed by the silence of Latino/a students in class, none of whom cared or dared to speak up. For even though 20 students made similar decisions to remain silent, not even the silence was democratic; while the muting of both white students and students of color may have been a defense strategy (neither group wanting to expose their positions nor incur the risky outcomes of speaking up in a class marked by staggering social inequalities), the stakes for remaining silent were grossly unequal.

After Ronnell spoke the entire class fell into a hush, but I took the "conversation" further by questioning the epistemic effects of white privilege and unexamined white identity. Specifically, I addressed the need for white students to become critical of how their social privilege and racial identity prompted them to reject new historical information and analyses that directly address the effects of institutional racism on Latino communities. I suggested to them that " . . . one's social situation enables and sets limits on what one can know; some social situations—critically unexamined, dominant ones—are more limiting than others in this respect, and what makes these situations more limiting is their *inability to generate the most critical questions about received belief*" (Harding 54–55, my emphasis). I also introduced the idea that emotions—such as those we were witnessing at that moment—do, in fact, have cognitive relevance.[3] I recommended to the class that we consider the theoretical premise that the anger deployed in class that day—mine, that of the white students, and Ronnell's—was grounded in specific social locations, concrete experiences, and cultural and political identity positions. Most students just sat there with semi-blank faces and we ended the class in tension and irresolution.

After nine years of teaching critical multicultural studies[4] in the U.S. Latino and Women's Studies classroom, I have come to expect defensive and offensive interventions by white students who claim that the Latino/a author in question isn't "qualified" as an authority because she or he isn't "rational," is too "emotional" or "angry" and therefore not "objective," is "biased" and fails to find the "middle ground" where one can see—disinterestedly—"both points of view." When, for example, white students read politicized revisionist accounts of the effects on Mexicans of white expansion into the Southwest in the nineteenth century—accounts written by Chicano/a intellectuals who rewrite the euphemism *Western expansion* as imperial conquest, theft of Mexican land, and subsequent internal colonization of its people— many delegitimize these oppositional narratives of U.S. history by questioning their "truths." As we study the militant Chicano version of the conquest of México's northwest in Acuña's *Occupied America* or Anzaldúa's *Borderlands/La Frontera,* white students will often support their skepticism by asking, sometimes defensively, "if this is the way it really happened, *why haven't we heard the story told like this before?*"[5] Some students will also cite what they consider to be the "hostile, bitter tone" of Acuña's and Anzaldúa's work— Acuña, for example, explains how the U.S. theft of Mexican land has left us with a "legacy of hate"—as further evidence of the dubious veracity of their historiographies. In a defensive and often angry manner students will argue that the authors' angry and emotional response to the historical event in question has biased them, preventing them from "seeing the whole truth," and motivating them to unjustly characterize whites as the "bad guys." Other white students (a consistent minority) react with remorse or regret at their manufactured ignorance about Latino history, but they still find it almost impossible to reject what they call the "objective" truth of official

North American history in favor of the "subjective" truth of Latinos/as. Thus these students tend to characterize Latino revisions of U.S. imperial history as "valuable" but "personally motivated." While admitting that official U.S. history assumes an exclusive, white positionality, they depoliticize this hegemonic exclusivity by seeing it as the inevitable representational bind of a national discourse that seeks to tell the story of the "majority" of Americans—and that therefore cannot detain itself in the micro-histories of its minority communities. What's clear is that although white students lament the suffering of Latinos/as who confront racist oppression, they still refute the institutional basis of Latino suffering. Both cases of white student response—the hostile defensiveness versus the subtler defense—are grounded in the unspoken assumption that "America" is white, middle-class, and exclusively English-speaking. This epistemological distortion of national history and identity decontextualizes the link between white, middle- and upper-class prosperity and the racist oppression of Latinos/as and other peoples of color, thus prompting white students to resist the decolonizing objectives of antiracist pedagogy.

I believe that the tendency of white students to characterize people of color as non-objective—whether they're theorists, other students, and/or professors—works as an epistemic strategy; in other words, white students—probably unconsciously—employ these arguments as a way of delegitimizing subjugated knowledges by framing them as personal, emotive, anti-intellectual, and therefore inaccurate. By refusing to question the partiality and exclusivity of hegemonic national history, white students are able to retain an unspoken cultural identity that conflates whiteness with righteousness. Since white students rarely encounter academic contexts in which their racial identities are recoded as historically "negative," the counterhegemonic curriculum of the U.S. Latino Studies classroom produces a hotbed of untheorized white emotion and contention.[6]

Pluralist Multiculturalism and the *Chiquitafication* of Latino History

What the art world wants is a "domesticated Latino" who can provide enlightenment without irritation, entertainment without confrontation.

—Guillermo Gómez-Peña, *"The Multicultural Paradigm"*

One can theorize about white defensiveness through many different lenses, but what interests me in this section is framing white resistance in the broader context of its inscription in pluralist multicultural paradigms that organize learning about "difference" in the educational system. Specifically,

I aim to place anthropolitical linguist Ana Celia Zentella's spanglish metaphor of *chiquitafication* in dynamic dialogue with the anti-historical project of multiculturalism. Zentella invokes the trope of *chiquitafication* to theorize how the exotified image of Brazilian "bombshell" Carmen Miranda exemplifies the ways that Latino cultures are trivialized and made small by racist tropes that disconnect Latino/a bodies from their historical context:

> When I was growing up in the fifties, the most significant Latina presence on television in the U.S. was a dancing banana named Chiquita. Decked out in a Carmen Miranda fruit-turban and conga skirt, she wiggled her hips while she sang, "I'm a Chiquita Banana and I'm here to say, bananas are delightful in every way. . . ." [. . .]World War II created a need for allies and markets south of the border, which resulted in the Good Neighbor policy. The U.S. was swamped with images that portrayed small people from small—i.e., poor, backwards, lazy—countries, terribly in need from their northern Big Brother. Mexicans in huge sombreros dozing siestas under trees was a favorite pose. . . . This propaganda coincided with the largest wave of Puerto Rican immigration the country has ever experienced . . . and with the movement of returning Mexican-American GIs and their families beyond their traditional border areas. (1)

As Zentella's example shows, the implicit racist logic of *chiquitafication* not only objectifies and sexualizes Latino images, but also works at the same time to obscure the histories that underlie those images: in Miranda's case, the commodification of her body distorts the real history of Central American women's labor on banana plantations and of the extremely exploitive and unsafe (not to mention "unsexy") conditions in which they work. Similarly, the image of the "lazy" Mexican who's always looking for a tree to sleep under belies the extensive and indispensable history of Mexican labor in building railroads across the United States, mining precious metals, producing in factories, construction sites and brickyards, seeding and harvesting the land, cleaning the houses of whites and raising their children, fighting U.S. wars, and so on. While Zentella is mainly concerned with how *chiquitafication* diminishes the complexity of the languages and cultures of U.S. Latinos[7] who reside in the United States and poses a threat to " . . . their linguistic security, language maintenance, and ultimately—their hopes for a good life"(1), in this essay I will employ her metaphor to address the ways that Latino history, identity, and epistemology continue to be *chiquitafied* by white students who have been inculcated in the dehistoricized epistemologies of institutional multicultural agendas.

Given that most students (white and non-white) have spent 12 or 13 years of their classroom experience in an educational system that has excluded or tokenized "minority"[8] narratives, histories, and perspectives, it isn't surprising that white students rebel in the face of discourses that reverse the white/brown binary by recasting white people as history's villains and people of color as its vanquished heroes. Sonia Nieto critiques the tendency of the educational system to dehistoricize the experience of peoples of color even as it "includes" them in the practices of a disembodied multiculturalism:

> The tendency to separate people from their experience may result in, for example, a treatment of the Navajo culture through an art project or a representation of the independence struggle in Puerto Rico through a single poem. These may indeed be worthy projects, but, decontextualized as they are from any sense of connection with the larger history of a people, they can easily become mere artifacts that have no meaning in and of themselves. (196)

Because the educational system reduces the histories and cultures of peoples of color to decontextualized artifacts, students' educational training prior to entering the college or university classroom has actually prepared them to reject the politicized truth claims of the radical classrooms as leftist "propaganda." Students whose exposure to minority voices has been limited to what Nieto refers to as the "brown heroes and holidays" programming of multicultural agendas are jolted by analyses of the United States as a racist society characterized by asymmetrical power relations between whites and peoples of color. Thus, the politics of institutional multiculturalism exotify and isolate the cultural and intellectual production of peoples of color, and as such they serve to mystify and obscure the social contradictions implicit in racist society.

"Celebrate diversity!" multiculturalism's favorite slogan, has taught students that the mention of multiculturalism should be followed by a party, exotic foods and dances, colorful costumes—anything but a political critique launched at the racial power structure and its hierarchies of domination and resistance. "Celebrate diversity" has become a *chiquitafied* institutional mantra that locates difference, in Chandra Mohanty's words, as "benign variation . . . that bypasses power as well as history to suggest a harmonious, empty pluralism"(42). It makes sense that the companion mantra to "celebrate diversity" is "tolerate difference," since in both cases what we seem to be celebrating is the willingness of white Americans to tolerate unwhite Americans who want to promote awareness of their cultural heritage. What these slogans don't address, of course, is the unmarked and unchallenged hegemony of whiteness that anchors both depoliticized images.

In U.S. colleges and universities multicultural desire has opened spaces for celebrating the diversity of salsa/merengue dances, international fashion shows, Chinese New Year celebrations, and "Arabian Nights" festivities (replete with belly dancers).[9] Multiculturalism is also focused through an academic lens that commonly provides a month-long inquiry into "multicultural" areas of U.S. history that are excluded or underrepresented in institutional curricula—African American History month, Latino Heritage Month, Women's History Month, and so on. Questioning the role of dehistoricized multicultural agendas in undermining the aims of race and ethnic studies courses is particularly relevant to me as a teacher of U.S. Latino literatures, since in the midst of the current "Latino Boom" in the art and the pop music world, in the midst of an Anglo consumer-binge on all things Latino, we are simultaneously witnessing virulent political and legislative actions perpetrated against Latinos, African Americans, immigrants, and so-called third-world countries. While "mainstream" America was recently "livin' la vida loca" with sexed-up Puerto Rican pop singer Ricky Martin, California's anti-immigrant, anti-Latino propositions 187, 202, 209, and 21 are aimed at the throats of Latinos/as all across the Southland.[10] In the midst of the implicit racist logic of anti-immigrant and anti-bilingual education legislation that has swept the nation, the criminalizing effects of racial profiling, and the exponential growth of prison populations of young men of color, the *chiquitafying* multicultural paradigms of higher learning continue to obscure the antiracist struggle of U.S. Latinos/as by objectifying and decontextualizing Latino/a life in the United States.

Multiculturalisms that see difference as "benign variation" stand—obtrusively—in the place where historical inscriptions of the political and spiritual struggles of subjugated peoples in the United States should be. Guillermo Gómez-Peña's assessment of the ambiguities of multiculturalism and its threat to politicized minority identities comes to life in the U.S. Latino Studies classroom:

> Multicultural . . . can mean a cultural pluralism in which the various ethnic groups collaborate and dialogue with one another without having to sacrifice their particular identities to the Big Blob. But it can also mean a kind of Esperantic Disney World, a tutti-frutti cocktail of cultures, languages, and art forms in which "everything becomes everything else," and nothing is really indispensable. This is a dangerous notion that strongly resembles the bankrupt concept of the melting pot with its familiar connotations of integration, homogenization, and neutralization. (52)

But taking the veil off the power-blind multicultural mystique is a serious intervention into students' worldviews, as well as into their notions of what constitutes legitimate forms of knowledge, since "many students, regardless of their race/class, have been socialized to believe that the U.S. is a 'just' society"(Tatum 2). Although my course syllabus outlines clearly that the intellectual/political focus of the semester will necessarily scrutinize not only U.S. Latino history but also its context within the racist history of whiteness, many students don't grasp the repercussions of this statement; specifically, they don't understand that their own social advantages and worldviews will be called into question as one of the legacies of the history of white domination (what I theorize below as "the wound"), and they are often not ready or willing to engage transformatively with what is, for them, this new "negative" information.

Clearly, when white students question the objectivity of Latino/a historians, one of the things they are trying to do is preserve an uncritical space for whiteness that has been granted them since birth; most white students are willing to admit that there are white racists out there, but they try to disconnect the history of whiteness itself from the distorted and grotesque gestures of white supremacy that they believe singlehandedly fuel racism. White students' characteristic unwillingness to scrutinize their own implication in structural racism—specifically the refusal to analyze racism as a system from which white Americans derive unearned advantages—leads them to question who can legitimately occupy the analytical spaces of the academy and the classroom to produce liberatory knowledge about national histories: *who is authorized to speak about what and in what way* (Giroux 1992). Hence, white resistance in the antiracist classroom at one level works to preserve operative myths held by students about "American" national character—myths that reverberate significantly in perceptions of their cultural identity and even their own personal worth. White resistance also works to *chiquitafy* the epistemic claims of politicized Latinos/as, thereby challenging not only the legitimate right of peoples of color to represent and critique white history, but also the validity and relevance of the insurgent knowledge we produce.

For the last several years I have been trying to situate my pedagogical strategies in this volatile conjunction of radical curriculum and resistant student response, by paying close attention to how these interactions transpire in my classes and how I anticipate and respond to them. I have begun a process of scrutinizing more rigorously the connection between theory, pedagogy, and politics in courses like U.S. Latino Studies that transgress intellectual/ideological/political boundaries in forceful ways. Giroux's happy image of teachers and students as "border crossers" gets marred in this wrenching, real-life struggle to find a pedagogy that gets us from one edge of the border to the other.

Unleashing the Demons of History/Theorizing the Wound

The U.S. Mexican border es una herida abierta [an open wound] where the Third World grates against the first and bleeds.

—Gloria Anzaldúa, *"The Homeland Aztlán"*

*[. . .]Who we are, how we act, what we think, and what stories we tell be-
come more intelligible within an epistemological framework that begins by
recognizing hegemonic histories.*

—Chandra Talpade Mohanty, *"On Race and Voice"*

The U.S. Latino Studies classroom, as I organize and focus it, is aimed at the
ethical and historical project of decolonizing knowledge production. Mapping whiteness is thus central to the project of decolonizing the classroom,
since, as Nelson Rodríguez argues, it "has the potential not only to raise consciousness about one's own possible complicity in supporting oppressive
regimes (that is, living whiteness oppressively); it also positions one to encounter a multitude of critical languages that can be used to rethink and live
whiteness in progressive ways" (31–32). Consequently, my goals in the
course are simultaneously directed at materializing the diverse but intercon-
nected histories of Latino communities in the United States, and at providing the pedagogical and political ground for both students of color and
white students to reassess the unspoken ideologies that frame their knowledge bases and their racial and political identities. To this end, I use the
tropes of *chiquitafication,* the *border,* and the *wound* to contextualize and historicize both Latino/a counterhegemonic narratives and students' locations
in relation to them, and to establish a possible ground for reinscriptions of
racial identity and for interracial coalition.

By organizing U.S. Latino Studies around a radical critique of white imperialist history, I try to highlight how U.S. Latinos/as question the hegemony
of national identity by scrutinizing *nation* and redefining what it means to be
"American"—for both Latinos/as and Whites. The examination of the economic, social, political, and cultural history of diverse Latino constituencies
helps me to situate and contextualize how we became "U.S. Latinos/as" and
how that process of identity formation is contingent upon the epistemological
project of reconstructing history.[11] The political framework of the course is at
one level oppositional, as I am interested in demonstrating how the internal
colonization of U.S. Latinos/as has helped to construct monolithic, inaccurate, and damaging stereotypes about Latinos/as—stereotypes that students
bring to class with them and that shade their perceptions of Latinos/as as literary protagonists, as artists, and as agents of political thought and action. But
I also insist on going beyond counterhegemonic analyses to build the class
around constitutive narratives that materialize the crucial role of Latinos/as as
primary producers in U.S. economic, social, and cultural spheres. Ultimately,
I hope to provide a politicized, aesthetic frame for expressing and interpreting
the beauty and dignity of diverse Latino communities who work, who dream,
who create, who love, who see the world from specific but multiple social lo-

cations, who make knowledge, who resist racist oppression, who nurture spirit and soul, who form community, family, and society.

The critical analysis of white hegemony grounds the course's subsequent study of Latino/a aesthetic production, much of which is concerned with inscribing and revising Latino histories and identities by critiquing and redefining the racial landscape of "America" and our historical struggles within it. Ultimately, as Juan Flores has argued, rewriting Latino histories engages the transformative qualities of reinscribing historical memory "in accordance with the needs and interests of the present" (49). For Latinos/as, the "needs and interests" of the present include prying open new spaces for the presentation and revaluing of subjugated histories and for the production of counterhegemonic knowledges—for new ways of conceiving of Latino/a self and community that call into question not only the colonizing structures of U.S. society but also the classism, [hetero]sexism, and colorism of our own communities. Latino/a writers interrupt hegemonic historical narratives by sidelining and objectifying white history while they center Latino/a lives as subjects of their own histories, as actors whose stories are shaped by but exceed the constraining social realities they confront. In this sense, Latino/a cultural production seeks to restore to Latino communities the historical body from which it has been severed in white master narratives.

I begin the conceptualization of the *border* and the *wound* by explicating three Chicano/a texts: Rodolfo "Corky" Gonzales's "I Am Joaquín"(1967), Gloria Anzaldúa's "The Homeland Aztlán"(1987), and Guillermo Gómez-Peña's "The Multicultural Paradigm"(1989). "I Am Joaquín" frames our discussions of the historical *wound* with a fierce inscription of Chicano nationalism that passionately articulates the goals of the Chicano Civil Rights movement of the sixties (including, unfortunately, its masculinist imperatives and exclusions—something I challenge explicitly in the classroom). Gonzales's poem theorizes the border as a hostile, racist space where Chicanos must struggle not only with economic and political oppression, but also with the lure of assimilation to white society: "My fathers / have lost the economic battle / and won / the struggle of cultural survival / And now! / I must choose"(207). Although the poem ends with the poetic voice asserting "I shall endure!" white students often complain that this poem is "depressing," "difficult," and "negative." Instead of seeing the speaker's dilemma to choose between economic and spiritual/cultural survival as an indictment of the degrading and dehumanizing effects of structural racism, white students often read this social predicament through a purely individualistic and dehistoricized lens, concluding that the speaker is unnecessarily "pessimistic" about his future, and that he has no "home."

I employ Gloria Anzaldúa's metaphor of the U.S./Mexican border as "an open wound" to crystallize the historical and contemporary effects of the collision of the imperial United States with a bleeding México. Anzaldúa locates herself as a queer historian in the physical and metaphorical wound of the 1950 mile-long U.S./Mexican border, grounding the historical genealogy of Chicanos/as in this heterogeneous, vulnerable space where social and cultural outcasts create new visions of national and cultural history. Anzaldúa redefines the history of the border by concretizing its ancient occupation by indigenous peoples who were eventually conquered by the Spanish. Thus Anzaldúa reverses the border binary "white natives/Mexican invaders" by coding illegal Mexican immigration into the Southwestern United States as a "return" to stolen ancestral lands. Her revision of both U.S. history and racist tropes about *mojados* (undocumented border crossers) points up the history and contemporary consequences of the internal colonization of Chicanos/as. I foreground Anzaldúa's trope of the *wound* throughout my course, as a way of surfacing and interpreting how Latino/a identities emerge within specific but varying contexts of imperial and colonial politics (I can therefore use the *wound* to organize inquiry into both Chicano and Puerto Rican history, for example, although the particular ways that México and Puerto Rico are/were subjected to imperial, colonial and neo-colonial rule are distinct and have had different effects on both groups). By refracting course analysis of the history of U.S. domination through the *wound,* I hope to help the class contextualize and evaluate both objective knowledge about Latino history (what happened, when, to whom, why, and so on) and also the meanings that students impute to that history from their specific social locations, experiences, and identities.

In Anzaldúa's metaphorical vision the border is war torn and unforgiving, but it is also a transgressive space where the dark, the queer, the female—the marginal, both in relation to Anglo society and within Chicano communities—encounter subversive possibilities for selfhood and community. Thus Anzaldúa's essay develops a parallel image of the border as a privileged, hybrid space for Chicano/a experiences and identities to be inscribed and reinscribed according to new historical imperatives. The text's code-switching, from English to Spanish, creates discursive border conditions for readers, at the same time that it expresses and documents the full range of Chicana cultural identity. Requiring the reader to "meet her halfway," Anzaldúa privileges other Spanish/English bilingual readers (especially Chicanos/as and other U.S. Latinos/as) who are best equipped to navigate the linguistic and cultural borderlands of her text. The text's disadvantaging of non-Spanish speaking white students pushes them to the margins of discourse, and produces strong effects in students who are unaccustomed to having their social experience and linguistic identity decentered. But in spite of Anzaldúa's productive reinscriptions of the border, her proud and defiant assertion of Chicana lesbian identity, and her emphatic insistence that Anglos—not

Mexicans—are the illegal invaders in the Southwestern United States, most white students reduce the complexity and epistemic validity of her text to "angry white-bashing." As in the case with "I Am Joaquín," white students often dehistoricize Anzaldúa's experience[12] by asserting that she doesn't "belong" on either side of the border, and that she doesn't feel that "America" (read "white" America) is her "home."

Gómez-Peña conceptualizes the "border" as an intercultural, interracial contact zone where privileged and subjugated communities have the opportunity to identify and redefine hierarchical relations of power and privilege. But he stresses that in order to facilitate intercultural dialogue, we must open, examine, and begin to heal the wounds of racist oppression. Like Anzaldúa, Gómez-Peña emphasizes that the racial border we share, in spite of all its cultural and social hazards, is a site of production where social experiences and cultural identities can be retheorized and mobilized in progressive political action. Gómez-Peña thus theorizes the border as a negotiating space for the "dominant" and the "marginal,"[13] an intercultural, dialogical zone where the dominant and the marginalized must come to the table as equals in order to enter into transformative communication and political coalition. For Gómez-Peña coming to the table as equals requires that Anglo-America begin to take seriously what Latinos/as are trying to tell them about our historical oppression in the United States. His utopian argument about intercultural dialogue supports me in establishing antiracist objectives for classroom discussion, since he stipulates that the work will be painful and fraught with misunderstanding, and that students' positionalities will largely determine the validity of their epistemologies:

> The social and ethnic fabric of the U.S. is filled with interstitial wounds, invisible to those who didn't experience the events that generated them, or who are victimized by historical amnesia. Those who cannot see these wounds feel frustrated by the hardships of intercultural dialogue. Intercultural dialogue unleashes the demons of history. (21)

Gómez-Peña's argument has deep epistemic relevance for both dominant and marginal communities, since it characterizes the historical and ever-present wound of racism as an epistemological beacon whose apprehension is contingent upon experience, cultural identity, and progressive political commitment. In this sense, he suggests that liberatory, antiracist knowledge is best constructed from the lives and the political initiatives of those who have experienced the *wound;* but he also suggests that white people must become willing to educate themselves about their implication in racist oppression by confronting, instead of avoiding, the "demons of history." Thus Gómez-Peña's border epistemology underscores the need to historicize not only the experience of Latinos/as and other marginalized peoples, but also that of white Americans. Each time I have taught "The Multicultural Paradigm," it has produced strong, negative emotions in white students who repeatedly claim that Gómez-Peña unfairly characterizes all white people as "demons." Although Gómez-Peña refers to both white America and also to the elite classes in Latin America as culprits in the essentializing and erasing of U.S. Latino history and cultural production, his essay is often interpreted by white students as a wholesale judgment of Anglo society as "evil."

White Resistance and Antiracist Pedagogies

Among the most powerful frameworks for maintaining the superiority of dominant voices, in the classroom as elsewhere, is the failure to understand the workings of whiteness: how assumptions of whiteness shape and even dictate the limits of discourse.

—Frances Maher and Mary Kay Thompson Tetreault, *"'They Got the Paradigm and Painted it White': Whiteness and Pedagogies of Positionality"*

The challenge here is to refrain from imposing meaning on our students' experiences and lead them, instead, to understanding how their experiences are shaped socially.

—Maralee Mayberry and Ellen Cronan Rose, *"Teaching in Environments of Resistance"*

I believe that what is really at stake for white students in the antiracist classroom, as Ronnell so rightly pointed out, is the loss of a sense of uncritical racial wholeness and dignity. By retelling imperial history through the heart of the historical wound of racism, the U.S. Latino classroom ejects white students from their invisible racial comfort zone as it casts an unrelenting spotlight on the material and ideological effects of whiteness. My struggle to unpack the perception held by many white students that U.S. Latino Studies is a "negative" affair has become one of the central pieces of my intellectual and pedagogical practice in the classroom. By using the *wound* as an icon that symbolizes the significance of our social locations and experiences in creating knowledge about ourselves and others, I am better able to dispute white students' unexamined imposition of their exclusive knowledge bases on the history and cultural production of U.S. Latinos/as. I ask the whole class to consider these questions: Who needs this history and why? Who needs to avoid it? Who is *able* to avoid its implications? I try to contextualize these questions by referring back to our scrutiny of the *wound* and of each of our locations in relation to it, so that students may begin to understand how experience focuses and organizes the ways that we see our shared social world. In other words, I try to turn the epistemic validity of students' problematic assertions about the nonpleasurable aspects of the course back on them and ask them to theorize how their own locations and racial identities motivate their evaluation of the "negativity" of course subject matter.

As I explicitly model for my students during the course, the epistemology of the *wound* is contingent upon how one situates oneself in relation to it and upon one's willingness to question one's implication in its historical context. In other words, the *wound*—the legacy of racist history—produces different outcomes for different "Americans," depending on one's racial/ethnic identity and one's political needs and desires. Students who descend from those who suffer and struggle to survive the *wound* have different needs and experiences from students who descend from those who inflict/ed the wound or who benefit from its infliction. In this way I hope to concretize for students how their judgments of course materials as "optimistic" or "pessimistic" are grounded in questions of social location, experience, identity, and power. I ask white students to consider how their ignorance of and/or resistance to the history of conquest and colonization of U.S. Latinos/as has allowed them to nurture a distorted view of Latinos/as as "foreigners" in search of a home.

The struggle to facilitate reliable interpretive practices in the U.S. Latino Studies classroom is often unproductive. Yet my/our repeated "failures" in this struggle continually motivate me to reflect on my progress as a teacher of insurgent disciplines in a conservative, racially homogeneous academic institution. I continue to reach for a pedagogy that can effectively engage diverse student constituencies and create a collective learning community with the resources to evaluate conflictive truth assessment and the partiality of experiential knowledge. At this point in my teaching trajectory, I am no longer interested in getting justifiably angry when white students interrupt my pace in the class to offer the opinion that the class is "negative," and that Latino/a writers are "hostile" and "emotional." Although I am often tempted, I am no longer content to climb onto my soapbox and deliver a righteous lecture about the blindness of white privilege. I have lost interest in "soap-box pedagogy," mainly because I realize that my efforts are not only fruitless, but they can also be poisonous. Antiracist monologues—no matter how many progressive truths they attempt to "share" with the class—consistently fail to impress or persuade white students or to move them to a place of greater consciousness. Furthermore, lectures from the soapbox can work deleteriously on both white students and students of color. For Latino/a students, authoritarian diatribes on the racist underpinnings of white resistance can be embarrassing and disorienting, as it tends to put Latino/a students even deeper into the hot-seat that they already occupy in the class. Students of color who struggle to find safe and sustaining spaces within the racist structure of a residential private white college may find it counterproductive to line up with the preachy Latina teacher and against the powerful community of white students who feel "attacked."

Although white students in my courses do not constitute a homogenous community—they are divided by gender, class, sexuality, politics, social affiliation, and so on—, in the radical classroom racial divisions become more dichotomous and polarized. By enacting an undemocratic pedagogical stance, I may give white students the impression that I am "speaking for Latino/a students" and their historical perspectives and interests (and indeed, I may at times fall squarely into this trap).[14] Snatching authority from the learning community also precludes the strong formation of epistemic *communities of meaning* in the classroom that could organically produce collective counterhegemonic knowledges within shifting classroom contexts (Macdonald 2000; Sánchez-Casal and Macdonald "Feminist Reflections").[15] By claiming supreme epistemic authority, I at times betray a lack of confidence in the promise of feminist pedagogy to produce collective knowledge-making in the classroom.

After much soul-searching and reality-testing, I have come to realize that in those moments of crisis, when I make quick decisions to filibuster my students out of their ways of seeing the world, nobody really listens to me. They may hear what I'm saying, but they are not adequately prepared to do anything productive with the signifiers that I produce. I have to face the fact that standing in front of my class delivering what I think is the rich and justified content of my objections to their ideas and opinions isn't teaching; it's preaching. Preaching is a presentational form that can be very effective when the listeners have signed up for it, but as a pedagogical practice I have found it to be spectacularly counterproductive. It is humbling to recognize that while my classes are providing me with perfect teaching moments, I don't always know what to do with them.

Somewhere, between my authority, knowledge, and desire for students to engage course material openly and willingly and students' desire to maintain and defend their ideological positions, somewhere in-between is a space for teaching, for organizing a progression of concrete steps that facilitate the possibility of collectively refining and transforming knowledges. Unfortunately, in positioning myself on the moral highground of universally valid propositions about human freedom and their relevance for U.S. Latinos/as, I often end up teaching my classes that the use of authority in the classroom is uneven and unpredictable—sometimes the teacher is diminutive and at other times supersized—and that students' commentaries can and will be used against them by someone much better equipped to argue the case. I have to confront the unsettling idea that I may be responsible for helping to make the classroom more "unsafe" and less participatory; at the very least I am helping to create a problematically ambiguous space in the classroom, by inadvertently discarding one of the central tenets of feminist pedagogy—the deconstruction of dominating, centralized authority.

I also recognize, however, that when I resort to soapbox pedagogy in the classroom I am doing so not only out of a desire to forcefully persuade students of the rightness of the ethical imperatives that frame my thinking, my teaching, and my life, and to pummel reactionary ideas out of the heads of those who oppose these sincere ideals, but also out of a sense of self-defense. Out of a desire to survive, to preserve integrity, and to remain whole. Like many radical teachers in conservative institutions, I often end the day twisted into dissonant threads of emotional pain, moral outrage, self-criticalness, negativity, discouragement, self-congratulatory reflections on my responses in class to confrontations, anger at students, anger at myself, a sense of futility, notions of what I should have said or not said, plans for what I will say next time, ideas about eliminating or adding course materials, ideas about eliminating students, questions about how to devise assignments that will bring the course material home to students, plans to change careers. . . . I know I am not alone in this. As feminist teachers begin to take more seriously the emotional effects of radical curriculum on our students and to investigate how they intertwine with, facilitate, and/or obstruct cognitive processing and political repositioning, I think we also have to take seriously the emotional effects of classroom resistance and aggression on the teacher. That antiracist feminist work is stressful and painful is not news. But how can feminist antiracist pedagogies help to support feminist teachers as we struggle with the tumultuous and sometimes pernicious consequences of student resistance in the classroom?

Reaching for Pedagogical Wholeness

> [. . .]The work of all our progressive teachers, was not to teach us solely the knowledge in books, but to teach us an oppositional world view—different from that of our exploiters and oppressors, a world view that would enable us to see ourselves not through the lens of racism or racist stereotypes but one that would enable us to focus clearly and succinctly, to look at ourselves, at the world around us, critically—analytically—to see ourselves first and foremost as striving for wholeness, for unity of heart, mind, body, and spirit.
>
> —bell hooks, "Toward a Revolutionary Feminist Pedagogy"

Feminist theorists of pedagogy like bell hooks (1989) have argued convincingly that we must restore a sense of struggle to feminist classrooms and ask ourselves not to abandon authoritative subject positions but to make sure that they work toward advancing antiracist, feminist imperatives. I would argue that the greater challenge for antiracist feminist educators is to continue to believe in the promise that we and our students (of any color) bring to the task of anti-oppression work in the academy. The task is daunting: at one and the same time we are called upon to theorize white resistance and white defensiveness, to recognize the seemingly insurmountable obstacles presented by unexamined and reactionary white racial identities, and to continue to believe that the work we're doing is worthwhile and productive, even when we do not arrive at the desired outcome. In order to maintain this posture, I have to take a warrior stance that is strong, but open—a hopeful, rooted, disciplined stance that supports me in staying on course in the classroom, even in the face of tremendous and continual resistance.

I strengthen myself by remembering that my interest in teaching U.S. Latino Studies originated in a desire to empower Latino/a students and other students of color by studying our rich histories and cultural productions. My own process of decolonization, of externalizing the racist oppression that I had internalized as a Latina child growing up in racist white America, was intricately tied to college classrooms where I learned the dignified history of resistance of my people and the social and historical context that we have actively and courageously confronted. So even though I may have only 3 or 4 Latinos/as in my classes, I try to remember that first and foremost I am teaching to them and for them. With respect for the intellectual and political challenge of white students in the antiracist classroom, I am beginning to learn not to make hasty judgments about what white students are taking from class—in spite of their defensiveness and resistance to question the historical implications of whiteness. I am also learning to detach from the racist comments that white students continually make, so that I can keep focused on the task at hand, so that I can stay open to the possibility that at some point they will be willing and able to see more clearly how their hegemonic knowledge bases are marked by the very relations of racial power that the class hopes to dismantle. In order to stay in this struggle for the long haul, I have to release myself from feeling like students need to "get it" the first time around. I have had to embrace the hard fact that white students "not getting it" is a crucial step in the pedagogical process of anti-oppression work.

I have come to believe that one of the most crucial steps in antiracist teaching is reminding ourselves of the successes of our classrooms. Thus I would like to highlight the progressive and encouraging participation of white students in my classes every semester. Some white students— especially those whose class positions or sexualities place them at odds with the hegemonic axes of whiteness—react to radical Latino/a historical/

aesthetic narratives with eyes wide open, with productive remorse for their ignorance about the role of whiteness in subjugating peoples of color in the United States, and with hunger for new knowledge and for new theories that can help them begin to reconsider their own racial identity in progressive terms. Students of color who take my classes—most of them Latino/a although in recent years more African American students as well—are inspired and encouraged by theorists, activists, artists, and historians like Zentella, Acuña, Anzaldúa, Flores, Moraga, Gómez-Peña, and others whose work and example provides them with an empowering analytical space that they rarely find in other classrooms.

Many Latino and Latina students report to me after the first or second week of the course that they feel an overwhelming sense of pride and acknowledgement in the classroom. Latino/a students often express this burgeoning epistemic transformation in the form of autobiographical poems and essays in which they express a deep and empowering sense of connection to robustly defined and historically contextualized images of U.S. Latinoness. For me, this is the greatest reward of teaching U.S. Latino Studies, which I have always defined as the work of decolonization; it is also a process that I intimately identify with, since my own positionality as a politicized Latina feminist came to life when, as a student, I discovered that there was an area of study that centered my historical experience and cultural identity as subject and object of intellectual inquiry. Ultimately, students who open themselves to antiracist theories and oppositional histories are most often those whose experiences link them with insurgent thinkers and writers who create the ground for politicized cultural identities. I remind myself that these students "need" a new theory and a new historical narrative in which to situate themselves, and that the U.S. Latino classroom—as messy and frustrating as it can be—provides it for them.

But the task of centering the counterhegemonic discourses of people of color in traditionally exclusive academic curricula and a predominantly white student population is a painful endeavor that presents formidable challenges to feminist educators. As Chandra Talpade Mohanty argues, "teaching about histories of sexism, racism, imperialism, and homophobia potentially poses very fundamental challenges to the academy and its traditional production of knowledge, since it has often situated third-world peoples as populations whose histories and experiences are deviant, marginal, or inessential to the acquisition of knowledge" (48). Moreover, our preparation for carrying out this difficult work is often piece-meal and erratic. Ellsworth is right when she points to the daunting and isolating conditions in which we work:

[. . .]In our classrooms we grope toward an "unknown," since those of us dedicated to critical, feminist and antiracist pedagogy teach in a way that . . . except for the desire and the political commitment, we have had little formal preparation for . . . with little support from our institutions and hardly any immediate rewards from our students (35).

As we take antiracist feminist pedagogies into the twenty-first century, we need to continue to focus on how to develop concrete pedagogies that unsettle white resistance and defensiveness in the classroom. By exposing and examining the interstitial wounds of racism, we can create classroom conditions that directly confront the historical amnesia of white America and its deficient epistemologies. Contextualizing and historicizing subjugated Latino/a experiences in the United States is a crucial step in subverting hegemonic racial narratives that *chiquitafy* Latino histories and cultures. But for antiracist feminist teachers, an equally significant step is focusing more intensely on how to sustain and nurture ourselves in adverse and stressful academic conditions, as we continue to commit ourselves—courageously—to the imperatives of liberatory pedagogies and the struggle for cultural democracy inside and outside the classroom.

Appendix to Chapter Two

213 "Introduction to U.S. Latino/a Literatures" Course Goals

To understand the diversity of U.S. Latino/a literatures and their historical/political content and aesthetic modes, from the Civil Rights movement to the present. To study the history and artistic expression of antiracist, feminist, gay/lesbian resistance in U.S. Latino/a cultural productions. To acquire basic knowledge of the history and practices of racism in the United States, particularly as they express themselves in relation to U.S. Latino communities (the internal colony, economic marginalization, anti-immigrant policies and ideologies, antibilingual education, English Only, Hispanophobia). To analyze the history and practices of *whiteness*. To engage and evaluate oppositional voicings of Latino/a authors in redefining *nation* and in rewriting the history of Latinos/as within the United States. To strive for these goals within the context and critical perspectives of antiracist feminist theory and pedagogy.

Notes

I would like to thank Amie Macdonald and Chandra Talpade Mohanty for their supportive and incisive readings of this essay in many earlier versions.
1. The essay that we read for class was Kincheloe and Steinberg's "Addressing the Crisis of Whiteness." This important essay argues for a critical pedagogy of whiteness that will support students who seek a progressive white identity to reorient themselves theoretically and politically. It is a pedagogy that demands that white students become "power literate" so that they may investigate the

racist imperatives of white intellectual history and their pernicious effects on knowledge-making and on the social lives of peoples of color; but the authors also insist that white students go further to scrutinize their own implication in the racist history of imperial and colonial rule (specifically, that this history is the cause of their current social privilege). The authors are ultimately arguing for a reinscription of white identity that goes beyond the attitudinal realm to support cross-cultural political coalitions; because of these goals, one of the central components of refashioning white identity is that whites actively seek new progressive experiences by beginning to adopt "new modes of living one's life, new methods of relating to the various individuals with whom one comes in contact"(24). "A pedagogy of whiteness," explain Kincheloe and Steinberg, " . . . seeks to engage students, teachers and other individuals in an ever-unfolding emancipatory identity that pushes the boundaries of whiteness but always understands its inescapable connection to the white locale in the web of reality"(24). I foreground the pedagogy of whiteness in my course as a way of demonstrating to white students that they have choices about *how* they are white and what being white means in their lives and in the world. I believe it would be unethical to subject white students to a rigorous critique of the history and practice of whiteness without providing them the means to reorient and reinscribe their racial identities according to the imperatives of antiracist pedagogy and political movement.

2. Not his real name.

3. For a rigorous and interdisciplinary inquiry into the cognitive and emotional relevance of emotion see de Sousa, Gilligan, Narayan, Nussbaum, Tatum, Harding, Lorde, Scheman, S. P. Mohanty.

4. I understand Giroux's use of "insurgent multiculturalism" and my use of "critical multiculturalism" (taken from other theorists of whiteness; see Kincheloe and Steinberg) to be consistent with the imperatives of antiracist pedagogy. By unearthing and centering subjugated knowledges and discourses in the radical classroom, both insurgent and critical multiculturalisms scrutinize the effects of asymmetrical racial power in the United States and the consequences of structural racism on institutional curricula and classroom practice. In this way, the theoretical and political frameworks of insurgent and critical multiculturalisms stand in direct opposition to the power-blinding lens of pluralist multicultural initiatives and pedagogies, since they scrutinize and call attention to the historically material effects of whiteness. As Kincheloe and Steinberg put forth: "Critical multiculturalists, thus, are fervently concerned with white positionality in their attempt to understand the power relations that give rise to race, class, and gender inequality. Those of us who claim the mantle of critical multiculturalism are concerned with the ways power has operated historically and contemporaneously to legitimate social/educational categories and hierarchical divisions"("Addressing the Crisis" 3)

5. This claim is of course perfectly justifiable, given not only the tendency of the educational system to exclude histories of peoples of color in the United

States from its curricula, but also its tendency to limit whatever subjugated histories are included within a strictly black/white paradigm. Thus while undergraduate white students do not balk when presented with evidence of the existence of black slavery in the United States, the great majority of them have never heard mention of the U.S. Mexican war nor its present historical consequences for Mexicans and Chicanos. As an example, my son's high school "history" book (2001) talked about the 19th century white conquest of almost half of México's land as peaceful "southwestern expansion," without ever mentioning the words "war" or "México." When my son pushed his teacher to comment on the significant absence of this historical fact in the text, she dismissed his objection and ended the conversation by saying that "Mexican people were there to help the [anglo] 'settlers,' but there really weren't enough of them to make the history books."

6. The role of emotion in white resistance is an area that demands more pedagogical analysis. Beverly Daniel Tatum highlights the significance of teaching students to recognize how their affective and psychological bases may impede or enhance learning in classrooms that provide openly political frameworks for social analyses. She argues that we can work toward dismantling student resistance to oppression-related content by teaching students to evaluate their negative responses to course material and classroom dynamics according to the progressive stages outlined in Racial Identity Development Theory. By making students self-reflexive about why they are feeling the way they are feeling, by theorizing their emotional responses and seeing them as part of a progression of cognitive stages that can eventually lead to a positive reinscription of racial identity (both for white students and for students of color), we can not only reduce resistance but enhance learning. Tatum elaborates:

   The emotional responses that students have to talking and learning about racism are quite predictable and related to their own racial identity development. Unfortunately, students typically do not know this; thus they consider their own guilt, shame, embarrassment, or anger an uncomfortable experience that they alone are having. Informing students at the beginning of the semester that these feelings may be part of the learning process is ethically necessary (in the sense of informed consent), and helps to normalize the students' experience. Knowing in advance that a desire to withdraw from classroom discussion or not to complete assignments is a common response helps students to remain engaged when they reach that point ("Talking About Race" 19).

7. In the seven years since Zentella published this essay, the Latino population has grown by more than 10 million. The U.S. 2000 census reports 32.8 million Latinos in the U.S.: 66 percent Mexican; 14.5 percent Central and South American; 9 percent Puerto Rican; 4 percent Cuban; 6.4 percent of "other Latino origin."

8. I am aware that the term "minority" is misleading, inaccurate and can be construed as demeaning. But I employ this term for economy of expression, as well as to highlight its recent resurgence in intellectual and scholarly production that reclaims the antiracist imperatives of academic "minority studies"—see Satya P. Mohanty, Paula M. L. Moya, and Linda Martín Alcoff, among others, for a discussion of the relevance of postpositivist realist identity theory and its application in the reevaluation of minority studies.

9. In the wake of the anti-Arab violence and discourse that followed the September 11 attacks on the World Trade Center, the Pentagon, and passenger airlines, the failure of pluralist multiculturalism to educate North American students about the contextualized histories of racial and cultural "others" becomes frighteningly clear. 'Celebrating diversity' is again revealed as a set of dehistoricized spectacles that disengage the cultural practices of "othered" U.S. and international communities from their insertion within the global context of U.S. imperialism.

10. Proposition 209 sought to end affirmative action in higher education and public agencies; 227 banned bilingual education in the public schools; 187 prohibits medical, educational and other social services to non-documented immigrants and their children; 21 reduces the civil rights of minors in gang-related crime (e.g., mandatory jail time and permanent criminal record for first offenders; a 14 year-old can be tried as an adult on murder charges).

11. The task of constructing and deconstructing notions of collective Latinoness in the undergraduate classroom is a daunting one, and one that I continue to struggle with. As Juan Flores outlines, constructing an overarching Latino experience that encompasses the differing social and cultural features of Mexicans, Puerto Ricans, Cubans, Dominicans and other groups runs the risk of erasing the historical specificity of each group in favor of an homogenizing assimilationist perspective. At this point in my practice, I situate our study of Latinoness through the collective and cross-cultural (intra-Latino/a) lens of race, class, gender and sexuality; in this sense I try to arrive at analyses of U.S. Latinos/as that take seriously the material and spiritual consequences of concrete social locations within existing structures of power and privilege in the United States.

12. Although I refer to the speaking "I" in Anzaldúa's text as "Anzaldúa," I am not attempting to conflate author and narrator; I use this denomination to facilitate my discussion of Anzaldúa's historicizing of Chicano/a history and white student response to it.

13. Although Gómez-Peña subverts the social dichotomy of "dominant" and "marginal" groups by arguing that the so-called dominance of the white experience obscures the social prevalence of "border cultures," he also signals the concrete social effects of unequal power relations between Whites and Latinos/as. It is in this way that I interpret his call for intercultural coalition as a meeting ground where the dominant racial group and U.S. Latinos/as set the historical record straight.

14. Although the purpose of this essay is not an exposé on the construction of my identity in the classroom, my status as a "white-looking" Latina provides

another revealing context for the performance of white resistance. The seemingly eternal challenge to my claim to Latinaness—by white students and at times by Latino/a students—expresses itself in what I have elsewhere called the "Light-Skinned Latina Test" (1998). I try to acknowledge simultaneously the very real privileges of my light-skin color and the divisive politics of colorism in Latino communities; but the emotional impact of the race-loyalty "test" and the ensuing urge to defend myself come crashing in on me in ways that feel threatening, alienating, and dislocating, at times robbing me of the ability to act according to the imperatives of antiracist pedagogies. When the authenticity of my status as a woman of color is questioned, I sometimes feel pressured to chastise white students harshly for their slowness to accept antiracist perspectives, rather than taking the time to cultivate in the classroom a collective awareness of the ideological pitfalls and defensiveness of uncritical white identity. While one of the explicit goals of my classroom is to engender a critical space for the reconstruction of progressive, antiracist identities, the pressure to prove to darker-skinned students of color that I am not "white" (this is what the "Latina Test" is all about) seriously undermines my pedagogical clarity and my willingness to risk being misunderstood by "my own people." The epistemic and emotional stakes for the embodiment of my cultural identity in the U.S. Latino Studies classroom underscore the volatile racial politics that characterize antiracist teaching and learning. Although I recognize the need to devise pedagogies that go beyond arguing white students out of their racism and Latino/a students out of their colorism and [hetero]sexism, and beyond the imperatives of self-defense, I am still cultivating a pedagogy that will engage the epistemic and political complexities of diverse classroom constituencies and put these forward in collective, democratizing knowledge production.

15. Amie Macdonald introduces and outlines the epistemic salience of "communities of meaning" in her important essay "Racial Authenticity and White Separatism: The Future of Racial Program Housing on College Campuses." Macdonald and I further develop the link between diverse communities of meaning and epistemic wholeness in our introductory essay to this volume "Feminist Reflections on the Pedagogical Relevance of Identity."

Works Cited

Acuña, Rodolfo. *Occupied America: A History of Chicanos.* New York: Harper & Row, 1988.

Alcoff, Linda Martín. "Who's Afraid of Identity Politics"? *Reclaiming Identity.* Ed. Paula M. L. Moya and Michael Hames-García. Berkeley: University of California Press, 2000, 312–344.

———. "Latina/o Identity Politics." *The Good Citizen.* Ed. David Batstone and Eduardo Mendieta. New York: Routledge, 1999, 93–112.

Anzaldúa, Gloria. *Borderlands/La Frontera: The New Mestiza.* San Francisco: Spinster/Aunt Lute, 1987.

————. "The Homeland Aztlán." *Borderlands/La Frontera: The New Mestiza*. San Francisco: Spinster/Aunt Lute, 1987, 1–13.

Deay, Ardeth and Judith Stitzel. "Reshaping the Introductory Women's Studies Course: Dealing Up Front with Anger, Resistance, and Reality." *The Feminist Teacher Anthology: Pedagogies and Classroom Strategies*. Ed. Gail Cohee, Elisabeth Daumer, Theresa Kemp, Paula Krebs, Sue Lafky, Sandra Runzo. New York: Teachers College Press, Columbia University, 1998, 87–97.

Delgado, Richard and Jean Stefancic. *Critical White Studies: Looking Behind the Mirror*. Philadelphia: Temple University Press, 1997.

de Sousa, Ronald. "The Rationality of Emotions." *Explaining Emotions*. Ed. Amelie O. Rorty. Berkeley: University of California Press, 1980, 127–51.

Ellsworth, Elizabeth. "Why Doesn't This Feel Empowering? Working Through the Repressive Myths of Critical Pedagogy." *Feminisms and Critical Pedagogy*. Ed. Carmen Luke and Jennifer Gore. New York: Routledge, 1992, 90–119.

Flores, Juan. *From Bomba to Hip-Hop: Puerto Rican Culture and Latino Identity*. New York: Columbia University Press, 2000.

Freire, Paulo. *Pedagogy of the Oppressed*. New York: Herder, 1972.

Gilligan, Carol. *In a Different Voice: Psychological Theory and Women's Development*. Cambridge, Massachussetts: Harvard University Press, 1982.

Giroux, Henry. "Radical Pedagogy and the Politics of Student Voice." *Interchange* 17 (1986): 48–69.

————. "Insurgent Multiculturalism and the Promise of Pedagogy." *Pedagogy and the Politics of Hope*. Boulder: Westview Press, 1997, 234–253.

Gómez-Peña, Guillermo. "The Multicultural Paradigm." *High Performance* (Fall 1989): 18–27

Gonzáles, Rodolfo "Corky." "I Am Joaquín." *Literatura Chicana 1965 - 1995: An Anthology in Spanish, English and Calo*. Ed. David William Foster and Manuel de Jesús Hernández Gutiérrez. New York: Garland Publishing, 1997, 207–222.

Harding, Sandra. "Rethinking Standpoint Epistemology: What is Strong Objectivity?" *Feminist Epistemologies*. Ed. Linda Martín Alcoff and Elizabeth Potter. New York: Routledge, 1993, 49–82.

hooks, bell. *Teaching to Transgress: Education as the Practice of Freedom*. New York: Routledge, 1994.

————."Toward a Revolutionary Feminist Pedagogy. *Talking Back: Thinking Feminist, Thinking Black*. Boston, MA: South End Press, 1989, 49–54.

Kincheloe, Joe et al. *White Reign: Deploying Whiteness in America*. New York: St. Martin's Press, 1998.

Kincheloe, Joe L. and Shirley R. Steinberg. "Addressing the Crisis of Whiteness: Reconfiguring White Identity in a Pedagogy of Whiteness." *White Reign: Deploying Whiteness in America*. Ed. Joe Kincheloe et al. New York: St. Martin's Press, 1998, 3–29.

Lowe, Lisa. "Imagining Los Angeles in the Production of Multiculturalism." *Mapping Multiculturalism*. Ed. Avery F. Gordon and Christopher Newfield. Minneapolis, Minnesota: University of Minnesota Press, 1996, 413–434.

Macdonald, Amie A. "Racial Authenticity and White Separatism: The Future of Racial Program Housing on College Campuses." *Reclaiming Identity: Realist Theory and the Predicament of Postmodernism.* Ed. Paula M. L. Moya and Michael Hames-García. Berkeley: University of California Press, 2000, 205–225.

Maher, Frances and Mary Kay Thompson Tetreault. "They Got the Paradigm and Painted it White." *White Reign: Deploying Whiteness in America.* Ed. Joe Kincheloe et al. New York: St. Martin's Press, 1998, 148–160.

Mayberry, Maralee and Ellen Cronan Rose. "Teaching in Environments of Resistance: Toward a Critical, Feminist and Anti-Racist Pedagogy." *Meeting the Challenge: Innovative Feminist Pedagogies in Action.* New York: Routledge, 1999, 23–46.

McIntosh, Peggy. "White Privilege and Male Privilege: A Personal Account of Coming to See Correspondences through Work in Women's Studies." *Critical White Studies: Looking Behind the Mirror.* Ed. Richard Delgado and Jean Stefancic. Philadelphia: Temple University Press, 1997, 291–299.

Mohanty, Chandra Talpade. "On Race and Voice: Challenges for Liberal Education in the 1990s." *Beyond a Dream Deferred: Multicultural Education and the Politics of Excellence.* Ed. Becky W. Thompson and Sangeeta Tyagi. Minneapolis: University of Minnesota Press, 1993, 41–65.

Mohanty, Satya P. "The Epistemic Status of Cultural Identity: On *Beloved* and the Postcolonial Condition." *Reclaiming Identity: Realist Theory and the Predicament of Postmodernism.* Ed. Paula M. L. Moya and Michael Hames-García. Berkeley: University of California Press, 2000, 29–66.

Moraga, Cherríe. *Loving in the War Years: Lo que nunca pasó por sus labios.* Boston: South End Press, 1983.

———. "La Güera." *Loving in the War Years: Lo que nunca pasó por sus labios.* Boston: South End Press, 1983, 50–59.

Moya, Paula M. L. "Postmodernism, "Realism," and the Politics of Identity: Cherríe Moraga and Chicana Feminism." *Reclaiming Identity: Realist Theory and the Predicament of Postmodernism.* Ed. Paula Moya and Michael Hames-García. Berkeley: University of California Press, 2000, 67–101.

Narayan, Uma. "Working Together Across Difference: Some Considerations on Emotions and Political Practice." *Hypatia* 3 (Summer, 1988): 31–47.

Nieto, Sonia. "From Brown Heroes and Holidays to Assimilationist Agendas: Reconsidering the Critique of Multicultural Education." *Multicultural Education, Critical Pedagogy, and the Politics of Difference.* Ed. Christine Sleeter and Peter McLaren. Albany: State University of New York, 1995, 191–220.

Nussbaum, Martha. *Love's Knowledge.* New York: Oxford University Press, 1990.

Rodríguez, Nelson A. "Emptying the Content of Whiteness: Toward an Understanding of the Relation between Whiteness and Pedagogy." *White Reign: Deploying Whiteness in America.* Ed. Joe L. Kincheloe et al. New York: St. Martin's Press, 1998, 31–62.

Roman, Leslie. "White is a Color! White Defensiveness, Postmodernism and Antiracist Pedagogy." *Race, Identity and Representation in Education.* Ed. Cameron McCarthy and Warren Crichlow. New York: Routledge, 1993, 71–88.

Sánchez-Casal, Susan. "In a Neighborhood of Another Color: Latino/a Struggles for Home." *Burning Down the House: Recycling Domesticity.* Ed. Rosemary Marangoly George. Boulder, CO: Westview Press, 1998, 326–354.

—— and Amie A. Macdonald. "Feminist Reflections on the Pedagogical Relevance of Identity." *Twenty-First-Century Feminist Classrooms: Pedagogies of Identity and Difference.* Palgrave Macmillan, 2002, 1–28 [Introduction, this volume].

Scheman, Naomi. "Anger and the Politics of Naming." *Women and Language in Literature and Society.* Ed. Sally McConnell-Ginet, Ruth Borker, and Nelly Furman. New York: Praeger, 1980, 174–87.

Sleeter, Christine E., and Peter McLaren. *Multicultural Education, Critical Pedagogy, and the Politics of Difference.* New York: State University of New York Press, 1995.

Srivastava, Aruna. 1997. "Anti-Racism Inside and Outside the Classroom." *Dangerous Territories: Struggles for Difference and Equality in Education.* Ed. Leslie G. Roman and Linda Eyre. New York: Routledge, 1997, 113–125.

Tatum, Beverly Daniel. "Talking About Race, Learning About Racism: The Application of Racial Identity Development Theory in the Classroom." *Harvard Educational Review* 62.1 (1992): 1–24.

——."Teaching White Students about Racism: The Search for White Allies and the Restoration of Hope." *Teachers College Record* 95.4 (Summer 1994): 462–475.

Trinh T. Minh-ha. *Woman, Native, Other.* Bloomington: Indiana University Press, 1989.

Zentella, Ana Celia. "The 'Chiquitafication' of U.S. Latinos and Their Languages, OR, Why We Need an Anthropolitical Linguistics." *Salsa III* Austin: University of Texas, (April 7–9, 1995): 1–18.

CHAPTER THREE

STUDENT RESISTANCE AND NATIONALISM IN THE CLASSROOM
Reflections on Globalizing the Curriculum

Michiko Hase

It was the tenth week of the 16 week semester at a state university in the western United States whose student population is predominantly white and middle- to upper-middle class. I had designed my "Global Gender Issues" course to direct student attention to the responsibility of the United States—the government, the military, its businesses—and the agency and activism of third-world women. The topic of the day was military violence against women in war and armed conflict, especially Japan's military "comfort women" system during World War II. In my classes, as in my writing, I use the term "military 'comfort women'" used by the Japanese military itself, although "sexual slavery" more accurately describes the brutal oppression under this system. By the use of quotation marks ("comfort women"), I intend to highlight both the inaccuracy of this historical term and the irony that the "comfort" supposedly provided to Japanese soldiers was made possible by the unbearably inhumane victimization of women, most of whom

The editors gratefully acknowledge the permission of *Feminist Teacher* to reprint this essay.

were Korean. Along with readings on the history of that system, I had assigned my own unpublished paper on the transnational feminist redress movement and the positionality of Japanese women, past and present, in that chapter of Japanese history and in the redress movement. In addition to teaching my American students about military violence against women and women's human rights violations, I wanted to raise issues about how women, an oppressed group in their own society, could also participate, albeit inadvertently, in the oppression of women (and men) of other nationalities, races, classes, and so on, and how women in such a situation might take responsibility and be accountable for their (inadvertent) complicity in an oppressive system. I also wanted to discuss the role of nation and nationality both in the historical "comfort women" system and in the contemporary redress movement. For example:

- How did the Japanese military define and treat Korean women and other women from nations colonized or occupied by Japan as expendable "receptacles" for Japanese soldiers' "sexual needs," while the Japanese imperial state prescribed for "good" Japanese women the role of wives and mothers of male subjects, especially soldiers?
- How is this different positioning of Japanese and colonized women in the wartime Japanese gender system reflected in their differing positionalities in today's feminist transnational redress movement that consists of women from both the victimized nations and Japan?
- Was the sexual violence against non-Japanese women a worse crime than that against Japanese "comfort women"? Why or why not?

I used the example of Japan's military "comfort women" system because of the gravity of the crime fraught with these complex questions, on the one hand, and because of my own struggle with the issues of complicity in and accountability for that history as a Japanese woman and feminist, on the other hand. I began my lecture by relating my personal engagement with the topic—how I had become interested in the issue and how I related to it—and discussed the issues of responsibility and accountability for me as a Japanese feminist for the history and contemporary redress movement of military "comfort women." Could I simply say, "I was not there," as a white historian said of slavery? (Farnham 112)[1] I talked about my experience of listening to horrific firsthand accounts by survivors of the "comfort women" system at the NGO (nongovernmental organization) Forum on Women held in China in 1995, and how I felt being at an international gathering of women hearing about heinous crimes committed by "my country." My students listened intently and with obvious interest. Following my presentation, the class had a very thoughtful discussion about positionality, accountability, nation, and the tension between feminism and nationalism.

This class meeting marked a significant turnaround in a course that had not gone as I had planned and hoped. Prior to this lecture, some students showed signs of discomfort with and resistance to the material and my approach to the topics. As I discuss shortly, in the previous several years in which I had taught about global gender issues, I had grown increasingly disturbed by students' attraction to "horrible" practices committed by native men on native women in other cultures and by their relative indifference to U.S. roles in the global economy and world politics. In the "Global Gender Issues" course, therefore, I put the United States, its government, its businesses, its military, and its influence in, and control of, international agencies at the center of the course, along with an emphasis on the agency and activism of third-world women. It was clear that this was a stark contrast to what the students expected to be the center of the course: "the plight of third-world women." My approach had been met with student skepticism and discomfort, until the class meeting described above.

After this "turnaround" class, the students appeared to become more appreciative of the course and me. There was one student who, earlier in the semester, had expressed in class her discomfort with the course material and the course's focus on U.S. responsibility, claiming that it was very difficult for her to see her country criticized because she was very patriotic. Having spent the previous summer in a program that took students to various parts of the world on a cruise ship, she had been excited about this course and had probably expected to discuss other cultures rather than the hegemony of the United States. Her statement was an expression of her nationalism, I felt, coupled with her disappointment and frustration with the course focus. Toward the end of the semester, after much delay she came to have a required individual conference with me. During this conference, she informed me that she hadn't been sure about the class at first, but had come to appreciate it. Eventually she wrote an excellent final paper with honest self-reflections and thoughtful insights about her positionality as a privileged upper-middle-class white American woman learning about global issues. At the end of the semester, to my relief and satisfaction, I received good student evaluations. I attribute much of this success to the impact of that one lecture that helped reframe the students' understanding.

I read this turnaround in the student attitudes toward the course and me in two ways. First, when I presented the "comfort women" issue in a way that was very critical of Japan, the students knew that I had not been "bashing" the United States but had been applying my critical analysis to *all* countries and issues. Second, I believe that discussing my own engagement with the "comfort women" issue and my own complicity in and accountability for Japan's war responsibility presented the students with an example of what I had been talking about when I had discussed U.S. citizens' complicity in and accountability for their government's and businesses's policies and actions. In the same vein, I have also used in my other courses writings by Japanese feminists that critically analyze Japan's role in the global economy, and the complicity and accountability of Japanese women in Japan's exploitation of third-world countries (Matsui; "Matsui Yayori"). Again, I have done so in the hopes not only of helping my students understand the global economy and interconnectedness in the lives of women in the first and third worlds, but also of providing a model for thinking about the complicity and accountability of women from the first world. Here, it is important to note that even though the Japanese economy is categorized as "first world," Japan is often grouped into the "third world" when it comes to "women's status" and the feminist movement (Jayawardena), although Japanese women in Japan probably do not conceive of themselves as "third-world women." Japan's indeterminate and shifting positioning in the series of geopolitical binaries (first/third world, West/East, North/South, and so on) is a problematic one and exposes the fundamentally arbitrary and unstable nature of such binaries. To avoid such confusions, in this essay I use "foreign-born women of color," though it sounds awkward, to refer to women of color (mostly from the third world but also from Japan) who teach in the United States.

Because my (mostly) American students and I do not occupy the same subject position of "we Americans" or "we American feminists," and because I am often perceived by some students as inferior and/or incompetent on account of my nationality, race, English, among other factors,[2] the teacher-student dynamics in my classes are quite different from those for American teachers, including Asian American teachers. In my classroom, nationality (in conjunction with race) readily becomes a demarcation line between my students and me. As a result, I have come to realize the significance of nation as a category in understanding and analyzing "women's" experiences and the role of nationalism as an element of the student resistance I have encountered in my classes. In this essay, then, drawing upon my experience of teaching American students about global gender issues, I argue for the need to consider issues of nationalism in the classroom and the relevance of "nation" as a category of analysis in Women's Studies teaching. After a brief review of the literature on the project of globalizing the Women's Studies curriculum, I relate some of my experiences, identify the challenges I have faced, and discuss how the category "nation" shapes women's varied experiences and positions. I close the essay by suggesting how the power dynamics in a "global classroom" where the professor is a non-U.S. woman of color and the students are Americans can be used as an opportunity to examine the issues of nation and nationalism.

Globalizing the Women's Studies Curriculum

In the 1990s, as negative consequences of globalization became more and more evident and widespread, Women's Studies teachers in the United States made a variety of efforts to bring "the global" to their classrooms (Bunch). These efforts ranged from offering courses on globalization and third-world women to transforming the curriculum by incorporating global issues and perspectives. As part of this growing trend, I have been teaching courses on global gender issues at U.S. institutions since 1993. An "international scholar" from Japan teaching in the United States, I have encountered challenges that are not addressed in the existing literature on internationalizing or globalizing the Women's Studies curriculum. I believe that as more and more foreign-born women of color are teaching in U.S. institutions of higher education, there is a growing need to address the challenges faced by them, as well as the significant contributions they can make to the project of globalizing the Women's Studies curriculum.

Published accounts of curriculum transformation projects from a global perspective include special issues of major Women's Studies journals, including a *Women's Studies International Forum* special issue *Reaching for Global Feminism: Approaches to Curriculum Change in the Southwestern United States* and a *Women's Studies Quarterly* special issue *Internationalizing the Curriculum,* as well as individual articles (Betteridge and Monk, De Danaan, Stetz, and Rosser). Many of these accounts show efforts to respond to Chandra Mohanty's critique that "assumptions of privilege and ethnocentric universality, on the one hand, and inadequate self-consciousness about the effect of Western scholarship on the 'third world' in the context of a world system dominated by the West, on the other, characterize a sizable extent of Western feminist work on women in the third world" (53). Many curriculum innovators are aware of the ways in which Western Women's Studies practice can reproduce unequal power relations between Western feminists and objects of their study. They have thoughtfully addressed such important problems as the hegemony of Western feminism, Western ethnocentrism in the Women's Studies curriculum, concerns with further marginalizing or othering non-Western women's experiences, tokenism, and problems of applying Western-originated concepts like feminism and gender to non-Western contexts. For example, mindful of "turning non-Western subjects into 'exoticized others'" (McDermott 90), they have asked some thoughtful, self-reflexive questions such as "What underlies European and American scholars' interest in knowing more about the status and conditions of women elsewhere—why are 'we'/ 'they' [*sic*] interested?" (Rosenfelt 13). To avoid reproducing stereotypes of third-world women and the hegemony of Western feminism, these innovators have tried to historicize and contextualize international material.

Most of the accounts of globalizing or internationalizing the curriculum are written from the perspective of Western feminists, assuming that the instructor is a Western feminist. One notable exception is "Internationalizing Theories of Feminism" by Seung-kyung Kim and Carole McCann. "As an expatriate Third World woman teaching feminist theory," Kim and McCann write, "Seung-kyung Kim is acutely aware of her own ambiguous location" (117). Here Kim and McCann are concerned with the instructor's positionality and raise issues of authenticity, instructor as native informant, and the danger of "essentializing 'Third World women.'" They quote anthropologist Aiwha Ong's question, "Do Third World feminists who now write in the anglophone world enjoy a privileged positionality in representing the 'authentic experiences' of women from our ancestral culture or not?" (117). Even though this is an important question, in this essay I approach the issue of instructor positionality in a globalized classroom from a slightly different angle: what happens when a foreign-born woman of color teacher presents herself not as a native informant or a representative of third-world women, but rather as a critic of U.S. hegemony in the world and in feminism?

My experiences teaching global gender issues in the United States from a perspective critical of U.S. hegemony include a set of challenges not addressed in the existing literature on curriculum transformation from a global perspective. Those challenges revolve around student resistance to critical examinations of U.S. hegemony in the global economy and of the hegemony of Western feminism. I characterize the resistance as nationalist in the sense that American students often become defensive about U.S. policies and practices as well as their own possible implication and investment in U.S. hegemony. I argue that this nationalist resistance to critical examinations of U.S. hegemony is intensified when such critical views are offered by a foreign-born woman of color. This student resistance, in my view, underscores the need to address the issues of nationalism in the classroom and the significance of "nation" as a category of analysis in a globalized Women's Studies curriculum. In the next section, I describe a prevalent pattern in student reactions that emerged in my courses on global gender issues courses.

Horrified Fascination with the "Barbaric" and Lack of Interest in U.S. Hegemony

Since 1993, I have been teaching courses on global gender issues in U.S. universities: first, as a graduate instructor at a state university in the Upper Midwest; next, at a state university on the West Coast; and currently at a state university in the West. My "global courses" typically cover such topics as the global economy, women's human rights, gendered violence in war and armed conflicts, militarization (including women in the military), the environment, and local and global women's movements.

Generally speaking, the students I have taught have shown much interest in "exotic" issues affecting third-world women while showing little interest in the ways in which the United States—its government, its corporations, and U.S.-dominated international institutions—shapes (and even dictates) the process of globalization. I have encountered much student resistance when attempting to engage my students in the latter perspective and issues. A disturbing pattern emerged: the American students I have taught showed lack of interest in the negative impact of policies and actions of the U.S. government, U.S. corporations, and U.S.-dominated international agencies (like the IMF and the World Bank) on the rest of the world. By contrast, these students showed marked interest in topics like female genital surgeries[3] and dowry deaths—namely, practices that concern sexuality and control/violation of woman's body and that are perpetrated by native men against native women in some distant societies. When I assigned a research paper and let the students choose the topic, there were always those who chose "genital mutilation" because it was "so interesting." They were simultaneously appalled by and attracted to those "barbaric" practices and could not stop talking about the grisly procedural details of "genital mutilation." I became increasingly troubled by my students' attraction to these particular issues and the matching lack of interest in and curiosity about the exploitative or unethical actions of their own government and U.S. corporations and the impact of these U.S. policies and practices on the rest of the world.[4]

This recurring pattern seemed to me to be a sign of American students' sense of superiority, mixed with their missionary attitude (they have to "rescue" "poor third-world sisters" from oppressive local cultures), their voyeurism, and their binary world view of "us" vs. "them." My students' horrified fascination with "barbaric" practices in non-Western societies confirmed time and again Inderpal Grewal and Caren Kaplan's observation that "Western culture continues to acknowledge difference primarily by differentiating the 'exotic' from the 'domestic'" (7). After learning about the "plight" of third-world women, my American students would typically come to the reassuring realization of "how lucky" they were and to the question of how they could help those poor third-world sisters. If these attitudes and assumptions were not challenged, I became convinced, global gender issues courses would end up reinforcing and reproducing such attitudes and preconceptions as well as Western representations of the third world (women) as the exotic/inferior Other, along with the binary view of "us" versus "them." I then decided to offer a course that challenged and critiqued Western feminist globalism,[5] which I discuss next.

Student Resistance to
Critical Examination of "Global Feminism"

It has been my experience that students more readily perceive me as having legitimacy and authority in courses that in some ways relate to my identity,[6] such as a course on global gender issues (my being an "international scholar") and on Asian American women (my being from Asia—a problematic association between course content and my country of origin because it is based on a conflation between "Asian" and "Asian American"). And yet I have encountered a variety of student resistance and suspicion even in courses dealing with global issues.

Thus far, student resistance was most pronounced in my "Rethinking Global Feminism" course, which critically examined the history and current manifestations of imperial Western feminisms and some recent theoretical contributions by third-world feminists. The class was small, with 13 students. All of the students were women and only two of them were women of color. The majority of the students were either Women's Studies majors or minors. Most of the students seemed to reject both the material presented in the course and me as an instructor. What made teaching that course even more difficult was the fact that I had not anticipated and, therefore, had not been prepared to deal effectively with the kind of strong resistance I encountered. The year before, I had taught a course titled "The Beijing Conference and Beyond," covering some of the major issues raised at the Fourth World Conference and the NGO Forum on Women held in China in 1995, but I had not encountered much student resistance. The difference between the two courses was that in the "Beijing" course, I covered some of the major global gender issues without critically examining the power relations within the "global feminist" movement or the notion of "global feminism" itself. The tendency to be drawn to sexual violence in other cultures and the "missionary" attitudes some of the students had exhibited in the Beijing course and other previous courses led me to rethink the teaching of global gender issues and to offer a course that critically examined "global feminism."

Early in the "Rethinking Global Feminism" course, I assigned Vietnamese American law professor Maivân Clech Lâm's article "Feeling Foreign in Feminism"—in which Lâm related her experiences of feeling dismissed and made invisible by white feminists—and critiqued white feminists' perception and treatment of third-world feminists. I assigned the article in the hopes that the article, rich with firsthand accounts of Lâm's personal experiences, would help expose the students to some of the issues faced by third-world feminists in the United States. Contrary to my hope and expectation, however, the students reacted to the article negatively and defensively. Instead of reading the article with empathy from Lâm's perspective, some of the white students clearly identified with the white feminists critiqued by Lâm. Rather than try to understand Lâm's perspective and examine the white feminists' attitudes, those students questioned and even dismissed Lâm's response to the white feminists, blaming Lâm for the problems she was raising rather than attempting to understand what she had to say. This negativity and defensiveness about the first assigned article set the tone for the rest of the semester.

For the rest of the course, as we read *Western Women and Imperialism: Complicity and Resistance,* edited by Nupur Chauduri and Margaret Strobel, and *Feminist Genealogies, Colonial Legacies, Democratic Futures,* edited by Jacqui Alexander and Chandra Talpade Mohanty, I increasingly sensed that many of the white students felt that *they* were under attack and that the *feminism* they had been taught and had embraced was challenged and discredited by the course material and by me. They often showed little interest in the readings or class discussions, evidence of which included lack of response to my questions, blank stares out the windows, and negative body postures.

In this course, I did not focus on the plight of third-world women and instead tried to problematize Western-defined, Western-imperial notions of "global feminism" and "global sisterhood." I wanted my students to understand that "Western feminist scholarship cannot avoid the challenge of situating itself and examining its role in . . . a global economic and political framework" (Mohanty 54). I used Alice Walker's video *Warrior Marks* on female genital surgeries as a case study of how an American feminist, albeit a woman of color and of African descent, engages herself with an issue affecting African women and how she represents African women and female genital surgeries in her campaign against the practice. By examining the example of a woman of color rather than a white American, I wanted to draw the students' attention to the problematic nature of such geopolitical binaries as the West/East, the first/third world, and the North/South because these binaries intersect in Walker's self-identification as a womanist in ways that complicate concepts like "third-world women/feminism" and "Western women/feminism." Walker, an American of African, European, and Native American descent, bases at least part of her reason for her interest in female genital surgeries on her ancestral connection to Africa (*Warrior Marks*). And yet, she is an American citizen born and raised in the United States, thus a Westerner and a citizen of a first-world country. Does she have a right to speak and act on behalf of African women? Is it fair to treat her as being emblematic of the Western feminist tendency, as her critics quoted below do, when Walker herself is aware and critical of *white* feminists' superior attitude (toward women of color) and their ethnocentrism, and pointedly avoids the designation of "feminism/feminist" in favor of "womanism/womanist"? Does she apply the same caution and critique to her own critical engagement with female genital surgeries?

In addition to Walker's own writing, I assigned an opinion piece written by two African women who were activists against female genital surgeries but critical of Walker's representation of African women. In their 1993 opinion piece, Seble Dawit, a human rights lawyer, and Salem Mekuria, a filmmaker, wrote:

> As is common in Western depictions of Africa, Ms. Walker and her collaborator, Prathiba Parmar, portray the continent as a monolith. African women and children are the props, and the village the background against which Alice Walker, heroine-savior, comes to articulate their pain and condemn those who inflict it. Like Ms. Walker's novel "Possessing the Secret of Joy," this film is emblematic of the Western feminist tendency to see female genital mutilation as the gender oppression to end all oppressions. Instead of being an issue worthy of attention in itself, it has become a powerfully emotive lens through which to view personal pain—a gauge by which to measure distance between the West and the rest of humanity.

Once again, however, my effort to have my students critically examine *Warrior Marks* and Walker's campaign backfired, despite my intention to engage them in a nuanced, complex discussion about representations of third-world women by Western feminists, a discussion that would go beyond that of "good" vs. "evil" and "us" vs. "them." The students seemed to see Walker as nothing but a feminist heroine who was bravely taking on the abolition of an objectionable practice by educating both African and Western women through her writing and this video. When I pointed out the filming and editing techniques that I thought served to present the local African women as mindless, helpless victims without agency, one student responded by suggesting that I was stereotyping African women. I got the sense that the students saw me as a villain who was trying to discredit and tarnish their feminist heroine.

I read this student backlash and resistance in two ways: my students' U.S.-centered education and their perception of me as unqualified and/or too incompetent to critique American feminists. First, before taking my classes, American students are generally taught U.S.-centered curricula that do not encourage critical examinations of the United States and Western-centered Women's Studies curricula and courses. It is conceivable, then, that the students in my "Rethinking Global Feminism" course were unhappy to have the feminisms they had been taught and had embraced and their feminist heroines criticized, particularly by a foreigner.[7] (A colleague, a white woman, who teaches about the global economy from a perspective critical of U.S. corporations and consumers, also reports student resistance to her critical approach, but not to the degree that I have experienced.)[8] When that critique and challenge came from a foreign-born woman of color, moreover, it is possible that my students could not appreciate, much less accept, such a critical reading of U.S. feminist work. In the end, I received poor teaching evaluations, an anomaly among the smaller, specialized courses I have taught.

Though in a different discipline, Lavina Dhingra Shankar's article "Pro/(Con)fessing Otherness: Trans(cending)national Identities in the English Classroom" sheds light on my experience described above. Shankar discusses the complexities surrounding teaching English composition and literature as "a 'nonnative' English speaker teaching a language and literature that are not her 'own,' in what is not Her land" (195). She asks, "What does it *mean* for a 'colored,' foreign female, triply an 'outsider' . . . to assume the position of power and authority in a 'First World' English classroom and to echo her (colonial) 'master's' voice?" (197; emphasis in original). Further, Shankar writes:

> Discussions focused on cultural diversity, racism, multiculturalism, and global awareness evoke a certain resistance even when a "white" teacher informs "white" upper-level undergraduate and/or graduate students, say, about slavery while teaching Toni Morrison's *Beloved*. . . . But the power dynamics may seem even more threatening to some eighteen-year-olds when the only colored person in the classroom also assumes the position of authority and informs them of the uglier parts of their cultural history, which they would rather not own (up to)." (197–8)[9]

Nationalism in the Classroom

Shankar's insights support my perception that had I not challenged students' assumptions and preconceptions about third-world women and Western feminisms, I would not have encountered so much resistance. However, I had grown too tired of and troubled by students' attraction to "horrible practices committed by native men on native women" in other cultures with their simultaneous indifference to the U.S. role in the global economy and world politics. I therefore made a considerably drastic change in my syllabus in the fall of 1998. In my "Global Gender Issues" course, which is meant to be an introductory course to global gender issues, I placed the United States—its government, its businesses, its military, and its influence in, and control of, international agencies—, rather than "the plight of third-world women," at the center of the course. Moreover, in this course revision I emphasized the agency and activism of third-world women.

At first, I was not aware of the problems of nationalism in the classroom, despite the difficulties with my "Rethinking Global Feminism" course. Instead I interpreted the student resistance primarily as a result of their racism and xenophobia. When, however, I heard a student in my "Global Gender Issues" course explicitly state that it was difficult for her to hear her country criticized, issues of nationalism became clear to me. The students' response to my lecture on military "comfort women," described at the beginning of this essay, further helped put the question of nationalism into relief. My experience in these two courses, then, taught me the need to identify and deal with nationalism as a component of student resistance and to integrate the category of "nation" into my courses. It is not only possible but probably pedagogically sound, I have come to realize, to use the *national difference* between me and my American students by foregrounding my nationality and positionality and my own engagement with critical analysis of Japanese imperialism. This approach can provide an effective pathway to my American students' self-reflexive, critical examination of U.S. government policies and U.S. businesses, as well as their own implication in U.S. hegemony. Next, I discuss some examples of how I have tried to bring to the fore the relevance of "nation" to women's lives by showing how women's experiences and positions are shaped by their nationalities (in conjunction with other categories of difference like gender, race, and class).

The Significance of Nation as a Category of Analysis in Women's Studies Teaching: Some Examples

The "comfort women" issue and the transnational feminist redress movement discussed at the start of this essay are a telling example of how "women's experience" and their positions can vary and even conflict depending on their nationalities and their differential relationships to the nation. ("Good") Japanese women and colonized women were positioned differentially within the prewar Japanese gender system and vis-à-vis the military "comfort women" system. That Japanese feminists and Korean (American) feminists working on the same cause can take divergent positions on nationalism was demonstrated in an exchange during a workshop on "comfort women" issues organized by Korean women residing in Japan and Japanese women at the 1995 NGO Forum on Women. A leading Japanese feminist contended that feminists should work to transcend nationalism because it was nationalism that had driven Japan to military aggression and war in the first place. A Korean American feminist in the audience, however, took strong exception to that view, asserting that for Koreans, nationalism was the key to their survival because it was Korean nationalism that had sustained the Korean nation and culture under Japanese colonialism.[10] Further, the "comfort women" issue raises at least two thorny, interrelated questions about sexual violence as a weapon of war. Is "nationed" sexual violence (to borrow from Nira Yuval-Davis's concept of "nationed gender") against women of other nationalities, carried out as part of national(ist) agenda, a worse crime than "in-nation" political sexual violence? And, as Rhonda Copelon asks, is sexual violence as a weapon of war, such as the "comfort women" system and mass rape in Bosnia and

Rwanda, more heinous than "ordinary" rape? Can any sexual violence be called "ordinary"?

On a topic closer to my American students, to help them become more aware of the relevance of the category of "nation" to them and, particularly, the differential impacts of the global economy on different populations in the world, I have created and used an in-class exercise that might be called "Where Were Your Clothes Made?" I have my students examine in which countries their clothes were made. First, I ask them if they know where the tops they have on were made. Typically no students do. Then, I have them form pairs and look at each other's labels on their garments. At this point, students usually become more curious about the topic and quite animated and vocal, voicing countries' names, often with surprises. I then ask them to say aloud the countries' names they have found on their garment labels. As they call out those names, I write them on the chalkboard, clustering them by continent. In addition to the familiar names like Hong Kong, students are often surprised to discover on their clothing labels some unexpected or unfamiliar country names that they don't even know how to pronounce or have never heard of, much less know where to locate (e.g., Lesotho and Lithuania). A number of their clothes are "made in the U.S.A.," a finding that gives me a chance to discuss American sweatshops that exploit recent female immigrants from the Third World and the transnational migration of labor as one aspect of globalization. Further, having the country names on the chalkboard clustered by continent aids me in discussing the historical process of globalization as well as its current situation. It also allows me to draw students' attention to the uneven effects of globalization on different parts of the world.

This exercise has proven to be both fun and instructive. First, it enables students to see in a very tangible way the connections they have to the world beyond the borders of the United States, even if they do not typically think about the rest of the world. Also, this exercise provides an effective passageway to exploring the impact of the global economy on their lives and the connections between their behavior as first world "consumers" and the work and lives of third-world women workers both here and abroad. Thus, this exercise helps students to realize how they, as (middle- to upper-class) American college students, and the women workers who sewed their clothing are *structurally* placed in differential positions within the global economy on account of their difference in nationality (in conjunction with class) and, therefore, in unequal relations of power to each other.

Another example of the relevance of nation to women's experience is the peace/anti-base movement among Asian and American women protesting the presence of the U.S. military in Asia. The East Asia-U.S. Women's Network against U.S. Militarism is an international coalition movement from South Korea, the Philippines, Japan (Okinawa, in particular, which hosts the largest U.S. military in Asia), and the United States. Created in 1997 as a result of trans-Pacific protests, initiated by Okinawan feminist activists, against the 1995 abduction and rape of a 12-year-old Okinawan schoolgirl by three U.S. servicemen stationed in Okinawa, the Network has so far held two international meetings where women from these countries reported the current conditions and issues around the U.S. military bases in each country, exchanged ideas and information, strategized action for change, and issued resolutions and statements. They have also made press releases and lobbied U.S. Congress and other government authorities. The main areas of concern have included violence against women by the U.S. military personnel, environmental problems caused by the U.S. military bases and practices, the unequal relationships between the U.S. government and military and the Asian host countries, and Amerasian children fathered but often discarded by U.S. personnel (Kirk and Okazawa-Rey, "Making Connections" 310–19). The American members of the coalition pointedly make their responsibility and accountability for these issues a center piece of their activism and acknowledge and respect the long and strong anti-base, peace activism their Asian counterparts bring to their movement. They are also keenly aware of the privileges that their U.S. citizenship or residency accord them in a variety of contexts. During the Network's second meeting in Washington, D.C., for example, sessions were conducted in English with volunteers translating. The American organizers of the meeting made a point of asking English speakers to speak clearly and of giving the translators and non-English speakers enough time to translate and to ask questions.[11]

In my "Global Gender Issues" course, I assigned writings by members of this network and discussed issues related to the large U.S. military presence in Asia and in the world. For example, the topics included the military budget (in comparison with welfare expenditures), the significance and power of the defense industry for the U.S. economy and other first-world economies, and the overall militarization of daily lives in American society, including violence against women. Much of this information was new to my students. In addition, through discussions of the activism and issues described above, my students were exposed to the perspectives of Filipino, Korean, and Okinawan (and other Japanese) women on the U.S. military and the U.S. government, perspectives they were not normally familiar with. Through this material, further, they learned a concrete example and model of how U.S. citizens and residents are working to protest against and change certain U.S. government policies and practices.

Earlier in this essay, I observed that the American students I have taught have tended to come to a comforting conclusion of "how lucky" they are after learning about the "plight" of third-world women. Asking questions about where that "luck" comes from is a way to probe the significance of

U.S. hegemony—economic, political, military, and cultural—in the world to the ways people live in the United States. In other words, I have them question how the material conditions in which they feel "lucky" are made possible and what symbolic messages influence their perception of how lucky they are. Similarly, Gwyn Kirk and Margo Okazawa-Rey, two of the founding members of the East Asia-U.S. Women's Network against U.S. Militarism and authors of the women's studies textbook *Women's Lives: Multicultural Perspectives*, comment on U.S. hegemony in the world:

> We argue that people in the United States need to understand the significance of this country's preeminence in the world, manifested culturally—through the dominance of the English language and in widespread distribution of U.S. movies, pop music, books, and magazines—as well as economically, through the power of the dollar as an international currency and the impact of U.S.-based corporations abroad. (*Women's Lives* 3)

In this passage, Kirk and Okazawa-Rey are referring to the privileges that U.S. citizenship (and residency) accord their holders. Those privileges directly and indirectly derive from U.S. preeminence in the world. To relate this point to the earlier discussion of the U.S. military bases abroad, some aspects of the "luck" of being a U.S. citizen—"national security"[12] thanks to the military dominance of the U.S. in the world and the military expenditures' contributions to the U.S. economy (both the defense and other related industries and the labor market), for example—are linked to the issues and problems confronting the women in the host countries in Asia. When these *structural* linkages between the "luck" Americans enjoy (albeit unevenly) thanks to their nationality, on the one hand, and the issues faced by third-world women, on the other, are exposed and analyzed, American students can begin to reflect critically on their attitudes of superiority, complacency, and rescue mission.

This self-aware, self-reflexive approach to U.S. hegemony is not the same as the feeling of "guilt"—far from it. As Audre Lorde writes in the context of white women's guilt about racism, guilt is not conducive to positive change but often an excuse for inaction and defensiveness: " . . . all too often, guilt is just another name for impotence, for defensiveness, destructive of communication; it becomes a device to protect ignorance and the continuation of things the way they are, the ultimate protection of changelessness. . . . Guilt is only another way of avoiding informed action. . . ." (130). What I strive to achieve in my classes in this regard is a constructive self-awareness and a structural analysis of one's privileges (based on nationality along with class, race, gender, sexual orientation, among other axes of power) as well as the structures of oppression. This awareness and analysis would enable students to grapple with their complicity as well as their own oppression and to form *equal* working relationships with individuals and groups from different (national, race, class, and so on) backgrounds so that they can work effectively and collectively for social change.[13]

Conclusion: Transforming the Women's Studies Curriculum by Incorporating Nation as a Category of Analysis

My experience of teaching global gender issues to American students as a foreign-born woman of color points to the need to address issues of nationalism and the relevance and significance of "nation" as a category of analysis in a "globalized" Women's Studies curriculum. American students generally feel more comfortable learning about the "plight" of third-world women and "exotic," "horrible" practices in other cultures. They tend to be resistant to critical examinations of ways in which the U.S. government, U.S.-led international institutions, and U.S. corporations might create or contribute to the "plight" of third-world women and ways in which they, the students, might be benefiting from U.S. hegemony in the global economy. If materials about women in "other" cultures are simply added to an existing curriculum without critically examining Western hegemony or problematizing the binary worldview that undergirds the curriculum, such an "innovation" will only result in feeding and fortifying preexisting student perceptions and prejudices. Moreover, such practices reinforce the well-established binary of the advanced, liberated West versus the backward, unliberated rest. This manner of "globalizing the Women's Studies curriculum" serves to reestablish Western feminist hegemony over third-world women and to reproduce Western imperial feminism.

To avoid this sort of "globalizing as othering," a curriculum transformation should be conducted in a way to challenge students' perceptions and assumptions of Western superiority, their voyeurism, and their missionary attitudes. Further, the goals should include educating students to become aware of and examine U.S. responsibility, as well as their own positionality and accountability in the U.S.-dominated global economy and politics. Having faced and dealt with particular challenges as a foreign-born woman of color from a "backward" country trying to bring about a transformative change in the teaching of global gender issues, I have come to acknowledge nationalism as a key issue in such a curricular and pedagogical transformation. My experience underscores the relevance and significance of "nation" as a category of analysis both in terms of course content and for examining the relationship between course content and instructor identity that shapes, at least in part, power dynamics in the classroom.

Margaret Andersen and Patricia Hill Collins, among other American scholars, have observed that "multicultural education" as it is practiced today tends to mean learning about "other cultures" and appreciating "diversity" (often reduced to the consumption of ethnic food, dress, music and dancing, and other cultural forms). This approach fails to examine critically and challenge the *structures of power and privilege* that produce and perpetuate inequalities and injustices (Andersen and Hill Collins 5–7; Miner). Such uncritical or liberal multicultural education may inadvertently serve to preserve and even strengthen the unequal social structure. Similarly, without critical examinations of unequal relations of power between the first and third world and between the scholar/student and the studied, a globalized Women's Studies curriculum has the danger of becoming an international version of liberal multicultural education, functioning to maintain and reinforce the structures and power relations that produce inequalities on a global scale. Such international or globalized liberal multiculturalism might also end up reproducing student prejudices and perceptions of the Third World (women) as the inferior Other as opposed to the superior, liberated America(ns). My experience suggests that non-American instructors (of color) may be suitably, if not uniquely, positioned to raise and explore global power imbalance within the context of a classroom. In a classroom in which a foreign-born (woman) professor of color teaches American students, instructor and students do not share the common subject position of "we American feminists." Instead, in such a classroom, the instructor-student power dynamics directly and indirectly are shaped by and reflect the larger power imbalance in the world. My experience suggests that these power dynamics can be utilized consciously and effectively as an opportunity to explore and critically examine the issues of nation and nationalism that should be integral to the studies of global issues. This way, then, the complex power dynamics between foreign-born instructor of color and American students around nation(ality), race, class, (and gender) can be a useful site of scholarship and learning, and not simply of struggle.

Notes

I would like to thank the *Feminist Teacher* Editorial Collective whose helpful comments and suggestions enabled me to clarify and sharpen the ideas discussed in this essay. I am greatly indebted to Joanne Belknap, Asunción Horno-Delgado, Janet Jacobs, and Lisa Sun-Hee Park, who read this essay in various stages and provided valuable comments and suggestions that were vital to its completion. Other colleagues and friends, including Lane Hirabayashi, Evelyn Hu-DeHart, Alison Jaggar, Joy James, Kamala Kempadoo, Katheryn Rios, Rachel Silvey, Timothy Weston, Haiping Yan, and Marcia Yonemoto, as well as my graduate advisors Professors Sara Evans and Elaine Tyler May, read an earlier paper from which this essay was developed, and their insightful feedback helped me write this essay. For their generous sharing of their time and ideas, I am most grateful.

1. Writing about her experience of teaching African American history as a white woman, historian Christie Farnham states: "Personally, I find it inconceivable that individuals should be held responsible for what other individuals and entire societies did before they were even born. Even though I am white, I do not feel any responsibility for slavery—I was not there" (112). To me, the point is that my existence and identity do not exist in a vacuum; they are a product of history and were born of a specific historical context and therefore cannot be understood without reference to that historical context. What I am interested in, then, is not how I might be *directly* responsible for something I personally did not do but how history shaped the context in which I was born and raised (and given certain privileges as well as disadvantages) and how my thinking and actions can be *accountable* for that history.

2. For a thorough and thoughtful overview of challenges and obstacles faced by Asian Pacific American (APA) women in higher education, including APA women professors, see Hune. Among many other issues, Hune discusses language bias and accent discrimination suffered by Asian-born women professors in the United States: "American society is generally intolerant of English spoken with Asian accents, but accepts, and even privileges, English spoken with European accents" (13). Hune's observation corresponds with my own experience as a nonnative speaker of English from Japan. I have repeatedly found that my Japanese-accented English marks me as the inferior Other in the minds of many American students; in the classroom, some of my American students have reacted to my English with open ridicule and mimicry to smirks and/or frowns on their faces.

3. Here I follow the practice of authors who have pointed out that the more commonly used term "female genital mutilation" "suggests a negative moral assessment before we have even begun the analysis" (Gunning 193), and use the expression "female genital surgeries" instead.

4. In an article that discusses transforming a survey course on U.S. women by incorporating international material, Cindy Himes Gissendanner writes, "I was surprised to discover how many of my students think that Africa is a country" (101), and "In my observation, students, particularly women students, often view national and international politics as remote from their lives and concerns" (103).

5. Critiquing the notion of "global feminism," Inderpal Grewal and Caren Kaplan write: "Conventionally, 'global feminism' has stood for a kind of Western cultural imperialism. The term 'global feminism' has elided the diversity of women's agency in favor of a universalized Western model of women's liberation that celebrates individuality and modernity" (17).

6. In her essay "Caliban in the Classroom," Indira Karamchetti, a literature professor, examines the "problem of the personal as it establishes or works against authority in the classroom for the teacher marked by race or ethnicity" (216). She writes:

As a postcolonial person teaching postcolonial literature, my authority, too, is somewhat dependent on my bloodlines, my physical and visible affinity with my subject matter. My authority is somewhat dependent on my status as native informant, providing others with data that can then be theorized, so that I serve as the representative figure for my entire field of study. . . . In my discipline, real power and authority lie, not in the role of native informant, not with Caliban, but in theory, with Prospero. (221)

7. Additionally, students, especially Women's Studies majors and minors, who consider themselves knowledgeable about women's oppression, tend not to take such challenges well. Colleagues of mine who teach Chinese and Japanese histories also made similar observations about their students who think of themselves as knowledgeable about China or Japan.

8. My gratitude to Kayann Short for sharing her experience and insights with me.

9. Shankar continues: "In my experience, often the 'white' (especially male) students either feel guilty and become silenced, or become defensive and/or (mildly) aggressive when the discussion centers around slavery or colonization" (197–8).

10. Although this particular exchange illustrated differing positionalities between Japanese and Korean (American) feminists quite dramatically, it is not to deny that there *are* diversities in positions on nationalism and other issues within each national group.

11. The author's personal observations during the Network's second international meeting, "Redefining Security for Women and Children," Washington, D.C., October 9–13, 1998. This practice contrasted sharply with what I had observed at the 1995 NGO Forum where many native English speakers spoke fast, often using colloquial expressions, without regard to nonnative speakers of English.

12. Whether or not the conventional, militarized notion of "national security" really ensures "security" in the sense that all members of society can live without threats of any kind to their life is highly debatable. Kirk and Okazawa-Rey, for example, reject the conventional definition of "national security" and propose an alternative definition of "security" to envision a society in which everyone leads a safe, secure life. ("Making Connections," 319; *Women's Lives,* 384–5).

13. I thank Karen Lozano for her antiracism work and her honors thesis, both of which influenced the ideas discussed in this paragraph.

Works Cited

Alexander, M. Jacqui, and Chandra Talpade Mohanty, eds. *Feminist Genealogies, Colonial Legacies, Democratic Futures.* New York: Routledge, 1997.

Andersen, Margaret L., and Patricia Hill Collins, eds. *Race, Class, and Gender: An Anthology.* 3rd ed. Belmont, Calif.: Wadsworth, 1998.

Betteridge, Anne, and Janice Monk. "Teaching Women's Studies from an International Perspective." *Women's Studies Quarterly* 18. 1–2 (1990): 78–85.

Bunch, Charlotte. "Bringing the Global Home." *Passionate Politics: Feminist Theory in Action.* New York: St. Martin's Press, 1987, 328–45.

Chaudhuri, Nupur, and Margaret Strobel, eds. *Western Women and Imperialism: Complicity and Resistance.* Bloomington: Indiana University Press, 1992.

Copelon, Rhonda. "Gendered War Crimes: Reconceptualizing Rape in Time of War." *Women's Rights, Human Rights: International Feminist Perspectives.* Ed. Julie Peters and Andrea Wolper. New York: Routledge, 1995, 197–214.

Dawit, Seble, and Salem Mekuria. "The West Just Doesn't Get It." *New York Times* Dec. 7, 1993, A27.

De Danaan, Llyn. "Center to Margin: Dynamics in a Global Classroom." *Women's Studies Quarterly* 18. 1–2 (1990): 135–44.

Farnham, Christie. "The Discipline of History and the Demands of Identity Politics." *Teaching What You're Not: Identity Politics in Higher Education.* Ed. Katherine J. Mayberry. New York: New York University Press, 1996, 107–30.

Gissendanner, Cindy Himes. "Transforming a Survey Course on U.S. Women." *Women's Studies Quarterly* 26. 3–4 (1998): 99–114.

Grewal, Inderpal, and Caren Kaplan, eds. *Scattered Hegemonies: Postmodernity and Transnational Feminist Practice.* Minneapolis: University of Minnesota Press, 1994.

Gunning, Isabelle R. "Arrogant Perception, World-Travelling and Multicultural Feminism: The Case of Female Genital Surgeries." *Columbia Human Rights Law Review* 23 (1992): 189–248.

Hune, Shirley. *Asian Pacific American Women in Higher Education: Claiming Visibility and Voice.* Washington, D.C.: Association of American Colleges and Universities, Program on the Status and Education of Women, 1998.

Internationalizing the Curriculum: Integrating Area Studies, Women's Studies, and Ethnic Studies. Spec. issue of *Women's Studies Quarterly* 26.3–4 (1998): 1–285.

Jayawardena, Kumari, ed. *Feminism and Nationalism in the Third World.* London: Zed Books, 1986.

Karamcheti, Indira. "Caliban in the Classroom." *Teaching What You're Not: Identity Politics in Higher Education.* Ed. Katherine J. Mayberry. New York: New York University Press, 1996, 215–27.

Kim, Seung-kyung, and Carole McCann. "Internationalizing Theories of Feminism." *Women's Studies Quarterly* 26. 3–4 (1998): 115–32.

Kirk, Gwyn, and Margo Okazawa-Rey. "Making Connections: Building an East Asia-U.S. Women's Network against U.S. Militarism." *The Women and War Reader.* Ed. Lois Ann Lorentzen and Jennifer Turpin. New York: New York University Press, 1998, 308–22.

———. *Women's Lives: Multicultural Perspectives.* Mountain View, Calif.: Mayfield, 1998.

Lâm, Maivân Clech. "Feeling Foreign in Feminism." *Sings: Journal of Women in Culture and Society* 19 (1994): 865–93.

Lorde, Audre. "The Uses of Anger: Women Responding to Racism." In *Sister Outsider.* Trumansburg, New York: Crossing Press, 1984, 124–33.

Lozano, Karen. "Beyond the 'Backpack' of Privilege: White Feminist Antiracism Strategies." Honors Thesis. University of Colorado, 1999.

McDermott, Patrice. "Internationalizing the Core Curriculum." *Women's Studies Quarterly* 26. 3–4 (1998): 88–98.

Matsui, Yayori. *Women's Asia.* London and New Jersey: Zed Books, 1989.

"Matsui Yayori." *Broken Silence: Voices of Japanese Feminism.* Ed. Sandra Buckley. Berkeley: University of California Press, 1997, 131–55.

Miner, Barbara. "Taking Multicultural, Antiracist Education Seriously: An Interview with Enid Lee." *Race, Class, and Gender: An Anthology.* 3rd ed. Ed. Margaret L. Andersen and Patricia Hill Collins. Belmont, Calif.: Wadsworth, 1998, 534–39.

Mohanty, Chandra Talpade. "Under Western Eyes: Feminist Scholarship and Colonial Discourses." *Third World Women and the Politics of Feminism.* Ed. Chandra Talpade Mohanty, Ann Russo, and Lourdes Torres. Bloomington: Indiana University Press, 1991, 51–80.

Monk, Janice, Anne Betteridge, and Amy W. Newhall, eds. *Reaching for Global Feminism: Approaches to Curriculum Change in the Southwestern United States.* Spec. Issue of *Women's Studies International Forum* 14 (1991): 239–379.

Rosenfelt, Deborah S. "Editorial." *Internationalizing the Curriculum: Integrating Area Studies, Women's Studies, and Ethnic Studies.* Spec. issue of *Women's Studies Quarterly* 26. 3–4 (1998): 4–16.

Rosser, Sue V. "International Experiences Lead to Using Postcolonial Feminism to Transform Life Sciences Curriculum." *Women's Studies International Forum* 22 (1999): 3–15.

Shankar, Lavina Dhingra. "Pro/(Con)fessing Otherness: Trans(cending)national Identities in the English Classroom." *Teaching What You're Not: Identity Politics in Higher Education.* Ed. Katherine J. Mayberry. New York: New York University Press, 1996, 195–214.

Stetz, Margaret D. "Globalizing the Curriculum: Rewards and Resistance." *Feminist Teacher* 12.1 (1998): 1–11.

Walker, Alice. "A Legacy of Betrayal." *Ms.* November/December, 1993, 55–57.

Warrior Marks. Dir. Prathiba Parmer. Exec. prod. Alice Walker. Videocassette. New York: Women Make Movies, 1993.

Yuval-Davis, Nira. *Gender and Nation.* London: Sage, 1997.

PART II

THE EPISTEMOLOGY OF EXPERIENCE

CHAPTER FOUR

FEMINIST PEDAGOGY AND
THE APPEAL TO EPISTEMIC PRIVILEGE

Amie A. Macdonald

Introduction

Recently a student—I'll call him Rafael[1]—in my course "Ethics and Law" drew heavily on personal experience to defend Kant's theory of the autonomy of moral reasoning. Citing that he has lived his entire life in a poor and violent neighborhood, that his family is heavily involved in selling drugs, that as a young Latino he has had oppositional interaction with the authoritarian and overtly racist police presence in the neighborhood, Rafael argued that Kant *must* be correct in asserting that there is a universal moral law, and that we can use reason independently of inclination to formulate this moral law. Rafael pointed out that despite the fact that in his "world" selling drugs is not only permissible but advisable, he knows that dealing is unethical and he therefore refuses to participate in the narcotics industry. Since he could not know through experience that dealing is wrong, Rafael continued, he must have made this moral judgment through reason alone. Therein, he concluded, is strong evidence of the truth of Kant's moral theory.

Centering student experiences such as this one in the learning process has been part of my standard operating procedure in over ten years of teaching at the university level—at the large public suburban University of Massachusetts at Amherst, the private, elite, and predominantly white Hamilton College, and now at John Jay College/City University of New York, one of our nation's vanguard urban public universities. While major demographic differences among these institutions have shown me a wide variety of classroom dynamics around the issue of student appeal to experience, the power and intensity of experiential learning is undeniable. In many instances my students' introduction of their experiences—sometimes as victims, sometimes as perpetrators (of sexual assault, racism, homophobia, anti-Semitism, homelessness, incarceration, homicide, police brutality, and so on)—have brought to the surface volatility, hatred, and hostility that are never resolved. These classroom encounters have often left me cold as I consider the long-term struggle for social justice and political equality. But as much as my students have disturbed me with, for example, starkly hateful remarks about poor people, I remain convinced of the epistemic influence of experiential learning when, on the other hand, women testify courageously about surviving sexual assault or young men of color retell their experiences as victims of racial profiling.

I think though that teaching at John Jay College—with a "majority minority" student population (i.e., approximately one-third black, one-third Latino, and one-third white, with a small but growing Asian contingent) ranging in age from 18 year-olds to middle-aged adults, where most students work at least one full-time job (many as police officers, corrections officers, or firefighters) and are responsible for the care of at least one child, grandparent, or other family member, where many students are recent immigrants or first-generation Americans and bilingualism is the norm—has more than anything motivated me to question the theoretical framework that informs my pedagogy of student experiences. At John Jay, the intense diversity and range of subjugated knowledges represented in the classroom outpaces most institutions, and thus the conglomeration of various student experiences is, at the very least, stunning. In my other jobs, privileged students (white, upper-middle/ruling class, moderately conservative, with college-educated parents, and so on) with hegemonic worldviews dominated my courses, and student appeals to experience typically produced either little conflict, or a kind of clear opposition between the views of students speaking from privilege versus those speaking from oppression. Now, in my courses at John Jay, there is a competition among divergent and contradictory subjugated knowledges that students mobilize from their experiences. Among these diverse learners, I can no longer ground my pedagogy in the fundamental claims about the epistemic privilege of oppressed people, since these claims cannot contend with the range and inherent complexity of people's identities. The realities that shape my current classroom have therefore pushed me to reexamine the pedagogical justifications and epistemic effects of experiential learning.

Although I position my analysis of epistemic privilege within the classroom, I am equally interested in the ways that institutional contexts enhance or impinge upon the practice of engaging student experience in the learning process. When I teach my courses in progressive philosophy departments or interdisciplinary departments (Women's Studies or Thematic Studies, for example), I am supported in applying feminist pedagogies. As an antiracist feminist philosopher, however, my pedagogy has been controversial in traditionally defined philosophy departments. Like many of my colleagues who teach from feminist/liberation/antiracist standpoints, some senior faculty members have scrutinized my teaching methods, and criticized (as too personal, not philosophical, not intellectual, ideological, prejudicial, and so on) my practice of encouraging students to bring their experience to bear on the issues at hand. I say this to make clear that I remain committed to enacting a feminist pedagogy that takes as central the inclusion of student experiences. But I am interested here—in the company of feminists—to scrutinize this practice of ours myself, and to sort out from the spurious criticisms some of what I take to be the reactionary effects of working with student experiences in the classroom.

While I believe that the experiences students and faculty bring to the classroom are an inherently valuable source of both evidence and point of view, I am disturbed by the way that students in my classes either appeal to an oppressed identity in order to substantiate an argument, or (just as commonly) appeal to their lack of experience of oppression in order to justify their "inability" to analyze an argument. In addition, I am critical of the role and epistemic value I have assigned to my own experience in the learning process. I therefore hope in this essay to reinvigorate a feminist pedagogy of experiential learning by examining my own contributions to the problematic functioning of epistemic privilege in the classroom. Through self-critique and an application of postpositivist realist theory,[2] I aim to elucidate a feminist pedagogy grounded in a collective struggle for knowledge, standpoint, and the experience of identity.

Feminist Standpoint Theory, Epistemic Privilege, and Experiential Learning

In her now famous essay "The Feminist Standpoint: Developing the Ground for a Specifically Feminist Historical Materialism," Nancy C. M. Hartsock constructs the theoretical framework of what she termed "the feminist standpoint." Her theory grows out of Marxist epistemology—specifically, the idea that people oppressed by capitalism are uniquely positioned to critique the system. Hartsock argues that under the social, political, and economic sexism structured by the sexual division of labor, women share a central and undeniable experience that gives us all the opportunity to develop a feminist standpoint—a unique epistemological and ontological relationship with the rest of the social world.[3] We must struggle to achieve this standpoint, and it is inherently liberatory since it allows us to see how sexism damages, distorts, and dictates our lives.[4] And while Hartsock argues for an epistemology where women have the potential to generate liberatory knowledge from this feminist standpoint, she is emphatic in her recent essay "The Feminist Standpoint Revisited" that she never theorized the feminist standpoint[5] as an epistemic position that is arrived at automatically or individually.[6] What interests me here is that feminist standpoint theories (and accompanying positions on epistemic "privilege") are often misinterpreted to mean that oppressed people *necessarily* occupy such a standpoint.[7] These misinterpretations in turn generate the conclusions that women presumably have a privileged view of sexism,[8] people of color have a privileged view of racism, GLBT[9] people have a privileged view of homophobia, immigrants or non-Americans have a privileged view of American nationalism, and so on.

I often inadvertently mobilize standpoint[10] theories in this very problematic manner when I encourage students to scrutinize their own life experiences, and to create analyses from those experiences. Especially in courses composed of primarily privileged students, I tacitly communicate that the analyses of experiences drawn from life in the margins (i.e., the margins of social power and privilege structured by racial, economic, gender, sexuality, and religious identity) are unassailable. This seems to be especially true when I am teaching about subject positions I do not share, subject positions about which I cannot be an experiential learner/knower. So in my own internal pedagogical confession (I am white, heterosexual, Jewish, professional, female, and so on) I delineate the boundary between where I can challenge students' analyses and where I can say nothing critical. Because I precast the epistemic framework of the course through self-evident experiential knowing, I effectively undercut my ability to generate critical standpoints on the experience-based analyses of my students who occupy subject positions that differ from my own. My curricula further reinforce this halting epistemic configuration by modeling for students the application of individualized standpoint theories. Texts from the rich bibliography of Second and Third Wave Feminism (*This Bridge Called My Back, Making Face/Making Soul, The Politics of Reality, Sister Outsider,* and so on) are overwhelmingly testimonial and often begin (or end) with a ritual of self-exposure by the author (e.g., "I am a white, working class origin, protestant, lesbian, who now enjoys the social and economic status of university professor").

But my admittedly faulted pedagogy of student experience has become untenable now that I am teaching at John Jay College. Among my students, it is utterly incomprehensible to create an epistemic framework where analyses of experience from the margins are unassailable. The fact of the matter is that nearly all of my students are occupying at least one subject position that marks them as oppressed. And of course, my students generate experienced-based analyses from the margins that are not only different from one another, but are oftentimes entirely contradictory to one another. For example, Rafael mobilizes his experience of racial and class oppression to prove that decisions to participate in the illegal drug economy are personal and individual. At the same time, Marissa[11] (another student in the class who identifies positively as Latina) says to Rafael (I am paraphrasing her remarks): "Where do you live? My neighborhood is exactly the same, and the pressures are real, and don't tell me that when someone has a bad education, and can't get a job, and has no options, and doesn't know people who have 'jobs' that their decision to deal is personal!" Clearly, I need a pedagogy that can focus on the role of experience and identity in the production of knowledge, but that can also contend with the ways that our experiences of our identities, and the theories we mobilize in understanding those experiences, may lead us to partial and distorted assertions and analyses about our shared social world.

In defense of my tactics, I offer the fact that I regularly confront in my students alarming ignorance, hatred, and general unwillingness to learn about people they define as "others." Let me share a few examples by way of illustration: a Hamilton student who prefaces her remarks by identifying herself as Jamaican is met with this response from a white woman classmate: "Oh, I know what you mean—my mother has two Jamaican maids"; a Black woman in a Hamilton course "Philosophy and Feminism" who has volunteered to present the assigned reading for the day (doris davenport's "The Pathology of Racism: A Conversation with Third World Wimmin") begins her presentation by saying that "Homosexuality is immoral and violates the law of God. All homosexuals are disgusting, and against God and my religion. I'm Jamaican and I don't believe in homosexuality;" in a discussion of a rape case (*State v. Rusk*[12]) many John Jay students (male and female, evenly divided racially among Black, Latino, and white, primarily working poor or working class) conclude that the victim (Pat) "deserved to be raped" because she never should have given the rapist a ride home; while viewing the Marlon Riggs film *Tongues Untied*[13] otherwise savvy and mature John Jay students groan, cover their eyes in mock horror, and murmur homophobic insults to their friends; in an interdisciplinary honors course at John Jay, 90 percent of the students argue that the internment of Japanese American citizens during World War II was necessary and ethical—they maintain further that America is for Americans, and anyone who doesn't love it should leave (interesting that more than half of them are immigrants themselves, or first-generation Americans).

In disturbing classroom interactions such as these I find myself anxiously searching for the necessary arguments to disabuse students of their oppressive thinking, concluding ironically that the most effective reply comes not from me but from my drawing out the oppositional experience-based views of other students. I therefore rely on student voices to give credence to the view that racist, classist, homophobic, and misogynist thinking is both un-ethical and illogical. Especially powerful though is the testimony of students who have been directly victimized by the kind of oppressive thinking demonstrated in the discussion. Consequently, I am relieved when two or three students in the rape discussion take their classmates to task for justify-ing a violent criminal act by appeal to whether the victim acted "prudently" or not. "Just because Pat (the rape victim) is not the sharpest knife in the drawer, this means she deserves to be raped? To have a crime committed against her?" one of the respondents asks. Another comes close to saying ex-plicitly that she is a rape survivor, and I can feel everyone shift uncomfort-ably; but the tenor of the discussion changes markedly now, with several students cautiously modifying their analyses of the case. The experiences of women who have survived, resisted, or avoided sexual assault, or simply lived with the day-in day-out reality of pervasive male sexual hostility there-fore prove to be exceedingly valuable in the unpredictable epistemic frame-work of the feminist classroom. My anxiety is similarly allayed when the four or five out lesbians in the "Philosophy and Feminism" course critique soci-etal heteronormativity and bombard the presenting student's homohatred with questions: "Just what do you mean by calling me disgusting and against God?" "What exactly do you mean by saying you don't *believe* in homosex-uality? You don't *believe* in me (i.e., a real live lesbian)?"

Each of these challenges—forged from personal experience—possesses tremendous power in the complex classroom calculus of value. And well they should possess such power, for these challenges are prime examples of subjugated knowledge—knowledge that is in these cases derived from the actual experiences of women living through oppression. As Patricia Hill Collins has argued (*Black Feminist Thought*), all knowledge claims exist within a knowledge validating process. Claims to knowledge that is created outside of that particular process cannot acquire status as knowledge since there is no process to name them as such—they are either anomalies or they are insignificant. I am gratified then when these student testimonials are ac-cepted as legitimate claims to know in my classroom, for this means that—at least in part—we have an alternative knowledge validation process in operation. And this is a major reason why personal experience remains a cen-terpiece in the feminist classroom, since prevailing epistemologies (in Collins's terms "Eurocentric masculinist epistemologies") often reject out of hand the epistemic practice of appealing to experience in general, and expe-riences of oppressed and exploited people in particular.

In the most general terms feminist inquiry is based on the assertion that the perspectives of women, our experiences and analyses of our existence, have been systematically excluded from mainstream social and intellectual thought. Thus, all varieties of feminist theory and practice are fundamentally concerned with women's experiences. This feature of feminist practice is no different in feminist teaching and learning. Institutionalized and interwoven oppressive forces, including racism, sexism, classism, and homophobia, obstruct women's access to formal education. Once we take our places in schools and universities (in the role of student, teacher, or administrator) we are forced continually to struggle for the legitimacy of girls' and women's ways of learning. Thus, feminist pedagogy is distinguished from other teaching strategies by making women's experiences central in the production of knowledge.

A wide range of testimonies from feminist teachers and learners evidences this appeal to experience in feminist learning. In their discussion of a feminist interdisciplinary course in geological science, Mayberry and Rees assert that "feminist pedagogy embraces a commitment to incorporating the voices and experiences of marginalized students into the academic discourse" (57), and go on to explain that because their "methodological approach is experiential" (57), that "personal experiences, therefore, provide the lens through which [the classroom] discussion is refracted" (58). In the essay "Building Feminist Praxis Out of Feminist Pedagogy: The Importance of Students' Perspectives," Bignell points out that "feminist pedagogy focuses on student experiences as a learning source" (315). Perhaps the most compelling empirical evidence comes from Frances Hoffmann and Jayne Stake, the authors of a new empirical study of feminist pedagogy, which is the first of its kind to assess directly the "nature [and] range of pedagogic approaches endorsed by a representative sample of women's studies faculty"(79). Hoffman and Stake have found "considerable congruence in the characteristics of feminist teaching approaches described by women's studies theorists" (79). They identify four teaching strategies articulated by a significant majority of those writing about feminist pedagogy as: 1) participatory learning, 2) encouragement of activism, 3) development of critical thinking, and 4) validation of personal experience (80). Hoffmann and Stake explain that "women's studies pedagogists view classroom structures that encourage students to contribute their experiences and perspectives through shared modes of inquiry" as a core element of feminist teaching. It is a broad consensus among feminist pedagogues that "students' active participation in their own education" is ensured by the "affirmation of the legitimacy of students' personal experiences as a source of evidence and perspective" (80).

The centrality of experience to the production of feminist knowledge is expressed in a variety of more theoretical perspectives on teaching and learning. Chandra Talpade Mohanty has argued that "knowledge, the very act of knowing, is related to the power of self-definition" (44). Given the contingency of knowing upon the process of self-definition, we can see why it is crucial for students in a feminist classroom to give voice to their experiences. Similarly,

Paulo Freire outlines a theory of education where the interests and experiences of the oppressed are the foundation of radical pedagogy. bell hooks maintains that even though the appeal to epistemic privilege in feminist classrooms can express an essentialist standpoint, the unique epistemic opportunity afforded by the "mixture of experiential and analytical ways of knowing" (*Teaching to Transgress* 90) is invaluable. Others, such as Elizabeth Minnich (*Transforming Knowledge*), Patricia Hill Collins (*Black Feminist Thought*), and Barbara Omolade ("Shaking and Trembling"), have argued similarly for the pivotal role of experience in the practice of feminist teaching.

Disenfranchisement of Knowers
by the Appeal to Epistemic Privilege

And while it seems to be with good reason that anyone engaged in feminist teaching would stand by the explanatory power of student experience to create and solidify knowledge, this pedagogy that foregrounds personal experience as the arbiter of truth tacitly, and I would add problematically, appeals to a distorted formula of epistemic privilege. According to this view, the experience of living an oppressed identity confers upon the oppressed a special privilege, a standpoint, a unique epistemic relationship to reality that permits anyone who has experienced oppression to formulate liberatory knowledge about that oppression. In Rafael's case, his experience of racist, economic, and political oppression actually does bestow upon him the ability to produce liberatory knowledge. For Rafael to establish the autonomy of his moral reasoning—in the face of numerous and offensive studies, policies, and ideologies all concluding that because of his upbringing and cultural identity he inevitably will become a drug dealer—is revolutionary. Bringing his personal experience to bear on the discussion of abstract moral theory enables Rafael to understand his life choices made under politically oppressive circumstances, at the same time as generating a relatively sophisticated understanding of Kantian moral theory. Rafael takes personal experience that many students would conceal out of a sense of privacy or shame,[14] and converts it into intellectually and politically useful analysis. This is the kind of classroom development that solidifies my commitment to retaining the practice of engaging students' experience in our feminist classrooms—despite the potentially reactionary outcomes of such a pedagogy.

Preserving the space in our classrooms for students to introduce their personal experience is a crucial element in engaging students who are often sidelined by prevailing systems of social domination. bell hooks, for example, suspects that the reaction against the appeal to experience in the classroom will become a convenient way to silence already marginalized students ("Essentialism and Experience"). I do share hooks's concern that marginalized students may become further alienated by the strategy of diminishing the role of personal experience in class discussion, but I am equally concerned about the negative effects of appealing to experience. The power of knowledge grounded in experience is significantly weakened when we examine some of the pedagogical consequences of structuring teaching and learning around such a premise.[15] The outcome of such knowledge production for Rafael is—in part—undoubtedly positive in the sense that it enables him to understand Kant as well as to gather moral strength from his decision to resist the dead-end life choices into which racism and classism push him.

However, the epistemic effects on Rafael and other members of the classroom community are more complicated. Inside our classrooms are the individual members of the very same social groups that exist in the larger world in complex and layered relations of dominance and oppression. Our commitment in feminist classrooms to dismantling the histories and ideologies of domination is crucial to the production of liberatory knowledge, but it in no way changes the immediate fact that dynamics of social and political power are fully operative in our classrooms. When one member of an oppressed social group claims epistemic privilege, others often presume that all similarly situated people share the same viewpoint. Ironically, this often has the effect of reinscribing racist, sexist, homophobic, and classist ideologies. Returning to the case above, for students in the class who have no similar experience of drug economies and police practices in urban Latino communities, Rafael's testimony can serve as confirmation of the racist, classist view that the decision to deal drugs or not is purely personal and individual, and has little to do with the social and economic forces that appear to militate the choice to deal. Moreover, for Rafael and other similarly situated students, unquestioned acceptance of his experiential knowledge contributes to seeing individual exceptionality (rather than systemic political, economic, and social transformation) as the method for overcoming oppression. This is what propels me to identify as reactionary—at least in part—the outcome of appeal to experience in the classroom.

Reflecting on the situation, I have tried to consider how I contribute to the reactionary outcome. Listening to Rafael chart out essential elements of Kantian philosophy in terms specific to his own life was exciting for me as a teacher—it confirmed that he was moving beyond the basic levels of interpretation and understanding, and engaging in application and critique. I was reluctant at the time to introduce—at that moment of triumph in his analysis—the suggestion that Rafael's account may be only partial, that it may eliminate from our consideration the impact of economic forces on so-called "personal" decisions to engage in criminal behavior or not. But in thinking about it, I see that directing the discussion in that way is precisely what I needed to do in order to reinvigorate the process of *collective struggle* for knowledge. Doing so could have led us to formulate and analyze important criticisms of Kant's theory, in particular the competing idea that individual rationality is not the only element involved in moral decision making. In addition, this line of thinking would help to explicitly dismantle the racist/classist presumptions that people choose to become drug dealers because they are morally weak or racially inferior. By drawing those—admittedly offensive—ideas into the discussion, I could have called into question the entire notion of a standpoint as an epistemic position that is arrived at automatically (as a byproduct of experiencing oppression) or individually (without collective struggle for meaning). For doing so would both substantiate and complicate Rafael's analysis, and show by example that his individual experience *is* a crucial element in the production of knowledge, but that left uninterpreted and alone, it simply cannot generate comprehensive knowledge.

I have therefore concluded that I need to restructure the epistemic framework of my courses in order to reflect the ways that knowledge is collectively produced and mediated by experience and identity. To this end, I would like to suggest the concept of *communities of meaning*,[16] epistemic communities that are defined not simply by identity markers (such as race, class, gender, sexuality, religion, or nation), but instead are defined by shared experiences and ways of understanding and being in the world.[17] I am therefore proposing that as feminist teachers, we introduce our students to an alternative epistemology that foregrounds the collective nature of knowledge production, and that we furthermore encourage our students to establish and align themselves with a variety of *communities of meaning* over the span of a semester, depending upon the course material under study. I want to emphasize that I do not envision these subsets of the classroom community of knowers to be separatist, divisive, static, or exclusionary. Instead, students and faculty would decide for themselves which community or communities they wanted to form or ally themselves within any given context. All members of any given community would aim to analyze the experiential knowledge claims asserted by any individual, investigate the theories mobilized in forming an understanding of the experience, and work especially hard to trace the epistemic trajectories of experience and identity.

In my "Ethics and Law" course, for example, students could decide to divide themselves into communities that are based on a provisional allegiance to any one of the ethical theories we study: Kantian virtue ethics, Utilitarianism, or a feminist ethics of care. As the professor, I would also have to locate myself within a community. Within these—in this example—three *communities of meaning*, members could advance experientially-based defenses and critiques of the theory in question (as Rafael and Marissa actually did in my course). Ultimately, members of the different communities would address, discuss, and critique each other's experience-based analyses. I am convinced that only through rigorous and collective examination—in conjunction with the experiences and analyses of others in the classroom— would Rafael's personal experience become a useful source of evidence and perspective. For it is in this collective context that Rafael can speak from his experience as a young Latino coming of age in a neighborhood and family filled with drug dealers, without anyone (including himself) presuming— explicitly or implicitly—that: 1) he speaks for all Latinos; 2) his experience gives him access to an unquestionable truth; or 3) that only people who are similarly situated can generate questions, analyses, and criticisms of Rafael's theory. If I had organized my students into distinct *communities of meaning*, then Rafael and Marissa and everyone else in the classroom could put their experiential knowledge to work within a collective epistemic framework from which we establish truth.[18]

Rethinking the epistemic foundation of my pedagogy will help me to avoid another unintended consequence of the appeal to epistemic privilege in feminist classrooms: the presumption that knowledge about difference is "attitudinal and interpersonal, rather than intellectual and constitutive" (Chandra Talpade Mohanty 51). Women students in introductory Women's Studies courses often appeal to epistemic privilege to argue against their male counterparts, and attest to the veracity of, for example, Marilyn Frye's claim that young women are caught in a double-bind in terms of sexual activity—the decision to forgo sex marks them out for homophobic accusations of lesbianism or prudishness whereas the decision to engage in sex makes them targets for sexual harassment and sexist innuendo as slutty. Having taught this theory at both Hamilton College and John Jay College, I can testify to the overwhelming similarities among men and women students in terms of their reactions to Frye's theory. The standoff between men who claim that Frye is wrong and women who claim she is right, both in virtue of their experience, solidifies the judgment among all members of the class that knowledge about difference (and thus that disciplines such as Women's Studies, Africana Studies, Puerto Rican Studies, and so on) is based not in intellectual judgment but instead in the consideration of whether one shares the opinion of the idea under consideration, for example, whether one "agrees" with the claims of feminists and/or whether one shares the social location of the theorist (or professor).

My unapologetic and explicit self-identification as a feminist therefore compounds the complexity of the situation even further. Many students (men and women) impute to me a kind of individual epistemic privilege that has the very real potential to truncate our collective struggle for knowledge. This takes a variety of forms, such as: "my professor knows that Frye is accurate because my professor is a feminist" or "my professor only thinks that Frye is accurate since my professor is a feminist and so is Frye." In this scenario, students become either reluctant to introduce into the discussion their criticisms of Frye, or alternatively, eager to demonstrate that their views match my own (and presumably thus are more authoritative). Both student strategies interfere with a collective struggle for knowledge in which everyone's social identities (and thereby experiences)—including my own—are understood as sources of both knowledge and mystification.

Moreover, such a learning process contributes to the epistemic disenfranchisement of knowers who cannot speak from the experience of oppression. When experience of oppression is the condition upon which one can know, anyone who occupies a dominant social position—in terms of race, class, sexuality, gender—is summarily excluded from the enterprise of creating feminist knowledge. The exclusion of white people, men, straight people, and rich folks from the process of creating feminist knowledge about social domination may be somewhat desirable, at least metaphorically, given that it is not the responsibility of the oppressed to educate their oppressors. However, such a strategy brings with it a curious outcome: people who cannot be experiential knowers are made utterly unaccountable for the creation and consideration of feminist knowledge. The utility of this disenfranchisement is dubious, for it makes students (and professors) who have lived experience of oppression primarily responsible for directing and defining the production of feminist knowledge, and it seems to say that people without oppressed identities are not responsible for constructing and justifying knowledge about difference, exploitation, and liberation. Once again, organizing ourselves into various and shifting *communities of meaning* immediately lessens the tendency of students and faculty to see feminist meaning-making through the lens of epistemic privilege: as an individual, oppression-driven, and identitarian process.

Giving Way to Epistemic Privilege, Making Way for Realism

Part of what seems to be wrong with the theory of epistemic privilege is that it formulates what is actually a political claim (oppressors should listen to the voices and give credence to the analyses of marginalized people), as epistemological (marginalized people have special and unassailable access to knowledge about oppression). This is what Bat-Ami Bar On argues when she observes that a socially marginalized group's "claims for epistemic privilege . . . are merely normative, compelling only for those who are theoretically persuaded by them, usually members of the socially marginalized group who find them empowering" ("Marginality and Epistemic Privilege" 96). For similar reasons, Marianne Janack recommends that we focus not on epistemic privilege, but instead on how to convey epistemic authority, since this authority is what really matters in the effort to make insurgent knowledge heard. But in diverse feminist classrooms, where the subject matter is based on histories of power, where students and teachers stand in complex relations of domination and subordination, the mandate that the oppressors grant either the epistemic privilege or the epistemic authority of the oppressed is both politically and epistemologically inadvisable, since doing so ultimately leaves unexplained the epistemic function of social identity.

The theory of postpositivist realism,[19] however, deepens and clarifies the relationship between identity and experience by accentuating the epistemic status of identity. Realists contend that the various components of social location (i.e., race, class, gender, etc.) shape the kinds of experiences an individual will have, and that in turn, those experiences will have some bearing on the identity an individual claims. For example, Rafael's race, class, and gender are definitively linked to his experiences of policing and the narcotics industry; Marissa's race, class, and gender are associated with her experiences of neighbors struggling to support themselves in a destitute community economy. In each student's case, their particular experiences are causally related to their identities, but not in a deterministic way. So a realist theory of identity can explain how Rafael and Marissa have many of the same experiences of social, economic, and racial oppression, but claim substantially different identities—Rafael who highlights his individual exceptionality and difference from other similarly situated young Latinos in choosing education over drug dealing, and Marissa who emphasizes solidarity and identification with other young Latinos/as who have not "made it"—as Marissa has—out of the neighborhood. For both Rafael and Marissa, their claimed identities affect what they come to know about concrete social conditions in their neighborhoods, city, and nation, and the abstract ethical theory under discussion in our classroom. Consequently, realists can assert that cultural identity has epistemic consequences.

A realist theory of identity therefore points to a progressive strategy for engaging students' experience in feminist teaching and learning—without reverting to the theoretically and politically untenable assertion that there is a direct and uncontroversially determinate relationship between the experience one has as a member of any oppressed (or privileged) social group, and the knowledge conferred upon the oppressed as a result of that experience. As Paula M. L. Moya argues: "[t]he advantage of a realist theory of identity is that it allows for an acknowledgement of how the social facts of race, class, gender, and sexuality function in individual lives without *reducing* individuals to those social determinants"("Postmodernism, 'Realism,' and the Politics of Identity: Cherríe Moraga" 135). Realism therefore highlights the central roles of experience and identity in the production of knowledge, without asserting that the experience of oppression and claiming an oppressed identity will necessarily lead people to produce revolutionary knowledge. In other words, people who have not experienced the oppression may also be able to produce knowledge about it. And, people who are oppressed may in fact be mystified about the causes and effects of that oppression. For feminist teachers, the crucial advantage of a realist feminist pedagogy is that we can now account for the epistemic role of social identities without grounding their epistemic function in the experience of oppression. Anchoring the epistemic framework of the feminist classroom in realist identity theory is therefore beneficial since doing so enables teachers to foreground experiential learning without reducing our students to the sum-total of their experiences (or the paucity of their experiences for that matter).

Organizing the feminist classroom by dividing students and teachers into self-determined and diverse *communities of meaning* allows for each individual's experiential knowledge to be interpreted within a collective context that declares cultural identity to be epistemically significant. If I had done so in my "Ethics and Law" course, then both Rafael's and Marissa's experiential knowledges would be subject to the analysis and scrutiny of diverse communities of knowers who may or may not be making assertions based on experiences similar to Rafael's and Marissa's. Doing so also would make it possible for others in the class—students and teacher—to participate in knowledge making through their own *communities of meaning,* and interaction with other *communities of meaning.* In this way, we can give way on the vexed claims of epistemic privilege and develop a feminist pedagogy that is responsive to the perspective that all experiences are potentially generative of evidence that we might marshal up to justify truth claims.

Importantly, giving up on the wholesale epistemic privilege of the oppressed does not preclude our seeking out the experiential knowledge of people who have experienced oppression. In fact, Satya Mohanty explains that "the possibility of accurately interpreting our world fundamentally depends on our coming to know what it would take to change it, on our identifying the central relations of power and privilege which sustain it and make the world what it is" (214). Because feminist educators are especially focused on teaching histories of domination and resistance, and producing revolutionary knowledge that is crucial to social change, feminist pedagogy will always provide a political and epistemic space for people to give voice to their experiences of oppression. It would simply be truncated epistemic practice to try to produce feminist knowledge without engaging the experiential knowledge of people who have lived through social domination and actively resisted it.

But epistemic practice on a postpositivist realist theory differs substantially from the standpoint/epistemic privilege theories in virtue of the fact that postpositivist realism understands the production of knowledge as primarily a collective enterprise, as opposed to the presumptions of epistemic privilege, which are marked by an inherent individuality. In the case of appeals to epistemic privilege in the classroom, the testifier to an experience of oppression produces knowledge on her own, knowledge that is personally felt and individually justified. Think again here of Rafael and Marissa: each student produces a theory about the context in which people become drug dealers. When I activate the tenets of epistemic privilege in my pedagogy, I create a model of individualized epistemology by affirming both the unassailable truth and personal origin of each student's theory. In this respect, the appeal to epistemic privilege denies the social production of knowledge by making it seem as though the knower in the privileged standpoint can both formulate and establish truths by herself.

But the knowledge derived from even our most personal experiences, and the emotions we have in relation to these experiences, is not necessarily transparent to us. Naomi Scheman has discussed at length the inherently political nature of our seemingly most private and inner emotions. This view leads Scheman to be able to explain how, for example, a woman's experience of depression and guilt in the wake of a sexual attack attains new meaning, and may actually be changed to something more like moral outrage and anger, when expressed in a social/political context such as a rape survivors' support group. As Satya P. Mohanty explains, "'personal experience' is socially and 'theoretically' constructed, and it is precisely in this mediated way that it yields knowledge" (*Literary Theory and the Claims of History* 206). A realist feminist pedagogy effectively expands the intellectual horizons of the feminist classroom by asserting further that all of our experiences and our claimed identities are mediated by theories, enabling feminist teachers and learners to examine and critique the theories each of us mobilizes to interpret our experience.

A realist perspective on identity therefore enables feminist teachers and learners to see how the personal experience of oppression (and all of the emotions, assertions, conclusions, and questions that inevitably arise in its wake) yields knowledge when it is expressed in a social/political context; and also to understand why it is misguided to maintain that an individual making a personal testimony has private, privileged, and conclusive epistemic access to (and accounting of) the knowledge that is derived from and conferred by that experience. Yet, I argue that it is terribly important that we preserve the opportunity to express and consider personal experience in the context of a variety of *communities of meaning*, including those that are defined by the social and political experiences of race, class, gender, sexuality, and nationality. For it is within these diverse *communities of meaning* that our personal experiences of oppression (and domination for that matter) become a part of objective knowledge.[20]

If I applied a realist feminist pedagogy to my "Ethics and Law" course, both Rafael's and Marissa's personal testimonies would yield knowledge in a totally different way. While I would encourage Rafael to introduce his experience of growing up in the world of drug dealing, our theoretical framework for the course would establish that Rafael does not have private, unmediated, and privileged access to the knowledge he formulates from his experience. Instead, students and teachers alike would accept that we are always testifying about our personal experiences within a social and political epistemic context. In Rafael's case, he is actually considering different interpretations of his experience against what Kantian theory says, against what John Stuart Mill's *Utilitarianism* says, and against what some feminist theory says about the relevance of social training to the development of moral knowledge; Rafael concludes in this theory-mediated fashion that Kant is correct. A realist feminist pedagogical framework would demonstrate how Rafael uses his personal experience to make such a conclusion, but specify that the knowledge he formulates is theory-mediated (in this case by ethical theories, by social theories of coercion, and by cultural theories of identity), and is not accessible only to him. Moreover, Rafael must agree to put his experience in dialogue with a community of meaning of his choice (which may or may not include Marissa's analyses), and ultimately in dialogue with other *communities of meaning* (and theories that oppose his own, as does Marissa's) that may find fault with his analysis. He does not have epistemic privilege in relation to the experience of racist and classist oppression, nor does he have epistemic privilege in relation to his emotions about drug dealers, university education, and his prospects for future employment. The meanings here are not self-evident or transparent, and the knowledge Rafael produces with this personal experience is necessarily mediated by both theories and diverse *communities of meaning*.[21]

Concluding Remarks

Ultimately, I am searching for a way to construct a pedagogy that leads to epistemic wholeness in the feminist classroom. To conclude this essay then I would like to consider some of the ambiguities and tensions inherent in such a process. I have tried to develop a theory that can engage students' experiences, like Rafael's and Marissa's, within a progressive and democratic epistemic framework. There is a real tension though in my effort to implement a pedagogy that could argue a student like Rafael out of his individual perspective on progress and success. I have faced a similar pedagogical challenge when teaching *The Communist Manifesto* to poor and working-class students who, in many cases, are demoralized by Marx's analysis since they envision the prospect of their success (or failure) as entirely dependent upon their own decisions and actions. Who am I, with my education and class privilege, to mobilize a pedagogy that stands to expose the superstructure of capitalism and the monumental task of fighting such an entrenched and exploitative system?

I am also trying to construct a pedagogy that can treat explicitly antifeminist analyses democratically: my students bring racism, womanhating, homohatred, xenophobia, anti-Semitism, and so forth into our classroom and I have concluded that my effort to quash these viewpoints by some combination of lecture, enticement, and testimony from "oppressed" people in the class is entirely counterproductive.[22] That said, I am wary of the epistemic, cognitive, emotional, and spiritual effects on my students and myself when one or more students articulate and defend hateful and oppressive thoughts, histories, and actions. I know that while I am not aiming to undercut student agency (of dominant or marginalized students) when I implement a pedagogy that tries to defeat racist or classist knowledge making, my teaching decisions within the politically and emotionally charged intellectual climate of a feminist classroom can inadvertently disempower students. It is my hope that engaging personal experience within a collective struggle for knowledge will enable my students and myself to theorize the complexity of the relationships between our experiences, our identities, and our assertions about the world, without reducing any of us to essentialized descriptions of who we are.

In this way, a feminist pedagogy built around the epistemic concept of *communities of meaning* stands a chance to give teachers and students crucial learning options that simply are unavailable when we precast the epistemic framework of the course according to the mandates of epistemic privilege. When everyone in the feminist classroom has the opportunity to affiliate with a community of meaning of their choice—and to shift among communities depending upon the course material under study—the pedagogy itself accurately and ethically reflects the ways that we all are experiential knowers while it highlights the contingency of knowledge upon identity. In this manner the collective epistemic framework of the feminist classroom— not the radical teacher, the testifier to oppression, or progressive curricula— is vested with the authority to establish truth.

Notes

I am very grateful to Susan Sánchez-Casal for her perceptive and encouraging comments on many drafts of this essay.

1. Not his real name.
2. In 1993 Satya P. Mohanty introduced the innovative theory of postpositivist realism in his essay "The Epistemic Status of Cultural Identity: On *Beloved* and

the Post-Colonial Condition." Since then, three more books that elucidate, apply and refine the postpositivist realist theory of identity have been published. See S. P. Mohanty 1997, Moya and Hames-García 2000, and Moya 2002. I have found the realist perspective on identity to be especially powerful in thinking about teaching and learning since it attempts to chart out the relationships between who we are, what we experience, and what we come to know.

3. See especially pages 111–117.

4. There is an interesting and important convergence between feminist standpoint theory and W. E. B. DuBois's theory of the "double consciousness" experienced by African Americans. DuBois writes: "After the Egyptian and Indian, the Greek and Roman, the Teuton and Mongolian, the Negro is a sort of seventh son, born with a veil, and gifted with second-sight in this American world,—a world which yields him no true self-consciousness, but only lets him see himself through the revelation of the other world. It is a peculiar sensation, this double-consciousness, this sense of always looking at one's self through the eyes of others, of measuring one's soul by the tape of a world that looks on in amused contempt and pity. One ever feels his twoness,—an American, a Negro; two souls, two thoughts, two unreconciled strivings; two warring ideals in one dark body, whose dogged strength alone keeps it from being torn asunder." (*The Souls of Black Folk* 2).

5. See Hartsock's original essay "The Feminist Standpoint: Developing the Ground for a Specifically Feminist Historical Materialism." Hartsock's basic argument in this essay is as follows: Marx theorized that the lives of the proletariat under capitalism give proletarians the ability to struggle for a unique epistemic standpoint (unavailable to the bourgeoisie) from which to critique capitalism and visualize liberation from capitalist exploitation. Analogously, Hartsock argues, women's lives under patriarchy give women the ability to struggle for a unique epistemic standpoint (unavailable to men)—the feminist standpoint—from which to critique sexist domination and visualize women's liberation from patriarchy. It is not my goal in this essay to rehearse arguments for and against the validity of a feminist standpoint. I raise the subject precisely because of the near ubiquitous focus on personal experience—through assigned texts or personal testimony of students and teachers—of oppression in feminist classrooms.

6. It is ironic then that many of the criticisms of feminist standpoint theory have proceeded from the assumption that Hartsock (and other so-called "standpoint epistemologists") defend a theory based on the ability of people living under oppression to adopt a liberation standpoint automatically.

7. See especially Hartsock's essay "The Feminist Standpoint Revisited" where she details widespread feminist misinterpretation of her version of standpoint theory. See also Uma Narayan: "The Project of Feminist Epistemology," Norma Alarcón: "The Theoretical Subject(s) of *This Bridge Called My Back*." While a taxonomy of the theoretical shift in the understanding and uses of standpoint theory may be very interesting, that process is actually somewhat beside the point for this discussion. Therefore I will not delve into

the theoretical mechanisms whereby feminists have applied standpoint theory and epistemic privilege as automatic accompaniments to living an oppressed identity.

8. As Hartsock argues in her essay "The Feminist Standpoint Revisited," she specifically chose the term *feminist* (as opposed to *woman's* or *women's*) to highlight the fact that the standpoint comes not from living an oppressed identity, but from struggling for political consciousness.

9. GLBT=gay, lesbian, bisexual, transgendered.

10. Let me be clear at this juncture to specify that by *feminist* standpoint theories I mean to encompass all of the various liberation standpoint theories that are based upon different forms of cultural identity and social domination, and allegedly generate a privileged standpoint on oppression and the route to liberation.

11. Not her real name.

12. In this case, the victim (Pat) gave the perpetrator (Rusk) a ride home from a bar. Before they left the bar Pat testified that she told Rusk she was giving him a ride home "only as a friend, as a favor, nothing more." When they arrived at Rusk's address (a city neighborhood completely unknown to Pat), Rusk repeatedly asked Pat to "come upstairs." Pat refused more than three times, at which point Rusk took the car keys from the ignition and then said "Now will you come upstairs?" Pat said she would—but only if Rusk would return her car keys to her. Once in the apartment—Rusk forced Pat to perform oral sex on him, and then to engage in vaginal intercourse. Pat testified that she repeatedly said she did not want to have sex, that she wanted her car keys back, and that Rusk should return to the bar if he wanted to find a willing sexual partner. Pat even expressed fear for her life, saying to Rusk, "If I do what you want, will you let me go without killing me?" and also testified that Rusk placed his hands on her throat, "lightly choking her."

13. *Tongues Untied* is a compelling documentary and autobiography of gay black men's sexuality where Riggs communicates the spiritually devastating effects of AIDS in black gay communities, and compares the struggle against homophobia to the Civil Rights movement.

14. Many of my students at John Jay College are disarmingly open about their lives in one-on-one conversations, while they routinely conceal in class discussion the fact that they are on welfare, or live in the projects, have served time in jail, are young single parents, or are survivors of sexual or homophobic assault, victims of police brutality, or are relatives of convicted criminals or drug dealers or drug users, and so on.

15. For example, several students who are rape survivors have dropped my applied ethics courses because they choose not to put themselves in situations where people engage in blaming victims of sexual assault. I have made flexible attendance arrangements for many more student survivors of sexual assault who wished to stay in the course.

16. I introduce the concept of *communities of meaning* in my essay "Racial Authenticity and White Separatism: The Future of Racial Program Housing on

College Campuses." There I argue that "The analysis of racial oppression and the formation of strategies for achieving political justice are contingent on communities of meaning that are racially identified. . . . The preservation of racially defined communities of meaning secures the continued diversity of interpretations of the social world, thereby providing a richer array of knowledges from which to construct social, political, aesthetic, spiritual, and scientific accounts of our experience"(213).

17. In our introductory essay to this volume "Feminist Reflections on the Pedagogical Relevance of Identity" Susan Sánchez-Casal and I argue that: "students and teachers in feminist classrooms see themselves as members of various and shifting *communities of meaning*. . . . This recommendation makes good epistemic sense, since feminist, postcolonial, queer, and racial identity theories all point to the fact that there is no such thing as "the black experience," "the gay experience," "women's experience," and so on (11).

18. For additional discussion and rationale for this pedagogy, see Susan Sánchez-Casal and Amie A. Macdonald "Feminist Reflections on the Pedagogical Relevance of Identity" (Introduction, this volume, 1–28).

19. See endnote 2.

20. There is a significant correspondence between the postpositivist realist understanding of theory-mediated objectivity and what Sandra Harding calls "strong objectivity."

21. Of course, the same holds true for Marissa's analysis.

22. For a brilliant discussion and analysis of feminist teachers' failure to engage the viewpoints of "dominant" students see Susan Sánchez-Casal's essay "Unleashing the Demons of History: White Resistance in the U.S. Latino Studies Classroom" (Chapter 2, this volume, 59–85).

Works Cited

Alarcón, Norma. "The Theoretical Subject(s) of *This Bridge Called My Back* and Anglo-American Feminism." *Making Face, Making Soul/Haciendo Caras*. Ed. Gloria Anzaldúa. San Francisco: Aunt Lute Books, 1990, 356–370.

Alcoff, Linda Martín. "Cultural Feminism Versus Post-Structuralism: The Identity Crisis in Feminist Theory. *Signs* 13 (Spring 1988): 405–437.

———. "What Should White People Do?" *Hypatia* 13.3 (Summer 1998): 6–27.

———. "Who's Afraid of Identity Politics?" *Reclaiming Identity*. Ed. Paula M. L. Moya and Michael Hames-García. Berkeley: University of California Press, 2000, 312–344.

———. "Latina/o Identity Politics." *The Good Citizen*. Ed. David Batstone and Eduardo Mendieta. New York: Routledge, 1999, 93–112.

Antony, Louise M. "Quine as Feminist: The Radical Import of Naturalized Epistemology." *A Mind of One's Own: Feminist Essays on Reason and Objectivity*. Ed. Louise Antony and Charlotte Witt. Boulder: Westview, 1993, 185–225.

Anzaldúa, Gloria. *Borderlands/La Frontera: The New Mestiza*. San Francisco: Spinster/Aunt Lute, 1987.

————. *Making Face Making Soul/Haciendo Caras: Creative and Critical Perspectives by Feminists of Color.* San Francisco: Aunt Lute Foundation Books, 1990.

Bar On, Bat-Ami. "Marginality and Epistemic Privilege." *Feminist Epistemologies.* Ed. Linda Alcoff and Elizabeth Potter. New York: Routledge, 1993, 83–100.

Bignell, Kelly Coate, "Building Feminist Praxis Out of Feminist Pedagogy: The Importance of Students' Perspectives." *Women's Studies International Forum.* 19.3 (May/June 1996): 315–326.

Collins, Patricia Hill. *Black Feminist Thought.* New York: Routledge, 1991.

davenport, doris. "The Pathology of Racism: A Conversation with Third World Wimmin." *This Bridge Called My Back: Writings by Radical Women of Color.* Ed. Cherríe Moraga and Gloria Anzaldúa. New York: Kitchen Table: Women of Color Press, 1983, 85–90.

DuBois, W. E. B. *The Souls of Black Folk.* New York: Dover Thrift Editions, 1994.

Fowlkes, Diane L. "Moving From Feminist Identity Politics to Coalition Politics Through a Feminist Materialist Standpoint of Intersubjectivity in Gloria Anzaldúa's *Borderlands/La Frontera: The New Mestiza.*" *Hypatia* 12.2 (Spring 1997): 105–124.

Freire, Paulo. *Pedagogy of the Oppressed.* New York: Herder, 1972.

Frye, Marilyn. *The Politics of Reality.* Freedom, Calif.: Crossing Press, 1983.

Fuss, Diana. *Essentially Speaking: Feminism, Nature, and Difference.* New York: Routledge, 1989.

Hames-García, Michael R. "'Who Are Our Own People?' Challenges for a Theory of Social Identity." *Reclaiming Identity: Realist Theory and the Predicament of Postmodernism.* Ed. Paula M. L. Moya and Michael Hames-García. Berkeley: University of California Press, 2000, 102–29.

Harding, Sandra. "Rethinking Standpoint Epistemology: 'What Is Strong Objectivity?'" *Feminist Epistemologies.* Ed. Linda Alcoff and Elizabeth Potter. New York: Routledge, 1993, 49–82.

Hartsock, Nancy C. M. "The Feminist Standpoint: Developing the Ground for a Specifically Feminist Historical Materialism." *The Feminist Standpoint Revisited, and Other Essays.* Nancy C. M. Hartsock. Boulder, Colorado: Westview, 1998, 105–132.

————. "The Feminist Standpoint Revisited." *The Feminist Standpoint Revisited, and Other Essays.* Nancy C. M. Hartsock. Boulder, Colorado: Westview, 1998, 227–248.

Hoffmann, Frances and Jayne Stake, "Feminist Pedagogy in Theory and Practice: An Empirical Investigation." *NWSA Journal,* 10.1 (Spring 1998): 79–98.

Hogue, Cynthia, Kim Parker and Meredith Miller. "Talking the Talk and Walking the Walk: Ethical Pedagogy in the Multicultural Classroom." *Feminist Teacher,* 12.2 (Autumn 1998): 89–106.

hooks, bell. *Teaching To Transgress.* New York: Routledge, 1994.

————. "Essentialism and Experience." *Teaching to Transgress.* New York: Routledge, 1994.

————. *Yearning: Race, Gender, and Cultural Politics.* Boston: South End Press, 1990.

Janack, Marianne. "Standpoint Epistemology Without the "Standpoint"?: An Examination of Epistemic Privilege and Epistemic Authority." *Hypatia* 12.2 (Spring 1997): 125–139.

Kant, Immanuel. *Groundwork of the Metaphysics of Morals.* New York: Cambridge University Press, 1998.

Lorde, Audre. *Sister Outsider: Essays & Speeches.* Freedom, Calif.: Crossing Press, 1984.

Macdonald, Amie A. "Racial Authenticity and White Separatism: The Future of Racial Program Housing on College Campuses." *Reclaiming Identity: Realist Theory and the Predicament of Postmodernism.* Ed. Paula M. L. Moya and Michael Hames-Garcia. Berkeley: University of California Press, 2000, 205–225.

Mayberry, Maralee and Margaret A. Rees, "Feminist Pedagogy, Interdisciplinary Praxis, and Science Education." *NWSA Journal,* 9.1 (Spring 1997): 57–76.

Mill, John Stuart. *Utilitarianism.* Indianapolis: Bobbs-Merrill, 1971.

Mills, Charles. *The Racial Contract.* Ithaca: Cornell University Press, 1997.

Minnich, Elizabeth. *Transforming Knowledge.* Philadelphia: Temple University Press, 1992.

Mohanty, Chandra Talpade. "On Race and Voice: Challenges for Liberal Education in the 1990s." *Beyond A Dream Deferred: Multicultural Education and the Politics of Excellence.* Ed. Becky Thompson and Sangeeta Tyagi. University of Minnesota Press, 1993, 41–65.

Mohanty, Satya P. "The Epistemic Status of Cultural Identity: On *Beloved* and the Post-colonial Condition." *Cultural Critique* 24 (Spring 1993): 41–80.

Mohanty, Satya P. *Literary Theory and the Claims of History: Postmodernism, Objectivity, Multicultural Politics.* Ithaca: Cornell University Press, 1997.

Moraga Cherríe and Gloria Anzaldúa. *This Bridge Called My Back: Writings by Radical Women of Color.* New York: Kitchen Table: Women of Color Press, 1983.

Moya, Paula M. L. "Postmodernism, 'Realism,' and the Politics of Identity: Cherríe Moraga." *Feminist Genealogies, Colonial Legacies, Democratic Futures.* Ed. M. Jacqui Alexander and Chandra Talpade Mohanty. Routledge, 1996, 125–150.

Moya, Paula M. L. "Introduction: Reclaiming Identity." *Reclaiming Identity: Realist Theory and the Predicament of Postmodernism.* Berkeley: University of California Press, 2000, 1–26.

Moya, Paula M. L. *Learning from Experience: Minority Identities, Multicultural Struggles.* Berkeley: University of California Press, 2002.

Moya, Paula M. L. and Michael Hames-Garcia, eds. *Reclaiming Identity: Realist Theory and the Predicament of Postmodernism.* Berkeley: University of California Press, 2000.

Narayan, Uma. "The Project of Feminist Epistemology: Perspectives From a Non-Western Feminist." *Gender/Body/Language.* Ed. Susan Bordo and Alison Jaggar. New Brunswick, New Jersey: Rutgers University Press, 1989, 256–69.

Omolade, Barbara. "Quaking and Trembling: Institutional Change and Multicultural Curricular Development at the City University of New York." *Beyond a Dream Deferred: Multicultural Education and the Politics of Excellence.* Ed. Becky W. Thompson and Sangeeta Tyagi. Minneapolis: University of Minnesota Press, 1993, 214–30.

Sánchez-Casal, Susan. "Unleashing the Demons of History: White Resistance in the U.S. Latino Studies Classroom." *Twenty-First-Century Feminist Classrooms: Peda-*

gogies of Identity and Difference. Ed. Amie A. Macdonald and Susan Sánchez-Casal. New York: Palgrave Macmillan, 2002, 59–85.

Sánchez-Casal, Susan and Amie A. Macdonald. "Introduction: Feminist Reflections on the Pedagogical Relevance of Identity." *Twenty-First-Century Feminist Classrooms: Pedagogies of Identity and Difference.* Ed. Amie A. Macdonald and Susan Sánchez-Casal. New York: Palgrave Macmillan, 2002, 1–28.

Scheman, Naomi. "Anger and the Politics of Naming." *Women and Language in Literature and Society.* Ed. Sally McConnell-Ginet, Ruth Borker, and Nelly Furman. New York: Praeger, 1980, 174–87.

State v. Rusk.

Wallace, Miriam L. "Beyond Love and Battle: Practicing Feminist Pedagogy." *Feminist Teacher,* 12.3 (Autumn 1999): 184–197.

CHAPTER FIVE

NEGOTIATING SUBJECT POSITIONS IN A SERVICE-LEARNING CONTEXT

Toward a Feminist Critique of Experiential Learning

Tamara Williams and Erin McKenna

Complicating "Experience":
Some Arguments for Authentic Heterogeneity

A student whom we will call Pilar[1] was born in the small village of Ixtepec outside of Guadalajara, Jalisco, over 20 years ago. She grew up in a small community of subsistence farmers. Her home was one room of rugged brick with a zinc roof, her bed a "petate." When Pilar was six, her mother left her and a brother with her maternal grandparents to make the long and risky trek to "el Norte" to join her husband and find work. Pilar's childhood memories were of soaking maize to grind and make tortillas, of the long walks across dry riverbeds to visit relatives in nearby villages, of other children, open spaces, and of the fading image of her parents. At age seven, Pilar was told that she and her brother would soon be going to the United States. A week later, a "legalized" and distant cousin would smuggle the two children across the California border and drive them to Oregon where her parents were farm-workers. The family of six lived in a small trailer owned by a farmer. The children's movements became restricted. Soon the two were sent to a predominantly white school in rural Oregon. They were singled-out, ridiculed, told to go back where they came from. As Pilar's English improved, she was teased less but her family's continued poverty made her feel ashamed.

She was ashamed, mostly, of where she had come from. However painful, she gradually forgot her grandparents, her friends, and the open spaces of Ixtepec. She hated being asked where she was from and began telling people she was from Guadalajara or Mexico City because these places were known and had a sophisticated ring to them. No one would believe her when she told them she was from Oregon. A few years later, Pilar "made it." At age 18 she enrolled in a predominantly white, middle-class, private college in the Northwest. Her major was Business. In her junior year, partly out of interest and partly to fill a requirement in "Alternative Perspectives," Pilar signed up for a course titled "Latino Experiences in the United States." The course had a service-learning component. That is, as part of the course requirement students had to do at least three hours of service at one of several agencies, organizations, and institutions that either were Latino or served the Latino community.

How did Pilar experience the class in which her classmates were required to "do service" in her community? Did or should such a course take into account her experience as a Latina in the United States? If so, could there be a balance between the course's scrutiny of her experience and that of her Anglo peers? Was there, for example, a balance between the scrutiny given to the Latino "text" and the implicit critique of the white "text" offered in the "alternative perspective"? How were Pilar's identity and Latino identities in general constructed by her predominantly white middle-class classmates who were "doing service" in a multiservice agency catering to mostly underprivileged, at risk, illegal Latinos? How was the identity of the majority of white middle-class students constructed? Was Pilar silenced and confused by a pedagogical process that unwittingly reproduced dominant views and familiar power dynamics in a classroom context that purported just the opposite objective?

At an increasing number of colleges and universities throughout the United States, "service" and "experiential learning" are becoming popular pedagogical strategies.[2] More and more students participate in "service" projects both as cocurricular and curricular enhancements to an undergraduate education. Specially designated administrative, faculty, and student leadership positions are being created to conceptualize, implement, and integrate this kind of learning into the classroom. At some institutions, service/experiential learning have become integrated into educational mission statements and long-range planning goals and commitments. College and university curricula, finally and more importantly, are being altered significantly as a consequence, as are their accompanying teaching approaches.[3]

Experiential/service components are added to higher education curricula for a variety of reasons. A frequent reason, for example, is to complement conventional academic learning with applied knowledge and practical experience. Another is to affirm an institutional ethos around public service or to promote and nurture the idea of a caring citizenry. More relevant to our discussion today, however, are those reasons that link experiential/service learning with attempts to transform and diversify traditional pedagogies and curricula. Integrating a service component into a course is perceived as a way to generate diversity at, for example, private predominantly white middle- and upper-middle class colleges and universities, where demographic, institutional, and/or political constraints severely limit authentic heterogeneity among the student body. It is also viewed as a means to enhance, clarify, or complicate ethical debates raised in accompanying textual materials. Related to the potential for service learning to generate diversity and enhance debate is the belief that, by affirming the value of experience, both the required readings and the placement experience become "texts." To the extent that service learning is also experiential, it closes the conventional gap between textual representation and the "real" world and between reading and encountering "the other" as subject/agent. This entire process is viewed as transformative. Students—mostly of the white middle- and upper-middle class—experience sustained encounters with people, situations, and institutions in contexts that stimulate consciousness about diversity and ethical issues and which are supplemented by relevant textual materials. This exposure often stimulates a concurrent self-reflection in which students' worldviews and deeply held assumptions about values, ethics, social relations, culture, and diversity are challenged and transformed. The process is perceived as nontraditional in its challenge to traditional categories of knowledge and models of inquiry. Privileging experience radically alters foundational assumptions, such as what constitutes a text, what constitutes knowledge, and what constitutes authority.

Not surprisingly, outside of Women's Studies programs, the feminist project is rarely, if ever, cited as a reason for adding service/experiential learning to courses at the college level. The development of feminist pedagogy and of experiential learning coincide historically. They also converge in their shared insistence on the authority of experience (Michelson 631) and their challenge to dualistic accounts of theory/practice, public/private, self/other, and knowledge/experience. Regardless of these convergences, however, there exists a gap—a lack of dialogue—between these two potentially radicalizing nontraditional forms of pedagogical practice.[4] Countering this trend, what we propose here is to bridge the gap between these parallel developments by sharing the ways in which feminist teaching in general, and feminist epistemologies in particular, have informed and complicated our implementation of service/experiential components in our classrooms.

Toward a Feminist Critique of Service and Experiential Learning

While we acknowledge the potential of experiential/service learning to generate diversity, to inform and enhance ethical debates, to challenge students' worldviews, and to subvert foundational assumptions about knowledge and authority in otherwise traditional academic contexts, we believe that this teaching practice has some hidden problems that require some scrutiny.

Some problems and concerns became central for me (Erin) in one of my earliest attempts at incorporating service learning into "Philosophy 125—Moral Theory." Even the title of the course is a problem. While everyone who teaches it does some "applied ethics," the title supports the traditional dualism of theory and practice. I added the service component to this course in order to help the students see how theories from the past can and do affect our lives today. I now call my section of Philosophy 125 "Ethics in Action." While it helps to alert the students to one of the goals of the class—putting moral theories into action in our everyday lives—it still seems to presuppose a possible split between theory and practice and fails to suggest the potential for experience in our everyday lives to affect our ethical theories.[5] This was brought home for me by my experience with a student whom I will call Tanya.

Tanya's best friend, Rob, died from AIDS during the fall semester of her junior year in college. That spring she enrolled in my (Erin's) moral philosophy course. That course had a service-learning component that required the students to do 30 to 40 hours of service and write four papers in which they applied the theories we studied to some particular aspect of their service experience. The students chose the focus for each paper themselves, with optional consultation with me. I let the students choose their service placement from a list of prearranged sites with little guidance from me. Tanya chose to work at a local AIDS hospice-care facility where she cooked, cleaned, and spent time with the residents.

The course began by covering traditional ethical theories such as virtue ethics, Kantian ethics, and utilitarianism. Toward the end of the semester, we covered feminine and feminist ethics (an order that I have since inverted). Tanya was asked to reflect on her experience at the hospice and apply the theories she was learning to some aspect of her experience. She was expected to do this through both class discussion and papers. But Tanya was paralyzed. She didn't want to talk about her experience because it had such personal importance. She knew this hurt her participation grade. She had trouble writing the papers because the theories (especially Kantian and utilitarian ethics) did not really have a way to account for her feelings. When she came to talk to me about rewriting one of her papers she ended up talking about Rob. My first thought was that Tanya should not have signed up for a service placement that brought up such deep personal issues. She needed to be able to keep some distance to apply the theories. But then, I thought, why did I teach a service-learning class? To help the students connect the philosophical theories to their lives! But this objective was proving to be difficult and messy. I realized how little preparation I had for dealing with service learning. I had hoped it would liven up the moral theories we had to cover but now it had taken on a life of its own. I suggested that Tanya read ahead to some of the feminine "ethics of care" material. I hoped these theories, which address emotions and relationships explicitly, would help her to bring theory together with her experience. She was able to connect to that material and it helped her make sense of her experience. Rather than dismiss her feelings or validate reason over relationships, these theories gave her a way to see and use her feelings and friendships as a source of knowledge. She ended up doing very well on the papers, but her participation grade did suffer.[6]

Like Pilar's story, Tanya's story reveals another level of difficulty we have encountered in teaching service-learning courses. First, there are shifting expectations. In the case of Tanya, I was forced to see that the "designated learning objective" might not have been important or even appropriate. Tanya was forced to realize that past expectations of providing "reports" on the class material didn't get her very far. This connects to a second difficulty—grading. Does one try to grade the quality of the service or the process of reflection? Are reflections about the material and reflections about one's self and one's beliefs equally important? Does Tanya get a better grade because she was able to demonstrate more profound reflection and change than the student who happily served lunches to seniors and spoke about her wonderful relationship with her grandmother? This also connects to a third problem—participation. The students who speak in class are rewarded. If they are going through self-transforming experience, can we really expect them to talk about it in a class of 35–40 students? And yet such sharing is one of the enriching elements of a service-learning class. These difficulties may be the result of seeing education in the traditional dualisms. We are lead to ask questions like is the learning about the students or about the course material, and if it is about the students then how does feminist learning claim to be "intellectual" in the same way as economics or physics?[7] Feminist pedagogy pushes us to take a different perspective. We cannot really separate the students and the course material. Service-learning courses make overtly apparent to us what is the case in all our classes—learning always involves some personal investment in the material.

As feminist teachers, the cases of Pilar and Tanya raise a range of concerns regarding courses with service/experiential components. These all merit careful consideration. There are three interrelated issues, however, that we wish to address specifically in this paper. The first is representation. The second is the failure among service-learning practitioners—particularly those who are feminists—to engage in active dialogue with the basic tenets of feminist pedagogy and the foundational assumptions of feminist epistemology. A third concern is the gap that exists between developments in feminist epistemology and feminist pedagogy involving service-learning components.

Experience and Representation

Representation, how alterities are constructed and the links between these constructions and larger societal dynamics involving difference and power, is of basic concern to feminist scholars. In the handling of written texts, the identification of issues and problems with representations of women and ethnic, sexual, racial minorities (particularly those that historically have been marginalized) is both a fundamental and an automatic strategy for the resistant reader. However, a parallel strategy is rarely practiced in approaching a "living" or "experiential" text. Has some thought been given, for example, to how service-learning projects construct these identities? Care-giving or "good works" placements are very popular as service sites but can be problematic as the loci of "textualized" experience. If, for example, predominantly white upper-middle-class students are only exposed to Latino men in a jail, or to African American women in a women's shelter, or to gay men in an AIDS hospice, or to the "poor" in the lines of a soup kitchen, there is a real risk of affirming pre-existing stereotypical views. Their encounter with "others" may well serve to reproduce rather than alter their personal investment in race, class, and gender privilege. The service/experiential component of the class, therefore, can backfire. Ultimately, our concern is that if left unchecked, a course with an experiential component can yield a situation where prejudicial perceptions of privilege and power are fortified and enhanced by "an experience" made legitimate by a given academic course of study.

Claiming a Feminist Epistemic Rationale
for Experiential/Service Learning

The second and more complicated concern is the failure, among service-learning practitioners, to engage in active dialogue with the basic tenets of feminist pedagogy and the foundational assumptions of feminist epistemology. In this regard, Elana Michelson has argued for a "feminist inquiry and intervention" illustrating convincingly that foundational theories of experiential learning, such as the one exemplified by the work of David A. Kolb,[8] are in much need of a feminist critque, for they assume

> both an unproblematized "reality" and the transparency of reason and language. It is grounded in what Alison M. Jaggar and Susan Bordo term "epistemological individualism," the notion that humans gain knowledge of the world "as solitary individuals, rather than as socially constituted members of historically changing groups." The model is, moreover, rooted in a liberal humanist view of the subject, "whose undeterred consciousness is the origin of meaning, knowledge, and action." In the end, because it fails to treat either experience or reason as socially constructed and historically contingent, Kolb's

theory, for all its important valorizing of experience, enacts an idealist episte-mology. Through the exercise of transcendent reason, certain knowledge is de-rivable from the raw data of experience by individual but largely interchangeable human beings (Michelson 633–634).

In addition to the concern over the kind of epistemology that is enacted in the experiential/service component, we consider how the failure to re-claim "service/experiential" learning as a teaching practice that is grounded in feminist pedagogy can lead to a superficial understanding and imple-mentation of service in a learning community. An understanding of feminist epistemology and pedagogy can deepen one's understanding and use of ex-periential learning of all kinds.

As I (Erin) argue elsewhere, feminist pedagogies are fluid and plural but they share some common commitments.

> First, feminist pedagogy challenges the notion that knowledge is a static and objective thing which one person can simply pass on to another. Instead knowledge is seen as emerging from one's position and molded by one's pur-poses. . . . Second, given the belief that knowledge is interactive, it follows that teaching becomes something other than the passing on of information and learning becomes something other than the passive receiving of such bits of wisdom. . . . It is generally a dialogue that is sought. Third, if teaching and learning are to be an engaged dialogue in which knowledge is seen as situated in who one is and what one's purposes are, it becomes important to be famil-iar with who is in the dialogue. Ideas and theories are not taken in as objec-tive and neutral, but they come with a past and are picked up by the students for some purpose. Hence the feminist classroom is both personal and politi-cal (McKenna 178–179).

Fluid, interactive, engaged dialogue—this grounds the feminist classroom. One could make the argument, moreover, that several core concepts under-lying the idea and practice of service or experiential learning grew out of, gained support from, and are complicated by developments in feminist ped-agogy. The feminist focus on, and legitimization of, experience, for example, takes a concrete form in a service-learning classroom. Further, feminist the-ory has long challenged the dualism of theory and practice as does the claim that theory influences practice and that practice should influence theory. The challenge to the public/private divide also comes from feminist theory. It is the collapse of these dualisms, moreover, that is necessary to see the value of bringing service into the classroom and the classroom into the com-munity. The degree to which service/experiential courses encourage partici-patory and active learning and encourage students to engage the material of the class from the standpoint that it actually matters in their lives can also be viewed as a legacy of feminist pedagogy. Along these lines, feminist classes have traditionally viewed personal experience as important to learning both as content and method. Students are asked to make connections between their lives and the theories they are studying and encouraged to develop both a personal relationship to the academic material and a critical perspective on their own experiences. This is a central goal of a feminist service-learning class: to ask students to move beyond their own experiences, to see life from other points of view in order to gain a critical perspective on how they have understood their own lives. Relatively little literature on service learning, however, explores the connections to feminist theories and pedagogies,[9] and we believe the failure to see these connections weakens many approaches to service learning.

These ideas and practices—from the legitimization of experience to the collapse of the dualism between theory and practice and between the personal and the academic—have been incorporated, in varying degrees, in the discourse about, and practice of, service/experiential learning and teaching. Overwhelmingly, however, these concepts and their attendant practices have been adopted without an accompanying epistemological rationale. Because the lack of an epistemological rationale, in turn, leads to a variety of problems in service-learning courses, we see a need to begin exploring what that epistemic rationale might be. This is what we attempt to do here. Without such work we run the risk of creating an environment where the service experience is used merely as a means of self-understanding and encouraging an instrumental approach to community service in general. It can also lead to self-absorption. The students may go about their service with little or no reflection about how and what they are doing, and the attitude they have about it affects those people with whom they are working. For example, students at a privileged Christian school like ours often assume they are doing their "Christian duty" by doing "for others." When it is suggested that we might be engaged in a project "with" others, this assumed equality can throw them off balance. They are more comfortable with charity than real service. Charity leaves their sense of place and self untouched. Service asks them to critically examine their sense of place and self. Their experiences, both prior to and during the service-learning class, are to be subjected to critical examination. Finally, when pushed to apply theory to personal experience, it is difficult to get students to move beyond the realization of seeing how their lives are or are not understood and affected by various theories to seeing the importance of being critical of their own perspective on their life experiences. In general, without a more critical approach, self-understanding may not come to include the socially constructed nature of the self and the social impact of perspectives on the self.

Revisiting the issue of experience as a legitimate source of knowledge, that is, looking at service/experiential learning from a feminist epistemological perspective, diminishes the risk of encountering the types of problems we described above. Historical developments in feminist epistemology foreground and complicate the issue of the nature, function, and value of personal experience as a source of knowledge. The work of feminist epistemology suggests that experience should no longer be discounted in the academic context as it has been in the past nor should it be uncritically valorized. In our experience, however, connecting service learning to feminist epistemological theory and pedagogical practice has presented some challenges. Speaking from the vantage point of experienced feminist teacher/scholars, we continue to find it extremely difficult to find pedagogical practices that take into account the more complex picture of knowledge and experience that evolves in a classroom community that critically valorizes the multiple positions of its constituents. Can and does our teaching affirm and validate knowledge derived from our students' positionality? Does it advocate for the social and historical contingency of all of the sites embodied in our students? The challenge of these questions are redoubled, of course, when we consider that we do this work in institutional settings that on all levels promote homogeneity.

Feminist Pedagogy and Multiple Subject Positions

Our final concern is the gap or lag that exists between developments in feminist epistemology regarding multiple subject positions and feminist pedagogy involving service-learning components. More specifically, we question whether feminist epistemology's recognition of the fact that experiencing, knowing, and learning are shaped and informed by variables such as race, class, gender, and sexuality, has substantially modified teaching practices in service-learning courses. It appears that the novelty and excitement of service-learning and the promise it holds for transforming traditional learning has led to some complacency in this regard. A major concern is that the service-learning component in courses is often presented to students, and dealt with by instructors, as course content. The following statement of objectives for a service-learning component in a course is a case in point:

> The service components fill an important textual gap that exists between the representation of the Latino experiences offered in the required readings and the "real" world that these readings attempt to represent. The course, therefore, assumes that both the required readings and the placement experience are "texts." Pedagogically, my goal is to facilitate a classroom experience where, on the one hand, students rely on the required readings as a means of interpreting the world that they will participate in as volunteers in the Latino community. On the other, they will rely on their volunteer experiences as a means of interpreting the texts read in class.[10]

At the time I (Tamara) used this description for the service component in a Latino Studies course (Spring 1996) I recall believing that the legitimization of experience through its "textualization" was a profoundly radical pedagogical move. In retrospect, such a perception, no doubt, was a projection of shifts in my own understanding of categories of knowledge and of related distinctions such as those believed to exist between theory and practice, the personal and the political, "real" life and the academy. Once I taught the course, however, I began to understand the limitations of this understanding of "service" or experiential learning. While my description underscored the value of experience by granting it equivalency with the written text and, therefore, undermined foundational assumptions about textual authority and knowledge, I failed to acknowledge the interpersonal dimension of service learning and, more importantly, to distinguish service learning as a specific kind of teaching/learning practice. In the description, the practice of service learning/teaching was subsumed, it appears, by the novelty of the experiential text as course content. The failure to distinguish service learning as a specific kind of teaching/learning practice with its own methods and goals has some implications. Like "reading," "experiential learning" is an activity that is unique, and that requires certain skills and strategies both for the teacher and the learner. Most unique to learning experientially is the activity's demand that students connect with people, organizations, and institutions in a way that renders their classroom learning more meaningful. Both students and teachers, however, lack training to deal with the intensity of cross-cultural relations outside the classroom as well as the complex nature of parallel dynamics inside the classroom. Awareness of the issue of multiple subject positions and learning styles make the need for training even more pressing if one begins to consider what silences might arise in a teacher-mandated experiential learning project around issues of race, class, gender, and sexuality. How will "textualized" experience of "other cultures" be experienced by minority students in the classroom? How does the minority student negotiate her subject position in the classroom when she is both a subject and the object of study simultaneously? Does this dual-positionality unwittingly privilege the white (male?) text? Or can it be deployed as a source of empowerment and difference?

In addition to the three concerns we have outlined above, there is a tendency among those of us who are feminist teachers to perceive the validation of "experience" as a crowning achievement in the process of transforming assumptions about knowledge and ways of knowing in the classroom. With this perception, moreover, comes a degree of self-congratulatory complacency that, unchecked, conspires against the need to complicate the notion of "the experiential text" by applying to it recent developments in feminist epistemological theory on women's ways of knowing, on learning styles, and on the nature, function, and content of knowledge.

To illustrate how the concerns we have discussed above are borne out in the classroom, we would like to return to the story with which we began the paper, the story of Pilar, the student enrolled in a service-learning class at our institution. Pilar's experience serves, in turn, as an opportunity to complicate the experiences of other students in this class and to explore strategies for teaching in a classroom environment that invites, nurtures, and yields a complex and multifaceted depth and breadth of diversity.

Strategies for Voicing:
Negotiating Subject-Positions in the Classroom

The case of the student we named Pilar, whose story we told in the introduction of our paper, illustrates the challenges I (Tamara) experienced using the service-learning model in a course whose objective is to teach about a minority perspective. At first Pilar, a Latina in a course on Latino Experiences in the United States, assumed that she was no different from her classmates. However, after a few days, her approach to both the readings and the service-learning components of the course began to shift, revealing some ambivalence. While attempting to maintain a critical distance from the material, she would project pieces of her own experience onto her clients at the service site. This is an early journal entry about her service site.

> I feel very excited about helping out with the ESL classes at Casa Latina. I am hopeful that I will be able to help these people in a way that will make their lives in the U.S. more manageable. People seem to make the choice to leave Mexico and their families thinking that coming to the U.S. will be better, but in many ways, their life will get worse.

Within a week, Pilar began to relate more directly to the reading materials and the people she was working with at Casa Latina and to recognize difference:

> For some reason, I felt drawn to the children, I think that this is because I relate strongly to what lies ahead for them as they get older. This reminded me a lot of when I first came to the U. S. I sort of have the feeling that I really need to help the children because the parents put so much hope in the children and many times the whole family becomes dependent on the children because usually the children pick up the language faster than the parents. So it becomes the children's responsibility to translate or communicate for the whole family with the outside word. For example, simple things like locating items not found in a grocery store to translating legal documents at the age of nine when other nine-year-olds are doing totally different things.

Finally, her position in the classroom shifted as she recognized her own difference. She became confused as she realized that who she had known herself to be was being contested by competing representations that seemed equally familiar. More than other students in the class, she expressed anger at having to discover her identity through the words of others and through the representation of texts. Her primary frustration resulted from not having a grounded sense of who she was in time and place; of feeling herself in the borderlands—a place she had not yet named. She did not know her history and she longed for a place to call home. She saw herself as a Latina on the one hand, but didn't feel she had the experience and knowledge to speak as a Latina, on the other. The combination of confusion, anger, frustration, and a perceived sense of weakness due to the lack of authority to speak as a Latina led to confusion and silence. In another journal entry, Pilar said:

> I hate it when people ask me where I'm from. I tell them I was born in Mexico City but my family is from Ixtepec, but I've lived in the U.S. since I was seven. SEE?????? I don't even know what Ixtepec is like, or Mexico City for that matter. I hate it when people come up to me and say, oh, I've been to Ixtepec. It's a beautiful place. I think to myself, "Is that right? I wouldn't know." And I just agree with them. I hate that!!! I hate not knowing these things; not having seen it with my own eyes, or not having experienced it myself. I have a lot of confusing feelings, because I feel as though I am here because this is what I know, but I wish I knew about living in Mexico because that is what I need to know. At the same time, I feel out of place here because I look different and right away people know I'm from some other place. I know the name of the place but I don't know the place. I feel like I'm somewhere in the middle but don't really belong here or there. I wonder if people are going to see me differently when I return. I wonder if they'll think of me as *Americana,* and will they, too, reject, me? I hope not.

Whereas the mostly Anglo students in the Latino Experiences class engaged the course material with varying degrees of passionate involvement and curious skepticism, Pilar's experience of the course was radically different in that she was learning about what it meant to be a "Latina." The process, as seen in the quotations above, angered and confused her and silenced her for most of the semester. Her silence was compounded by the nonwhite students' perception that she was an expert because of her Latina identity. Non-Latino students, on the other hand, were able to engage with the material and discussions in the class more dispassionately. Although they understood the "alternative perspective" dimension of the course to be a critique of their own privileged "white text," they still felt safe enough—as a majority—to speak confidently, drawing all too frequently on the use of difference-making pronouns such as "us"/"them" and "we"/"they." This type of discourse was intensified by class and privilege dynamics. Because the students worked in service sites mostly of the "care-giving" variety—with Latinos at homeless shelters, in remedial programs in schools, in free health clinics, in homes for the elderly, or illegal immigrants, and so on—their difference was pronounced and their privilege reaffirmed or reproduced. The high participation rates of non-Latinos in classroom and small-group discussions contrasted markedly with Pilar's ongoing silence. Pilar, unlike her non-Latino peers, could not find the words to match, characterize, or locate her experience as a Latina in the classroom. Not only was she navigating in class through the psychosocial challenge of, quite literally, finding herself, she also was not always able to find herself in the experiences of the drug-addicted, the homeless, the gangs, the elderly, that the service sites represented. Ultimately, she felt marginalized and could not utter "I" as a subject in a discursive arena that had placed her, unwittingly, at the center. As was the case of her unfolding relationship to, and identity within, the borderlands between Latino and dominant U.S. culture, Pilar's ambiguous sense of place and her anxiety about not belonging were reproduced in the confines of a classroom context that purported to be safe, open, and democratic.

Pilar finally did speak during a classroom presentation at the end of the semester required of all students in lieu of an examination. She walked to the front of the class and sat down at the desk. She was empty-handed. No note cards, no yellow pad. Quietly at first, she began to speak. "My name is Pilar," she began, "and I'm going to tell you my story." She shook and composed herself several times and then continued uninterrupted for about 45 minutes. She told about Ixtepec, her border crossing, her childhood and schooling in racist eastern Oregon. She told her classmates about the course on Latino experiences and her experience within classroom dynamics. She told them about her confusion, her anger, and the pain of her protracted silence. Her classmates were stunned. The challenge of the class materials was intensified instantly.

That Pilar voiced her story constituted a visible manifestation of student empowerment and a radical shift in the established classroom dynamic. When the course began, Pilar struggled with questions about the legitimacy of her claim to Latino identity and with her ability and willingness to speak authoritatively on the topic of *her* Latino experience. Ultimately, however, she intervened as an "I"—as subject and agent—disrupting the "we" versus "they" discourse that had dominated classroom discussions throughout the semester.

The opportunity to teach Latino Studies for a second time encouraged me to reflect further on Pilar's experience in the classroom, on the process that might have led to her breakthrough, and most significantly, on the role I might have played in hindering or nurturing Pilar's agency in the classroom. Not surprisingly, my reflections pointed to the need to transform my pedagogical practice, in particular, to revisit, and recommit to, assumptions about the classroom that are fundamental to feminist pedagogical practice.

To address my concerns about how the Latino community was being represented in the service-learning component and how this played out with Pilar, in particular, I experimented with several strategies. The first was to foreground the issue of representation in the service/experiential component of the course just as I would in my approach to a written text. This foregrounding required a dual emphasis first on how differences based on race, class, gender, and sexuality have been constructed historically, and second, on the diversification of the kinds of sites where students work in order to more accurately represent the diversity within the ethnic groups being studied. Additionally, I had to problematize and develop some degree of self-consciousness among students regarding the power positioning that often accompanies the act of "doing service." This latter strategy is even more important when students are placed in sites to explore social problems or ethical issues. If the students' perceptions and power relationship to the site in which there is an embedded social problem/issue is not dealt with up front, students will most likely either detach or attempt to rescue; they will "work for" rather than "work with" the communities at their sites. Second, I had to make an equal effort to break down the notion that the classroom represents a homogeneous community that is distinct from the world "out there" and in which, and from where, the "outside world" could be discussed without real challenge. If—as a feminist teacher—I was serious about claiming a legitimate space for experience in the academy, then I had to be willing to conceptualize, affirm, and interact with the classroom as a community characterized by equally (if not more) complex dynamics as "the world out there."

Our role as teachers, then, must include the need to facilitate learning through the *experience* of the classroom as a community characterized by difference and by common goals of mutual understanding, mutual recognition, empowerment, and transformation. Only in this way can we begin to blur the boundaries between us and them, between inside and out, between naming (theory) and experiencing (praxis) the mechanisms of social oppression that impede change and invite action and innovation.

In addition to experimenting with the strategies of foregrounding representation, problematizing the power position of students vis-à-vis service sites, and putting forth the notion of classroom as heterogeneous community, I worked with another cluster of strategies aimed more specifically at the issue of multiple subject positioning in the classroom. The first of these strategies was to foreground silence both as a "process" issue emerging as a classroom dynamic and as a "content" issue linked thematically to assigned readings and journal assignments. In both journal assignments and in-class discussions, students were asked to read texts and consider their service placement sites in terms of the kinds, the degree, the causes, and the responses to silence that they encountered there. They were also asked to reflect upon their own silences and the possible connections between their silences and the silences they had observed in their reading and experience. These exercises succeeded in raising the consciousness of students about silence as a mechanism of oppression. It also revealed other dimensions of silence in the classroom. The most helpful was one most frequently articulated by the non-Latino students and involved a silence generated by a fear of not having the authority to "speak for" the Latino experience:

> I'm generally quiet in class and I have to put an effort into speaking. That is part of the reason for my own silence. But the other reason is that I feel like I lack the authority to speak on the subjects we discuss. My background does not allow me any real understanding of the Latino experience in the U.S.

This student felt doubly disadvantaged because, for personal reasons, she was not able to participate in a service/experiential project. Having had the experience of working with the Latino population in our community, she argues, would have given her more confidence and authority to speak about the issues at hand. Implicit in her position is a fundamental distrust of the "text" and a privileging of experience:

> As I sit at my desk on Tuesday and Thursday mornings, I listen intently to the various discussions that go on around me, specifically those concerning our class topic of Latino experiences in the U.S. and how the students see issues we have discussed play out in their service placements. People in my class are experiencing first hand [sic] some of these issues. These experiences have created such intense responses and brought about such involved discussions that I cannot help but feel as though I have missed out on something by not being able to participate in the class's service-learning component. Aside from my own disappointment, I would go even further to suggest that the experience of a service placement allows students to take on issues discussed in class with more authority than those students who do not have a similar experience. To see problems play out in front of you has a value beyond simply discussing an issue you will never come into contact with.

A second strategy was to encourage voicing not only through carefully organized activities that encouraged more even class participation but also through the use (with students' permission) of "anonymous" journal entries that spoke particularly eloquently to a topic being covered in class. This latter practice proved particularly effective as a means of validating and affirming the ideas of students who might otherwise not venture to speak. More significant though, was that the journal entries (more so than open class discussion) tended to place a multiplicity of "I's"—subjects—front and center, which in turn succeeded in transforming—democratizing, if you will—the dynamics in the classroom.

A final and related strategy was to foreground the issue of authority. Questions such as: Who can and cannot speak? Who does and does not speak and why? For whom does I/we/they/he/she speak and why? These issues were a major obstacle to breaking down the silences and building democracy in the classroom. Addressing these questions yielded thoughtful and lively discussions on, for example, the authority of experience versus the authority of knowledge and on the nature and function of authority and hierarchy in academe. More important, however, was that this thematic emphasis proved to be one of the most effective mechanisms for transforming/liberating students. Like the naming of *multiple oppressions,* naming *multiple authorities* broke down the rigidity of the dominant/oppressed binary, but it also succeeded in diversifying the sources of, and access to, authority and power in the classroom community.

Active encouragement to reflect upon silence, conscious affirmation and valuation of student's "voicing"—either written or spoken—in the classroom arena, and the identification and nurturance of *multiple authorities* precipitated numerous breakthroughs like Pilar's much earlier in the semester the second time the course was taught.

Because of its transformative power we have found service learning to have many benefits, all of which outweigh the difficulties that we have described above. To deal with the problems of participation we recommend— in addition to the use of journals mentioned above—the use of e-mail and related technologies. These allow students to participate without having to expose all of their thoughts and feelings to a classroom of strangers. We also suggest allowing the rewriting of papers. This allows students the freedom to experiment with new modes of exposition with less risk. It also allows the student time and the professor space to require that their rigorous expectations be met despite the new challenges being presented. This leads to the last concern and possible solution. One must set expectations as a class. It is very important that the class be involved in setting the expectations for the course. This is usually a new mode of learning for students and it does not fit their past experience. If they can participate in the setting of goals and expectations they are more likely to buy into the validity of the learning experience. If the students are not involved in this way, they often try to proceed with business as usual. They will report on the texts of the course in a distanced and detached manner. Service learning, as we have tried to argue, is not business as usual.

Concluding Remarks: The Challenge to the Teacher

As feminist teachers committed to the idea of the classroom as a safe and empowering space, our students have taught us that there is much more at stake in the service-learning classroom than we had anticipated. By affirming experiential learning—foregrounding experience—silences among students were intensified and learning took on a multidimensional personal quality that radically shifted our designated learning objectives. We realized that while service learning picks up on the feminist rejection of the practice/theory dichotomy and hierarchy, we had much to learn about the practical implications, or, more literally, the *teaching practice,* of such a position. Our goal here has been to share this learning process with you.

Our experience raises a range of questions that help us to clarify our own perspectives on the nature and function of knowledge and experience, and to transform our teaching and learning practice. More specifically, and from the standpoint of the teacher's role, the issues that emerged out of our courses with experiential components pointed to the possibility of reorienting our learning objectives toward three interrelated processes that, not surprisingly, coincide with three fundamental principles of feminist pedagogy: the affirmation of the personal, the personal made political, and the call to action.

The first of these processes, which we will call "subject positioning," encourages self-representation and authentication for our students and is best represented by Pilar's remembering and assuming her Latina identity. A second and concomitant process requires a concurrent examination of one's identity as a construction. The question, "Who am I,"? that is, must be accompanied by the following related questions: Who have I been defined as? Who has defined me? What has defined me? How do I define others? Why have I defined and been defined in given ways? These questions involve students in a process that moves them beyond the claim of "I" as an endpoint, toward a critical and theoretical examination of the self and its position in the classroom and in the world. The third process, finally, enjoins the student— once the political dimensions of the personal have been explored—to commit to, and act upon, the need for continued internal/external transformation.

We have two final considerations. First, these learning objectives serve as a dynamic framework for identifying breakthroughs, measuring progress, and setting goals for students' transformation. Second, the teacher, while maintaining the role of instructor, must be equally and personally committed to this threefold process. The teacher must be willing, therefore, to model her self-positioning, to model the critique and theorizing of the self, and to articulate/implement her concomitant plan for action. The teacher's position, along with that of her students, therefore, also will shift and be modified depending on how the identities of the community members evolve. The learning process, finally, will be characterized by less pre-dictability and more open-endedness and will assume a diverse, personalized, dynamic, and embodied nature.

Notes

1. The student stories told in this paper are true although names, dates, and places have been changed to protect their privacy.
2. The difference between the terms "service" and "experiential"—subtle and easily blurred in the literature—resides primarily in the intended purpose and outcome of each of these teaching/learning strategies. Both, of course, rely on personal experience rather than traditional academic learning as a source of knowledge. However, "experiential" learning places most of the emphasis on the experience as an end in itself or as a means of learning about, and gaining personal experience in a particular field (in corporate, medical, or international internships, for example); "service" learning, how-ever, purports to provide personal experience with the concurrent goal of teaching about, and providing service or outreach to people and organiza-tions in less advantaged communities. Institutionalized examples of this dis-tinction can be observed in the differences between, for example, the American Association of Higher Education Service-Learning Initiative (see their website www.ahaa.org/service/srv.lrn.html) and the Council for Adult and Experiential Learning (www.cail.org) or the Institute for Experiential Learning (www.ielnet.org). We deliberately chose to combine the two terms throughout the text (service/experiential) because our primary emphasis is on the need to begin problematizing both the increasing popularity and le-gitimization of experience as a category of knowledge and the possible mis-use or application of this knowledge in contexts of difference.
3. The degree to which service/experiential learning is visible, administra-tively supported, funded, encouraged, and integrated into either curricu-lar or cocurricular programs varies significantly from institution to institution. Moreover, it does not appear to be determined by an institu-tion's church-relatedness. At Pacific Lutheran University, the commitment to service/experiential learning is visibly reflected in the institution's motto, "Educating for Lives of Service." To lend support to this mission, PLU funds a full-time administrative position—"Director of Public Ser-vice"—whose job description includes the coordination of the Center for Public Service as well as the task of encouraging, supporting, and assisting faculty in the process of implementing service/experiential components into their courses. Recently, the director also administered a generous grant from the Aid Association to Lutherans that was designed to infuse service/experiential learning into new and existing courses across the cur-riculum. Stanford University funds a similar position and center (The Haas Center for Public Service). In increasing numbers, colleges and uni-versities are adding nonacademic service requirements for graduation.

Some of these include Monmouth University in New Jersey, the University of Wisconsin Eau Claire, and Cal State Monterrey Bay. Other institutions are requiring a course with a service-learning component for graduation. Cedar Crest College—a small, private, women's college in Eastern Pennsylvania—instituted a mandatory service requirement for first-year students in the fall of 1998 to be followed by a required course in Ethics with a two-hour experiential component in the sophomore year.

4. Few studies exist that bring into dialogue feminism, feminist pedagogy, or feminist epistemology with experiential learning. These include: Ludlum Foos 1998, Michelson 1996, and Rhoads 1997. Finally, Kerrissa Heffernan with Campus Contact at Brown University and Barbara Balliet of Rutgers University have co-edited *The Practice of Change: Concepts and Models for Service Learning in Women's Studies*, a Women's Studies and Service Learning monograph for the AAHE disciplinary series which provides some provocative contributions to this much needed conversation.

5. See Michelson 1996 for a helpful characterization of the challenge of collapsing the split of theory and practice in the experiential learning context.

6. I do not mean to imply that the "ethics of care" is the better theory—it has many problems. It did help Tanya gain a different perspective on her experience. Further discussion of the ethics of care is beyond the scope of this paper. See McKenna "The Need for a Pragmatist Feminist Self."

7. Thank you to Amie MacDonald and Susan Sánchez-Casal, editors of this volume, for posing these questions.

8. We refer here primarily to David A. Kolb's classic *Experiential Learning: Experience as the Source of Learning and Development*, 1984.

9. See Ludlom Foos 1998, Rhoads 1997, Heffernan and Balliet 2000.

10. Text from syllabus for Spanish 341, "Latino Experiences in the U.S.," taught by Prof. Tamara Williams.

Works Cited

Belenky, Mary Field, Blythe Clinchy, Nancy Goldberger, and Jill Tarule. *Women's Ways of Knowing: The Development of Self, Voice, and Mind*. New York: Basic Books, 1986.

Flax, Jane. "Political Philosophy and the Patriarchal Unconscious: A Psychoanalytic Perspective on Epistemology and Metaphysics." In *Discovering Reality: Feminist Perspectives on Epistemology, Methodology, and Philosophy of Science*. Ed. Sandra Harding and Merrill Hintikka. Dorcrecht: D. Reidel, 1983, 245–281.

Heffernan, Kerrissa and Barbara Balliet. *The Practice of Change: Concepts and Models for Service Learning in Women's Studies*. Washington, D.C.: American Association of Higher Education, 2000.

Kolb, David A. *Experiential Learning: Experience as the Source of Learning and Development*. New Jersey: Prentice-Hall, 1984.

Ludlum Foos, Carolyn. "The Different Voice of Service." *Michigan Journal of CLS* 5 (Fall 1998): 14–21.

McKenna, Erin. "Some Reflections Concerning Feminist Pedagogy." *Metaphilosophy* 27 (1&2): (January/April 1996): 178–183.

———. "The Need for a Pragmatic Feminist Self." In *Feminist Interpretations of John Dewey.* Ed. Charlene Haddock Seigfried. University Park, Pennsylvania: Pennsylvania State University Press, 2002, 133–159.

Michelson, Elana. "'Auctoritée' and 'Experience': Feminist Epistemology and the Assessment of Experiential Learning." *Feminist Studies* 22. 3 (Fall 1996): 627–656.

Rhoads, Robert. *Community Service and Higher Learning: Explorations of the Caring Self.* Albany: State University of New York Press, 1997.

CHAPTER SIX

ANTIRACIST PEDAGOGY
AND *CONCIENTIZACIÓN*
A Latina Professor's Struggle

Maria Eva Valle

As the youngest daughter of a first generation immigrant family, I am not your traditional "academic." My father, Miguel, was from the popular tourist resort of Mazatlán, Mexico. In the United States he labored as a journeyman brick mason for most of his life. Miguel took great pride in his profession, working hard to remodel the homes of the rich and famous in La Jolla, California. Rosalía, my mother, was born in San José del Cabo, a small fishing village on the tip of Baja California. In San Diego, she toiled as a domestic worker in the homes of moderately wealthy Euro-American families. Born and raised in San Diego, I had family on both sides of U.S.-Mexican border and traveled frequently between these two countries. These conflicting yet coexisting worldviews shaped my culture, identity, and consciousness. As a transborder person the languages and cultures of these countries comingled in me, and I utilized them interchangeably; yet English predominated over Spanish, creating a Chicana identity, distinct from that of a Mexicana.

As an undergraduate college student at University of California at San Diego's Third College during the early 1970s, I became active in various student and labor organizations. I served as cochair of the Movimiento Estudiantil Chicano de Aztlan (MEChA); I was a founder of Mujeres Unidas Para Justicia Educación y Revolución (MUJER), and a student coordinator for the United Farm Workers (UFW). The political vision of professors such as Angela Davis and Herbert Marcuse inspired me to question the nature of capitalism, to promote student activism, to explore the changing roles of women, and to strategize the relationship between ethnic identity and political empowerment. My direct participation in broad social movements—including the struggle for Civil Rights, opposition to the Vietnam War, and the Women's movement—further shaped my educational and political experience. As student leaders we formed study groups where we analyzed the writings of Karl Marx, Che Guevara, Frantz Fanon, Carlos Mariátegui, Amilcar Cabral, Mao Zedong, and many other leaders of national liberation struggles. We learned that revolutionary political consciousness is an essential component of social change, which in turn is contingent upon a profound restructuring of social institutions. This political knowledge forms the foundation of my argument in this chapter, that personal strategies for retaining and graduating students of color, hiring and tenuring faculty of color, and institutionalizing insurgent disciplines such as Chicano/a Studies are ultimately bankrupt since they do not address the overarching power relations that permeate institutions of higher learning. In support of this argument, I will analyze the concept of *concientización*[1] within the context of my personal journey through academia and my struggle as a professor to create a pedagogy that empowers faculty and students of color.

Class Consciousness and Feminist Ideals

My history of work and education leads me to conclude that without a clear political framework—i.e., *concientización*—I would not have been able to succeed as a student and as a professor. Upon completing my undergraduate education, I diverged from the traditional academic path and sought employment in various industries throughout San Diego. I became one of the first women of color to enter the male world of the aerospace industry when I accepted a job in a plant that made cruise missiles. I also worked as a secretary, high-school teacher, an apprentice, and eventually a journeyman machinist in a shipyard. I labored in a male-dominated world where I challenged unions to address women's issues. At the shipyard where most women swept floors or did secretarial work, I worked in a machine shop. Working within the shipyard proved dirty; women had to earn the respect of all male crews and had to confront unsafe working conditions daily.

I was assigned to a work crew that included Euro-Americans, Mexicans, African Americans, Filipinos, and Vietnamese. While working we engaged in lively discussions about our families, cultural traditions, immigration, the union, politics, and our future goals. From the outset, I made clear my commitment to feminist ideals. My presence challenged the men to avoid certain topics of discussion, especially those related to sex. I distinctly recall one incident during lunch where "the guys" passed around the latest copy of *Playboy*. When the magazine reached my side of the table the foreman quickly intervened by saying "I am sure you are not interested in what this has to offer," but to his surprise I indicated that I would gladly take it home. The next day the foreman asked what I had done with the *Playboy* and I told him that I had used the paper as kindling in my fireplace. Eventually I was elected as a representative to the leadership conference for our local union where I addressed the need for greater gender representation and more inclusive policies that incorporated the concerns of a racially diverse membership. Although most men were generally hostile to the idea of being directed by a woman, in the end the union elected more Latinos/as and African Americans to leadership positions and agreed to translate union documents into Spanish.

After ten years of working in the labor movement, I returned to the university and pursued a Ph.D. in Sociology. Within the ivy-covered walls, I quickly learned that I did not conform to the dominant racial "aesthetic" of academia. This became evident when I visited the home of a professor to submit a research paper and was mistaken for a friend of the maid by a family member who asked me to enter through the backdoor. More than once I was advised that to succeed in academia, I would have to relinquish my "cultural baggage"—my working-class background, my racial/ethnic identity, and my feminist perspectives. As the only Chicana graduate student in a Sociology department, I came to understand that these instances of cultural imperialism were predicated on the fact that the university did not value my form of cultural capital; this realization served to reinforce my political convictions.

The personal discrimination I experienced led me to a new level of consciousness, infusing my political beliefs, cultural experiences, and theoretical perspectives with a yearning for a new way of life based upon equality. First and foremost, I have concluded that I only survived these "cultural wars"— earning my doctorate and becoming a professor—because of a heightened level of *concientización*. While some of my cohorts—other women of color— either dropped out or transferred to another campus, I had a different vantage point from which to evaluate the unequal gender relations, the contentious class dynamics, and overt and covert cultural subordination that we encountered. I did not view my particular situation simply as a personal trial but understood it as part of a broader systemic structure of power and exclusion. My politicized *concientización* provided me a framework from which to identify the issues of discrimination and inequality, and a position from which to critically reflect upon these issues and their possible solutions. When it became obvious that I could not rely upon academia to validate my cultural identity and experiences, I searched for other sources of support and meaning.

To complicate matters further, by the late 1980s the political orientation on the UCSD campus had dramatically shifted. The students I encountered appeared more interested in working "within the system" rather than radically altering the power relations that structurally subordinated working people, women, Latinos/as, and other people of color. Nonetheless, through an arduous process of contestation and negotiation I managed to carve out a "safe place" within the university to advance my education. After overcoming many odds, I became the first Chicana to receive a Ph.D. in Sociology from the University of California, San Diego. I presently teach at California State University, Dominguez Hills within the Department of Chicana/o Studies. However, I have multiple areas of interests and my approach is interdisciplinary. I work with Women's Studies, coordinate the service-learning component within Chicana/o Studies, and teach courses on cultural diversity in the School of Education. Like many of my students, I am the first one in my family to acquire a college education. My parents labored long and hard to provide their family with a better life with the hope that someday their children could become professionals, so that we could achieve our goals and make a worthy contribution to society. They never imagined, however, the challenges involved in becoming a university professor.

Developing a Pedagogy of *Concientización*

Within academia I seek to unite my personal and political journey with the new critical approaches implemented in various disciplines. I locate myself within the political framework of the late Brazilian sociologist, Paulo Freire, who defines *concientización* as a process that rejects individualism and stresses an understanding of our relationship to community, nation, and the world. Yet he also cautions that this " . . . discovery cannot be purely intellectual but must involve action, nor can it be limited to mere activism, but must include serious reflection"(23). Freire sees that through a continual process of "dialogue, reflection and communication," people can direct their political action and achieve praxis. Central to the idea of *concientización* is an understanding of how power is disseminated within academia, replicating economic structures and maintaining privilege (La Belle and Ward 152). This process encourages us to challenge hierarchical structures of authority and develop participatory mechanisms that lead to self-actualization and empowerment for faculty and students. Self-actualization, according to Aruna Srivastava, is a process involving:

> . . . political realization—a recognition of ourselves in history and in the context of differential and fluid relations of power; indeed the actualization of the self necessarily entails the ability to articulate ourselves in institutions, to rec-

ognize how our actions are oppositional, how they are complicit in academic structures of oppression. (115)

This self-realization is a political process of consciousness—a rebirth of sorts—in which we gain a critical understanding of differential power relations and our role within them. *Concientización* requires us to engage structures of power and domination and to question our complicity in oppression. Furthermore, Freire argues against the notion that faculty are objective conveyors of knowledge and students passive observers of the educational process (24). Instead, he encourages faculty and students to examine our social conditions in order "to see the world not as a static reality, but as a reality in the process of transformation"(70–71). This type of transformation is not immediate, but requires a protracted process of contestation and negotiation at the individual, local, and national level.

The pedagogy of *concientización* highlights the interdependence of critical reflection and political action. Our obligation as educators centers on providing students the analytical tools and practical knowledge that enables them to comprehend the underlying causes of inequality within the contexts of racism, sexism, and classism. Part of this mission includes the imperative to empower students by demonstrating the link between critical thinking in the university and social activism in at-risk communities. For their part, students need to practice democracy by developing and implementing strategies that can help counteract racism and sexism—in their selection of courses, involvement in campus activities, service to their communities and through their participation in the political process. To understand oppression, teachers must adopt an antiracist pedagogy where our experiences, beliefs, and opinions are no longer "neutralized" but instead play a crucial role in the formation of antiracist feminist knowledge (Nieto 169).

Reaching consciousness can be a complex and conflictive process. Gloria Anzaldúa discusses how cultural "collisions" and "incompatible frames of reference" between marginalized and dominant communities produce new forms of a hybrid "mestiza consciousness" (1987, 78). Although the notion of mestiza consciousness can motivate people to engage in general social/political activism, this racialized and cultural consciousness often fails to consider the more complex issues of class, culture, national origin, gender, and even sexuality. Theories that focus on individual solutions fail to address the overarching power relations that permeate educational and civic institutions. While individual change is a significant first step, *concientización* requires the application of broader forms of analysis capable of influencing large segments of the population. Since outlooks that center solely on individual circumstances or culturally based solutions can lead people astray, it behooves us to move away from personal reflections as our unit of analysis and examine more systematically the structural relationships that exist within education including class background, school resources, and social environment.

Using Freire as a guide, bell hooks expands upon the notion of *concientización* in her book *Teaching to Transgress*. She agrees that education should involve the "practice of freedom" and that classrooms should be an exciting and transformative place to learn. Teachers must be flexible, inclusive, and create an open space for change and invention with the objective of providing students a safe place to dialogue and debate issues with their peers. According to hooks, the " . . . classroom remains the most radical place of possibility in the academy" since teaching is a performative act where teachers become catalysts and active participants in learning (1994, 12).

Some educators have equated the role of teacher to that of a "bridge" providing students access to knowledge, avenues of communication, and the resources to support their interests (Nieto 115). All students have particular strengths, reflecting specific experiences that should be publicly acknowledged, evaluated, and incorporated into the classroom. One method I have successfully employed requires students to make themselves and their families the object of study. They engage in "free writes" about their neighborhoods, peer groups, gender differences, family socialization, and overt experiences of discrimination and share this information with the class. In this manner they begin to explore new paths of knowledge, linking the home and the school, validating hooks's assertion that the manner in which radical educators think, write, and speak constantly evolves in dialogue with our students.

One of our goals as educators is to create a communal place of learning that can be sustained by a collective process of engagement. No one strategy is complete—nonetheless our approach should take into consideration our students' skills, social environments, and cultural backgrounds. By allowing students to take control of their education, giving them voice in the selection of themes, course assignments, and participation in the evaluation of their peers, we can contest the political apathy endemic in many classrooms. The challenge is to make learning real and meaningful by demonstrating to students how various forms of knowledge can be integrated into the transformation of everyday life. As hooks suggests:

> Progressive professors working to transform the curriculum so that it does not reflect biases or reinforce systems of domination are most often the individuals willing to take the risk that engaged pedagogy requires and to make their teaching practices a site of resistance. (1994, 21)

Furthermore, hooks underscores the need to transgress from coercive hierarchies—building democratic relationships premised on mutual control and participation.

Drawing from her own experiences, Sonia Nieto demonstrates how the inequities of poverty and "unrelenting oppression" can place working-class students of color at an educational disadvantage. Adopting Freire's notion of *concientización*, she professes the need for educators to undergo personal transformations in which they step outside of their own worlds and learn about the languages, cultures, values, and experiences of their students. From Nieto's perspective "being antiracist means paying attention to all areas in which some students may be favored over others, including the curriculum, choice of materials, sorting policies, and teacher's interactions and relationships with students and their communities" (169). Similarly, schools need to undergo a radical institutional transformation that rejects sterile curricula and fosters quality education by acknowledging the importance of nurturing positive social relationships. Developing an "antiracist" pedagogy remains a prolonged process that requires constant attention to unlearn the racist stereotypes that permeate education, the media, and society. Roxana Ng takes this notion a step further declaring "antisexist and antiracist means seeing sexism and racism as systemic and interpersonal problems"(51). Ng therefore recommends that we combat sexism and racism collectively, not just personally, since, as Chandra Mohanty states, "resistance that is random and isolated is clearly not as effective as that which is mobilized through systematic politicized practices of teaching and learning"(1994, 148).

Feminist pedagogy demands resistance to normative educational practices, for it perceives them neither as neutral nor as the "great equalizers" that many liberals advocate. It is no surprise that the marginalization of faculty of color, women, gays, and lesbians in the academy ultimately leads to their radicalization. Marginalization, according to hooks, need not lead to deprivation, but can provide creative insights or "sites of radical possibility," or "a space of resistance" (1990, 149). My radicalized political consciousness, i.e., my process of *concientización*, emerges out of the conjunction between specific social movements in which I participate—Chicano/a, women, student, and the workers movement—and antiracist feminist theory.

Conflicts and Contradictions
Confronted by Faculty of Color

Labor historians and many social scientists have documented the ways in which academia discourages social activism, while claiming to value individual merit and "objectivity." Within this depoliticized context it is not surprising that academic institutions are unprepared to deal with faculty of color who regard their commitment to the political objectives of their communities as an integral part of their intellectual mission. As one Latino faculty member succinctly states:

Faculty of color's circumstances are quite different from other people in that if you have any social consciousness and any identification with your respective ethnic or racial group you are going to want to help in some way, through your discipline or otherwise. (Baez 133)

Within this context, faculty of color who question the patriarchal Eurocentric views of their colleagues suffer negative consequences and are perceived as "oppositional"—or worse, "un-collegial." Faculty who challenge the "status quo" place themselves "at risk" and can incur reprisals from administrators and senior faculty. Under these circumstances, it becomes difficult for progressive intellectuals of color to remain in academia. The solution for progressive and radical faculty, according to the pedagogy of *concientización*, is not to acquiesce to this coercive hierarchy but to search for creative ways to transform hegemonic structures and, in Freire's words, "become beings for themselves" (61). Following the theoretical legacy of Freire, Anzaldúa, Nieto, and hooks, I attempt to infuse a feminist critique and bicultural orientation into the predominantly male structure that persists in viewing race through an exclusionary black and white paradigm. I have put myself at risk by defending programs, perspectives, and individuals that are crucial to a meaningful and democratic form of education. By assuming the imperatives of institutional reformation—challenging the traditional canon, creating unique course offerings, designing a variety of cultural activities, and promoting community involvement—Latino/a and Ethnic Studies can successfully increase students' interest and establish an antiracist presence on campus.

Nonetheless, the academy as a whole continues to resist these changes, reinforcing the marginalized status of minority professors and forcing us to confront overt and covert forms of racism. For example, a Euro-American female professor once questioned my ability to teach a course on cultural diversity by asking: "What do you know about ethnicity, anyway?" Despite these ongoing conflicts, minority faculty are still expected to assume the role of the "token representative" of our particular racial/ethnic group by assuming responsibility for "multicultural" administrative duties, advising, mentoring, and programming.

Whether or not they embrace the concept of *concientización*, faculty of color in higher education are expected to be more than traditional conveyors of knowledge. We confront a broad array of responsibilities and conflicting sets of obligations that tend to counterpose the demands of the academy against the needs and desires of students to improve the conditions in their respective racial/ethnic communities. While academia generally stifles community activism by faculty of color, it also perceives their cultural identity as a liability that needs to be "managed"; thus many of us are forced to confront the contradiction between the intellectual practices of the academy and our own cultural identities. Two Chicanos prominently featured in the 1997 video documentary *Shattering the Silences*—Gloria Holguín Cuádraz, a sociologist at Arizona State University, and Alex Saragoza, a Latin American historian at the University of California, Berkeley—illuminate the cultural clash and class antagonism exhibited at their universities. Cuádraz and Saragoza echo the same sense of alienation and marginalization that María de la Luz Reyes expresses in her essay "Chicanas in Academe: An Endangered Species." These professors of color underscore the absence of institutional support and the sense of exclusion they confront at their universities. Cuádraz stresses the feeling of being invisible in the eyes of the administration while de la Luz Reyes addresses how Chicana professors confront Euro-American students and colleagues who question their credentials and even their ability to teach.

Alienation in academia represents more than simple intellectual isolation; it can also involve significant personal sacrifice. Many promising faculty of color have paid a heavy price for their refusal to conform to the status quo. In some cases, the mere presence of a faculty member of color is perceived as a challenge to those who hold the reigns of power in the academy. As de la Luz Reyes points out, academia suppresses our voices, dismisses our ideas, and devalues our contributions. Many faculty of color work in academic departments that neglect to mentor us or promote our professional and political interests. Additionally, some of the more established faculty of color regard their racial identity, class background, and/or feminist ideals as "problems" that generate tension and conflict within their predominantly Euro-American departments.

I have personally experienced the trauma of marginalization and racism. My racial and ethnic identity as well as my sociological approach has unsettled some of my colleagues in traditional disciplines. In one department where I worked, I was asked to adapt to a middle-class Euro-American experience that served as the operative intellectual and cultural framework. Far from an isolated incident, three other faculty of color in different departments faced similar circumstances. Although my colleagues claimed to support diversity, in practice they impeded its implementation. Nevertheless, I continued to interact in Spanish when appropriate, to encourage students to connect with local Chicano/Latino communities and to explore cultural perspectives different from their own. Unfortunately, the effects of racist practices in academia disrupt political alliances among faculty of color: in this case, some Chicana/o faculty, even those with tenure, quietly acquiesced to white, middle-class normativity. As Freire states, the "struggle for freedom threatens not only the oppressor, but also their oppressed comrades who are fearful of still greater repression"(32).

While those of us situated within insurgent departments such as Ethnic or Latino/a studies may enjoy the support of our departments, we are often racially segregated from the Anglo majority in mainstream departments. Within these segregated conditions, faculty of color are given exclusive responsibility for promoting and building our departments and are forced to continuously recruit students and majors in order to justify and maintain our presence on campus. Significantly, this burden is not shared equally among minority faculty, since unpoliticized faculty of color may not share this critical consciousness and thus may feel no obligation to serve the intellectual and cultural interests of their ethnic group. Moreover, it is seldom the case that Euro-American colleagues encounter these types of perplexing and contradictory situations that divide faculty "communities" on campus.

While confronting these complex sets of conditions, faculty of color nonetheless must establish their reputations within academic institutions dominated by a Euro-American aesthetic. For example, at the 23 California State University campuses, nearly 80 percent of the faculty are Euro-American, and men constitute a two-thirds majority. Latino/a professors, as well as other faculty of color, remain dramatically underrepresented and constitute less than 7 percent of the faculty system-wide (CSUDH Institutional Research Website). As Barbara Robles has noted, the "lack of diversity within the academy hinders collegial collaboration, joint intellectual inquiry, and the formation of an academic environment dedicated to discovery" (102). This white and male-dominated administration sets institutional policies, hires the faculty, and dictates the mission of the university. They pass judgement on faculty of color and stand as a "disquieting reminder that white male academics continue to set the parameters of what is considered acceptable research within their own disciplines and, in so doing, pass on their own intellectual preconceptions and limitations" (Robles 103). At a time when significant demographic shifts have occurred in society, we must address the glaring underrepresentation of faculty of color in academic institutions. Under these adverse conditions, even the individual successes of minority faculty, no matter how significant, do not alter the dramatic racial gap in faculty representation. We need concerted antiracist action to mobilize faculty, students, and other constituencies to pressure university administrations to concretely address institutionalized racism and sexism.

Regardless of the political commitment of faculty of color, the rigors of academic life rarely allow faculty of color the opportunity to adequately conduct research, teach classes, serve on committees, mentor students, and tend to their personal lives. Research requires time away from classes, students, and campus activities in order to think, read, and write. Furthermore, university administrators and senior colleagues often devalue the research areas and publication venues of faculty of color, since innovative topics and controversial perspectives that question the hegemonic structures and policies of the academy are often deemed to be purely ideological, and nonintellectual. The underlying tensions that result from being pulled in opposing directions are often difficult to reconcile. María de la Luz Reyes refers to this tension as walking a tightrope between the demands of our professional career and the need to contribute to our ethnic community while maintaining our own cultural identity (17). Undoubtedly, this balancing act requires much skill and places faculty of color at constant risk of failure.

Faculty of color face an ongoing dilemma as we continually confront questions of how to prioritize academic and political objectives, since conventional definitions of merit privilege scholarship and teaching and disparage service and community activities as a misuse of minority scholars' time. Paradoxically, while the service of minority faculty is rarely taken into account for promotion and tenure, colleges and universities insist upon minority faculty labor in order to adequately serve students' nonacademic needs. Thus, service is a doubled-edged sword that creates much controversy. At one level, multicultural service duties can be the downfall of faculty of color, since it causes dispersal and may undermine scholarly productivity. But this criticism does not take into account the view explicit in *concientización* that critical education involves creating political communities that work to restructure existing relations of power in academia. Freire reminds us that isolating ourselves in the "ivory tower" does not produce transformative results. He states: "Authentic thinking, thinking that is concerned about reality does not take place in ivory tower isolation, but only in communication. It is true that thought has meaning only when generated by action upon the world. . . ."(64). Service that is linked to activism remains essential if one seeks to improve the status of people of color within academia and the broader community. As both Exum and Baez point out, service fulfills a variety of important functions "for both the faculty member and institution, because such participation increases the diversity of perspective, ensures sensitivity to the needs of people of color, and may be personally and politically rewarding to faculty of color" (Baez 132).

Official service on departmental or campus-wide committees is regularly validated since it augments the mission and reputation of the university. In contrast, work with students or ethnic groups is not formally acknowledged but instead viewed as disconnected from the academic realm. Rather than privilege one arena over another, we should require the university to expand the ethical dimensions of service to students and community whether inside or outside the classroom. The establishment of an equitable system of acknowledgement and rewards for the time and dedication professors invest in their students and prospective communities would situate college campuses as part of the total reality in which we live and learn. For as Astin suggests, the sole outcome of an education is not for students merely to earn "As" but to encourage them to become lifelong learners by exposing them to experiential forms of knowledge applied in real life situations.

Challenges and Expectations of
Working-Class Latino/a Students

To complicate matters further, rarely do students fully comprehend the conflicting dilemmas that faculty of color face within the university. The academy expects professors to conduct research and serve on departmental and
academic committees. Students, on the other hand, want faculty of color to
be mentors, provide meaningful courses, and "protect" them from an insen-
sitive university system that is often blind to their specific academic and social needs. Students look to faculty of color to serve as role models, as
advisers/counselors and in emergencies, as surrogate parents. The faculty
member fills the gap that exists between the family, community, and the
campus environment. This becomes an arduous responsibility that doesn't
"fit" conveniently within office hours, nor within the constraints and limitations faculty confront within an educational environment in which the dynamics of domination, oppression, and competition are still the normative
mode of operation.

As Freire informs us, students are not empty vessels for us to write
upon—or for educators to imprint their ideas upon—but human beings
whose feelings, expressions, and experiences have to be recognized and engaged in the classroom. Thus, our classes must provide new insights and interpretations of diverse social realities, since they are populated by students
of all races, ethnicities, languages, classes, and cultures. In addition, faculty
must diversify the perspectives from which we teach in order to dethrone
prevailing Eurocentric curricula and modes of thought. The public university or college must not reproduce a "plantation system" in which the students from predominantly diverse racial/ethnic backgrounds are governed
and instructed by a majority Euro-American faculty. As critical educator Antonia Darder explains:

> The dominant pedagogy of American schools predominantly reflects the val-
> ues, worldview, and belief system of the dominant culture's middle and upper
> classes, while it neglects and ignores the lived experiences of subordinate cul-
> tures. Hence students of color are silenced and their bicultural experiences
> negated and ignored, while they are systematically educated into the discourse
> of the dominant culture—an ethnocentric ideology that perceives the dis-
> course of the other as inferior, invaluable and deficient in regards to the aims
> of American society. (68)

Darder clearly depicts the process by which Latino/a students' voices have
been systematically silenced and their experiences negated or ignored. Until
recently, the history, culture, and contributions of people of color have been
conspicuously absent from public discourse and thereby excluded from most

universities. Consequently, the level of engagement of students of color within the classroom has been limited. Under these conditions, some students of color have become alienated and disinterested in traditional areas of study. Conversely, when students of color enroll in ethnic/gender studies and engage relevant ideas, they develop a strong sense of inclusion and intellectual solidarity (Flores 209). We can learn from this how racial and ethnic difference among our students forces us to grapple with the complex and contradictory ways that individual beliefs, personal experiences, institutional norms, and political ideologies converge in the classroom and dictate policies within the university.

By employing a critical analysis and continual reflection that draws upon common lived experiences and a willingness to take risks, faculty can devise antiracist feminist pedagogies that enlighten and empower. We must have the courage to step outside our own frame of reference so that we can relate to "others," nurture mutual trust, and establish the conditions for cultural democracy on our campuses. Even on the most diverse campuses, racial stereotyping and segregation continue to inhibit students of color from working in coalition across racial lines.

Students must build bridges between the diverse elements of the Latino/a community while at the same time engaging the broader society. Only by shattering the prominent stereotypes that continue to shape negative behavior and produce low expectations can this be accomplished. The general orientation may lead us to critically examine or debate conflicting perspectives such as ethnocentrism, racism, homophobia, cultural nationalism, *machismo* or *marianismo*. Our goal is to instill a higher level of consciousness, or *concientización*, with the distinct understanding that "cada mente es un mundo" (each mind is a world). Once developed, students will have to situate this knowledge to suit their own circumstances, frames of reference, and political desires.

The goal of ethnic studies should not be to promote the sort of romanticized ethnic pride that characterized the male-dominated cultural nationalist ideas of the Chicano movement in the 1960s. Ethnic studies should provide students the theoretical tools to address issues of class, racial/ethnic identity formation, immigration, gender and sexuality, and other complex issues. This is particularly true for Latinos/as since the process of globalization has created dynamic exchanges between the homeland and the immigrant communities within the United States. Consequently, Chicano/Latino studies have become more broadly defined and culturally diverse—addressing the transnational, cross-cultural realities of U.S. Latino communities that now join together Mexican, Central, South American, and Caribbean people. These immigration and demographic changes force us to also address the concerns of Latinos/as from different racial and ethnic backgrounds, including African, Asian, Indigenous, and mixed race peoples. This diversity and geographic diffusion create new fissures as well as points of convergence, or as Flores and others have noted "more complex, interactive and transgressive notions of hybrid and multiple social points of view" (210). Some scholars have envisioned the emergence of a new level of pan- ethnic unity. Unity, however, cannot be premised upon imaginary cultural ties. Given the profound and expansive cultural transformation in Latino communities, we are now faced with the challenge of creating pan-Latino coalitions across differences of class, gender, generation, national origin and ancestry, color, religion, and other distinguishing factors.

Classroom Dynamics:
Creating A Community of Engaged Learners

Underrepresented students offer a unique set of challenges for faculty of color. To better understand student expectations, I queried several groups at California State University, Domínguez Hills. The students who shared their views were mostly children of immigrants who live in the inner city and have working-class backgrounds. Students' concerns centered around two basic areas: first, hiring faculty who are sensitive to students' ethnic and cultural backgrounds and working to integrate these subjugated areas into the curriculum; second, ensuring access to faculty by encouraging meaningful intellectual engagement and greater opportunities for interaction between faculty and students. These expectations address the dramatic needs confronted by the majority of Latino/a students who attend community colleges, state universities, or even prestigious private institutions.

One way to address students' needs is to employ the concept of "modeling." Central to liberatory pedagogy, modeling allows us to lead by example, utilizing real life experiences to exemplify a point. Once we demonstrate the courage to expose our lives by inviting students' evaluations and comments, we forge open lines of communication. Under these conditions, classrooms can become places of active dialogue that promote intense contestation and negotiation. In these discussions, divergent worldviews and political perspectives intersect. This pedagogical strategy rigorously interrogates ideas, opinions, and ideologies. As Aruna Srivastava informs us:

> The classroom cannot help but be, at times chaotic, confusing and disordered, a place of pain, denial, anger, and anxiety—all of which we expect, we have to expect, when challenging others and ourselves to examine, even simply reveal, the ways in which all sorts of racism have inflected our/their identities. (121)

To move beyond abstract concepts of knowledge, I encourage students to consider new forms of writing including personal narratives, oral histories, plays, and poems. My goal is to use their personal experiences to promote growth and inspire their creative imaginations. To counter notions of individualism, I underscore the importance of collaboration and self-critique—combining group projects with individual endeavors. By using various mediums such as music, films, and plays to present concrete information from multiple perspectives, I am able to challenge students to broaden their visions and deepen their understanding of the world and their places in it. I attempt to make critical theories meaningful to their life experiences, regardless of whether the topic is gangs, teen pregnancy, immigration, or labor. As Manuela, a Salvadorian student, pointed out in March of 2000:

> The courses I enjoyed the most during my college years were psychology, sociology, and Chicana/o Studies. In all these courses, facts were not enough. In class, we all gave our personal points of view in regards to social and educational issues that in many cases ended up in serious debates among students.

As students become engaged in their education within the context of antiracist classroom practices, they are more likely to develop an interest in the political process. For example, Rogelio, a history major from El Salvador, criticized his classmates who were quick to accept hegemonic racist views about Latinos/as. At times, his politicized consciousness brought him into conflict with other students over the role of gangs, the nature of discrimination and police brutality. But even politicized students like Rogelio may encounter difficulty in distinguishing between individual, group, and institutional responsibility for discrimination. In these cases, a pedagogy of *concientización* prompts students to examine the structural apparatuses that support racism.

Students may just as likely react to antiracist feminist pedagogy by retreating into silence or denial. Silence ensures invisibility; it provides protection and masks the rage students can feel when confronted with racism and sexism (Srivastava 117; Montoya 536). Speaking about politically motivated but deeply personal issues requires not only courage and conviction but also academic preparation. Thus, our task in the classroom centers upon convincing students that their experiences matter and are relevant to the production of revolutionary knowledge, that they can become agents of change, that they have the power to challenge racist and sexist domination. I teach students that rather than internalizing their anger or passively accepting discrimination, they need to engage in collective action that fosters social change. This response demonstrates how a liberatory classroom encourages the pedagogical goals of discovery and learning.

Linking Service to Activism:
Empowerment and Transformation

Besides engaging critical issues, the pedagogy of *concientización* requires that professors step outside of the classroom and connect with students in multiple ways. I see mentoring in a politicized context, thus I believe, along with Freire, that its main purpose is to facilitate revolutionary learning outside the classroom and thereby refocus our energy on institutional, as opposed to personal or individual strategies for liberation. Mentoring students presents multiple challenges. As a female professor of color, I find myself in a perpetual catch–22. Many of the dilemmas I face are framed by my racialized feminist and political principles or what Patricia Hill Collins defines as the "ethic of caring." Female professors of color who mentor students encounter a host of gender biases that most men never confront. Many students expect women academics to assume the role of surrogate mother, providing them with "unconditional nurturing." Students' socialization leads them to become dependent on female professors who they anticipate are open and approachable. However, they do not put these same burdens on male colleagues whom they may perceive as distant, disinterested, and authoritarian. This places women faculty of color in a paradoxical situation. For example, when, because of my own multiple responsibilities, I am unable to immediately attend to my students' needs, they are quick to criticize me and label me as "*creída*" (uppity). In their minds, my image shifts from the "all forgiving nurturing mother" to the heartless "bearded mother" who exercises power over her students (Friedman 206; Morgan 50).

Alexander Astin and others document the importance of faculty and student interaction inside and outside the classroom as an essential factor in a quality education. Astin emphasizes that within the California State University system, the potential failure or success of students is ultimately determined by the quality of the interaction with the professor. He argues that students at elite institutions possess the expertise required to maneuver through complex systems. Faced with substandard educational systems and limited resources many students of color who enter the CSU system are academically vulnerable. The importance of establishing personal connections with students is reinforced by Stanton-Salazar, Vásquez, and Mehan who claim that "in order to be successful, students need to establish social relationships with those people who are not only technically capable of providing support, but who are also committed to doing so" (124). Once the student and professor establish a democratic relationship based on trust and mutual respect, direct intervention can lead to transformation.

Beyond academic mentoring we are being asked to compensate for the inequities of the secondary educational system that fails to train students to think analytically, research their own projects independently and produce the expository essays required at the university. Moreover, students whose writing skills need attention often view critical comments as a personal affront and not as constructive criticism. I have overheard student's say that "I bloodied their paper" precisely because they are so unaccustomed to receiving any type of detailed critique of their written work. Under these circumstances mentoring students can, for many, become a burden. In contrast, Robles notes the high level of commitment of Latina faculty and their willingness to "engage in multiple leadership roles by sharing information on career opportunities, establishing networks of scholarly support, providing necessary research and instructional guidance, and generally helping ensure that future Latino women leaders and young intellectuals avoid the adobe ceiling that many encounter" (98). This type of commitment is admirable, but are we creating expectations for ourselves as unrealistic as those held by the students? Are we placing an undue amount of responsibility on the shoulders of minority faculty to ensure the academic success of the students? Faculty are not solitary agents of change; alone they cannot compensate for the lack of public commitment, or the absence of institutional support for students of color. Politicized and/or well-meaning faculty who unselfishly assume these multiple roles can, in the end, simply absolve the institution of its ultimate responsibility for addressing students' needs.

Conclusions

Latina professors, as María de la Luz Reyes insightfully illuminates, remain an "endangered species," since very few of us actually complete our degrees, enter academia, or receive tenure. But equality within higher education is not a privilege; it is right that many have struggled to establish. We must have the courage to defend the principle of equality within higher education in order to create the conditions for others to follow. The changing racial/ethnic composition of our students forces us to grapple with the contradictory ways that traditional canons have undermined educational opportunities for students of color. Eurocentric institutional norms and political ideologies continue to shape the subject matter we teach and related social attitudes. Under these circumstances, it is no longer sufficient to merely promote a "liberal" tolerance for differences that incorporates the experience of people of color as a postscript in the curriculum. This additive approach leads to indifference or worse yet, reproduces existing patterns of exclusion and segregation. The limited resources, hostile environment, and lower academic expectations that permeate public schools leave marginalized students ill-equipped to cope with the demands of the university. Consequently, students' shortcomings do not reflect their lack of personal initiative, but rather underscore the structural and economic inequity that places people of color and those from working-class origins on an unequal footing with their Euroamerican and class-privileged peers.

In keeping with the philosophy of *concientización,* the mission of radical educators of color is to empower students to take control of their own destinies, both inside and outside of academia. Through critical reflection and self-actualization, we can raise the level of consciousness among students and transform classrooms into sites of antiracist, feminist resistance and hope. By providing students of all backgrounds the public space necessary to voice their opinions and the power to make decisions about their educational process, we can create the conditions for a community of learners who possess the vision and commitment necessary to help transform the broader society.

Note

1. *Concientización* is a conceptual framework originated by Paulo Freire in his theory of radical education and political reform; I will be mobilizing this concept throughout this chapter. Gloria Anzaldúa takes up Freire's concept in her theory of *mestiza consciousness,* which she elaborates in *Borderlands: La frontera* and *Making Face, Making Soul/Haciendo Caras: Creative and Critical Perspectives by Feminists of Color.*

Works Cited

Anzaldúa,Gloria. *Borderlands: La Frontera.* San Francisco, Calif.: Aunt Lute Foundation Books, 1987.

———. *Making Face Making Soul/Haciendo Caras: Creative and Critical Perspectives by Feminists of Color.* San Francisco: Aunt Lute Foundation Books, 1990.

Astin, Alexander. Public Lecture. California State University, Dominguez Hills, April, 2000.

Baez, Benjamin. "Faculty of Color and Traditional Notions of Service." *Thought and Action: NEA Higher Education Journal* 15. 2 (Fall 1999): 131–138.

Collins, Patricia Hill. *Black Feminist Thought: Knowledge, Consciousness and the Politics of Empowerment.* New York: Routledge, 1991.

Darder, Antonia. *Culture and Power in the Classroom.* New York: Bervin and Garvey, 1991.

De la Luz Reyes, Maria. "Chicanas in Academe: An Endangered Species." *Radical In<ter>ventions—Identity, Politics, and Differences in Educational Praxis.* Ed. Suzanne de Castell and Mary Bryson. Albany: State University of New York Press, 1997, 15–37.

Exum, William "Climbing the Crystal Stair: Values, Affirmative Action and Minority Faculty." *Social Problems* 30. 4 (1983): 383–399.

Flores, Juan. *From Bomba to Hip-Hop: Puerto Rican Culture and Latino Identity.* New York: Columbia University Press, 2000.

Freidman, S. S. "Authority in the Feminist Classroom: A Contradiction in Terms?" *Gendered subjects: The Dynamics of Feminist Teaching.* Ed. M. Culley and C. Portuges. Boston: Routledge and Kegan Paul, 1985.

Freire, Paulo, *Pedagogy of the Oppressed.* New York: Herder and Herder, 1972.

hooks, bell. "Choosing the Margin as a Space of Radical Openness." *Yearning: Race, Gender and Cultural Politics.* Boston, Mass.: South End Press, 1990.

——. *Teaching to Transgress: Education as the Practice of Freedom.* New York: Routledge, 1994.

La Belle, Thomas J. and Christopher R. Ward. *Multiculturalism and Education: Diversity and its Impact on Schools and Society.* Albany: New York State University Press, 1994.

Mohanty, Chandra Talpade. "On Race and Voice: Challenges for Liberal Education in the 1990s." *Between Borders: Pedagogy and the Politics of Cultural Studies.* Ed. Henry Giroux and Peter McLaren. New York: Routledge, 1994, 145–166.

Montoya, M. "Un/Masking the Self While Un/braiding Latina Stories." *Critical Race Theory: The Cutting Edge.* Ed. R. Delgado. Philadelphia: Temple University Press, 1995, 529–39.

Morgan, K. P. "The Paradox of the Bearded Mother: The Role of Authority in the Feminist Classroom." Unpublished paper, University of Toronto, 1988.

Nieto, Sonia. *The Light in Their Eyes: Creating Multicultural Learning Communities.* New York: Teachers College Press, 1999.

Ng, Roxana. "A Woman Out of Control: Deconstructing Sexism and Racism in the University." *Radical In<ter>ventions—Identity, Politics, and Differences in Educational Praxis.* Ed. Suzanne de Castell and Mary Bryson. Albany: State University of New York Press, 1997, 39–57.

Pardo, Mary. *Mexican American Women Activists.* Philadelphia: Temple University Press, 1998.

Robles, Barbara J. "Latinas in the Academy: Profiling Current and Future Scholars." *Reflexiones 1999: New Direction in Mexican American Studies.* Ed. Richard Flores. Austin: University of Texas Press, 2000, 91–113.

Srivastava, Aruna. "Anti-Racism Inside and Outside the Classroom." *Dangerous Territories: Struggles for Difference and Equality in Education.* Ed. Leslie G. Roman and Linda Eyre. New York: Routledge, 1997, 113–126.

Stanton-Salazar, Ricardo, Olga A. Vásquez, and Hugh Mehan. "Engineering Success Through Institutional Support." *Strategic Interventions in Education: Expanding the Latina/Latino Pipeline.* Ed. Hurtado, Figueroa, and Garcia. Santa Cruz: Regents of University California, 1996, 100–134.

Video Productions. *Shattering the Silence.* Gail Pellettin, Executive Director, 1997.

CHAPTER SEVEN

QUEER THEORY AND FEMINIST PEDAGOGY[1]

Nancy Sorkin Rabinowitz

I have been writing (and not writing) this essay for more than a year now. What has made it so difficult to finish? For one thing, like most college teachers, I was trained in a field (literary studies) not in teaching, and I don't usually write about pedagogy—I just do it. More significantly, the problems I planned to address here—specifically my teaching of a queer theory course ("Practical Feminist Criticism: Across Gender, Race, and Sexuality") in a particular semester (Fall 1996), from a particular identity position (heterosexual woman)—can't be contained in a neat narrative of what happened that semester; they refuse to stay put for at least two reasons. One, what I experienced in teaching illuminates and is illuminated by current theoretical debates between feminism, gay/lesbian studies, and queer theory; two, the issues of identity and authority surrounding my teaching the course have been replicated (though with a difference) in working on this essay. The question of who gets to teach or speak in the classroom also becomes a question of authorial authority: Who am I to write this essay? The anxiety surfaced in a different form when I attended seminars with Judith Butler and Leo Bersani in the summer of 1999; there I was a student not a teacher, and a novice compared to my classmates (especially in the Bersani seminar) who were on the whole much younger than I am. In addition, there still seems to be a risk to doing this work. While in Berkeley, I often found myself explaining what I was doing to people outside academia. As I moved around from location to location I was intensely aware of how I changed my presentation of what I was writing because what seemed totally acceptable (even de rigueur) in the seminar setting seemed unspeakable outside of it. Thus, at a dinner table with a therapist, a businessman, and a lawyer, I called it a paper on "Gay and Lesbian Studies"; talking to my friends, I called it "queer theory and pedagogy." Clearly, there was a charge attached to the word "queer." Finishing the essay has been more difficult than usual, then, because the problems I address are not securely located in the past, nor located in another scene (the one where I am the teacher and others are the students). Finally, to make matters worse, I do not have answers for most of my own questions; thus, I offer no miracle cure here, but will instead try to lay out some of the issues raised by teaching what you "are" not.

"Why Are You Teaching this Course?"

Let me start with the history of the institution at which I teach because that context was crucial in my developing the course. Hamilton is a well-established, highly selective, liberal arts college; all-male since 1812, it founded a coordinate women's college, Kirkland, in 1968. It was a very traditional men's school, and in many ways Kirkland College was designed to be its polar opposite. In 1978 Hamilton dissolved the women's school and absorbed it; in a bit of unproblematized heterocentrism, those of us fighting the merger wore T-shirts proclaiming that "Living together is better than being married," but we did not carry the day. A more traditional arrangement—whereby the woman's college changed her name and lost her identity—ensued. But given the Kirkland history, Hamilton is not quite the school it once was and is full of interesting paradoxes. It is still very male-dominated on the administrative and trustee levels (and to a lesser extent in the faculty, especially at the senior ranks); students' social lives remain closely tied to a vigorous system of private societies, although men can no longer live in fraternity houses (the sororities never did have houses). But, at the same time, feminism and Women's Studies are very strong at Hamilton, and I have been privileged to be part of a progressive Women's Studies community dedicated to doing antiracist work and to forming multiracial alliances. In part because of the nasty transition to coeducation, in part because of the larger social context of the 70s, some of us joining the faculty in the early days of Second Wave feminism felt a seamlessness between scholarly work (feminist criticism was an exciting new field), work in the classroom (challenging the canon[s]), and political work for women. That unity is now gone, but I still hanker after it. "Practical Feminist Criticism: Across Gender, Race and Sexuality" was the latest incarnation of my first "Images of Women in Literature" course at Kirkland; thus, it grew out of that earlier moment in feminist organizing and thinking and it retained the political motivation. Much had changed, however, and I now think that it was problematic to assume that queer theory could simply be a subheading of feminist criticism.

The title of the course (carefully chosen, a variation on the title of an essay by Eve Kosofsky Sedgwick on Willa Cather [Sedgwick 1989]) and the course description were somewhat vague, in other words, closeted, as much for the sake of students who might not want to have "queer" on their transcript as for ease of passage through the committee structure. Indeed, students had asked another instructor to change the name of an explicitly titled "Queer Theory" course after they were already enrolled because they did not want parents or prospective employers to know that they had even taken such a course. In this instance, to study the theory was to run the risk of *being or seeming to be* queer. Since many students in any case don't read the catalog carefully, on the first day of the semester, I announced that this feminist criticism course was really a queer theory course. I also announced that I intended it to be gay-affirming and antihomophobic. After I made my statement, the leader of the gay/lesbian/bisexual/transgendered/questioning student group (the Rainbow Alliance) asked me whether I had thought about why I was teaching it. Though I don't remember her exact words, I translated them, correctly I believe, into the question of "Who was I to teach this course?"

Who indeed? I had been moving toward offering a course on sexuality since 1986 when students in an earlier feminist criticism course designed a syllabus in lesbian literature as their final project. Lesbian feminism already occupied a large portion of the readings, and sexuality made up a significant topic of conversation, but these students wanted an entire semester's course taught by a lesbian, for women only. In our discussion of their project, I explained the institutional structure that made it unlikely that the Comparative Literature department could insure either part of their requirement, but I took their desire seriously,[2] and in the end the department did find a one-year replacement (who turned out to be a lesbian) who was delighted to teach a course on lesbian writing. I did not teach the course myself after she left, out of respect for my students' insistence on the importance of a lesbian instructor, though I did team-teach a course on women's sexuality with a colleague in Sociology who was out on campus as a lesbian.

As you can see, the backdrop to the course was tied to a certain moment in feminism where identity politics was a strong presence. As is often noted, identity politics, articulated by women of color in response to feminism's early elision of racial and sexual difference in its concentration on the universal subordination of "woman," pushed feminism from a focus on wom*an* to a recognition of differences between wom*en*, and to a demand for a curriculum expanded to include many different "women's voices." It also seemed to line up who we are with what we do, thus with what we teach. Certainly there was an expectation that women would teach Women's Studies, that women of color would be central to the transformation of the Women's Studies curriculum, that faculty members of African descent would teach Africana Studies. Gay and Lesbian Studies, as a scholarly initiative growing out of the Gay Liberation movement, fit within that model and might correspond to a demand that gay and lesbian teachers teach Gay and Lesbian Studies, and that they be out as they do so (Silin, cf. Khayatt). Identity politics provided a base for an educational movement that could include new knowledges, act affirmatively in hiring, and provide role models for students at risk. These advantages were not without attendant difficulties, however—did we want to expand beyond our identity groups? If so, how did we do it? We have not been able to solve the problems that Bernice Reagon pointed out almost 30 years ago when she analyzed the necessity as well as the pain of doing coalition politics. As she puts it, you can't stay in your little barred room. How do you deal with the other people you have to let in the room? Classrooms are not our homes; they are more like places for building coalitions, but students and teachers alike are often looking for "safe spaces" or the comfort of home there and are unpleasantly surprised when we find out that we don't all agree.

Queer Theory or Gay and Lesbian Studies

I described the course as about "queer theory" that day and not Gay/Lesbian studies. The phrasing was a matter of timing (before 1991 queer theory can hardly be said to have existed, but by 1996 it was common parlance),[3] but also strategic, for queer theory is not just a synonym for Gay and Lesbian Studies.[4] As is clear from my ambivalence at the dinner table, the word "queer" is much more "in your face" than "gay" and "lesbian"; Queer Nation and queer politics in general seem more confrontational than (and present themselves as radical in opposition to an assimilationist) gay politics. Teresa de Lauretis uses the term "queer theory" to "mark a certain critical distance from the latter [lesbian and gay], by now established and often convenient, formula" (iv). Similarly, in the initial issue of a new journal, *GLQ: A Journal of Lesbian and Gay Studies*, the editors say that the "Q" stands for the "academic legitimacy of *quarterly*" but is also a gesture "towards the fractious, the disruptive, the irritable, the impatient, the unapologetic, the bitchy, the camp, the *queer*"; with growing institutional recognition, "lesbian and gay studies runs the risk of losing its edge and narrowing its desires" (iv).[5]

Because of this in-your-face status, queer might have been threatening to the "typical Hamilton student." Intended as the reclaiming of an insult, "queer" can still sound pejorative to those who are not aware of its new meanings, or for those who are aware but don't accept that usage and cringe at the echoes of shame it sets off.[6] I used it anyway in part to avoid the very problems of identity politics; though more aggressive, queer is paradoxically much more inclusive than the label "gay/lesbian." On the simplest level, the term provides an umbrella so that we don't have to keep adding "identities" or resort to LGBT"W" (for "whatever," to quote Michael Warner).[7] The term can refer to many sexualities (and may even refer to other forms of dissent).[8] At the same time, as Douglas Crimp has suggested, queer may be a form of identification, based on a political affiliation, instead of a form of identity on the analogy of ethnicity. Thus it is potentially more accepting of straight-but-not-narrow allies.

There is a corollary intellectual expansiveness to queer theory, because it tends to problematize heterosexual orthodoxy without necessarily tracing out an alternative history and identity for gay sexuality. The name "Gay and Lesbian Studies" (like "Women's Studies" or "African American Studies") appears to take for granted the existence of an entity with a recognizable identity that one can study, whereas queer theory claims not to study some one thing but to displace, decenter, and problematize the cultural assumptions of heteronormativity. The difference between Gay/Lesbian Studies on the one hand and queer theory on the other has been structured as that between "minoritizing" or "universalizing" discourses. Eve Sedgwick's formulation (1990, 1) has become all but canonical: "The book will argue that an understanding of virtually any aspect of modern Western culture must be, not merely incomplete, but damaged in its central substance to the degree that it does not incorporate a critical analysis of modern homo/heterosexual definition; and it will assume that the appropriate place for that critical analysis to begin is from the relatively decentered perspective of modern gay and antihomophobic theory." Further down on the same page, Sedgwick distinguishes between the minoritizing view (seeing the "homo/heterosexual definition" as of importance to a "small, distinct, relatively fixed homosexual minority") or the universalizing view (which sees that relation as "an issue of continuing, determinative importance in the lives of people across the spectrum of sexualities"). Similarly, Michael Warner argues that queer "represents, among other things, an aggressive impulse of generalization; it rejects a minoritizing logic of toleration or simply political interest-representation in favor of a more thorough resistance to regimes of the normal" (1993, xxvii). The movement from Gay and Lesbian Studies to queer theory, from minoritizing to universalizing perspectives provides a powerful way of reading. At the risk of oversimplifying and positing an identity for queer theory (which is based on resistance to such moves), I would say that the two correspond roughly to identity-based movement/discipline and postmodern antimovement and antidiscipline. In calling the course queer, then, I was throwing my lot in with those who look at queerness as a way of destabilizing all norms, and who are not necessarily interested in tracing out a single history of any one group.

First Day of Class

To return to the first day of class, it now seems to me that I had attempted to foreclose the question of "who was I to teach" by naming the subject matter as queer theory; as I indicated earlier, I was encouraged to teach the course because of these developments and the seeming inclusiveness of the word "queer"—its potential for staking out a post-identitarian politics as well as its exciting intellectual claims. That did not mean that identity politics and its concerns were eliminated in me or in the class, however; you could say that identity politics were the unarticulated repressed of the course.[9] I see now that because of the hold of identity politics on me I *assumed* I knew what my student meant; I never asked.[10] That moment and my blushing reaction consolidated an identity for me, outed me as hetero sexual. Of course, I was already implicitly "out," for though I do not announce my sexuality in class, I *am* married and my students know it: my husband teaches at the same institution; I wear a wedding ring, and we share a last name. In beginning literature classes, when we are discussing sexuality, I often tell my students that knowing all those things does not mean that they know my sexuality (for they do not know the particulars of my sexual history or my desire or forms of pleasure), but that is something of a cheat; if they make the crude assumption, they are in large part correct not about some essential me, but about the privileged position I occupy.[11] Let's face it; most of the world makes the same assumptions and *treats me accordingly.*

In answering my interlocutor, I replied that of course I had asked myself whether I should teach the course, and that such questions were built into the course material because we would be discussing identity formation. Though I didn't say this at the time, I hadn't wanted to foreground the issue of my position the first day because to do so seemed defensive. I had assumed that my history as an ally would stand in place of some hardened notion of identity; moreover, I think I hoped that teaching the course would be a way to continue to act as an ally. In my answer I focused on the question of epistemology. I took a deep breath and answered that there was more than one way to know something; we might not know a great deal about those things we are born into (for instance, I am not equipped to teach Jewish Studies just because I have Jewish parents). Of course, our positions often lead us to educate ourselves because we may care more and take the time to find out about things that affect us closely, but that is not the only motive for education. I pointed out that while my students indisputably had lesbian and transgender experience, I did have much to teach them about how to read, think, and write, and I had studied "the subject." I also have a knowledge based on lived experience of political struggle within the institution, which could be useful for those attempting to make progress on similar fronts.

Feminist Pedagogy

The fact that I had to take a deep breath, and that I felt my ears burning, indicate that I also responded on another level, one that is not purely epistemological. What else was going on? Such a question was not an example of the obvious sort of ideologically-based "resistance" that we so often encounter in the classroom when teaching about race or sexuality to members of dominant groups; rather, it was based on the success of feminism and identity politics—the recognition that people bring different knowledges to bear on the material.[12] The fundamental feminist observation that the personal is the political, that knowledge is partial, and a matter of perspective led to the claim that experience "counts," and to a consequent emphasis on the importance of hearing different voices, valuing diverse experience, and empowering the disempowered.[13]

Not only was my student's question premised on a certain feminist ideology, but my teaching style grew out of that same tradition. Like many feminists, I have sought out for myself a position of teacher as liberator. If the traditional classroom was masculine and depended on teacher's "power over" students, feminists felt that the teacher should share that power and give visibility and voice where it had been denied. At first these powerlines seemed clear, if not easy to change. Women students (compared to men) were silent in class and should be encouraged to speak up because that was the way they would get the most out of their education. That single axis has become a much more three-dimensional grid.[14] First, not all student silence is a result of disempowerment or timidity; it may be a sign of arrogance ("I don't have to explain to *you*."); it may be a means of protection ("You couldn't understand anyway."). Second, the power does not go in one direction from teacher to student in a simple way. The teacher's race, sexuality, and gender may mitigate against her authority, and student claims of authority on the basis of identity can do the same (as they did in my classroom). In this case, my student did not seem to need me to empower her. How did her question affect other students? Was it an attempt to disempower me? Which brings me, third, to the teacher's legitimate authority. Like many of my colleagues, I have increasingly emphasized that allowing space for silenced voices does not mean simply accepting every statement uncritically.[15] In general, I know more than my students, I am highly trained, and I have a more grave responsibility for the classroom. In practice, there may be a conflict between the expectations of the empowering function of feminist education and education's obligation to question assumptions. Indeed, the classroom may not feel empowering when the teacher and other students challenge a student's newly acquired sense of identity.

So far I have been discussing the prioritization of experience in early feminist pedagogy. Given queer theory's distrust of identity positions and its assertion that to name oneself is to place oneself under a sign and thus potentially to support the very regimes the label was designed to oppose, what is or should be the status of experience in the queer theory classroom?[16] In the wake of postmodernism, I now often sit in rooms full of feminist/queer teachers who proudly announce that they refuse to allow any personal narrations, that they are not therapists. I agree, we are not trained as healers, but in classes where the family, rape, gay bars, or crossdressing is the topic, our discussions are not simply a matter of intellectual consequence; moreover these classrooms may be the only site for discussion of these issues without blame. Thus, personal experience will come up and is relevant. But experience without examination does not necessarily constitute good evidence, and the teacher has the job of pushing students if no one else does. Students and teacher alike must be open to the possibility that the reading can and will change their perspective, otherwise what is the point of reading? In class I negotiate the critical divide between what I have to offer as teacher and scholar, and how that relates to the experiences that the students (and I) brought to the discussion. Here as elsewhere, we can (must?) continue to refuse the "either/or" formulation and instead foreground the tension in our classrooms.[17] What I mean by that is that we have to be bold enough to call attention to problematic reliance on untheorized experience, as much as we have to allow the use of experience to interrogate theory.

Queer Theory and Curricular Politics

As Women's Studies, African American Studies, and Gay and Lesbian Studies grew out of identity-based political movements, so queer theory has a political aspect, and as some fear the dilution of Gay and Lesbian Studies by queer theory, so too there is a concern that queer theory and postmodern strategies in general are apolitical, and that the anti-essentialism of queer theory undercuts the particularity of lesbianism and gay activism.[18] The tension between identitarian and post-identitarian thought and politics (the gay and lesbian vs. the queer) may also have created friction between my political (antihomophobic) and intellectual interests in teaching the course. On the one hand, the course grew from my recognition of the oppressive nature of heterocentrism and homophobia and how they affect all of us: self-identified queers, those passing for straight or queer, and self-identified heterosexuals. The climate at Hamilton was such that teaching a course on sexuality seemed radical; it was the most silenced site of struggle in the sense that including racial difference in courses was acceptable and desirable, but sexual orientation is still not widely understood as a significant factor of analysis. At the same time, homophobic harassment seemed a fact of life at

Hamilton, and one of the student leaders in the class had been a target of threatening phone calls for two years and was to be the target of violent graffiti outside her door, as well as a physical attack before she would graduate (in 1998). There were upsurges in activism, well-organized demonstrations, in response to these events, but the college was unable to stop the harassment or to find the culprits.

I do this work in the classroom, as Bonnie Zimmerman (21) puts it,

> to save our lives. And by that I mean the lives of lesbian and gay students and faculty, but also the life of society in general . . . we provide an education that validates the reality of gay and lesbian students; second, we liberate heterosexual students, and thereby lesbian and gay students, from the prejudices and misconceptions of the dominant society; third, we expand the boundaries of what is knowable; and fourth, we push to the extreme the limits of social tolerance and the acceptance of cultural diversity.

Curricular transformation work relies on the assumption that our courses can work for social justice—by teaching old material differently (e.g., by pointing out the gaps in heterocentrist readings), by teaching new material (either queer theory or specifically gay/lesbian/bisexual texts), and by revealing and confronting attitudes and assumptions that we bring to bear as we read, speak, and write. How easily does that project cohere with the agenda of queer theory? Queer theory implies that there are no queers, only self-identified "queers"; even more to the point, it claims to be about challenging the very categories themselves. Thus, queer theory is good for analyzing what discursive forces are constructing the "boundaries" and what is behind the "prejudices and misconceptions," but how does it "validate the reality of gay and lesbian students" if it denies such categories as the basis for identity? Though a gay/lesbian focus would, strictly speaking, ignore many other sexualities also outlawed by compulsory heterosexuality, it has the advantage of increasing the visibility of lesbians and gays in history; it is important to reveal that Wilde, Whitman, Plato, and Shakespeare loved other men, that male homoeroticism of at least one sort was acceptable even praiseworthy in antiquity, and that you can read *for sexuality*. A queer perspective would ideally include many different kinds of sexualities, would problematize the subject of sexuality in general, and would reveal structures of heteronormativity. While the universalizing strand of queer theory makes it a powerful teaching strategy, it is not without costs for self-identified or closeted queer students who are steeped in the hetero-world from birth. Queer theory challenges authority based on identity, but how useful is it to deconstruct the subject position that has been won with difficulty? This is not an idle question but one with personal ramifications for young undergraduates.

What should a queer pedagogy be? Syntactically, the word "queer" can refer both to subject and object: teaching queer materials and teaching any material from a queer perspective.[19] William Haver and Deborah Britzman have been working on a radical formulation of what queer pedagogy can do. For Haver (291) it is a way of interrupting and making "strange, queer or even cruel what we had thought to be a world." This pedagogy would seem to be totally distinct from the necessity of teaching as a gay man and being out, as asserted by Jonathan G. Silin. The relative merits of these strategies depends on what (or who) we take teaching to be for.

Angus Gordon places some of the most advanced work in queer theory in the context of discussions of queer adolescence. Gordon cites Butler and Sedgwick at length; he analyzes what he takes to be Sedgwick's problematic (1993a, 1) citation of statistics on the rates of queer youths' suicide, which she says are "haunting" Gay and Lesbian Studies. His critique of the sentimentality of the appeal to dying youth makes me uncomfortable because I found those same statistics and Sedgwick's implicit point—that teaching is a way to combat gay youths' suicide—very moving. The statistics on gay youth and suicide seem to me to be evidence of the power of homophobia and a compelling argument for "doing something." As teachers, that means teaching something. Nonetheless, as Gordon points out, these statistics are very easy to question: what is a "queer" teenager anyway? So what do we do? Gay and Lesbian Studies might present those figures on suicide as part of the story of what it is like growing up gay, or as evidence of the costs of homophobia. Queer theory might interrogate the categories and the very heterosexual matrix out of which they (and the youth behind them) come. I would like to try to do both: use queer theory's interrogation of assumptions to encourage us to take committed positions that do not later trap us.

The point of our teaching is both to move to thought and to move to action—action based on clear thinking. We need to hold onto the activist source of the push for identity-based studies (Africana, Latino/a, Women's, Gay/Lesbian)—the belief that our classes could make a difference, could fight racism, sexism, homophobia.[20] At Hamilton, we now have a first-year seminar in "diversity" because we hope to open people's minds by making them take difference seriously. Can we do so? Is it logical to think that there is a causal connection between a course and behavior? Sometimes it works. Richard Mohr describes his success in teaching "Gay 101":

> One of the most up-tight suburbanite women in the class, someone who made dramatic strides through the three weeks in shedding mental and social encrustations, works part-time at a local shelter for runaways. . . . That these gay people, completely unknown to me, have ended up in a gay support group in a little Midwestern town rather than staring vacantly around the

New York Port Authority bus terminal, reduces to insignificance the class's mentioned and unmentioned disasters, and increases my sense of pride and hope. (57).

To make heterosexual students see that they have something to gain by understanding the work of subjection performed by notions of sexuality would be a productive task for "queer" classrooms to take on. Some of the most powerful moments in my teaching have come when I have turned the light on the constructedness of heterosexuality and what makes it appear natural, when we have discussed the constructedness of the very hetero-homo binary.

I find myself ambivalent about the pedagogical efficacy of the expansiveness of queer theory as the whole story, as I do about the analogous moves from women to gender, from race to racialization. The rise of queer theory has been challenged of course. First, there is a fear that the specificity of gay and lesbian lives may be lost in the shuffle. What if queer ceases to have a relation to sexuality and comes to mean anything in opposition (as it sometimes seems to do now)? What then happens to people oppressed on the basis of their sexuality? Second, the inclusiveness leads to suspicions about the very ease with which presumably straight people like myself can take it up. Its expansiveness might mean that anyone can teach queer theory because queerness isn't about "being" in some fixed concept of identity but about performance and positions one can take on. One can be queer in one's reading however straight one's sexuality might seem. It is a problem if we end up with queer studies without any queers (cf. Modleski on feminism without women; Halperin, 39; Savoy). Thus while I agree that heterosexuality must be denaturalized and interrogated, that work should not be done in isolation from the work of giving students a sense of the literature and history that might be "legitimately" labeled gay or lesbian.

On the other hand, the total collapse of identity with field of study is not desirable either. That way lies the requirement that you (always? only?) teach what you "are," and pragmatically speaking that can be very difficult for an untenured gay or lesbian faculty member in an unsympathetic department. The difficulties that I face in teaching as an outsider to gay and lesbian life are perhaps no less daunting than those facing an insider. For instance, when I team-taught the course on women's sexuality, my untenured colleague felt less comfortable privileging lesbianism in the syllabus. It seemed like special pleading to her, whereas it was easy for me to say that we had to introduce lesbianism early and as a central framing element of the course. I believe that those of us with heterosexual privilege and other kinds of protection (like tenure) have the responsibility to articulate the political significance of sexuality. As Women's Studies faculty we have pushed ourselves to get beyond a white women's heterosexual past; we have trained ourselves in reading groups and pedagogy study groups; we have insisted that it is the responsibility of everyone to do this work. To the statement that "we can't have the experience," I can reply that I can't fully know Euripides' life conditions either, and that does not stop me from teaching Greek tragedy.[21] The point has to be, of course, that it's not just your race, gender, or sexuality that qualifies you; it's also a matter of scrupulous attention to the material.

It seems that a difficult balancing act is required. Just as affirmative action is related to (but not coextensive with) multiculturalism, so civil rights for sexual minorities is related to teaching gay/lesbian history, literature, and queer theory. And as you can't make a revolution without coalition, so we can't change the curriculum without allies either. The point is, of course, that one course can't do it all. My course was offered in isolation, not as part of a program where we could have courses in gay and lesbian history, material on gay and lesbian authors within mainstream courses, and courses in queer theory. We need many different people teaching from many different positions and institutional locations so that the questions don't always appear to come from one place. As there are many sites for teaching Women's Studies (in departments as well as in the Women's Studies programs), so we need a multifaceted approach to queer studies. By approaching homophobia along with racism and classism in the Women's Studies classroom we can raise consciousness about it; we can resist the hegemony of heterosexuality, for instance in literature classes, by exposing the complicated lines of sexual desire underlying apparently "straight"-forward romantic plots; but there also needs to be a place for the sustained study of sexuality if we want to accomplish all of Zimmerman's aims.

"Who Gets to Speak?"

All of these issues are related to the one question of who was I to teach the course; other related issues came up as the course went on and developed its personality. For classes do indeed have characters; we plan our courses for some ideal audience, but we teach them to those who enroll. The class was small (eight students at first), all female, and I knew five of them. Four of the students were lesbians active in the Rainbow Alliance, and three of those women presented themselves as butch-identified; one identified as femme. Only one of the students spoke as a woman of color, though one might have observed that there were two women of color in the room. Most were not from privileged class backgrounds by Hamilton's standards. There was also quite a range of experience with Women's Studies or feminist criticism: one of the straight women in the class had taken no Women's Studies courses, one had started but dropped an introductory Women's Studies course, while the others all had some background, and most were Women's Studies majors. Their inexperience with postmodern theory and ignorance about it was considerable: not one of them knew that Foucault was a gay man.

In designing the course, I was unprepared for this diversity of background. In upper-level courses, I emphasize the fact that this is "our" course not "my" course, and I typically leave room at the end for their selections because the syllabus is a work in progress. We often go through several versions of the syllabus. Nevertheless, faculty members do have to order the books without knowing who will be in the class. I was working on the basis of the notion of queer theory that I have sketched out here, as a powerful tool for understanding the constructedness of identity, but most of my undergraduate students did not yet have a concept of a lesbian or gay canon to deconstruct. Thus, the course needed to reveal and validate sexualities that have been rendered invisible or denigrated (yes, Wilde "was gay") at the same time that it questioned those very identity categories. I assigned readings that attempted to come to terms with the problem of identity formation, but which nevertheless made a place for some provisional identity categories carefully considered. For instance, I foregrounded Maria Lugones's conception of "Playfulness and World Travelling" and Gloria Anzaldúa's *Borderlands;* Douglas Crimp's notion of identification fit here as well.²²

As the course developed "who gets to speak?" replaced "who gets to teach?" as an issue for the students. This was not an explicit question, but an enacted one nonetheless. In the beginning, the class atmosphere was intimidating; people did not feel comfortable together, particularly because of the difference in background. Perhaps I was working on the basis of a fantasy of a seminar, one where we would engage in the free exchange of ideas without rancor or reservation. As I write this, I realize that we do not often manage to meet that standard even as professionals. Trust takes time to develop and only grows when you take risks to make it happen. Some problems arise that are particular to teaching such a course in a small-college setting, where there is an even smaller queer community. In this situation, the potential for self-censorship is enormous, and the obstacles to free and open conversation came as much from the fissures within the class as from any authority residing in my faculty status (Ellsworth 314). Unfortunately the identity issue remained underground except for a very few conversations in class where it was brought explicitly to the surface by me or my early interlocutor. People did not speak from their experience or about their experience; I did not often put people on the spot demanding that they do so. Thus, their experiences remained unarticulated though it was inferred (perhaps wrongly) from the signs of gender/sexual identity or race that students presented. This pattern made for multileveled conversations, one enunciated in the room, and one silent below the surface.

In a predominantly white college, the chances are very good that classes will be predominantly white and that issues of race will be difficult to address. This class was no exception. I was committed to discussing sexuality in relation to race not apart from it, so I started with works that bring together race and sexuality. While that decision meant that race would not appear to be an afterthought, it also meant that we had to discuss racial politics while the students were still getting to know one another. The Women's Studies concentrators were used to that kind of work, but the others were not, so there were many different tensions in the room. After we read Audre Lorde's *Sister/Outsider*, the conversation was very stilted (almost nonexistent) particularly on the question of "silence"; on the second day, I insisted that we discuss our own silence. One Latina woman asserted that silence was a privilege, but she did not go further than that statement. I took her to mean that the classroom was a much more important space for her, that if race did not get discussed it was significant because it allowed the dominance of whiteness to go unchallenged; if some white students did not speak up, it did not matter to them because race does not "have" to be an issue for them. Did I get it right? I had to guess, because she did not want the responsibility for explaining Audre Lorde to the class. And given the history of students of color being called on to answer "for the race," I certainly did not want to give her that responsibilty. But was I wrong? Did she owe the group something more? I did not ask her to be explicit, and it seems to me now that I lost a valuable opportunity out of a misguided sense of politeness. Was I right in my assumption? Was she right in her assumption that the complete silence of one heterosexual white student was a power play? Was that student perhaps just insecure, afraid of making a mistake? Given that it was a small class and that students were being graded at least in part on class discussion, one could see her silence as a form of resistance to the teacher's power. On the other hand, it is very possible that the white student felt that she did not lose anything by not contributing to a conversation about racism.

There was also something of a straight/queer axis. Two of the straight-identified students were probably looking for a literature course or a non-threatening feminist course when they signed up, and were at first only comfortable with a literary analysis of texts.[23] But they stayed in the class even after my announcement that first day (one other woman did drop at that point). Was there an element of voyeurism at play, or even homophobia in their behavior? They hardly spoke up unless asked a direct question. Calling on them might have lowered the level of conversation given their unfamiliarity with the material as well as lack of experience (from their written work I could tell something about their preparation); allowing them to stay in silence meant not knowing what that silence meant. The Women's Studies concentrator who did not identify as lesbian but was not a femme-y straight woman was best able to bridge the gap; her openness and ability to speak her mind came from her familiarity with the terrain, with her fellow students, with the classroom style, as well as with me. I take her participation as a model to strive for.

Among the self-identified queer students and the lesbians, there were also strains. The dynamics between them, their reluctance to disagree with someone presumed to know more or to be a campus leader, their reluctance to hurt the feelings of a friend, turned out to be as problematic as the challenges to my credibility. I tried to explain to my most advanced students, who were also the most committed and most radical women, that their role in the class had to be in part that of teacher, which meant facilitating the participation of others by respecting their contributions. In order for that to have happened, I needed to have serious conversations with them about my philosophy of teaching, needed to pay them, or do something formal to acknowledge their level of knowledge. It is hard to handle a small class with such divergent levels of expertise, even when the subject matter is not sensitive—dividing up a Greek class according to level of ability would only be a question of time commitment, but on what basis could I have made the divisions in this case? My advanced students were entitled to a course on their level, but I could not provide it without making distinctions that I wasn't prepared to make. In retrospect, that was a mistake; different students have different needs, and as the teacher, I could have done more to address them.

It is hard to generalize on the basis of this experience because it is difficult to distinguish class dynamics from personal dynamics. As teachers we must remember that our class occupies only a few short hours of students' lives; especially at a small college, there is much seepage under the doorsill of the classroom even when the door is closed. My students inhabited a world (of political groups and sororities) that I knew little or nothing about, and that world was a factor in our class. What was subtly playing itself out in my classroom was the exclusionary force of silent identity politics. Taking queer theory as the method as well as the subject matter, I would have put that politics in question and asked more pointedly about what was going on, not to reify the categories but to unpack them. According to Butler (1993, 19), queer theory constitutes "a self-critical dimension within activism, a persistent reminder to take the time to consider the exclusionary force of one of activism's most treasured contemporary premises." If self-identifying as a member of any resistant group is both freeing and complicit with the power it sets out to resist, what is the analogue in the classroom? We can read for this double tendency not only in the authors we study but also in class discussion or in the community surrounding us. Body language (glances, smiles) revealed that the political vanguard was constituting itself as an exclusive group in my class. I found it hard to get past my most advanced students' sense that they knew it all; questioning the power of their behavior more directly would have been fruitful. At the time, I left those conversations for my office out of a misplaced desire to avoid confrontation.

There was one more element in the mix, which was the resistance to the combination of feminist and postmodern or Foucauldian assumptions in my thinking. In designing the course, I had put at the center not only race, but also those theoretical formulations that would lead to a questioning of fixed sexual identity. Thus I assigned readings that focused on butch/femme roles and transgender issues, such as Elizabeth Kennedy and Madelyn Davis's *Boots of Leather, Slippers of Gold* and Leslie Feinberg's *Stone Butch Blues*. In our discussions, the greatest tension was around questions of agency, in particular, around how much choice is revealed in butch or trans deployment of masculinity. I was stressing that masculinity is a social construct inseparable from male human beings, no matter how it is queered; the students would ask "What about their agency?" as I pointed out how narrow the cultural definition of masculinity and femininity is. In challenging the freedom of the choice to change sex, in pointing out that if there were more ways to be male or female, one would not have to change genitals, I seemed to my students to be the enemy. My postmodern feminist questioning of the constructedness of roles seemed oppressive to them. I saw myself pointing out how subject positions subject and constrain; they saw me as the source of the subjection that I was trying to critique.

Twenty-Twenty Hindsight

The atmosphere in class improved by the end of the semester, but it took time, as it always does, to make us into a group. Because the tensions I have described here were for the most part undercurrents, which occasionally surfaced in aggressive questioning of me, I tended to deal with them obliquely. My techniques were simple, based on a desire to break the tension. For one thing, I tried to make space for the heterosexually-identified women to feel welcome in the discussion. I praised them for their work on the literary texts and for their citation of specific passages. Moreover, I tried to create social occasions where we would be "more equal." Those gatherings misfired, however, in part because of the closeness of the queer group—among themselves and with me—there ended up being a lot of in-jokes but things did loosen up and we laughed together. I am not sure I could have done better with the mix of students I had. I similarly tried to encourage the silent lesbian women to speak up by having frequent office hours and by writing copious responses in their journals. It was hard to accomplish my goal of open conversation without making people speak more personally in class discussion than they were willing to do in the early part of the semester. I also tried to break the silence by speaking of my experience of being split, how I was gendered a proper woman, and so on, in order to make their questions of agency apply more generally. In retrospect, I wonder how freeing that was for others or whether it was not an assertion of privilege. Perhaps my speaking, too, needs to be problematized next time I offer such a course. Perhaps I spent too much time worrying about the barriers to open discussion; was that a result of my own position (as a "well-brought up" woman) or was it simply good pedagogy? As I have replayed the course in my head to write this essay, I have questioned my assumption that speaking is important; in the end, I remain committed to discussion as a method and reluctant to write some people off, particularly in a small seminar. It is my firm belief that students won't learn if they are not engaged. For me, that engagement is usually shown by participation in discussion.

What made the crucial difference was that the students were all required to work on a project together; they each had different strengths, and they had to use them to come up with something they could all agree to. They had originally planned to go into the local high schools and do sexuality workshops; I was amazed that they all agreed, but in the end they could not get the permission they needed. That was an education for them in itself because they had assumed that they would be welcome in any school. For their final project they made a video that did succeed in getting them all engaged, though it allowed one of the quietest students to hide behind the camera; nonetheless it did call on her very good technical skills. Clearly the switch from talking to doing something together was positive: they had to work out their differences for the project to succeed, and in working together they developed camaraderie at last. In a small way, it got them beyond their multiple positions into a new (temporary) position as collaborators. Thus, projects may be a good way to bridge gaps; in the future I won't have only one as the culmination but will introduce them into the semester at an earlier point.

You cannot plan your teaching strategies too far in advance because you cannot predict the classroom dynamics without knowing who will be taking the course. But in terms of that first question of "who was I," next time I will explain my commitment to the material; I will change the title so that the topic is more obvious, and then ask students openly why they are there and what their investment is. After all, I do this in the case of my course on "Twentieth-Century Fiction," why not with this much more politically loaded class? Moreover, I would confront openly the question of announcing or not announcing sexual identity; it is a complicated issue after all and one that reveals the difference between courses about sexuality and those about gender or race. I know that some teachers forbid announcements as a way of preempting heterosexually-identified students from distancing themselves from the material by claiming a heterosexual position. But what constitutes an announcement anyway? References to boyfriends or girlfriends? This is a conversation I would hold next time, for clearly the possible invisibility of sexual orientation means that there is a difference in the ways that race/ethnicity, gender, and sexuality play themselves out in education. The racialized other is hypervisible, while the sexualized other may be invisible.[24]

The possibilities of a radically destabilizing pedagogy, one which queers the classroom by challenging fixed positions, is attractive as a strategy for the next time I teach the course. Perhaps that first day I should have turned the conversation around more forcefully and more personally than I did; instead of simultaneously explaining myself and asking them who should study queer theory, as I did, it might have been powerful to challenge the presumption of stable subjectivity itself and the relationship between who I am and what I do. It is not clear that such a strategy would work on the first day of class at a liberal arts college with students who are at such different levels. Thus, in addition to needing more courses, we need more finely calibrated practices. Some approaches might be more useful for graduate students or for our scholarly work; we must remember that teaching is a matter of relationships as well as of material and approach.

The underlying question behind this essay has been whether "straight" people *should* teach Gay/Lesbian Studies or queer theory. The construction of a significant difference between queer theory and Gay and Lesbian Studies does not mean that there are two watertight categories; much of what queer theory claims to do could be done in Gay and Lesbian Studies by problematizing the categories. From the most expansive queer perspective, there would seem to be no problem because of queer theory's explosion of stable identities. From a more moderate stance, everyone can gain from the study since queer theory turns its lens on the constitution of the hetero/homo divide itself; it is the purview of no one group. The answer to the question of who gets to teach this material has to be "both/and," that is, people like me but not exclusively so; gays and lesbians have been at the forefront of the field, and it would be a serious loss if, as I said earlier, we have queer theory without any "queers." Similarly, the answer to the question of "who gets to speak" has to be "both/and"; the silencing that takes place as a result of the granting of authority to experience needs to be confronted. Though I would not want to segregate the groups in my class, we need more classes, so that we would not have to lump together students of disparate levels. "Practical Feminist Criticism: Across Race, Gender, Sexuality" was overdetermined; perhaps I was trying to accomplish too much—personal and political transformation as well as education in subject matter. I might narrow it down next time, but I won't give up (as I have been tempted to), for if we don't try, we most assuredly won't succeed. It is popular these days to seek a third position, beyond the binary construction; in the present instance I come back to the importance of making alliances so that we can do "both/and"—both expand curricular opportunities and make the connection between politics and knowledge.

Notes

1. Thanks go to Hamilton College for generous support, in particular Dean of Faculty Bobby Fong and President Eugene M. Tobin for making my attendance at the Berkeley Seminar possible. I owe a huge debt of gratitude to the students in my seminar, Comparative Literature 391, for pushing me to think through the issues I raise here. I also want to thank Sascha Arbouet, Adinah Bradberry, Rebecca Libed, and Stuart Murray for their crucial research assistance; Patricia Cholakian, Lydia Hamessley, Stuart Murray, Peter Rabinowitz, John Ricco and Julie Zuckerman for their perceptive and challenging comments on earlier versions; the members of the Butler and Bersani Berkeley Summer Research Seminars for conversations about queer pedagogy (especially Chris Nealon, John Ricco, Kelly Younger, Heather Lukes, Britt-Marie Schiller). And I thank my dear colleagues and editors, Amie and Susan, for inviting me to contribute to the volume, for waiting for my paper, and for their careful and rigorous reading.

2. In the summer of 1999 the administration of Boston College barred Mary Daly from her office and attempted to force her to retire at 70 for excluding men from her classes. Superior Court Justice Martha B. Sosman ruled that "a coeducational institution of higher learning may insist that all courses be open to both male and female students" (Goldberg). I was willing to fight for a women's college, but not to make gender a prerequisite for a course I was teaching at a coeducational institution.

3. In introducing Michael Warner to our seminar, Judith Butler recalled that when he interviewed her in 1993 and asked her what she thought of queer theory, she said "what is that?"

4. Judith Butler (1997, 1–3) moves back and forth between the two; for a strong working out of the differences between Gay/Lesbian and Queer Studies, see Savoy.

5. John D'Emilio and others would disagree. For him, Gay Studies is political, as is education in general: "Our social characteristics, our values, and the vantage point from which we gaze at society shape the conclusions we reach. And the ideas that we put forward in print or in the classroom help to reproduce, or to modify, or to subvert, the order of things. . . . But we are involved in an effort to reshape a world view and an intellectual tradition that has ignored, debased, and attacked same-sex relationships and that has, in the process, impoverished our understanding of human experience and human possibilities" (158). He is clear that "Colleges and universities are important institutions. . . . For me, the purpose of education . . . is to offer and refine an accurate description of reality" (159). He argues that "By having a gay studies program, we are making a statement about values, about society, and about our vision of the future" (159).

6. On shame see Sedgwick 1993b, 4; she argues that "The main reason why the self-application of 'queer' by activists has proven so volatile is that there's no way that any amount of affirmative reclamation is going to succeed in detaching the word from its associations with shame and with the terrifying powerlessness of gender-dissonant or otherwise stigmatized childhood. If 'queer' is a politically potent term, which it is, that's because, far from being capable of being detached from the childhood scene of shame, it cleaves to that scene as a near-inexhaustible source of transformational energy." Similarly, Judith Butler says: "The term 'queer' emerges as an interpellation that raises the question of the status of force and opposition, of stability and variabilitiy, *within* performativity. The term 'queer' has operated as one linguistic practice whose purpose has been the shame of the subject it names or, rather, the producing of a subject *through* that shaming interpellation. 'Queer' derives its force precisely through the repeated invocation by which it has become linked to accusation, pathologization, insult" (18). A question remains: Is queer going to turn out to be as constraining as any other liberatory slogan?

7. Address to Berkeley Summer Research Seminars, July 1999. See also de Lauretis 1991, v. Cf. Probyn (1995, 7) who associates queer theory with the way it deploys desire and resists stabilizing it.

8. On exclusiveness of gay and lesbian, see Dinshaw and Halperin (1991, iii). The capaciousness of queer theory may be a mirage, for it constitutes an "inside," as this passage from Sedgwick (1993a, 13) makes clear: "Everyone knows that there are some lesbians and gay men who could never count as queer, and other people who vibrate to the chord of queer without having much same-sex eroticism or without routing their same-sex eroticism through the identity labels lesbian or gay." Butler (1993, 20) acknowledges as much: "As expansive as the term 'queer' is meant to be, it is used in ways that enforce a set of overlapping divisions."

Halperin (1995, 61–2) makes an extensive argument that queer is not a positivity but a strategy by which "the homosexual subject can now claim an identity without an essence. . . . Those who knowingly occupy such a marginal location, who assume a de-essentialized identity that is purely positional in character, are properly speaking not gay but *queer*." What constitutes that homosexual subject? Is it same-sex desire? It seems that within this queer negativity, there is an unquestioned gay identity: "What makes 'queer' potentially so treacherous as a label is that its lack of definitional content renders it all too readily available for appropriation by those who do not experience the unique political disabilities and forms of social disqualification from which lesbians and gay men routinely suffer in virtue of our sexuality" (65). I will return to this oscillation later.

9. See Butler (1999, 17) on problems with the slogan of "acts not identities" that stands in for Foucault's idea that "bodies and pleasures" should replace regimes of sexuality. She suggests that "the regime of 'sex-desire'" returns and becomes "the 'unconscious' of the time of bodies and pleasures." Identity was working in a similar (unconscious) way in my class. We cannot do away

with identity; for some clear statements from Foucault on the importance of identity for politics, see Foucault (1984, 56).

10. I recognize what was going on then from the *effect* on me, cf. Sedgwick on the shame reaction of political correctness (1993b, 14).

11. Special thanks to Stuart Murray for pressing me to think through these issues more clearly. Any lingering lack of clarity is due to my own struggle with these formulations.

12. On feminism and experience, see the work, for instance, of Hartsock 1998, 36–37; for her standpoint theory, see Hartsock 1983; 1998, 227–48; see also Scott 1991. My experience here leads me to wonder whether in other classes I would benefit from recasting "resistance" as another knowledge instead of seeing it as ignorance. For a psychoanalytic reading of teaching, see Felman. For a non-psychoanalytic view of students' voices and students' understanding, see Ellsworth, especially 307–309.

13. On feminist pedagogy for change, see de Castell and Bryson 1997; hooks; Maher and Tetreault; Mayberry and Rose; Mohanty 1989/90. Emphasis on silenced voices in feminist pedagogy was attached to certain models of the early stages of Second Wave feminism—for instance to consciousness-raising groups where (mainly white middle-class women) learned that their experiences were not idiosyncratic but like those of other women (on the significance of consciousness raising, see, for instance, Gornick and Moran, xviii-xxii; MacKinnon; Anonymous, 1–5; Hanisch). The movement went in different directions with this fundamental realization, some seeking universal causes of what seemed to be women's universal oppression (e.g., Rosaldo 1974; cf. Rosaldo 1980; Reiter) and some seeking to understand gendered roles as socially constructed (for summaries see, de Lauretis 1986; Echols; Eisenstein 1983; Eisenstein and Jardine 1980). Early radical feminists coming out of the civil rights movement did not overlook race and class, but bourgeois feminism (as it came to be called) did. For examples of the critique of the exclusivity of feminism, see Smith 1983; Moraga and Anzaldúa; Mohanty, Russo and Torres 1991; Hull, Scott and Smith.

14. On complicated scenarios of gender and power, see Walkerdine 3–6, 9, 14.

15. Feminist pedagogy shares much with progressive pedagogy, in particular its conflicts over control in the classroom; as Walkerdine (18) says, "There was joy in my classroom. There were also terrible problems: how to control the children, for example."

16. See Butler (1991, 13) on her reluctance to speak "as a lesbian" for fear of the term's regulating power. For a statement of lesbianism as consistent with postmodernism, both constituting challenges to heteronormativity, see Kitch. Feminism has been read as the stodgy other of queer theory, forgetting that at least one sex radical critique also began within feminism though in contestation with it.

17. Although Foucault is taken to be the spokesperson for "acts not identities," he also saw narrating one's own experience as a form of resistance to the hegemonic construction (Halperin 25).

18. For a vitriolic statement of feminist problems with queer theory, see Jeffreys. Less tendentious is de Lauretis 1991, vii. Cf. Savoy, Meyers. Wilson (114) argues that feminism has become the "wicked stepmother" of queer activism; she further asserts that socialist feminism is being over-looked; she fears that emphasis on "transgression" is the "aestheticization of politics."

    For the concern about deconstructing lesbian/gay before "they have been acknowledged within the school context . . . and while invisibility remains a major problem for young lesbians and gays, but especially for young les-bians," see Epstein 281. See also Bersani on the perils of "The Gay Absence." Bersani notes "Never before in the history of minority groups struggling for recognition and equal treatment has there been an analogous attempt, on the part of any such group, to make itself unidentifiable even as it demands to be recognized" (31–32).

19. For a view of the positive results of using queer theory materials, see Greene. He believes, as I do, that "As teachers of English literature and composition, our job is to encourage and provide opportunities for students to think about and ask questions of the world, of reality, politics, and the possibility of mean-ing and truth" (337). He also holds that it is intrinsically political: "To intro-duce queer theory into the literature or composition classroom is to do a variety of things: It is first of all to immediately and intimately engage our analyses of texts with the political world" (337). That does not strike me as a necessary conclusion, though I would agree it is a desirable one.

20. This assumption has not been examined sufficiently. Clift's research showed that including a section on gay/lesbian issues into a general education course did not make a significant difference in attitudes (46). Others argue for bringing in gay/lesbian speakers on gay/lesbian topics. My experience has been that the personal acquaintance with "the other" (in one of my classes, students participated in a workshop on welfare with a former welfare recip-ient) can at least cause an awakening of sympathy. This strategy presupposes, however, someone's willingness to speak from a particular position; it also presupposes the value of "sympathy." It may also allow students to remain too comfortably the observer and thus may encourage voyeurism, pity in-stead of analysis.

21. Stuart Murray reminds me that no one in the Euripides class can claim first-hand knowledge, so these are not really parallel examples.

22. Diane Fowlkes would build a new form of identity politics based on inter-subjectivity, on the model of works like *Borderlands*. But there is a risk here too. White students in particular found it a relief to read Lugones and An-zaldúa and to look for the ways in which they were themselves constituted on borders; when that got too cozy, then my job was to point out there are borders and borders—because of their race and class privilege, they can ig-nore the borders when they are too uncomfortable.

23. See Bryson and de Castell for a similar experience: "In their journals, white straight-identified women did not make use of textual or in-class discussions

of identity to reflect on the constructedness of their own identities, but chose, rather, to consume or reject the material on the basis of abstract arguments and 'critical' rationality." (291) One of the women in my class almost failed the course because she could not get her work in, although she actually came a long way in her thinking and participation in class discussion.

24. The position of "queer" faculty member in these situations is of course different than that of a "straight" professor, and there are issues of power conferred by tenure (Bryson and de Castell, Silin, Khayatt).

Works Cited

Anonymous. *Liberation Now: Writings from the Women's Liberation Movement.* New York: Dell, 1971.

Anzaldúa, Gloria. *Borderlands/La Frontera.* San Francisco: Spinsters/Aunt Lute, 1987.

Bersani, Leo. *Homos.* Cambridge, Mass: Harvard University Press, 1995.

Britzman, Deborah P. *Lost Subjects, Contested Objects: Toward a Psychoanalytic Inquiry of Learning.* Albany: SUNY Press, 1998.

Bryson, Mary and Suzanne de Castell. "Queer Pedagogy: Practice Makes Im/Perfect." *Canadian Journal of Education* 18.3 (1993): 285–305.

Butler, Judith. "Against Proper Objects." In *Feminism Meets Queer Theory.* Ed. Elizabeth Weed and Naomi Schor. Bloomington: Indiana University Press, 1997, 1–30.

———. "Critically Queer." *GLQ: A Journal of Gay and Lesbian Studies* 1 (1993): 17–32.

———. "Imitation and Gender Insubordination." In *Inside/Out: Lesbian Theories, Gay Theories.* Ed. Diana Fuss. New York: Routledge, 1991, 13–31.

———. "Revisiting Bodies and Pleasures." *Theory, Culture & Society* 16.2 (1999): 11–20.

Clift, S. "Lesbian and Gay Issues in Education: A Study of the Attitudes of First-Year Students in a College of Higher Education." *British Educational Research Journal* 14.1 (1988): 31–50.

Crimp, Douglas. "Right On, Girlfriend!" In *Fear of a Queer Planet.* Ed. Michael Warner. Minneapolis: University of Minnesota Press, 1993, 314–18.

de Castell, Suzanne and Mary Bryson. *Radical In<ter>ventions: Identity, Politics, and Difference/s in Educational Praxis.* Albany: SUNY Press, 1997.

de Lauretis, Teresa. *Feminist Studies, Critical Studies.* Madison: University of Wisconsin Press, 1986.

———. "Introduction." *Queer Theory: Lesbian and Gay Sexualities* (special issue of *differences*) 1 (1991): iii–xviii.

D'Emilio, John. *Making Trouble: Essays on Gay History, Politics and the University.* New York: Routledge, 1992.

Dinshaw, Carolyn and David Halperin. "Introduction." *GLQ: A Journal of Lesbian and Gay Studies* 1 (1993): iii–iv.

Echols, Alice. *Daring to Be Bad: Radical Feminism in America 1967 - 1975.* Minneapolis: University of Minneapolis Press, 1989.

Eisenstein, Hester. *Contemporary Feminist Thought* Boston: G. K. Hall, 1983.
————and Alice Jardine. *The Future of Difference.* Boston: G. K. Hall, 1980.

Ellsworth, Elizabeth. "Why Doesn't This Feel Empowering? Working through the Repressive Myths of Critical Pedagogy." *Harvard Educational Review* 59.3 (1989): 297–324.

Epstein, Debbie. "Practicing Heterosexuality." *Curriculum Studies* 1.2 (1993): 275–86.

Feinberg, Leslie. *Stone Butch Blues.* Ithaca, New York: Firebrand Press, 1993.

Felman, Shoshana. "Psychoanalysis and Education: Teaching Terminable and Interminable." In *Jacques Lacan and the Adventure of Insight: Psychoanalysis in Contemporary Culture.* Cambridge, Mass: Harvard University Press, 1998, 69–97.

Foucault, Michel, with Bob Gallagher and Alexander Wilson. "Interview: Sex, Power, and the Politics of Identity." *The Advocate* 400 (August 7, 1984): 26–30.

Fowlkes, Diana. "Moving from Feminist Identity Politics to Coalition Politics Through a Feminist Materialist Standpoint of Intersubjectivity in Gloria Anzaldúa's *Borderlands/La Frontera: The New Mestiza.*" *Hypatia* 12.2 (1997): 105–24.

Garber, Linda. *Tilting the Tower: Lesbians Teaching Queer Subjects.* New York: Routledge, 1994.

Goldberg, Carey. "Facing forced Retirement, Iconoclastic Professor Keeps on Fighting." *New York Times,* August 15, 1999, Section 1.13.

Gordon, Angus. "Turning Back: Adolescence, Narrative, and Queer Theory." *GLQ: A Journal of Lesbian and Gay Studies* 5.1 (1999): 1–24.

Gornick, Vivian and Barbara Moran. *Woman in Sexist Society: Studies in Power and Powerlessness.* New York: Basic Books, 1971.

Greene, Frederick. "Introducing Queer Theory into the Undergraduate Classroom." *English Education* 18 (1996): 325–39.

Halperin, David. *Saint Foucault: Towards a Gay Hagiography.* New York: Oxford University Press, 1995.

Hanisch, Carol. "The Personal Is Political." In *Women's Liberation: Notes from the Second Year, Major Writings of the Radical Feminists.* New York, 1970, 76–78.

Hartsock, Nancy C. M. "The Feminist Standpoint: Developing the Ground for a Specifically Feminist Historical Materialism." In *Discovering Reality.* Ed. Sandra Harding and Merrill B. Hintikka. Boston: D. Reidel, 1983, 283–310.

————. *The Feminist Standpoint Revisited and Other Essays.* Boulder: Westview, 1998.

Haver, William. "Queer Research; or, How to Practise Invention to the Brink of Intelligibility." In *Eight Technologies of Otherness.* Ed. Sue Golding. London and New York: Routledge, 1997, 277–92.

hooks, bell. *Teaching to Transgress: Education as the Practice of Freedom.* New York: Routledge, 1994.

Hull, Gloria T., Patricia Bell Scott, and Barbara Smith. *All the Women Are White, All the Blacks Are Men, But Some of Us Are Brave: Black Women's Studies.* New York: Feminist Press, 1982.

Jeffreys, Sheila. "The Queer Disappearance of Lesbians: Sexuality in the Academy." *Women's International Forum* 17 (1994): 459–72.

Kennedy, Elizabeth Lapovsky and Madelyn D. Davis. *Boots of Leather, Slippers of Gold: The History of a Lesbian Community.* New York: Routledge, 1993.

Khayatt, Didi. "Sex and Pedagogy: Performing Sexualities in the Classroom." *GLQ: A Journal of Lesbian and Gay Studies* 5.1 (1999): 107–139.

Kitch, Sally L. "Straight but Not Narrow: A Gynetic Approach to the Teaching of Lesbian Literature." In *Tilting the Tower.* Ed. Linda Garber, 1994, 83–95.

Lorde, Audre. *Sister/Outsider.* Trumansburg, New York: Crossing Press, 1984.

Lugones, Maria. "Playfulness and World Travelling." *Lesbian Philosophies and Cultures.* Ed. Jeffner Allen. Albany: SUNY Press, 1990, 159–80.

MacKinnon, Catharine. "Feminism, Marxism, Method, and the State: An Agenda for Theory." *Signs Reader.* Chicago: University of Chicago Press, 1983, 227–56.

Maher, Frances A. and Mary Kay Thompson Tetreault. *The Feminist Classroom.* New York: Basic Books, 1994.

Mayberry, Maralee and Ellen Cronan Rose. *Innovative Feminist Pedagogies in Action: Meeting the Challenge.* New York. Routledge, 1999.

Meyers, Helene. "To queer or not to queer: that's not the question." *College Literature* 24: (1997):171–82.

Modleski, Tania. *Feminism Without Women: Culture and Criticism in a 'Postfeminist' Age.* New York: Routledge, 1991.

Mohanty, Chandra Talpade. "On Race and Voice: Challenges for Liberal Education in the 1990s." *Cultural Critique* (1989/90): 179–208.

Mohanty, Chandra Talpade, Ann Russo and Lourdes Torres. *Third World Women and the Politics of Feminism.* Bloomington: Indiana University Press, 1991.

Mohr, Richard. "Gay 101: On Teaching Gay Studies." *Christopher Street* 89 (1985): 49–57.

Moraga, Cherríe and Gloria Anzaldúa. *This Bridge Called My Back.* New York: Kitchen Table, 1983.

Probyn, Elspeth. "Queer Belongings." In *Sexy Bodies. The Strange Carnalities of Feminism.* Ed. Elizabeth Grosz and Elspeth Probyn. New York: Routledge, 1995, 1–18.

Reagon, Bernice. "Coalition Politics: Turning the Century." In *Home Girls: A Black Feminist Anthology.* Ed. Barbara Smith. New York: Kitchen Table Press, 1983, 356–69.

Reiter, Rayna R. *Toward an Anthropology of Women.* New York: Monthly Review Press, 1975.

Rosaldo, Michelle Zimbalist. "The Use and Abuse of Anthropology: Reflections on Feminism and Cross-Cultural Understanding." *Signs* 5 (1980): 389–417.

———and Louise Lamphere. *Woman, Culture, and Society.* Stanford: Stanford University Press, 1974.

Savoy, Eric. "You Can't Go Homo Again: Queer Theory and the Foreclosure of Gay Studies." *English Studies in Canada* 20.2 (1994): 129–52.

Scott, Joan. "The Evidence of Experience." *Critical Inquiry* 17 (1991): 773–97.

Sedgwick, Eve Kosofsky. "Across Gender, Across Sexuality: Willa Cather and Others." *South Atlantic Quarterly* 88.1 (1989): 53–72.

———. *Epistemology of the Closet.* Berkeley: University of California Press, 1990.

Sedgwick, Eve. "Queer and Now." *Tendencies.* London: Routledge, 1993a, 1–20.

Sedgwick, Eve. "Queer Performativity: Henry James's *The Art of the Novel,*" *GLQ: A Journal of Lesbian and Gay Studies* 1 (1993b): 1–16.

Silin, Jonathan G. "Teaching as a Gay Man: Pedagogical Resistance or Public Spectacle." *GLQ: A Journal of Lesbian and Gay Studies* 5.1 (1999): 95–106.

Smith, Barbara. *Home Girls: A Black Feminist Anthology.* New York: Kitchen Table Press, 1983.

Walkerdine, Valerie. *Schoolgirl Fictions.* London: Verso, 1990.

Warner, Michael. *Fear of a Queer Planet.* Minneapolis: University of Minnesota Press, 1993.

Wilson, Elizabeth. "Is Transgression Transgressive?" In *Activating Theory: Lesbian, Gay, Bisexual Politics.* Ed. Joseph Bristow and Angelia R. Wilson. London: Lawrence and Wishart, 1993, 107–117.

Zimmerman, Bonnie. "Lesbian Studies in an Inclusive Curriculum." *Transformations* 5 (1994): 18–27.

Part III

Contextualizing Difference

CHAPTER EIGHT

"WHITE GIRLS" AND
"STRONG BLACK WOMEN"
Reflections on a Decade of Teaching Black History
at Predominantly White Institutions (PWIs)

Allison Dorsey

Higher education has been transformed in the last quarter of the twentieth century. The "multicultural revolution" has mandated an increasingly diverse core curriculum and faculty in the nation's colleges and universities. Neither as broad nor as deep a change as conservative pundits fear, the landscape on America's ivy-covered campuses has been significantly altered. The history of the African American people, once limited in the curriculum and minds of many academics to a study of slavery and "gritty" ghetto life, has moved toward the mainstream. Students majoring in political science, engineering, art history, and literature find the experience of African Americans relevant to their course of study. Unfortunately, mere exposure to the subject matter does not transform the way Americans, first as students, then as real world actors, understand black historical experiences or interact with people of African descent. Certainly, it takes more than the study of history to foment change in American race relations. History, well taught, does however have the power to inspire serious contemplation about our nation's past, present, and future.

Teaching African American history has its own special set of challenges. The American Historical Association newsletter, *Perspectives,* addressed some of these challenges in 1993 (Vince Nobile's provocative essay "White Professors, Black History: Forays into the Multicultural Classroom") and again in 1998 (Robert L. Harris's "Dilemmas in Teaching African American History"). Nobile wrote of the difficulties of bridging the gap of trust between a white male professor and black students enrolled in a community college. He suggested black students were inherently distrustful and unreceptive to his understanding of history. Leon Litwack, senior scholar in African American history at University of California, Berkeley, responded to Nobile, encouraging all scholars to consider the ways "skepticism about African American history [. . .] as a serious academic endeavor" has engendered a suspicion of mainstream "paternalism," in an increasingly savvy student body. Brenda Stevenson, a scholar of African American history at UCLA, joined the discussion. She reminded Nobile and others of the "national history of racial oppression and the institutionalized distortions and marginalization of African American history" that has led black students to challenge the assumptions and perspectives of all professors who teach black history. She continued noting that "black professors [. . .] also confront the same kinds of questions and threats of rejection that Professor Nobile describes" but bear the additional burden of being deemed "sellouts" or "worthless" in the eyes of black students. Robert L. Harris's commentary focused on the tensions involved in trying to teach the stories of a separate African American experience while understanding and acknowledging the inseparable link between "mainstream" and "minority" history. "The dilemma," argues Harris, "is how to select an appropriate medium . . . which lens to use at what times, for understanding the African American past."

The experience of teaching black history at small liberal arts colleges, predominately white institutions (PWIs) has something to add to the discussions concerning the multicultural classroom and the dilemma of black history. PWIs, long-established elite institutions of higher learning, produce (and reproduce) America's ruling elite. The role such colleges play in grooming successive generations of the nation's leaders, be they corporate CEOs or heads of progressive nonprofits, is not to be underestimated. The way students at these institutions do or do not understand race has a significant impact on the national conversation about multiculturalism, diversity, and social justice.

The following discussion grows out of personal observations of the young people who have enrolled in my courses in black history during the last decade. My own teaching, with the exception of one quarter while a fellow at the Center for Black Studies at the University of California Santa Barbara, has been limited to PWIs in the east. The student bodies have been considerably less diverse than either Nobile would find at a community college or Stevenson at UCLA, though we share other challenges. All instructors of

African American history must be cognizant that students who have self-selected our courses, but pass through having missed or sloughed off under-standing, move into the real world convinced of their progressive motivations. Often they reinforce the very hierarchy that first necessitated challenges by the marginalized oppressed and excluded. Consequently, an analysis of the experiences of teaching black history at PWIs is significant in that it reveals the ways students develop understanding or reject the knowl-edge to be gained from such courses. Specifically, I believe my experiences with the use of feminist pedagogy in the classroom offer some insights into the strengths and limits of education as a tool to facilitate understanding. The following essay will detail some of the patterns of student motivation, discuss student experiences in the classroom, and comment on their under-standing of African American history. I offer my insights into the academic and political relationships that develop in the classroom, report on the ways feminist-inspired pedagogy has informed my teaching (and affected those relationships), and make suggestions that might positively influence the out-come of the study of African American history at the undergraduate level.

The Instructor

I was drawn to the study of the past because of the great stories of challenge, of resistance, and of change. Historians are, if nothing else, storytellers. We can be storytellers of great power and sometimes wisdom, modern day *griots*. A *griot* is a storyteller in the West African tradition. Most often a male, a *griot* commits to memory the entire historical record of his people. When new events and details are added to this oral history, they are centered within the context of past understanding. Contemporary historians can act as *griots*, imparting knowledge about the past, generating understanding, and giv-ing meaning to the present. This is the reason to study history, to look "at the past only by means of understanding more clearly what and who they are so that they can more wisely build the future"(Freire, 65).

I am a scholar of Southern history who specializes in the study of the African American experience. I wanted to know what newly freed blacks did to recreate their lives, families, and communities in the aftermath of slavery, (which skills learned in their time of bondage were applied to crafting their freedom). The majority of the newly freed remained in the American South, hence my interest in Southern history between the burning of Atlanta and the Great Migration. My graduate program at the University of California at Irvine, "Southern History in Southern California" prepared me to address the history of slavery, the economics and politics of Reconstruction, and black culture and traditions. The racial and gender dynamics, pedagogy and political finesse in the classroom I learned on my own. I anticipated neither the ways in which the essence of the storyteller or the complexion, status, and/or class of the listeners would condition their understanding of the stories nor the ways I would be conflated with my subject matter. I did not consider how white female students (who invariably self-identified as "just white girls") would be drawn to the stories of black women as if they were talismans designed to ward off suffering. I did not anticipate how black female students, who name themselves Strong Black Women (SBW), would use those same stories to deny the past (and present) pain associated with racism and in the process undermine the very strength to which they were laying claim. My experiences at three predominantly white elite liberal arts colleges have provided a superior, if at times frustrating, on-the-job training.

The Feminist Classroom

She puts history through a sieve, winnows out the lies, looks at the forces that we as a race, as women, have been part of.

—Gloria Anzaldúa

Anzaldúa, in "La conciencia de la mestiza: Towards a New Consciousness," begins her discussion of "The Mestiza Way" noting, "Her first step is to take inventory. Just what did she inherit from her ancestors?"(381). Anzaldúa's words have significance for historians of the black experience in the United States Students of black history must begin by confronting the idea of the ancestors, by considering the Africans in the story. The conceptualization of Africans is problematic for many Americans. The key is to explain the ways in which Africans were both the same and different from their European peers. We must consider the histories, cultures, languages, and social organizations African peoples brought to the encounter. People from Senegal were different from people from Liverpool—in religion and political organization, style of dress and courtship rituals. Yet the similarities, the shared humanity, were more important than the obvious differences. Educators should never underestimate students' acceptance of the fantastic when considering people of "the Dark Continent." The task is to help them move away from considering Africans and by extension, the enslaved and their descendants, as so different from Europeans as to be outside the human family. I have occasionally been taken off guard by the difficulty involved in this process.[1] Contemporary historians are right to criticize each other for works that merely celebrate black agency, though those of us who teach undergraduates must be ever mindful of the way successive generations of students are socialized to accept notions of black passivity and dependence. Often times it is the progressive, liberal student who simultaneously speaks of the need for equality of the races while stressing the need for whites to guide blacks to freedom. Students who are unable to imagine Africans making a way in a world of their own creation are equally incapable of asking how African Americans planned to use their post–Civil War freedom.

Introducing gender as a category of analysis helps students see the African American experience as a fully human experience that includes challenges common to all human experiences. Black people and their experience appear more "real" rather than remaining some "exotic" ideal when viewed through the lens of gender. A feminist ethos that stresses shared responsibilities and the essential dignity of persons helps challenge students to rethink the past and work toward a just, more equitable future. I have crafted a feminist teaching style that incorporates tools of feminist pedagogy—the dialectical notebook and journal, life narratives, and the student-led discussion into my teaching. Some tools have more utility than do others. I have at times, yielded my authority in the classroom, recognizing the value of a more democratic learning space.[2] At other times, the reality of being a racial minority in a largely white classroom has precluded engaging in this feminist exercise. While the ideal goal is to change classroom culture so that students are empowered to set the agenda for learning, one must control for class and race. The assumption of class (elite) and gender (male) involved in a feminist critique of academic authority that calls for marginalizing the professor does not apply to me as a working-class black female. My authority in the classroom is rooted neither in my class, nor my gender or my race. Indeed, in the eyes of most students and faculty at PWIs, my authority is tied specifically to my body of knowledge as marked by the Ph.D. in American history. I reject, therefore, the assumption that the professor's voice should be used sparingly in the feminist classroom on the grounds that to set aside my professorial status is most often to reinscribe traditional class (upper middle over working class/poor), sex (male over female), and race (white over black) dynamics. I have found it difficult to use a democratic approach to my teaching precisely because of student skepticism and the resistance rooted in their assumptions. My task as a feminist teacher of African American history is to challenge students to become conscious of position and privilege and to denaturalize social structures of power in the process of discussing and analyzing information about the past. Ideally the challenges, shifts in consciousness and greater knowledge will contribute to the process of social change. My place at the front of the classroom, behind the podium and in authority goes a long way toward beginning that process.[3] I am open to experimenting with different teaching methods, some of which I refer to in this essay, remain committed to mastering the art of cultivating knowledge of the past, telling the stories, and hoping to inspire future storytellers.

The Students

There are as many reasons to study black history as there are students who enroll in courses. Still I am struck by the patterns of student reasoning that have emerged over a decade of teaching. Some years ago, in the process of trying to explain the patterns to a fellow faculty member, I developed the code of the four Ds: Discovery, Dismay, Denial, and Dismissal. These make up the points on an emotional road map, which reveals the course followed by the vast majority of students who have enrolled in my courses at PWIs. A brief discussion of each offers the reader an insight into this academic experience.

Discovery

Curiosity brings most students at predominately white liberal arts colleges to the study of black history. For most privileged white students, people of African descent are exotic objects of study whose lives serve as a link to an oppositional culture and styles of expression. For many, this black culture is perceived as inherently radical, "outside the box," certainly outside the norms of American culture and history. I have often been struck by the ways in which students engage in the "otherizing" Langston Hughes identified among whites during the Harlem Renaissance. Too often students are drawn to the history because, to paraphrase, "the African American is in vogue." Students use black history as a measuring stick by which they might gauge the success of Western civilization. They do not study black history to understand the diversity of people of African descent, nor to contemplate the contributions the African American experience and the resulting jeremiad has made to American consciousness, culture, and identity. They want to study black history to understand the roots of hip-hop and rap, the origins of Jackie Robinson or Ali and ultimately to get why "you" are not like "us." This reasoning is unconscious, which is to say that students operate from racial innocence. Most students at PWIs are confident that neither they nor anyone they know act from any kind of racialist thinking or bias.

Most students have had no serious or concentrated exposure to black history before they arrive on campus. They have learned: slavery existed and had something to do with the Civil War, black folks did something called the Harlem Renaissance, Martin Luther King, Jr. and Malcolm X were in conflict during the Civil Rights movement, and Clarence Thomas "replaced" Thurgood Marshall as a Supreme Court Justice.

Other students come to college at a different point of discovery. Well versed in one particular aspect of black history, they hope to expand their knowledge in particular ways. Having read selected works of Frederick Douglass or W. E. B. Du Bois, they take courses that they believe will deepen their understanding of the black leaders and intellectuals, e.g., a sort of Great Black Men study of history. Still others, having read one of each of the novels by Alice Walker, Zora Neale Hurston, and Maya Angelou (rarely Toni Morrison), seek the history that will help them substantiate the fiction. Broad or focused, the curiosity of young minds is exhilarating, even electric. The professor's daunting task is to harness the charge. C. S. Lewis correctly identified the disappointment that grows in the breast of every student when he or she "has been enchanted in the nursery by Stories from the Odyssey" then "buckles down to really learning Greek" (17). Certainly the weekly tasks of reading and analyzing historical monographs, examining evidence, and perfecting oral argument sometimes lower the voltage for the less than committed student. Unfortunately, the next stage in the student's progress, dismay, is not a product of facing the actual work in the course, but the side effect of beginning to confront the unrelenting story of America and race.

Dismay

Dismay is the startled discomfort many students express in reaction to the first serious discussions of the construct of race and slavery. I first encountered this phenomenon a decade ago. A sophisticated, long post-Roots generation of students who were cutting their intellectual teeth on the "social construction of race, class, and sex," were nevertheless, thrown by the details of barracoons, Middle Passage, and the auction block. They began to shift in their seats when discussing slave narratives, to develop a sudden inability to look at the instructor when responding to questions about rape in slavery. Visits to my office hours grew into extensions of classroom discussions. An enthusiastic first year (white) burst into tears and confessed that she was "just a white girl," overwhelmed by the horrors of slavery. She was undone by the reading, and was seeking advice as to how to gain emotional distance from the material so she might be able to engage in discussion without tears.

Taken in isolation, this experience could be dismissed as the dramatics of an immature teen. Visits from many more students, including juniors and seniors graduating in history and Women's Studies, required I make a different analysis. A paper conference with a serious and committed rising junior clarified matters. She interrupted our discussion to ask if I believed racism was genetic. Specifically, did I consider racial prejudice and the corresponding abuse of power to be a disease, which affected the entire human genome or just whites? Further discussion narrowed the focus of the conversation to the real concern: did I think she, "a white girl from the 'burbs," by virtue of her whiteness, was racist and if so, what cure would I recommend? However, I soon figured out that the label, "just a white girl" was designed to exempt students from any responsibility for race relations in the present, past, or future by highlighting their youth and inexperience with the world—their innocence. Such students were, of course, simultaneously, though somewhat apologetically, reinscribing their privileged race position by noting their whiteness. The dismay exhibited by so many white students in the process of studying black history is rooted in their first real confrontation with the concept of race. To study American history through the lens of the black experience is to make race a central, if not dominant, point of analysis. Acknowledging racism as an essential part of our heritage means realistically to consider it as a factor in our present and future.

For many white students, this is their first serious challenge to racial innocence. A protective insulating mindset, racial innocence is best understood as part of the package of "white skinned privilege" as identified by Peggy McIntosh in her 1988 paper, "White Privilege and Male Privilege." McIntosh notes that white skinned privilege "confers dominance [. . .] gives license to some people to be, at best, thoughtless and, at worst, murderous" (293). Racial innocence is the product of being born and socialized as white in a white supremacist society. Young children learn to expect safety, acceptance, and opportunity by virtue of their whiteness (and especially if that whiteness is underscored by class privilege). They approach the world with a marvelous sense of freedom of choice and trust in outcomes. This sense of innocence may begin to recede as their understanding of the historical realities of blackness in America grows. Their reaction is the *"dis - ease,"* a lack of peace or comfort that occurs at the first stages of any critical shift in consciousness or understanding. Dismay flows into the next step in the process. Denial of or distancing from the cause of distress is natural and can lead to a rejection of the subject matter.

Denial

Denial is the most dangerous stage in the learning process. Students engage in denial as they come to understand the consequences of accepting the idea of a raced American history. A raced America calls into question concepts of liberty, of individual rights and equal opportunity—hence it significantly challenges American liberalism. Students understand that if the history of black people does not conform to the traditional story of equality, justice, and democracy, then the entire notion of America is in question. The mythology of American liberalism can remain intact only if the *idea* of America is protected from a history that includes white supremacy and reveals a necessary tie between white privilege and black oppression.

Black history taught with the "radical black subjectivity" envisioned by bell hooks, challenges the traditional rationalizations that support American liberalism and identity. I encourage students to consider the daunting prospect that black subjects—*people* who were enslaved, transported, sold, abused, killed—were capable of being fully realized humans with consciousness and plans for their own cultural existence. I urge students to consider commentary found in Freire's *Pedagogy of the Oppressed* in the context of Orlando Patterson's *Slavery and Social Death,* and Edmund Morgan's *American Slavery and American Freedom.* They learn black enslavement and "social death" purchased white freedom, making American liberty a product of perversion that granted a few greater individual opportunities, while reinscribing racial oppression for the majority.[4] Freire's assertion, "No one can be authentically human while he prevents others from being so," when presented within the context of a discussion of slavery and racial discrimination, challenges progressive notions of the independent Individual and free Self at precisely the moment young students are striving to create both (66).

Their denial is then a logical response to a subject matter that threatens to undermine (upper middle class, white) American selfhood. When confronted by the details of the black experience in America and forced to interface with a "woman of color" in a position of authority, a student's denial can be ferocious. Armed with moral outrage at "unreasonable attacks on the founding fathers who were after all only men of their time" or "being made to feel guilty because some white people were racist 200 years ago," students engage in one of two types of self-protective denial.

The first type of denial, the "that's just what she says" variety is preferable and often productive. Students indulging in this type of denial are eager to visit my office to discuss historiography as it relates to the use of slave narratives, or details on the numbers of people lost in Middle Passage or lynched following Reconstruction. One male student was shocked to hear Abraham Lincoln's views on race as espoused during the Lincoln-Douglas debates. The young man in question stormed into my office and demanded to know where I had gotten the information. I wisely resisted the urge to tell him I had just made it up while writing the lecture Sunday afternoon, choosing instead to pull Benjamin Thomas's *Abraham Lincoln* off the shelf so that he might read the quote in its entirety. I referred him to other works and encouraged him to seek out primary sources on Lincoln. I am delighted to direct such students to historical monographs, textbooks, and journals to be found in the library. I encourage them to investigate the voices of other scholars, to consider the ways in which Eugene Genevose and Herbert Gutman or Barbara Fields and Evelyn Brooks Higgenbotham agree or disagree about the black experience. Indeed, I was surprised to learn that some of my colleagues were reluctant to expose their students to arguments that differed from their own sense of orthodoxy in the field, though it did help explain why students thought of me as a maverick![5] Some of them will return, having checked the sources, ready to argue their case with supporting data.

These students are still engaged in the process of studying history. Most discover their discomfort fades as they work through the material. The "extra" work helps reinforce the difference between then and now, creates the very space the teary first-year student was seeking. Such work cannot return them to their belief in the perfection of American liberalism, nor can it restore a belief in white innocence. Still, they are able to discern change over time and to investigate ways in which persons in the past worked to produce such change.

This is especially helpful for self-described progressive students who have been drawn to the study of African Americans by a magical thinking that posits complete eradication of racism and inequality in the simple act of learning the history of oppressed black people. They are initially distressed to learn that an end to race-based injustice requires more than just "learning each others' stories." As Freire reminds us, "To affirm that men and women are persons and as persons should be free, and yet to do nothing tangible to make this affirmation a reality is a farce" (32). Discussion helps students understand that learning the stories without taking action is "verbalism [. . .] an alienated and alienating 'blah,'" while action without proper reflection on and dialogue with the subjects of the stories, produces a self-indulgent student activism (68–69). Greater study conveys the understanding that social change (past and present) necessitates a recognition of their positionality, as well as a change in their thoughts and actions if they are to live in step with their own progressive image.

Many more white students engage in the second kind of denial: the variety that suggests black history is not real American history. This denial is considerably more resistant and more likely to aid students in their desire to escape discomfort by avoiding the provocative subject matter altogether. This second form of denial is rooted in privilege of both race and class.[6] Such students cultivate a vision that disavows the effectiveness of race as a category of analysis. This denial further relies on arguments rooted in cultural bias and supported by contemporary intellectual discourse, to avoid considering race as a factor in understanding either the past or the present. Borrowing from a postmodern commentary on the construction of reality, students argue the "obvious" position that given race is not "real" but "a social construct," therefore racism, oppression caused by race, must not be "real." In their view, scholars who record and analyze data about injury based on race are not presenting real histories of the American experience, but rather writing biased polemics. First, such students fail to comprehend how the construction of any social reality and corresponding relations of power are tied to the hegemony of the group doing the constructing. Then students fail to recognize the fallacy involved in simply asserting the social construction of race. They do not grasp the limitations placed on actual human lives in the moment when race, or gender, or class is being constructed. Rather they latch on to the lyricism of the language and indulge in high-toned discussions of "essentialist" thinking.

In their rush to invalidate the concept of race, students fail to grasp the negative "implications of a critique of identity for oppressed groups"(hooks, 1990, 26). Many students will resort to naïve comparisons between black and white ethnic experiences. They fail to consider the historical experiences of black people, specifically the ways negative stereotyping and law, products of racism and essentialist thinking in the past, have worked to prevent African Americans from reaching their full human potential. Confronted with course materials (literature, legal statues, and religious tracts) that clearly endorse the nation's past belief in the reality of race, students counter by focusing on the absence of words that directly highlight race in the official documents of American democracy. The Declaration of Independence and the Constitution are favorite examples. Pressed further to consider the spirit of those documents rather than their letter, most will admit that some misguided and lost souls, in the past, may have been racists. Yet students argue such racists were certainly outnumbered by the legions of good "normal" whites that were not. For example, one young man from Virginia disrupted two class periods to forcibly interject his understanding that Jefferson clearly meant all people, rather than white males, when he penned "all men are created equal." In this equation, race, racists, and racism are products of illusionary and long since dead reasoning, tied to only the most overt and heinous acts of rape or murder. Persons in the past who engaged in said actions were clearly deviants by whom America and Americans cannot be analyzed or judged. Such students are unwilling to consider the ways in which a) racism and racist acts were commonplace or b) the sheer number of "normal" educated and professional persons in the past who were overtly involved in white supremacist groups and actions. Run-of-the-mill racism, which denied education to black children or employment in positions above factory janitor or railroad firemen to black males, is not part of the equation. The fact that sheriffs, states attorneys, or federal Supreme Court justices, well into the twentieth century, proclaimed proudly their Klan membership while simultaneously serving as legitimate officers of courts across the country is also lost in this discussion.

Such students refuse to consider the way free-floating racial stereotypes enter into their own reasoning. Many have argued that Reconstruction-era disfranchisement was wrong only because it locked out educated blacks while protecting the vote from "illiterate former slaves"; white culpability for slave illiteracy was lost in the translation. Others have been slow to critique the development of chain gangs or lynching because Southern legislatures were "only trying to keep order." Two young men, deep in this form of denial, asserted quite boldly that lynching was "clearly the last resort of Southern white males who were trying to protect the virtue of white women." No amount of literature on the history of lynching could draw them into a discussion of the recorded events. These students felt no need to read literature on lynching, which of course contains the details of the lynching of women, children, and marginally white ethnic (Italian, Greek, Jewish) males, to challenge my presentation of Ida B. Wells's arguments on the subject. Rather, they handily dismissed her work as politically inspired and biased, because the black male desire for white women was "common knowledge!" Educators should not underestimate students' ability to maintain such denial despite the necessary permutations of logic. Students are committed to this form of denial because it allows them to circumvent feelings of discomfort by erasing the historical realities that cause them pain. They then segue beautifully into the final stage of the process, dismissal.

Dismissal

Dismissal proves to be the ultimate escape for a frightening number of students at PWIs. Frightening because it closes the door both to a critical part of intellectual development and to understanding an important part of the American experience. A liberal arts education requires the development of critical thinking skills. Students must engage an idea, view it from all sides, and use both their reason and their emotion to create understanding and intuit meaning. Shutting the door on ideas that challenge and/or create discomfort deprives their minds of necessary training and development. Students will go on to enroll in other courses with less threatening subject matter. Successive courses with talented professors will have a cumulative effect, eventually wearing down the student's resistance to critical thought. Unfortunately, while they will master this academic skill, many will have missed the connection between race and equality, injustice and privilege in American society. These students will carry their petrified belief in racially blind liberalism into their professional schools, their political life, and their social and parenting activities.

I am frustrated by the prospect of this outcome. I fear my teaching may not have "transgressed," that while I have indeed struggled to make education a "practice of freedom," it has failed to inspire social change.[7] While I would agree with the necessity of transgressing the norms to make social change, I am also aware of the ways in which thoughts, actions, and persons who transgress are frequently discarded by those who are threatened and unwilling to engage in dialogue. Students leave my classroom having been exposed to radical black subjectivity, challenged to rethink American history as they know it, yet a depressing number of them fail to rise to the challenge.

The feminist premise that community and action in the classroom will contribute to community and action in the world is not borne out when there is little or no secondary reinforcement for the ideals presented in class readings and discussions. I have no power to make real the ideas expressed in the classroom and with no support in the actual world, challenging/discomforting ideas fade away and established thought patterns and beliefs prevail.

Thankfully only the second form of denial delivers students to the door of dismissal. Students who react with self-defensive denial yet continue to ask questions are open to greater knowledge, understanding, and the possibility of intellectual epiphany that can be singularly transforming. The struggle is to guide students through the necessary paradigm shift (more realistically, the first tweak in consciousness) that comes from a new way of knowing, by confirming the existence of solid ground on the other side. The instructor must encourage students to consider ways selfhood can be defined in opposition to structures of domination. How can one be fully realized as a part of a group committed to human liberty rather than as a pseudo-independent individual whose freedom rests on the backs of the oppressed? How can the Individual exist with a lower-case, less oppressive and imposing i?

Feminist and Freirean theory have often proved useful in helping students work on staying the course despite discomfort. My courses have been most successful when the classroom climate was one of trust, mutual respect, and community. Unfortunately, such a climate has been more often the result of serendipity than of choice or planning. I strive to lay the proper groundwork, yet I am well aware of the limits of my power to create such a climate. I can and do address the importance of safe space, of mutual respect and open honest dialogue. However, I am also conscious of Freire's commentary about the nature of dialogue.

> Dialogue cannot exist, however, in the absence of a profound love for the world and for people. . . . How can I dialogue if I regard myself as a case apart from others—mere "its" in whom I cannot recognize other "I"s? [. . .] How can I dialogue if I am afraid of being displaced, the mere possibility causing me torment and weakness? (70–71).

Different classes, races, genders, sexualities, nationalities, and political affiliations are present as each class begins to negotiate the study of black history. White students who approach the classroom with the assumption that the course will be about the way black people have related to the white/European traditions are sometimes instantly put off by my assertion that the course will center on the black experience. Minority students who are looking for their own stories are often cool toward white students, whom they consider interlopers. Still other minority students are reluctant to engage if their minority story does not fit the expected stereotype. Clearly the expectation that a class of 16 undergraduates of diverse background will reach Freirean level of respect and love is somewhat unrealistic. The key is to set the bar high, to let my students know I hope and expect us to reach that pinnacle. We can then proceed, being sure to check ourselves when we stray off course, and hopefully thrash out conflicts when they arise.

bell hooks's work has also contributed to my teaching style. In "toward a revolutionary feminist pedagogy" found in *Talking Back,* she writes of her early frustrations with teaching, especially the negative feedback she received from students with regards to her "very confrontational" style. Her insistence that those students "come to voice" proved to be in conflict with her "longing for immediate recognition of my value as a teacher." Later she came to understand that "courses that work to shift paradigms, to change consciousness, cannot necessarily be experienced immediately as fun or positive or safe and this was not a worthwhile criteria to use in evaluation"(53). I read these words in my first year of teaching. I have returned to them many times, to encourage myself to stay true to my methods and hold fast to critical storytelling.

Students have often told me that I share hooks's "confrontational" style. I do not perceive my teaching style to be hostile or combative. Rather, I do believe that spirited debate between student and professor as well as between students helps sharpen the ability to reason and spark new ideas. I do require that those who speak be able and willing to clearly and as fully as possible articulate the arguments and reasoning behind their statements. Students must support their arguments with evidence drawn from the course materials, make their case from reason, and be willing to take their remarks through to their logical conclusions. Those students who are accustomed to being rewarded simply for speaking are often startled by my pedagogical choice to challenge speech that is uninformed by the reading and/or thin analytically. This is seen as "intensity," or "having attitude."

I also begin my classes with a discussion of the importance of viewing the past with a lens broader than one's personal life story. Black people must be the core subjects of study to teach African American history effectively. Young, white, upper-middle-class privileged students are the primary constituents at PWIs. Most have been conditioned to see themselves as the proper subjects of American history. These students must be decentered, moved from their unexamined assumptions and privilege, to be open to the process of studying the black experience. Students can learn from their own narratives, yet they must also understand that history did not happen solely to arrive at their existence.

As for coming to voice with their own truths, I too understand the dangers of silence. "Quae tacet, videtur consentire."—She who is silent is understood to consent. Therefore, speaking one's truth is essential if education is to be liberating. However, there must (as noted) be a link between speaking and the premise of safe space. Safety, which requires some sense of connectedness and community, is in fact quite rare in academic circles. Indeed, I regularly warn my students against assuming connectedness based on ideology or race. I have struggled with ideas about the nature of connectedness in my research on the black community in turn-of-the-century Atlanta. I have concluded that connectedness and community of any kind must be made and remade in a thousand small ways each day. Neither the adjectives "feminist" nor "black" ensures connection or blanket safety for students/faculty if they are speaking "out of turn," i.e., in such a way as to challenge the orthodoxy of the group. Sherene H. Razack reminds us that "there are penalties for choosing the wrong voice at the wrong time, for telling an inappropriate tale"(53). I have both witnessed amongst undergraduates, and experienced with academic peers, the punishment that members of a "shared community" (feminist or black) can mete out to those whose speech threatens a sacred tenet. I am reluctant to encourage students to speak aloud a critique for which they are neither willing nor able to pay. I encourage those in my African American Women's history seminar to record in a journal both their analyses of the texts and their own commentary. Commentary taken from such journals is frequently more concise and insightful than off-the-cuff remarks. Journal entries can also be shared anonymously for the purposes of discussion. Those students who feel secure can claim authorship, yet all can consider and offer critique while preserving safety.

"We're rough and tough, and we don't take no stuff!"

Though sometimes few and far between, there are also students of African descent at PWIs. Some come to such elite institutions from similar upper-middle-class backgrounds and subsequently share much of the worldview of their white peers. Others, including some first generation college students, find themselves engaged in a rather personal anthropological study while simultaneously working to secure their degree. Courses in black history can become places of sociological and psychological therapy for both sets of students. Contentious issues of classism, colorism, and internalized racism often rise to the surface as students begin to study the black past. They enroll in history class to get at the root of the race problem in America: slavery. While they are correct to begin with the study of the past, history offers answers only if one studies the actual human interactions, rather than projecting fantasies onto the past. Unfortunately many students, black and white, arrive on campus well versed in urban legends and sacred "truths" about African American history.[8]

Young black women make up the majority of black students both in the African American survey courses and in the seminar in African American

Women's History. (Black male students do take both courses, but tend to prefer the course on Black Reconstruction or my courses on the American West.) Two things stand out from my experiences with young black female students. The first has to do with the ways such students self-identify, the second with the ways they identify or label me.

One can argue that choosing to identify as "Strong Black Women" is a manifestation of a positive self-identity in the minds of young women who live within a society that regularly endorses negative and dysfunctional images of black females. Long-lived stereotypes: domineering matriarch, lazy welfare queen, sexually deviant jezebel, or selfless mammy (more on her in a moment) continue to pepper popular dialogue, contemporary literature and film, and political commentary relating to black women and the black community. So how can one criticize a self-selective identity that dwells on strengths rather than its purported deficiencies?

Feminist pedagogy encourages us to engage in both serious self-reflection and self-criticism as part of a process of creating social change that ultimately results in greater freedom and equality for all members of society. The Strong Black Woman created by the young women in question is not a by-product of such reflection and critique. She is a larger than life mannequin, a stiff unyielding figure erected to fend off external critique and shield internal pain and sorrow. The Strong Black Woman is a reactionary being who grows out of the fears and very real dangers that confront black women on a daily basis, and her presence is often an obstacle to the self-reflection and growth necessary to create change.

The strength in the title Strong Black Women is more often an illusion than a reality. Asked how they came to think of themselves, their peers, or historical figures they idealize—Sojourner Truth, Ida B. Wells, Anna Julia Cooper—as strong, students focus on the ability to survive their oppression. These women were strong, they tell me, because they "took it, and took and kept going." They are especially fond of quoting the much-dissected Sojourner Truth's "Ain't I a Woman?" speech. "Just think how strong Sojourner had to be to lose all those children and survive." Survival, regardless of the obvious costs, the real emotional or spiritual consequences for the women in question, is most significant. The less they know or think about the actual burden, the wearing away of self involved in the domination by others of their heroines or themselves, the better. These students have confused strength with endurance. Endurance focuses upon surviving great stress. Strength is the power to resist force, to respond creatively in the presence of coercion. While I am not interested in reviving old arguments about black pathology rooted in slavery, I am unwilling to set aside serious discussions of the injury, suffering, and deprivation inflicted upon black people during two centuries of slavery and under a brutal system of racial apartheid.[9] These young Strong Black Women are often unwilling to engage with the negative fallout associated with living within systems of domination, choosing instead to valorize the survivors. They have been unwilling to consider the lives of those who did/do not endure, but succumbed to the beatings, rape, exploitation, and loss. Such women do not fit the mold, as they are weak (read white), and must be discarded or else their presence risks tarnishing the image. Black womanhood is equated with the mythological superwoman, who is not only all things to all people, but impervious to pain, to sorrow, to loss. In other words, she is not fully human.

The humanity of African Americans is undermined if the history of their experience in the United States is reduced to stories of survivors (or victims). Black history cannot, as Robert L. Harris noted in his *Perspectives* article, be reduced to images of the "Catastrophic or Survivalist." The study of the African American experience should not be reduced to a listing of black firsts and also-rans, or recitations of the deeds of black heroes and heroines. I combat the survivalist/SBW model by telling stories that contain the positive and the negative of the black experience. I frequently use counter factual exercises to help students better grasp a multidimensional understanding of history. What, for example, would have had to happen in order for Gabriel's rebellion to have been successful?[10] Students are assigned roles and asked to identify what alternative decisions they must make to change the outcome of the events. I ask students to read and analyze materials specific to women's experience in slavery, to consider a gendered variation on the theme of enslavement. Talking to students about the ways in which a woman might in one moment choose to acquiesce to her abuser and in the next respond with righteous and murderous rage (see Melton A. McLaurin's *Celia, A Slave*) helps move them past the oppositional dynamic that suggests that one was either a sell-out or a radical. I have had some success challenging the SBW with these techniques, but I have also learned the survivalist mindset endures because of factors outside the classroom.

Julia A. Boyd in *Can I Get A Witness? Black Women and Depression* notes that black women have as children been given the message that "we had to be tough in order to survive." The image of what she calls the "don't take no stuff sista" has settled into the stereotype of the "angry Black woman." Many young black women find they "aren't always comfortable being defined" so negatively, cannot or do not wish to "live up to that image"(Boyd 43). The result of being trapped inside a stereotype is often great stress and depression. College age Strong Black Women who find themselves racially threatened, injured, or attacked as part of the process of attending elite PWIs then can have only one response: they must endure. They are not allowed moments of weakness. They often feel they must remain within the scripted role, even if it means passing on the opportunity to seek assistance and failing the class or passing up counseling and languishing in depression and fear. Better to fail privately than show weakness publicly. This superhuman vision of themselves and the corresponding pattern of behavior undercuts the potential sisterhood among black female students, preventing them from reaching out to each other to create a network of care and support. Ironically, it was a network of sisterhood, black female collegiality rooted not in blood ties but in shared commitment to improving the conditions of their lives in the face of racism and slavery, that allowed their heroines of the past to be truly strong.

Students often expand the SBW ideal to include faculty. Faculty members are included in or excluded from this club somewhat randomly. Marital status, class background, complexion, sexual orientation, or teaching style can be used for or against various black female faculty. One faculty member was "not really a sista" cut from the SBW cloth because she let it be known that she visited a therapist. Another was discounted because her husband was white and her style of dress too conventional, yet another because there were "too many books by white men on her syllabus." The fickle nature of the standards is not to be underestimated. Teaching the same courses, with the same politics and texts, wearing the same clothing, I have been alternately labeled a SBW and been dismissed as less than. Ultimately for these students, black female faculty must uphold the correct, essential image of SBW to the larger society in order to be granted approval as a "real sista." Failure to pass muster often results in tensions that play out in the classroom or, as more than one black female colleague has related, show up in damning and inaccurate teaching evaluations. Forcing faculty/student relations into a rigid, self-deprecating, and unrealistic framework paradoxically undermines the potential sisterhood of black women. Freeing young women who are trapped behind the mannequin façade requires far more work than can be done within the classroom.

Important issues may be raised in the classroom, though courses on black women and work are not realistically the place for the necessary dialogue. I do believe feminist ideals that celebrate both the value and truth of individual life experience can help, but in a different framework. I regularly encourage college-age black women to organize themselves into consciousness raising groups in which they can create community—plan activities, get involved with campus politics, but most importantly talk, share, and learn to trust one another with their fears.

"How I love ya, how I love ya, My dear old mammy!"

Second to the image of the Strong Black Woman is that of the intellectualized mammy. The image of the black mammy is well-established in American history.[11] Forced to leave her own home and family to become the care-taker of white children, mammy is a tragic figure. The surrogate mother, wet nurse, nanny, maid, cook, cleaning lady, caricatured as obese, dark-skinned, thick-lipped with nappy hair wrapped in the favorite red bandana, mammy is much "loved" and simultaneously much abused. Poorly paid, made to eat in the kitchen, and subject to sexual exploitation by males in white house-holds, she is, nevertheless, identified by whites as "one of the family." Mem-ories of mammy color images of black women in media, in politics and, as I have discovered, in the classroom.

The intellectualized mammy varies from the historical model by degrees. Students, regardless of race or gender, regularly assume female faculty will ful-fill certain gender roles. Female faculty will naturally grant extensions, write letters of recommendation, make time to see them, and provide a sympathetic ear—especially with regard to personal issues, by virtue of their gender. I have been stunned at the intimacy of conversations with students who visit my of-fice. Many are centered on lost loves, abortions, and extreme family dysfunc-tion. Male colleagues note that they have encountered some students who wished to address personal issues but that such interactions were rare.

In a brief 1993 article published in the *Sociological Forum,* John Pease re-ports that teaching, in and of itself, was most often equated with women's work, as opposed to scholarly research that faculty and students associated with men's work. Students, who self-select faculty with whom they will share their troubles, may be predisposed toward female faculty whom they see as teachers rather than researchers. Junior faculty who teach lower division and general survey courses or faculty who specialize in black, women's, or Latino studies (work about people who are not "central" to the American drama) and who are also female, are most likely to be asked to serve in a mothering role. Race and feminist politics add complexity to this gender quandary.

Black students, both female and male, can envision black female faculty as substitute mothers and therefore conjure the intellectualized mammy. Not only are such faculty members endowed with certain desirable female traits, they share their racial orientation. The circumstances of being an extreme racial minority at a PWI lend themselves to such misperception. Isolated, sometimes stigmatized, and perhaps lonely, young students cast about for some familiarity and source of comfort. While the action is on some level logical, it is not without consequence. Locking black female faculty into the role of surrogate mother/mammy weighs teacher-student relations down with familial emotional patterns, including inappropriate displays of anger, resistance to authority, and misplaced feelings of sibling rivalry.

Feminist pedagogy that focuses upon the link between the personal and the political and the democratic classroom contributes to this dilemma. For the faculty member in question, being held to the role of mammy, brings the unnecessary burden of additional caretaking and responsibility while discounting the faculty member's intellectual abilities and contributions. Students (and some faculty peers) operate from the belief that feminist faculty are supposed to be open to intimate, even faux familial relations with their students as a necessary counterpoint to patriarchal tradition.[12] The idea that such intimacy might undermine professorial authority and produce greater democracy in the classroom is seen as a positive outcome. Such theories however, fail to consider either freedom of choice or the dangers involved in such modes of extreme connectedness. Feminism has given me the power to make life choices, including the right to reject expectations rooted either in biology or social constructions of gender. I have, and will continue to freely form close relations with individual students, yet I reject wholeheartedly the assumption that I must be open to all students upon demand. On demand is key here, for more than one minority faculty member has been told what she "ought" to do, as the student in question "paid her salary." Good teachers do nurture their students—encourage independent thought, help them improve academic skills, perhaps even guide them toward graduate programs that fit their talents. There is, however, a distinction between nurturing and mammy work. A few examples of my experience in the intellectualized mammy role may help make the case.

My first experience involved a bright but brittle young black woman who began the term by coming to my office to welcome me to campus. A soon to be graduating senior, she asked about my research and expressed her interest in pursuing a graduate degree in history. Our meeting ended with her noting how many things we had in common and that she was looking forward to taking my courses. Over the course of the year both her enthusiasm and amazing hard work were nearly eclipsed by her approval-seeking behavior and angry outbursts. Our relationship began to deteriorate as I disagreed with her SBW characterization of female slaves. The situation worsened in the face of criticism of her written work. Unable to separate critique of her paper from critique of her person, she flew into my office in rage, accusing me of judging her more harshly than I did her white peers. "I do expect white men to diss me out, Professor Dorsey, but I do not expect it of a black woman, a big sister." She continued, asking if I understood my role as a black female faculty member—which was to sister/mother young black women like herself who were looking for mentors. When I explained that mentors were required to offer both help and criticism to encourage students to rise to their potential, she countered that black female students "caught enough hell" from "white boys" and expected love from their own. The relationship continued to decline, though it did not prevent this young woman from asking me to write a letter of recommendation for graduate school. I refused, encouraging her to secure a letter from a more senior faculty member with whom she had a better relationship. Our relationship bottomed out, resulting in a teaching evaluation in which she noted that while I was a professional, competent teacher and potentially a good scholar, I clearly needed to rethink my relationship to "the race" as I "hated all black students."

Other experiences as the intellectualized mammy are less painful but equally problematic. A fifth-year senior, committed to graduating, came to my office and expressed her difficulties in financing her last year in college. I offered to loan her the extra copies of all the books for my course to help reduce costs, suggested she make an appeal to the office of financial aid, and did my best to reassure her of a positive outcome. Shortly after the third week of the term, the student disappeared from class. She failed to respond to either email or phone calls and I began to fear that she had succumbed to the pressure of her situation and withdrawn. At the beginning of the next class period, I asked if anyone had seen her and encouraged her peers to have her contact me if they encountered her. Three weeks later, I ran into the student in question. Noting that she knew I was looking for her, she reported the following conversation with "Que" her ace (best friend), also in my class.

Que: Professor Dorsey is gonna kill you girl! She was asking everybody if they had seen you, were you okay. You haven't been in class in weeks.
Student: I know. I haven't done the reading and you know how she is.
Que: Yeah, but you know she is worse on people who just plain don't show up. You better get your behind to class.
Student: Girl, just like you, I have a black mother. I know I'm gonna catch hell from Professor Dorsey.

She apologized for failing to either make it to class or make contact and promising to do better, ran off.

I doubt that either of the two students spent time deconstructing their conversation. I am sure they did not think about the way they equated "black mother" with "catching hell," and certainly not about the way they had equated my role as the professor in their history class with the role of mother. The stereotype of the black matriarch, the controlling figure who strides through much of the early revisionist history of slavery (and through government sponsored literature designed to justify or condemn social welfare programs) is alive and well in the minds of young black college students. Sadly, they paint their mothers and grandmothers with the same broad brush.[13] The continued existence of this image is troublesome and, when projected onto black faculty, highly disruptive. It undermines authority, diminishes the constructive power of criticism, and mires faculty and students in a muddy jumble of assumptions and mixed emotions.

White students also possess the power to call up the intellectualized mammy. They do not confuse black female faculty with their mothers in as direct a fashion, but they are capable of envisioning black female faculty as caretakers who exist to offer them succor. Two young women who had enrolled in African American Women's History expressed their mutual discomfort speaking, as they were "just two white girls in a class full of Black Women." When asked why they hadn't considered their whiteness (in advance), they assured me that they had thought about their whiteness but, "well, it's just that Black Women are so strong. You are so strong, Professor Dorsey; we just want to get some of that, to borrow some of that strength from you." Black women's stories of struggle were so much nourishment to be drawn out of me to calm the fears of "white girls." Both the instructor and the subject were being fetishized, *and* I was being asked to smooth their path. This exchange opened the door to conversations about people, "beings for themselves" as opposed to things "beings for others," and the dangers of objectifying black experiences. (The two reported that they "got it" by the end of the term, though I am unsure.) I have, in the face of such experiences, redoubled my efforts to include more personal narratives in which black female actors speak about their life and times. The challenge remains of how to help students connect with the humanity of historical actors yet how to avoid the narrow identification that blurs lines of position and promotes appropriation.

Creating Empathy

"If humankind produces social reality . . . then transforming that reality is a historical task, a task for humanity."

—Paulo Freire

There is more to teaching black history effectively than getting past denial, the survival outlook, and disengaging from misplaced emotional connections. Students of history must be moved from interest to compassion and eventually to understanding and empathy for those who have experienced injustice if the subject matter is to retain the cathartic power touted by W. E. B. Du Bois and Anna Julia Cooper. Both scholars argued that education, especially knowledge of the past, was a necessary precondition (rather than the sole cause), of the eradication of racial oppression. Empathy, which requires identifying with the circumstances of the oppressed, is the most difficult part of the process. It is easy to evoke sympathy, empathy's anemic cousin. Readings on children in slavery often produce tears of pity and discussions of public lynching festivals open the door to guilt. These emotions are pedagogically counterproductive. The key is to help students see the selfhood of all historical actors and see all such actors (including themselves) as both oppressors and oppressed.[14] Such a shift in mindset can successfully challenge both the fearful mentalities, which leads students of color to overcompensate with SBW syndrome and the aforementioned racial innocence of white students.

My attempts at producing empathy begin with conversations about the importance of positionality with regard to race, class, gender, and time. I encourage students to think, talk, and write about the real differences between historical figures and themselves: what barriers did Harriet Jacobs face that they do not?[15] Then, risking the presentism and essentializing to which undergraduates are prone, I ask them to consider what challenges of the modern world they share with Jacobs. Sometimes it works. A student will consider the dilemma of this historical actor and be able to identify with the anguish of her impossible choice. Instead of feeling sorry for Jacobs, they can begin to see themselves negotiating a sexual harassment scenario, yet still recognizing the privileges of status and law they have as twentieth-century actors. The experiment does sometimes falter. Students lose their grasp on their position in the time. They ask why Jacobs fails to seek assistance from authorities (the same authorities duty bound to keep her enslaved) or "resist" (as if her refusal to concede to her master's sexual demands was not resistance). Or they begin to talk about how *women* in *all* cultures and *all* times have been sexually vulnerable—universalizing the female experience and failing to draw the distinction between legally free and enslaved women. Despite the setbacks, I have found bringing students to the point of identification to be the single most effective tool in cultivating empathy with the oppressed.

Education can have the liberating power that is central to the idea of liberal arts colleges. The study of African America history, inextricably linked to the study of race, liberalism, and democracy is at the core of that power. The impact of such history is lost if students deflect knowledge and reject understanding. Feminist-inspired pedagogy has helped me to work on my teaching in hopes of increasing the number of students who "get it," who understand the structure of oppression, the link between narrow visions of national identity and the history of racism, and the way racism corrodes democracy and freedom. I hope I am catching more white students before they opt out. I know I have more conversations with young black women about the right to embrace their humanness—weakness and all. Yet feminist pedagogy, as detailed above, presents other dilemmas and challenges. I continue to study feminist thought and remain hopeful.

Notes

1. I recently assigned Jennifer Morgan's insightful essay "'Some Could Suckle Over Their Shoulder': Male Travelers, Female Bodies and the Gendering of

Racial Ideology, 1500 - 1770," *William and Mary Quarterly,* 54(1997): 167–192. While discussing the passage in which Morgan addresses reports of slave women who could allegedly sling their breast over their shoulders to nurse infants on their backs, a white female senior history major raised her hand to ask if in fact black women had such ability. I encouraged the class to consider the implications of the question, especially the similarities between the gaze of the student and that of the seventeenth-century European travelers. The senior did not consider the implications of her question until a peer inquired as to whether she would assume white women had such ability. She had not considered the common human physiology that would identify the humanity of the enslaved Africans.

2. Frances A. Maher and Mary Kay Thompson Tetreault, *The Feminist Classroom: An Inside Look at How Professors and Students Are Transforming Higher Education for a Diverse Society* (New York: Basic Books, 1994). The issue of teacher authority is quite complex. "Traditionally," the authors argue, "professorial authority comes from superior knowledge of the academic discipline; it is lodged in the hierarchical relationship of expert teacher to students, and enforced institutionally by the power and duty to assign grades"(127). Such authority is linked to the broader patriarchal authority wielded in institutions of higher education. Feminist emphasis on positionality and voice suggests all learners, professors and students, possess authority rooted in their life experiences and their ability to engage with the material. In this model, knowledge is created then in a democratic dialogue between learners rather than disseminated by the authoritarian professor to students. Maher and Tetreault comment on efforts of feminist teachers who "model themselves as knowers and learners for their students . . . (and) fashion multiple identities and grounds for authority"(128). I have found the issue of classroom authority to be complicated by race.

3. My identity as a woman of African descent is inextricably linked to students' perception of my professorial authority and my ability to experiment with feminist pedagogy. Students at each of the PWIs have felt comfortable pointing out my unique role in their lives, as in "Wow, I've never had a black woman professor before." Such statements are most commonly followed by, "So where *did* you get your degree?" leaving me to draw the logical connection between their surprise that I hold a doctorate with their need for me to reassure them that it did not come out of a Crackerjack box. Maria de la Luz Reyes, Roxana Ng, and Homa Hoodfar, writing in *Radical in<ter>ventions: Identity, Politics and Difference/s in Educational Praxis,* eds. Suzanne de Castell and Mary Bryson (Albany: State University of New York Press, 1997), comment on the ways race and racism complicate the use of feminist pedagogy. Reyes notes that Chicana faculty often experience a lack of "deference, power and authority" in interactions with white students. One of the informants who participated in Reyes's study notes, "students are confrontational, questioning; they want [to know] my credentials. . . . They can't stand that I'm down there on the platform, as the professor. They resent that

a brown woman is telling them their business"(29). Ng in "A Woman Out of Control" recalls her experiences with a white male student who reported feeling "marginalized" by her teaching. "As a member of a racial minority and a woman, I have no authority despite my formal position." She continues, "The knowledge I embody and transmit is also suspect—I am a woman out of control"(48). Lastly, Homa Hoodfar reporting on her efforts at using feminist pedagogy in her Women's Studies class on third-world women notes "The legitimacy of my occupying the powerful position of teacher in a classroom is, at best, shaky"(219). She continues arguing that her authority was especially challenged if she "deviated from conventional norms or [. . .] criticized an anthropological or feminist approach to so called Third World women"(221). Ultimately, Hoodfar, like Ng, recognizes "that my being a racial and cultural minority has compromised my authority in the classroom despite my occupying the position of teacher"(223).

4. Edmund Morgan's work highlights the link between slavery and freedom in colonial Virginia, noting that Americans rooted their economy in slave labor, which allowed their financial emancipation from Britain and cemented political liberty for the white males in the Early Republic. Orlando Patterson defined slavery as "The permanent violent domination of natally alienated and generally dishonored persons." His work details the experience of slavery in many times and locations, noting that while slavery may have developed as substitution for death on the battlefield, it grew to have other, including racial, justifications.

5. I have experienced this maverick status on two levels. I have often worked with colleagues whose understanding of race, slavery, and gender are somewhat stale. Such scholars have mastered the arguments involved in a historical debate and have not moved from that position despite new literature and new arguments in the field. Consequently, their syllabi may be frozen chronologically and historiographically. Students have expressed surprise that I assigned a variety of old and new works, including those of scholars with whom I disagree. More than one student has suggested that I must not have "mastered" my material as my arguments about the nature of slavery differed from that one of my colleagues who was devoted to a singular, dated understanding of black/white relations in the antebellum South.

The maverick label can also be applied outside of the discipline. Students and fellow faculty comment on my "positionality" vis-à-vis "legitimate" subjects of study. I study the history of Americans of African descent. Despite more than 20 years of "history from the bottom up," scholars who study those relegated to the lower rungs of American society continue to struggle with notions of academic significance when working to center "minority" traditions and culture. Faculty members have argued that stories of "others" have value to "others" but offer little to the "center" or mainstream. Some faculty members have also explained that black history is not "really" American history. Scholars and disciplines that remain focused on the experiences of the white, male, and upper class continue to hold the academic center.

Scholars, who focus on nonwhite, female, or poor subjects, despite our employment in institutions of higher learning, remain at the margins.

6. My experience is similar to that noted by Maher and Tetreault in *The Feminist Classroom.* They report the ways in which students are frequently incapable of acknowledging either their class or race position in America. For example white middle-class students, "tended to perceive themselves only as individuals, missing their own connection to the economic and political structures that privilege them in relation to other women and men" (220). While, "The white students had trouble seeing themselves in their own lives as white, in seeing racism as part of a social structure in which their own lives were embedded, and therefore, had trouble coping with their own racism except, sometimes in terms of individual guilt" (221).

7. This is in reference to bell hooks's *Teaching to Transgress: Education as the Practice of Freedom* (New York: Routledge, 1994). The book is a collection of passionate and hopeful essays that speak to hooks's desire to make the process of education "a movement against and beyond the boundaries," by celebrating "teaching that enables transgressions."

8. The most persistent urban myth is the belief that all mulatto children in slavery were the offspring of their slave masters and granted special treatment. Students insist all house slaves were "light skinned" and pampered and all field slaves were dark skinned and abused. The historical reality is all slaves were abused, skin color and birth parent were no guarantee of treatment, and house slaves were not pampered.

9. See Nell Painter's "Soul Murder and Slavery: Toward a Fully Loaded Cost Accounting," in *U.S. History as Women's History: New Feminist Essays,* eds. Linda K. Kerber, Alice Kessler-Harris & Kathryn Kish Sklar (Chapel Hill: University of North Carolina Press, 1995).

10. Gabriel Prosser was the organizer of what historian Douglas Egerton calls "the most extensive slave conspiracy in southern history." Gabriel's plans for rebellion and revolution in Virginia in 1800 were foiled by a combination of treachery amongst his fellow slaves and bad weather. He and his co-conspirators were captured and executed. See Egerton's *Gabriel's Rebellion: The Virginia Slave Conspiracies of 1800 & 1802* (Chapel Hill: University of North Carolina, 1993).

11. Patricia Hill Collins, *Black Feminist Thought: Knowledge, Consciousness, and the Politics of Empowerment* (Boston: Unwin Hyman, 1990) devotes an entire chapter "Mammies, Matriarchs and Other Controlling Images," to dissecting the constructs of black womanhood/mothering created by American society as part of the process of objectifying black women. Of the mammy she writes, "Created to justify the economic exploitation of house slaves and sustained to explain Black women's long-standing restriction to domestic service, the mammy image represents the normative yardstick used to evaluate all Black women's behavior. . . . Even though she may be well loved and may wield considerable authority in her white 'family,' the mammy still knows her place as obedient servant. She accepts her subordination."

Collins, like Gloria Joseph (see below) draws a distinction between the understanding black women have of mothering and that imposed upon them by white society.

12. Commenting on the variations in authority found the classroom, Maher and Tetreault note the ways feminist professors and their students approach the issue. I was particularly struck by the way they reported the tendency of students at Spelman College to compare classroom dynamics to familial relations. The concepts of family (and by inference mothering) as presented in this chapter on authority, are situated as if they are without complication. Family, motherhood, (and to some degree sisterhood) are to my mind quite complicated and potentially places of conflict as well as support and connectedness. A feminist strategy that encourages students to draw parallels between the classroom and the family runs the risk of tapping into tensions rooted in dynamics that may be less benign than envisioned by a more beneficent vision of family.

13. Gloria Joseph writes of the tensions between black mothers and daughters. Black daughters learn "that their mothers are not personally responsible for not being able, through their individual efforts to make basic changes in their lives or the lives of their children." (96) This understanding engenders an immense respect for their mothers and the efforts they do make to protect their children from the abuses of a racist society. At the same time those same daughters learn to fear their mothers' anger born of the intensity of their struggle, which may be manifest in physical punishment and/or erratic mood swings. See "Black Mothers and Daughters" in *Common Differences Conflicts in Black and White Feminist Perspectives*. Patricia Hill Collins also addresses black motherhood and mother/daughter tensions. "Black mothers' ability to cope with race, class, and gender oppression should not be confused with transcending those conditions. Black motherhood can be rewarding, but it can also extract high personal costs. The range of black women's reactions to motherhood and ambivalence that many Black women feel about mothering reflect motherhood's contradictory nature" (133). Black daughters who are being raised to be "strong" so they might thrive within the race/class/gender triad sometimes find themselves yearning for more lighthearted and loving relationships with their mothers (127).

14. Dr. Papusa Molina addresses this idea in, "In Alliance, In Solidarity," *Making Face, Making Soul: Creative and Critical Perspectives by Feminists of Color*, ed. Gloria Anzaldúa and in her workshop on shared oppressions. Writing of the tendency to "blame the white, upper class, Christian, heterosexual, able-bodied man as the Oppressor with a capital O," Molina suggests "assuming some responsibility for our contributions to this patriarchal, imperialist system" by first "looking at every human being—including ourselves—as victims *and* perpetrators of oppression" (330).

15. Harriet Jacobs was a female slave whose tale of years of sexual harassment and mental torture at the hands of her master were documented in an 1861 narrative. *Incidents in the Life of a Slave Girl: An Authentic Historical*

Narrative Describing the Horrors of Slavery as Experienced by Black Women, was edited by L. Maria Child though written by Jacobs under the pseudonym Linda Brent. Jacobs escaped from her sadistic master after hiding in an attic crawlspace for nearly seven years. Literary critics and some historians assumed the tale to be a work of fiction written by Jacobs's white editor. The work has since been authenticated.

Works Cited

Anzaldúa, Gloria, ed. *Making Face, Making Soul: Creative and Critical Perspectives by Feminists of Color.* San Francisco: Aunt Lute Foundation Books, 1990.

Boyd, Julia A. *Can I Get A Witness: Black Women and Depression.* New York: Plume, 1999.

Collins, Patricia Hill. *Black Feminist Thought: Knowledge, Consciousness, and the Politics of Empowerment.* Boston: Unwin Hyman Inc., 1990.

De Castell, Suzanne, and Bryson, Mary, eds. *Radical In<ter>ventions: Identity, Politics, and Difference/s in Educational Praxis.* Albany: State University of New York Press, 1997.

Domhoff, G. William, Richard L. Zweigenhaft. *Diversity in the Power Elite: Have Women and Minorities Reached the Top?* New Haven: Yale University Press, 1998.

Egerton, Douglas. *Gabriel's Rebellion: The Virginia Slave Conspiracies of 1800 & 1802.* Chapel Hill: University of North Carolina Press, 1993.

Freire, Paulo. *Pedagogy of the Oppressed: New Revised Twentieth-Anniversary Edition.* New York: Continuum, 1999.

Harris, Robert L. "Dilemmas in Teaching African American History." *Perspectives* (32) 1998.

hooks, bell. *Talking Back: thinking feminist, thinking black.* Boston: South End Press, 1989.

———. *Yearning: Race, Gender and Cultural Politics.* South End Press, 1990.

———. *Teaching to Transgress: Education as the Practice of Freedom.* New York: Routledge, 1994.

Joseph, Gloria. *Common Differences: Conflicts in Black and White Feminist Perspectives.* Boston: South End Press, 1986.

Lewis, C. S. *The Screwtape Letters.* New York: The Macmillan Company, 1943.

Maher, Frances A., and Mary Kay Thompson Tetreault. *The Feminist Classroom: An Inside Look at How Professors and Students Are Transforming Higher Education for a Diverse Society.* New York: Basic Books, 1994.

McIntosh, Peggy. "White Privilege and Male Privilege: A Personal Account of Coming to See Correspondences through Work in Women's Studies." *Critical White Studies: Looking Behind the Mirror.* Ed. Richard Delgado and Jean Stefancic Philadelphia: Temple University Press, 1997, 291–299.

McLaurin, Melton, A. *Celia, A Slave.* Athens: University of Georgia Press, 1991.

Morgan, Edmund. *American Slavery, American Freedom: The Ordeal of Colonial Virginia.* New York: Norton, 1975.

Morgan, Jennifer. "'Some Could Suckle Over Their Shoulder': Male Travelers, Female Bodies and the Gendering of Racial Ideology, 1500 - 1770." *William and Mary Quarterly* 54 (1997): 167–192.

Nobile, Vince. "White Professors, Black History: Forays into the Multicultural Classroom." *Perspectives* (31:6) (1993): 1–19.

Painter, Nell Irvin. "Soul Murder and Slavery: Toward a Fully Loaded Cost Accounting." *U.S. History as Women's History: New Feminist Essays.* Ed. Linda K. Kerber, Alice Kessler-Harris, Kathryn Kish Sklar. Chapel Hill: University of North Carolina Press, 1995.

Patterson, Orlando. *Slavery and Social Death: A Comparative Study.* Cambridge: Harvard University Press, 1982.

Razack, Sherene H. *Looking White People in the Eye: Gender, Race, and Culture in Courtrooms and Classrooms.* Toronto: University of Toronto Press, 1998.

Williams, Patricia. *The Alchemy of Race and Rights.* London: Virago Press, 1993.

Yellin, Jean Fagan, ed. *Incidents in the Life of a Slave Girl: An Authentic Historical Narrative Describing the Horrors of Slavery as Experienced by Black Women, written by Herself, Harriet A. Jacobs.* Cambridge: Harvard University Press, 1987.

CHAPTER NINE

TEACHING (ABOUT) GENOCIDE

Bat-Ami Bar On

I

A while back I was assessing my teaching during the academic year that just ended in order to bring some closure to it, as well as create an opening into the new one about which I was beginning to think. I was focusing in particular on my genocide course in preparation for a course on Hannah Arendt since, for me, both were connected; this led me further into a questioning of modern and postmodern Western ethico-politics and what ethico-politics may mean in light of the *shoa*[1] or Nazi Judeocide[2] and other genocidal events that seem so very entwined with Western modernity and postmodernity.[3] These include, for example, the murderous annihilation of indigenous peoples in the process of European incursion into and conquest of the Americas, the greedy cruel indifference toward the death of millions in the process of the European enslavement of Africans, the dispossession and slaughter of Armenians by the Turks while the Turks were consolidating a nation-state that was intended to replace a fallen empire, and the mass politicides[4] in Cambodia and Argentina. Thinking about my genocide course, and in conjunction with it about other courses that I teach, I was again aware that there is something about those of my courses that thematize oppression or violence, and especially "extreme" or "limit cases" of it, that tends to engender resistance to rather than a deep engagement with the course materials in a fair number of undergraduate students.

There are a few elements to what I take to be a "depth of engagement" with a course. Of these, the most important is experimentation with ways of thinking that do not necessarily fit perfectly into one's existing thought habits.[5] This is, I think, one of the aims of the teaching of philosophy. In particular, though, it is the goal of any oppositional critical pedagogy, including feminist pedagogy, insofar as it takes upon itself the teaching of analytic interrogative skills and competencies, as well as prepares students to form creative new syntheses.[6] While these may be generally useful, in many of my courses I want the students to put their critical skills and competencies to use in some form of ideology critique. In my genocide course, projecting my own trajectory of questions, the ideology I wanted investigated was that of modern Western liberal ethico-politics, which centers abstract individuals with conflicting desires and a reason that can, nonetheless, bring them into social collectivities from which they protect themselves with a semi-permeable wall of rights. Marxist readings have exposed some of the contradictions of this ideology. Feminist readings have shown this ideology to be male. Antiracist and postcolonial readings have shown it to be European white.[7] What I anticipated from the study of genocide is that it may add to and perhaps even radicalize these already critical readings.[8]

Though wishing for this from the course, I generally do not expect students to become convinced that a different way of thinking is better than what they are used to. However, I do request that they try things out, believing that it is through thought experiments that one best navigates among and can come to a better comprehension of alternative conceptual frameworks. Since no choice among alternative conceptual frameworks is merely rational and habit weighs heavily on how one thinks, thought experiments are particularly important in the case of nonordinary or not yet habituated "knowledges" because this is in part how they get "tested."

I do not conceive of my request for and insistence on thought experiments in the liberal terms of "open mindedness." I suspect with Althusser that performance subjectifies and that, therefore, when one tries out a way of thinking one risks a change of one's identity.[9] At the same time, though, I also believe that subjectification is a complicated process and that if honest self-reflection is possible, one can become proficient in a new way of thinking without it automatically replacing an old way. If so, then generally speaking, the risks to the stability of an experimenting student's identity are the fairly ordinary risks of education under nontotalitarian conditions, a risk that is exemplified by bell hooks's description of the conflict that she felt between ideas learned at school and values and beliefs acquired at home. She writes,

> School was the place of ecstasy—pleasure and danger. To be changed by ideas was pure pleasure. But to learn ideas that ran counter to values and beliefs learned at home was to place oneself at risk, to enter the danger zone. Home was the place where I was forced to conform to someone else's image of who

and what I should be. School was the place where I could forget that self and, through ideas, reinvent myself (3).

Perhaps because I myself find genocide so puzzling and in some ways as even defying understanding, which always takes shape within some conceptual framework, and because I organized the syllabus for my genocide course in a manner that emphasized the need for new approaches to ethics and politics, I thought that the course materials themselves will lead to the kind of thought experiments that I wanted the students to undertake as part of their engagement with the course.[10] Reading poems from *Against Forgetting: Twentieth Century Poetry of Witness,* selections from *I Rigoberta Menchu: An Indian Woman in Guatemala,* or essays from *Echoes from the Holocaust: Philosophical Reflections on a Dark Time,* or viewing films such as *The Official Story* or *The Revolt of Job* is thought provoking.[11] However, many of the students did not seem to be galvanized by them to think. This time, instead of immediately assuming that my choice of materials for the course was wrong, I suspended the usual flurry of activities with which I tend to respond to students responses to my courses and did not tinker with the syllabus. Instead, I allowed the problem to be a problem and decided that before I take on the restructuring of my genocide course I needed to make sense of why, with some exceptions, undergraduate students appear to resist the kind of substantive materials with which one could almost anticipate them to become seriously involved.

Reviewing what students did in my genocide course, I realized that their resistance took several nonverbal forms, all of which included a presentation of themselves that implied a kind of boredom with suggestions that this was due to previous exposure to the same materials. Verbally their resistance was usually expressed through the question—"What can be done to prevent the repetition of genocide?" The students asked this question whenever they could and then discussed it very passionately. Though there may be other explanations of a resisting student's conduct,[12] what I want to explore is the possibility that the "boredom" and the excited and earnest turn toward issues of "prevention" are about a defensive kind of inattention.[13]

Since for most of the students the texts and films that I assigned in my genocide course were new, the students did not actually already know the course materials. And even if they knew some of the texts or films, each was quite rich and could be looked at again without one becoming bored. I, therefore, suspect that to the extent that the students presented themselves as bored because they already knew what they were supposed to learn, they enabled themselves to simulate an absence from the course, excuse this simulated absence, and also hide it. Something quite similar happens when the "prevention" question is asked. At face value, the question may look like the most urgent question one could ask with regard to genocide. But, what the question accomplishes is the redirection of attention away from genocide and to an imaginary genocide-free possible world. By redirecting one's attention away from something, one simulates an absence relative to it. In this case, because the simulated absence is achieved through attention to an important related and relevant question, it is simultaneously excused and covered up.

I think that if the students indeed excused and covered up their simulated absences, then they probably had quite a dilemma to deal with as a result. The simulated absence is a lack of a presence with respect to and a distance from the substantive materials of the course. Doing this and implying that they knew all there is to know about genocide and trying to "fix" the world so as to render it genocide-free, the students could both disassociate themselves enough from the course and keep enough of a felt trace of a connection to it, all of this while also asserting themselves openly in the classroom as perceptive, sensitive, and concerned since they affirmed their knowledge of and were searching for a good solution to genocide.

II

Understanding the students' resistance as an excused and covered up simulated absence makes intuitive sense of their behavior. However, I remained bothered by what now looked like the students' need to flee what they were studying in my courses. As I pointed out, I hoped that a focused concentration on genocide would enable the students to perceive and be moved by the need to ask critical questions regarding the continued reliance on and use of a modern Western liberal ethico-politics. I wanted them, for example, to ponder seriously Eichmann's claim that he was a good Kantian and whether his kind of banality was made possible by modern Western ethico-politics, or wonder if given the dimensions of most genocides, how it is that they are still taken as a kind of ethico-political mistake that permits the reinscription of modern Western ethico-politics. Yet, using the routes that the students seemed to have used for their escape, they reaffirmed just what I wanted them to question and did not distance themselves from modern Western liberal ethico-politics in a manner that encouraged them to reexamine it in light of what they were encountering in the course. What this meant for me was that despite my plans for my genocide course in particular, and perhaps in the case of all my courses that thematize violence, these courses are undermining themselves and not facilitating the development and refinement of interrogative understandings at the levels that I desire. Moreover, it now looks like my courses fail in this way because I assign particular substantive materials.

Due to my own readings in and for my genocide course, I began thinking of how it was that the substantive materials of my courses were undermining my pedagogical intentions in terms of psychological trauma. What
I started wondering about is the possibility that my courses were traumatizing my students. This is a disturbing idea not least because this suggests a
much higher risk to the students than the risk of education-related ordinary
change. And yet, I was thinking about my courses this way, initially following Eric Santer's analysis of a debate among German historians regarding
Germany's Nazi past.[14] What Santer suggests is that the work of many of the
historians involved in the debate displays a narrative fetishism. Santer describes narrative fetishism as follows:

> By narrative fetishism I mean the construction and deployment of a narrative
> consciously or unconsciously designed to expunge the traces of the trauma or
> loss that called the narrative into being in the first place. The use of narrative
> as fetish may be contrasted with that rather different mode of symbolic be-
> havior that Freud called *Trauerarbeit* or the "work of mourning." Both narra-
> tive fetishism and mourning are responses to loss, to a past that refuses to go
> away due to its traumatic impact. The work of mourning is a process of elab-
> orating and integrating the reality of loss or traumatic shock by remembering
> and repeating it in symbolically and dialogically mediated doses; it is a process
> of translating, troping, and figuring loss. . . . Narrative fetishism, by contrast,
> is the way an inability or refusal to mourn emplots traumatic events; it is a
> strategy of undoing, in fantasy, the need for mourning by simulating a condi-
> tion of intactness, typically by situating the site and origin of loss elsewhere.
> Narrative fetishism releases one from the burden of having to reconstitute
> one's self-identity under "posttraumatic" conditions; in narrative fetishism,
> the "post" is indefinitely postponed (144).

Given Santer's description of narrative fetishism I wondered whether
students in my courses were deploying a narrative of "boredom" with its
implied claims to "preexisting knowledge," or a narrative of "prevention," with its display of passion, fetishistically; whether like the German
historians, their simulated absence was a mode of refusing to acknowledge and of denying a psychological trauma and an indefinite postpone-
ment of the "reconstitution" of their "identity under posttraumatic
conditions." If this is what my students were doing, then, on the one
hand, my courses do shake students out of their habituated "dogmatic
slumber," but apparently the substantive materials of my courses some-
how traumatize students.

I believe that the literature on "secondary trauma" can help make some
sense of this. Thus, Judith Lewis Herman, a therapist specializing in in-
cest, states that,

Trauma is contagious. In the role of a witness to disaster or atrocity the therapist at times is emotionally overwhelmed. She experiences to a lesser degree,
the same terror, rage, and despair as the patient. This phenomenon is known
as "traumatic countertransference" or "vicarious traumatization" (140).

According to Herman, therapists become traumatized because when listening
to their clients, they witness traumatizing events. One may object to Herman
and point out that insofar as therapists are witnesses, at most their witnessing
of traumatizing events is a secondhand kind of witnessing because what therapists witness is their clients' experience of trauma. Yet, the situation is not so
simple since, as Cathy Caruth notes,[15] what marks a trauma is some kind of
a lack because traumatizing events are not assimilated or integrated events. By
witnessing their clients' experiences of trauma, then, therapists cannot even
be secondhand kind of witnesses to traumatizing events. And, indeed, according to Dori Laub, a psychoanalyst who works with *shoa* survivors, this is
not what goes on in the case of therapeutic witnessing.

Laub suggests that due to their work with unassimilated material, as they
listen to their clients, therapists are participating with their clients in the
construction of the traumatizing events as known events. Therapists are,
then, not exactly witnesses of witnesses; their witnessing and their clients'
witnessing are in an important sense co-temporal and interdependent. Laub
explains the resultant psychological trauma of the therapists, saying:

> The listener to the narrative of extreme human pain, of massive psychic
> trauma, faces a unique situation. In spite of the presence of ample documents,
> of searing artifacts, and fragmentary memoirs of anguish, he comes to look for
> something that is in fact nonexistent. . . . The listener [by listening] . . . is a
> party to the creation of knowledge de novo. . . . By extension, the listener to
> trauma comes to be a participant and co-owner of the traumatic event; through
> his very listening he comes to partially experience trauma in himself (57).

An analogy between therapists and students of traumatizing events is, I believe, warranted. Students of traumatizing events are as much "listeners to
the narrative of extreme human pain" as therapists. While not necessarily directly listening to witnesses or even reading or watching memoirs, even their
working with secondary materials brings them into contact with what they
usually recognize as outside of their "ordinary" experience and what they
take as outside "ordinary" human experience, and therefore something that
is not at all easily assimilated. Their studies, though, require some kind of
integration insofar as they involve a thinking through, an attempt to understand and make sense of, and a response to what they encounter. As a result,
through their study of traumatizing events, the students participate in mak-

ing them known. As knowledge producers they become the events' "co-owners," and as "co-owners," the students, just like therapists, are bound to become traumatized by the traumatizing events that they study.[16]

III

When Shoshana Felman realized that students were becoming traumatized in her graduate course on testimony, she address them, stating:

> What your responses most of all conveyed to me was something like an anxiety of fragmentation. People talked of having the feeling of being "cut off" . . . some felt very lonely. It struck me that Celan's words were very accurate to describe the feeling of the class:
>
> > A strange lostness
> > was palpably present.
>
> There was a sense of panic that consisted of both emotional and intellectual disorientation, loss of direction. . . . There was a great need to talk. . . . People frantically looked for interlocutors, but expressed their frustrations at the fact that everything that they could say . . . was just fragmentary: they could not convey the whole experience. . . . I suggest that the significance of [this] . . . was, not unlike Celan's . . . something akin to the loss of language (49–50).

Felman responded to her students' crisis not only with a clarifying description of what was happening to them as witnesses. Taking their experience as traumatic and trauma as manifesting itself as a rupturing destabilization resulting in the loss of intelligible speech, she designed therapeutic assignments that were intended to facilitate her students reentry into intelligible speech. The need for such a reentry is one felt by many survivors of traumatizing events because the possibility of reentry promises some kind of relief from alienation due to the connection between speech and community.[17] But, as James E. Young points out, reentry into intelligible speech might be costly since it seems to normalize atrocities. Intelligible speech requires using known patterns and styles and Young claims:

> It is almost as if violent events—perceived as aberrations or ruptures in the cultural continuum—demand their retelling, their narration, back into tradition and structures they would otherwise defy. For upon entering narrative, violent events necessarily reenter the continuum, are totalized by it, and thus seem to lose their "quality." . . . For once written, events assume the mantle of coherence that narrative necessarily imposes on them, and the trauma of their assimilability is relieved.[18]

It seems as if trauma forces a binary choice between disconnection and connection and the choice of connection as a connection through speech requires a certain betrayal of a truth that cannot be told. Some form of "narrative fetishism" seems, then, inevitable because there is no way to have a narrative and to not, as a result of that, be "undoing in fantasy" that which caused the need to mourn. If so, my students' "boredom" narrative can be seen as an attempt to reenter intelligibility by turning toward "normality" and their "prevention" narrative as a way to reenter intelligible speech with "standard" philosophical means. The extent to which these narratives are implicated in some form of "narrative fetishism" is, perhaps, simply unavoidable.

Reentry into intelligible speech, though, might not need to take the form of "narrative fetishism" and Hannah Arendt's struggles for intelligibility illustrate this point well and are also pedagogically instructive. Arendt was a victim/survivor of Nazi Germany, as well as a student of the Nazi Judeocide. She negotiated her need for intelligible speech among other ways, by examining and analyzing how others attempted to speak about Nazi Germany and the *shoa*. This led her to offer a distinction between two kinds of writing about the concentration camps experiences.[19] One of the two kinds that she identifies is "the immediate experience report," which she describes as an "unmediated recording" that fails to communicate because the record is of things that evade human understanding. The second kind is the "assimilated recollection," which is mediated and written purposefully in an attempt to communicate, hence, in an attempt to understand and make it possible for others to try and understand.

It is not only the two kinds of writings that are distinct, according to Arendt, but also the attitudes of those who write in these two distinct ways. She believes that writers of "unmediated records" do not trust people who have not partaken in the same, or similar enough, experiences to be capable of understanding the concentration camps experiences, while the writers of the "assimilated recollections" do trust others' capacity to extend themselves beyond their own experiences. For Arendt, the difference in writers' attitudes is significant not merely because it results in two kinds of writings, but because the two kinds of writings have different effects on the writers and on others. These effects are diametrically opposed because "unmediated records" do not but "assimilated recollections" do form a bridge between their writers and others. Where no bridging happens, Arendt claims, the readers stay distant from the writers who stay alienated from the world. And she points out that "[o]nly a few [reports by survivors of the concentration camps] have been published, partly because, quite understandably, the world wants to hear no more of these things, but also because they all leave the reader cold, that is apathetic and as baffled as the writer himself" ("The Concentration Camps" 743).

It may seem from Arendt's distinctions that even though she prefers the "assimilated recollection," because it is mediated, it will not escape "narrative fetishism," though the "unmediated record" might. Yet, Arendt believed that the totalitarianism of Nazi Germany contributed to a rupture with tradition and that the known categories of right and wrong cannot be used meaningfully anymore. Moreover, she says in "Social Science Techniques and the Study of Concentration Camps" that the concentration camps cannot be understood in ordinary scientific terms. So, her preference for "assimilated recollections" and a communicative kind of writing that bridges between those who have and those who have not had the traumatizing experiences of genocide firsthand, should not be construed as a preference for familiar emplotment strategies, structures, and styles, hence as a preference that entwines one necessarily in "narrative fetishism." Rather, they should be taken as a preference for intelligibility by other means.

But how does one communicate intelligibly by other means? Arendt herself does so by using familiar concepts differently, giving them new meanings, and allowing these meanings to develop in her writing, many a time by returning to the same or similar events and issues and trying out her reworked concepts again. As she ends her report on the Eichmann trial, for example, Arendt suggests that the Nazi Judeocide problematized the idea of crime since many of the acts constituting it did not necessarily involve an intent to do wrong, among the traditional criteria for the distinction between criminal and noncriminal conduct. Arendt does not, as a result, shy away from the use of the idea of crime. Rather, she tries out the notion of a crime without an intent to do wrong and argues that it is not Eichmann's motivations but his active participation in the execution of a genocidal policy that is criminal. Because she emphasizes Eichmann's "active participation," she implies that it is important to distinguish between "activity" and "passivity" in the case of complicity and that "passive" complicity is not criminal.

Arendt's conceptual innovation in this case is not too complex. She articulates the conceptual problem posed by the Nazi Judeocide clearly and she works out a resolution that makes it possible to hold some people legally culpable for genocide. Still, as an example of an interpretive work that deployed concepts that my students were familiar with critically and differently, thus perhaps not fetishistically, it did not work. Indeed, none of the textual examples that I gave them worked.

IV

The various examples that I gave the students in my genocide course seemed particularly lacking in the context of the kind of inclusive learning community that I try to facilitate in the classroom, a learning community that I was inspired to take seriously by critical pedagogy. Like many others of my generation, I turned to critical pedagogy due to ethico-political commitments and my disappointments with the kind of teaching that I was usually subjected to. With the aid of critical pedagogy I learned to imagine the classroom in a manner that was more congenial to me, thus, as a place where students should learn to think for themselves and with others, and of course, as a site of opportunities for students to participate in the production, rather than just the consumption, of knowledge. The kind of thought experimentation that I talked about earlier as something that I expect my students to undertake is, from the perspective of critical pedagogy, an exercise in the production of knowledge. Though, as time passed and I thought more, I have learned to assert my authority as a teacher, nonetheless, I still conceive of my classrooms and courses along the basic guidelines of critical pedagogy.

My genocide course met these guidelines. But, what I did not take into consideration when designing the course is that in the case of a course centered on genocide, the expectation for independent yet collaborative critical learning and for animated participation in the shaping of knowledge may be, at the same time, an expectation for a reconstitution of oneself posttraumatically via a reentry into intelligible speech by means other than "narrative fetishism." Were I to think more carefully about how complicated this has been for me and the extent to which this is still a very unfinished project to which teaching contributes—thinking I have been doing retrospectively since I taught the course—I might have understood better that I expected too much from the students in my genocide course. I was parceling out more responsibility than was appropriate.

The students can be taken as telling me this indirectly with their two "narratives." One implication of their "boredom" narrative is that they already have been responsible, as is evidenced by their previous study of the course materials. The "prevention" narrative also performs responsibility and its repetition functions as an index of quantity showing how much responsibility has already been accepted.

I was not able to hear the students. I tend to respond to indications of "boredom" with pedagogical strategies that are intended to make ideas and their discussion exciting. Yet, intellectual excitement is pleasurable and I did not know how to reconcile the pleasure with the horrors of genocide. I also did not know how to respond to the interest in "prevention." Critical pedagogy usually mobilizes students' feelings in an attempt to ignite a liberatory imagination. Yet, I thought that my students should first "stay with" and not move on the feelings that they had and experience more of the ruptures and the loss of sense that come with the study of horrifying injustices.

While I believe that I now hear the students more complexly and fully, I still do not know how to assign them the right kind and amount of responsibility. I have, however, clarified some of my expectations; I would think that my genocide course did not fail if the students taking it would feel conflicted about the intellectual pleasure that they have while studying genocide and the tension between an imagined genocide-free world and the emotional toll of facing as fully as possible a world shackled to and by genocide.

Notes

I read an earlier version of this essay at a conference on teaching the Holocaust. I would like to thank members of SOFPHIA for comments on another early version of this paper. Lisa Tessman commented on the current version as did Mary Jane Treacy, Amie Macdonald and Susan Sánchez-Casal.

1. 'Shoa' is the Hebrew term for the Holocaust and it literally means a great disaster. It is the term I prefer using, though within the context of Jewish History it too is as problematic as the term "Holocaust," since the expulsion from Spain in 1492, for example, was also quite a great disaster.

2. I am borrowing the term "Judeocide" from Arno Mayer, who introduces it without much argument in *Why Did the Heavens Not Darken? The "Final Solution" in History* (New York: Pantheon, 1988). I like the term because much more than a term like "the Holocaust," which is extremely controversial, the term "Judeocide" combines the particular with the general and acknowledges both historical uniqueness and conceptual similarity. I tend to use "Nazi Judeocide" rather than just Mayer's "Judeocide" in order to emphasize locatedness and historicity. According to Charles Mills, Mayer, who criticizes people who believe that the *shoa* is unique, fails to admit enough of the similarity between the Nazi Judeocide and other genocides and betrays his Eurocentrism with the title of his book. (*The Racial Contract* (Ithaca: Cornell University, 1997), 102).

3. Modernity has had a high share of genocidal events. Max Horkheimer and Theodor Adorno were the first to argue that there is a relationship between the two in their *Dialectic of Enlightenment* ([German, 1944], New York: Continuum, 1972). The thesis is developed differently and further by Hannah Arendt in *The Origins of Totalitarianism* (New York: Harcourt Brace Jovanovich, 1951). George Mosse returns to this thesis in *Toward the Final Solution: A History of European Racism* (Madison: University of Wisconsin, 1978), as does Zygmunt Bauman in *Modernity and the Holocaust* (Ithaca: Cornell University Press, 1991). While, with the exception of Arendt, these studies center racist anti-Semitism and the *shoa,* Mills in *The Racial Contract* centers the experiences of "non-European" indigenous populations and argues that the modern liberal idea of the social contract is "underwritten" with the modern unliberal reality of a racial contract that excludes "people of color" from personhood and legitimizes their exploitation, torture, and murder. Mills points out that this idea has been suggested by anticolonial thinkers like Frantz Fanon (see his comments in *Black Skin, White Masks* ([French, 1952], New York: Grove, 1967, 115–116)

and Aimé Césaire (see his comments in *Discourse on Colonialism* ((French, 1955), New York: Monthly Review, 1972), 13–15) who, in addition, believed that by beginning with the experience of "people of color," one could easily see a continuity of genocidal events from the beginning of modernity till the Nazi Judeocide. Postmodernity, if it is a global rather than a local condition, has its own share of genocidal events like those in Rwanda and the former Yugoslavia. The relationship between postmodernity and genocide is not yet theorized and explored. Much of the work on these latest of genocides follows the models set by the examinations of the relationship between modernity and genocide. Still, one may want to look at Etienne Balibar's "Is There a Neo-Racism?" (in *Race, Nation, Class: Ambiguous Identities* by Etienne Balibar and Immanuel Wallerstein ((French, 1988), London: Verso, 1991), 17–28) and Zygmunt Bauman's "'Anti-Semitism' Reassessed" (in *Life in Fragments: Essays in Postmodern Morality* (Oxford: Blackwell, 1995), 206–222) for attempts to rethink at least the European situation.

4. I use the term "politicide" to refer to politically implicated killings. I take the term "politicide" to be morally neutral and allow for the possibility that some politicides may while others may not be justifiable. My sense of politicide encompasses political assassinations like that of President Saadat of Egypt or Prime Minister Rabin of Israel by members of underground conservative oppositional groups, as well as the politically motivated killing of Tzar Nicholas II and members of his family by the almost victorious Bolshevists. Politicides, however, need not have members of current, declining—or as in the case of the killing of Stephen Bikko—possibly ascending political elites as their victims. Their targets can even be people who do not necessarily involve themselves politically but are used so by others, as has been the case with many peasants in El Salvador who have been killed by the ruling elite to terrorize the larger population into submission. Following the same logic, I would say that insofar as terrorism is practiced politically and involves killing, the killing in question is a form of politicide and so are certain acts of war, perhaps like the dropping of the atomic bombs on Hiroshima and Nagasaki. I think that some genocides are politicides, since what they are about is a radical alteration of the "body politic." In this sense the Nazi Judeocide was a politicide. While genocides seem to tend to be politicides, the connection between them is not a necessary one.

5. For a discussion of the place of this kind of experimentation in the case of liberatory movements see Diana Meyers, *Subjection and Subjectivity: Psychoanalytic Feminism and Moral Philosophy* (New York: Routledge, 1994), particularly 106–119.

6. The tradition of critical pedagogy uses Paulo Freire's *Pedagogy of the Oppressed* ([Portuguese, 1970], New York: Seabury, 1973), as its founding text. Ira Shor and Henry Giroux have contributed significantly to its developments, as have feminists since the earlier days of the Second Wave of the

feminist movements. Antiracist and postcolonial critiques have also added to its developments. Among the latest contributors to critical pedagogy are those that, in addition, query it.

7. Liberal ideology seems to have been Karl Marx's target of criticism from very early on. His "On the Jewish Question" ([German, 1844], in Karl Marx and Frederick Engles, *Collected Works, Vol 3: Marx and Engles 1843 - 1844* [New York: International Publishers, 1975], 146–174) provides an excellent example of his reading of the liberal theory of rights. For examples of early Second Wave feminist critiques see Lorenne M. G. Clark and Lynda Lange, ed. *The Sexism of Social and Political Theory* (Toronto: University of Toronto, 1979); Ellen Kennedy and Susan Mendus, ed. *Women in Western Political Philosophy* (New York: St, Martin's, 1987). For examples of antiracist and postcolonial critiques see Lucius T. Outlaw, Jr., *On Race and Philosophy* (New York: Routledge, 1996); and Anne McClintock, Aamir Mufti, and Ella Shochat, eds., *Dangerous Liasons: Gender, Nation, and Postcolonial Perspectives* (Minneapolis: University of Minnesota, 1997).

8. As I pointed out before, following the Nazi Judeocide, Max Horkheimer, Theodor Adorno, and Hannah Arendt were quite critical of modernity. While they were not always openly critical of liberalism, their critique of modernity has a built in implied critique of liberalism. But, their work is the kind of work that needs a radical revisioning in light of feminist, antiracist, and postcolonial work.

9. This is an idea that one can find already in Plato and Aristotle who, though essentialists about some aspects of character, were also quite concerned with habituation and its place in character formation. It is, however, probably Louis Althusser who has first used it in the current strong sense that leaves no room for the liberal assumption of a rationality that simply weighs and chooses. See his "Ideology and Ideological State Apparatuses," (French, 1969) in *Lenin and Philosophy and Other Essays* (New York: Monthly Review, 1971), 127–186. Foucault develops this thesis further, most notably in the first volume of *The History of Sexuality* ((French, 1976), New York: Random House, 1978). Judith Butler's *Gender Troubles: Feminism and the Subversion of Identity* (New York: Routledge, 1990) adds to it further.

10. This is not an exaggerated claim. I do believe that course materials have intense intellectual effects. But, I also use a variety of pedagogical techniques to try and facilitate students' engagements with the materials. Among the techniques I used in the genocide course was that of "buddy" journals in which journal writing was also a site for a conversation between two students. I used the "buddy" journals rather than ordinary journals to help students have a safer space than that of the classroom to talk about what disturbed them most about the course materials.

11. Carolyn Forché, ed. *Against Forgetting: Twentieth Century Poetry of Witness* (New York: Norton, 1993); Rigoberta Menchu, *I Rigoberta Menchu: An*

Indian Woman in Guatemala ((Spanish, 1983) London: Verso, 1984); and Alan Rosenberg and Gerald E. Myers, ed. *Echoes from the Holocaust: Philosophical Reflections on a Dark Time* (Philadelphia: Temple University, 1988).

12. I do not tend my exploration here to be definitive. Students "turn-off" to course materials for many reasons, for instance, because the materials may be too complicated to grasp even with hard work and mutual good intentions by students and teachers alike.

13. I learned to consider boredom as a form of inattention in a meditation workshop with Aikido and Laido master, Sensei Michele Benzamin-Masuda. While I am not sure that Benzamin-Masuda is right and all boredom is inattention, I now examine mine more suspiciously than before the workshop.

14. This debate is known as the *Historikestreit*. It began in 1986 and was carried out for a while in the German media. For an initial description and analysis see Charles Maier, *The Unmasterable Past* (Cambridge: Harvard University, 1988); and Richard Evans, *In Hitler's Shadow: West German Historians and the Attempt to Escape the Nazi Past* (New York: Pantheon, 1989). For later discussions see Dominic LaCapra's "Representing the Holocaust: Reflections on the Historian Debates" in *Probing the Limits of Representation: Nazism and the "Final Solution,"* ed. Saul Friedlander (Cambridge: Harvard University, 1992), 108–127), and his "Revisiting the Historian Debates: Mourning and Genocide," *History and Memory* 9/1–2 (1997): 80–112.

15. Cathy Caruth "Introduction to Psychoanalysis, Culture, and Trauma," *American Imago* 48/1 (1991): 1–12.

16. The analogy between students and therapists accentuates the contagiousness of psychological trauma. Lora Brown discusses contagiousness or what she calls a "lateral spread" of psychological trauma in the case of members of oppressed groups in "Not Outside the Range: One Feminist Perspective on Psychic Trauma," *American Imago* 48/1 (1991): 119–133. Her discussion calls attention to the loss of a sense of invulnerability that accompanies the realization that psychological trauma is common rather than rare. See also Sofia Salimovich, Elizabeth Lira, and Eugenia Weinstein's "Victims of Fear: The Social Psychology of Repression," in *Fear at the Edge: State Terror and Resistance in Latin America,* ed. Juan E. Corradi, Patricia Weiss Fagen, and Manuel Antonio Grretón (Berkeley: University of California, 1992), 72–89.

17. See Kai Erikson's "Notes on Trauma and Community," *American Imago* 48.4 (1991): 455–472.

18. James E. Young, *Writing and Rewriting the Holocaust: Narrative and the Consequences of Interdependence* (Bloomington: Indiana University, 1990), 15–16. Young returns to the issues that normalizing intelligibility pose in his examination of memorials in *The Texture of Memory: Holocaust Memorials and Meaning* (New Haven: Yale University, 1993).

19. Hannah Arendt "The Concentration Camps," *Partisan Review* 15.7 (1948): 743–763.

Works Cited

Althusser, Louis. "Ideology and Ideological State Apparatuses" (French, 1969). *Lenin and Philosophy and Other Essays.* (NY: Monthly Review, 1971), 127–186.

Arendt, Hannah. "The Concentration Camps." *Partisan Review* 15.7 (July 1948): 743–763.

———. "Social Science Techniques and the Study of Concentration Camps." *Jewish Social Studies* 12 (1950): 49–64.

———. *The Origins of Totalitarianism.* NY: Harcourt Brace Jovanovich, 1951.

Balibar, Etienne. "Is There a Neo-Racism?" *Race, Nation, Class: Ambiguous Identities.* Ed. Etienne Balibar and Immanuel Wallerstein (French, 1988). London: Verso, 1991, 17–28.

Bauman, Zygmunt. *Modernity and the Holocaust.* Ithaca: Cornell University Press, 1991.

———. "'Anti-Semitism' Reassessed." *Life in Fragments: Essays in Postmodern Morality.* Oxford: Blackwell, 1995, 206–222.

Benjamin, Walter. "Critique of Violence." (1921). *Selected Writings: 1913 - 1926.* Ed. Marcus Bullick and Michael W. Jennings. Cambridge: Bolknar, 1996, 236–252.

Brown, Lora S. "Not Outside the Range: One Feminist Perspective on Psychic Trauma." *American Imago* 48.1 (1991): 119–133.

Butler, Judith. *Gender Troubles: Feminism and the Subversion of Identity.* New York: Routledge, 1990.

Caruth, Cathy. "Introduction to Psychoanalysis, Culture, and Trauma." *American Imago* 48.1 (1991): 1–12.

Césaire, Aimé. *Discourse on Colonialism* (French, 1955). New York: Monthly Review, 1972.

Clark, Lorenne M. G. and Lynda Lange, ed. *The Sexism of Social and Political Theory.* Toronto: University of Toronto Press, 1979.

Erikson, Kai. "Notes on Trauma and Community." *American Imago* 48.4 (1991): 455–472.

Evans, Richard. *In Hitler's Shadow: West German Historians and the Attempt to Escape the Nazi Past.* New York: Pantheon, 1989.

Fanon, Frantz. *Black Skin, White Masks.* (French, 1952). NY: Grove, 1967.

Felman, Shoshana. "Education and Crisis or the Vicissitudes of Teaching." *Testimony: Crises of Witnessing in Literature, Psychoanalysis, and History.* Ed. Shoshana Felman and Dori Laub. New York: Routledge, 1992.

Forché, Carolyn, ed. *Against Forgetting: Twentieth Century Poetry of Witness.* New York: Norton, 1993.

Foucault, Michel. *The History of Sexuality: Volume I: An Introduction.* (French, 1976). New York: Random House, 1978.

Freire, Paulo. *Pedagogy of the Oppressed.* (Portuguese, 1970). NY: Seabury, 1973.

Herman, Judith Lewis. *Trauma and Recovery.* NY: Basic, 1992.

hooks, bell. *Teaching to Transgress: Education as the Practice of Freedom.* NY: Routledge, 1994.

Horkheimer, Max and Theodor W. Adorno. *Dialectic of Enlightenment.* (German, 1944). New York: Continuum, 1972.

Kennedy, Ellen and Susan Mendus, ed. *Women in Western Political Philosophy.* NY: St. Martin's Press, 1987.

Kushner, Tony. *The Holocaust and the Liberal Imagination.* Oxford: Basil Blackwell, 1994.

LaCapra, Dominick. "Representing the Holocaust: Reflections on the Historian Debates." *Probing the Limits of Representation: Nazism and the "Final Solution."* Ed. Saul Friedlander. Cambridge: Harvard University, 1992, 108–127.

———. "Revisiting the Historians' Debate: Mourning and Genocide." *History and Memory* 9.1–2 (Fall 1997): 80–112.

Laub, Dori. "Bearing Witness or the Vicissitudes of Listening." *Testimony: Crises of Witnessing in Literature, Psychoanalysis, and History.* Ed. Shoshana Felman and Dori Laub. New York: Routledge, 1992.

Levinas, Emmanuel. "Ethics and the Spirit." (French 1952). *Difficult Freedom: Essays on Judaism.* Baltimore: John Hopkins University, 1990.

Maier, Charles. *The Unmasterable Past.* Cambridge, Mass.: Harvard University, 1988.

Marx, Karl. "On the Jewish Question." *Collected Works: Marx and Engels 1843–1844.* New York: International Publishers, 1975, 146–174.

Mayer, Arno J. *Why Did the Heavens Not Darken? The "Final Solution in History.* New York: Pantheon, 1988.

McClintock, Anne, Aamir Mufti, and Ella Shochat, ed. *Dangerous Liasons: Gender, Nation, and Postcolonial Perspectives.* MN: University of Minnesota, 1997.

Menchu, Rigoberta. *I Rigoberta Menchu: An Indian Woman in Guatemala.* (Spanish, 1983). London: Verso, 1984.

Meyers, Diana Tietjens. *Subjection and Subjectivity: Psychoanalytic Feminism and Moral Philosophy.* New York: Routledge, 1994.

Mills, Charles W. *The Racial Contract.* Ithaca: Cornell University, 1997.

Mosse, George L. *Toward the Final Solution: A History of European Racism.* Madison: University of Wisconsin, 1978.

Outlaw, Lucius T. Jr. *On Race and Philosophy.* New York: Routledge, 1996.

Rosenberg, Alan and Gerald E. Myers, ed. *Echoes from the Holocaust: Philosophical Reflections on a Dark Time.* Temple University, 1988.

Salimovich, Sofia, Elizabeth Lira, and Eugenia Weinstein. "Victims of Fear: The Social Psychology of Repression." *Fear at the Edge: State Terror and Resistance in Latin America.* Ed. Juan E. Corradi, Patricia Weiss Fagen, and Manuel Antonio Garretón. Berkeley: University of California, 1992, 72–89.

Santer, Eric L. "History Beyond the Pleasure Principle: Some Thoughts on the Representation of Trauma." *Probing the Limits of Representation: Nazism and the "Final Solution."* Ed. Saul Friedlander. Cambridge, Mass.: Harvard University, 1992, 143–154.

Wiesenthal, Simon. *The Sunflower.* (French, 1969). New York: Schocken, 1976.

Young, James E. *Writing and Rewriting the Holocaust: Narrative and the Consequences of Interdependence.* Bloomington: Indiana University Press, 1990.

———. *The Texture of Memory: Holocaust Memorials and Meaning.* New Haven: Yale University Press, 1993.

CHAPTER TEN

DECENTERING THE WHITE
AND MALE STANDPOINTS
IN RACE AND ETHNICITY COURSES

Margaret Hunter

Universities have increasingly become a site of contestation for issues regarding race, class, and gender. As more universities add a "diversity requirement" to their list of courses necessary for degree articulation, the politics surrounding these courses intensifies. Although it seems generally positive that universities offer more courses about racial and ethnic inequality, the way that many of these courses are organized is extremely problematic. The epistemological standpoint of the course is particularly important. From whose knowledge base is this course organized? I have found that many courses are organized from a white and male knowledge base. "Ethnic studies is grounded in an epistemological assumption of multiple standpoints that coalesce around socially constructed racial categories . . . and stand in opposition to whiteness."[1] Chun, Christopher, and Gumport argue for multiple perspectives in courses on racial inequality, particularly those that challenge white and male hegemonic notions of race and reality. Unfortunately, many courses do not challenge reified notions of race and reality, and some actually reinforce them.

I am currently an assistant professor at a private liberal arts college in Los Angeles. Before this position, I taught at a "majority-minority" public university in the Los Angeles area. That university was primarily comprised of African American and Latino working-class, working adults, with smaller populations of Asian Americans, Pacific Islanders, and whites. As a biracial, black and white, woman, I was one of few women of color faculty members on campus.[2] Teaching at a university, where the vast majority of my students were students of color, provided me a space to reconsider the meanings and methods of teaching about racial and ethnic inequality. My experiences on that campus combined with my experiences, as both teacher and student, on predominantly white campuses form the basis for the following critique and proposed transformation of courses on racial and ethnic inequality.

Teaching in a university classroom, comprised primarily of students of color, has revealed to me the limitations of "traditional" courses on racial and ethnic inequality. In this case, "traditional" race and ethnicity courses are courses constructed from the standpoint of whites and men. Courses that are created from epistemologies of whiteness and maleness perpetuate the ways that whites and men view the world. These courses rarely challenge whites' and men's problematic assumptions about race and racism or challenge them to think outside of their life experiences. The racial epistemologies of whites and men are *unspoken knowledge systems* that dominate the public discourse on race.

In my courses, the students of color bring their own unique racial epistemologies that undergird how they approach the topic of racial inequality and structure the knowledge that they subsequently gain from the course. From my experiences in a racially diverse environment, I have devised three frameworks that describe *subjugated knowledge systems* of students of color: the black/white racial paradigm, the colonial framework, and the immigrant framework. I invoke Collins's concept of subjugated knowledge to illustrate the asymmetrical power relationship between the unspoken dominant knowledge systems of whites and the subjugated and insurgent knowledge systems of people of color.[3]

The knowledge systems of women of color are part of the insurgent systems of knowledge that are imperative for courses on race and ethnicity. Despite the fact that many women of color scholars have written about the inextricable relationship between race, gender, and class, many courses on race and ethnicity still exclude gender analyses because gender issues are seen as a separate course topic (The Sociology of Race and Ethnicity *or* The Sociology of Gender, not both).[4] Creating courses from the knowledge base and experience of women of color decenters the traditional white and male standpoint in our current curricula. I assert that courses on race and ethnicity would be more beneficial to everyone if the courses take into account, and teach from, the unique knowledge bases of students of color.

Courses on race and ethnicity should privilege the subjugated knowledge of people of color instead of the unspoken knowledge of whites. This requires teaching courses from the standpoint of students of color, and more specifically from the standpoint of women of color. Teaching from the standpoint of women of color exposes authentic community understandings of race and the particular ways that race is experienced by women. For instance, teaching from the standpoint of Native American women will allow us to see how Native Americans as a group have been oppressed, and how the oppression affects Native American women in particular ways: increased community sexism, violence against women and children, and so on. Studying from the lives of women reveals not only women's unique experiences with racism, but also men's gendered experiences with racism. For example, if Native American women experience higher levels of violence from Native American men in colonized communities, then there is something about the Americanization/degradation of Native peoples that encourages hatred of women. Native American cultures of egalitarianism are taken over by Anglo patriarchal culture.[5] This is an example of how studying racism from the lives of women of color reveals that racism is gendered. It structures different types of oppression for women and men.

When we use the lives of women of color as a starting point for our inquiry into racism we learn of a larger breadth of experience with racism than if we only studied men. However, it is important to note that teaching from the standpoint or knowledge base of women of color does not require the teacher to actually live a particular social identity. Racial or gender group membership never guarantee one's ideology or politics.

I agree with Mohanty's contention that, "it is not color or sex which constructs the ground for these struggles. Rather, it is the way we think about race, class, and gender—the political links we choose to make among and between the struggles."[6] Mohanty argues that social identities, themselves, do not create resistance to hegemony. Instead, she points out, it is the connections we make between struggles for liberation that ultimately determine our political goals. I agree with Mohanty's contention that it is politics and ideology that connect people in struggle more than race, class, and gender identities. Therefore, a pedagogy of liberation should not be limited to people embedded in particular identities. However, in order to teach from the standpoint of women of color, one must rely on scholarship and knowledge created, at least primarily, by women of color. This chapter outlines the disadvantages of teaching from the unspoken knowledge of whites and men, the benefits of teaching from the subjugated knowledge of students of color, particularly women of color, and the intellectual and political importance of transforming our curricula.

As a scholar-teacher of the sociology of race and ethnicity, I follow new developments in teaching race and ethnicity; I dialogue with colleagues about teaching strategies and syllabi; and I review the latest scholarship on race, as well as current textbooks in the field. This research has led me to the conclusion that many courses on racial and ethnic inequality used to "sensitize" students are actually designed for imagined white audiences.[7] This means that the courses are organized in specific ways, include certain authors, and have particular epistemological assumptions that privilege whiteness. That is, they are organized around the unspoken knowledge of whites. Epistemologies of whiteness are ways of seeing the world, or ways of knowing, that perpetuate the material and ideological position of white supremacy.[8]

White unspoken knowledges of power maintain their power through invisibility.[9] The white racial identity is rarely problematized in survey courses of racial and ethnic inequality.[10] Instead, courses on race and ethnicity say they will cover African Americans, Latinos, Native Americans, and Asian Americans. The white identity is often absent from the list. Also, both professors and students avoid naming whiteness, covering it up with terms such as "mainstream," "majority," or even "Caucasian." Using the terms "white" or "Anglo" is more useful because they are part of a discourse on racial domination that names a group by its power and exclusion rather than by physical features or numbers.

Nonwhite ethnic and racial identities do not exist without whiteness. When students and scholars speak of them in isolation, it is as if they stand alone. Morrison takes up this exact point when she writes, "There seems to be a more or less tacit agreement among literary scholars that, because American literature has been clearly the preserve of white male views, genius, and power, those views, genius, and power are without relationship to and removed from the overwhelming presence of black people in the United States."[11] She goes on to say that, " . . . one can see that a real or fabricated Africanist presence was crucial to their [American writers'] sense of Americanness."[12] Morrison shows that the black identity, perceived or actual, is crucial to the creation of a white identity. She shows that being white or "American" is not to be black. It is imperative that critical scholars convey to their students the relational nature of racial identities. The same can also be claimed for gender identities.

Many courses on racial and ethnic inequality are organized around the unspoken knowledge of men. The male standpoint is a standpoint of privilege, like whiteness, even for men of color, and it excludes the experiences and knowledge construction of white women and women of color.[13] Men's standpoint in many subjects, including the study of race and ethnicity, dominates. Men occupy a standpoint from where they view the world and this view dominates our current curricula. For example, many courses focus on the "Crisis of the African American Male" and display the harrowing statistic that more African American men are incarcerated than enrolled in college. Race and ethnicity courses often ignore the gender differences in rates of Asian men and women marrying whites. Instructors may describe the human rights abuses of the Tuskeegee Experiment on African American men, but ignore the sterilization procedures forced upon thousands of Puerto Rican and African American women. A focus on the social movements of men and the creation of men as the "heroes of the race" is further evidence of the dominant male standpoint. These courses rarely address the existence of women's social movements on the behalf of their co-ethnics, and the unique methods and organizing aspects of women-based movements appear even less frequently. I have gathered these examples of the dominant male standpoint in courses on racial inequality from a variety of sources including conversations with other race and ethnicity scholars, reviews of race and ethnicity textbooks, reviews of syllabi from various universities, and of course personal experience as both student and teacher.

Male epistemologies have been so universalized throughout academia that many professors, both male and female, have internalized this view and unreflexively teach from a male standpoint. This happens because, by and large, the accepted and canonized set of topics to cover in racial and ethnic relations courses ignores the experiences of women. Textbooks reinforce this by only covering such things as: intermarriage rates with no discussion of the racial politics of beauty, incarceration statistics, unemployment rates, racism in housing, whites' racial attitudes, self employment rates among immigrants, and so on.[14] There is no question that these are all important topics, but they exclude women's experiences with racism: the sexualization of women of color in the media, the criminalization of poor women of color (i.e., abolition of welfare), the increasing presence of the global sex trade for third-world women, and more.

Smith asserts that male knowledge dominates the discipline of sociology. Male knowledge is dominating because it only validates the experiences it can understand, and these experiences are all from the standpoint of men. In the following quotation, Smith describes how graduate students of sociology learn to think as sociologists. "We learn to think sociology as it is thought and to practice it as it is practiced. We learn that some topics are relevant and some are not. We learn to discard our experienced world as a source of reliable information or suggestions about the character of the world; to confine and focus our insights within the conceptual framework and relevances which are given in the discipline."[15] Smith reveals how knowledge construction is restricted when a male standpoint dominates a discipline. It can stifle any dissent and rearticulate or dismiss any experiences that it cannot understand. Race and ethnicity courses may also restrict insurgent knowledge if they are dominated by a white and male standpoint. These courses exist as a part of other disciplines, such as sociology, and may be subject to the same types of gendered or racial restrictions on knowledge creation.

For example, I have reviewed several textbooks on racial and ethnic relations for possible course adoption and none of those textbooks include topics on the degradation of women of color's bodies, forced sterilization, discrimination in government removal of children from the homes of poor women of color, or the cult of white womanhood.[16] The exclusion of these topics that address the specific way that racism affects women is evidence of exclusion of women's knowledge. This is why it is so important to move away from teaching within a white and male standpoint, and to begin teaching from the standpoint of women of color.

Courses that privilege the unspoken knowledge of whites and men do not provide alternative viewpoints that serve to actually *educate* students. One of the most important missions of higher education is to offer critical and alternative viewpoints to prevailing hegemonic understandings of the world. This requires that our courses challenge our most privileged students and their worldviews. Freire outlines a dialogic, problem-posing pedagogy that takes its content from the needs and experiences of the oppressed, not the oppressors.[17] The program content, or curriculum, is key to the liberation process. "Thus, the dialogical character of education as the practice of freedom does not begin when the teacher-student meets with the students-teachers in a pedagogical situation, but rather when the former first asks herself or himself what she or he will dialogue with the latter about. And the preoccupation with the content of dialogue is really preoccupation with the program content of education."[18] Freire's concern with the content of education reflects the importance of curricula in creating freedom or heightening oppression. He opposes the oppressor's knowledge as the knowledge base for learning; this is what perpetuates a colonized mind. For Freire, colonized minds mimic their oppressors. The oppressed simultaneously reject and model the behavior and values of the oppressors. Both teachers and students must work to decolonize our minds. In order to do that we must challenge hegemony and move toward teaching from the standpoints of one of the most oppressed groups of people in the country: women of color.

These examples of white and male privilege set the stage for this chapter's discussion of decentering the white and male standpoint in courses on race and ethnicity. There are several underlying epistemological principles guiding curricular organization and we must guard against using the white and male gaze as our lens of the world. First, I discuss several enduring problems with courses that are taught primarily for white students. Second, I describe three alternative epistemologies for understanding racism typically found in the knowledge bases of students of color. Lastly, I outline several concrete strategies for curricular improvement in courses on racial and ethnic inequality and implementing curricula constructed from the knowledge of people of color.

The Unspoken Knowledge of Domination

The unspoken knowledge systems of whites and men dominate and regulate the content of race and ethnicity courses. The knowledge bases are unspoken because they are often taken for granted assumptions that remain unquestioned by the instructor and/or the students. Whites' unspoken knowledge works as a barrier to antiracist education because it denies the reality of racism and it maintains the invisibility of whiteness as a racial identity. Men's unspoken knowledge continues the myth that men's experiences are universal experiences, and excludes women, and especially women of color from history and knowledge construction.

One of the most noticeable weaknesses of mainstream courses on racial and ethnic inequality is that they spend a significant amount of time "convincing" the students that racism actually still exists in the United States and around the world today. Although most students will admit that there was a chapter of U.S. history that included some racist acts, most students believe that is now behind us. This is particularly a problem for white students who have been fed a steady diet of "colorblind society" and "post Civil-Rights era" sound bytes.[19] With the help of California's Proposition 209,[20] white students have convinced themselves that not only is there no more discrimination against people of color, but that any discrimination that does exist is in "reverse" and directed toward them as white people.[21]

Unspoken knowledge can be a powerful force to contend with in a classroom, especially when the subject matter is contemporary U.S. racial and ethnic relations. Because of the current political climate and the brainwashing effect of the media on whites' perceptions of racism, or lack thereof, many professors spend most of the time trying to convince white students that it really exists. They may do this with an infinite number of charts and graphs, studies, and experiments. From my experiences observing several race and ethnicity classes at universities in southern California, I have been exposed to the common practice of offering "evidence" to the fact that discrimination still affects people of color. Usually, these statistics describe income and wealth differences, educational disparities, or residential segregation indices, and are displayed in textbooks, handouts, and overhead projections to drive home the point that racial equality is not yet a reality.

This is also troubling because the way that we typically prove that racism still exists is not in the deeper and least tangible forms of racism, but in the most superficial forms of discrimination. We cite examples of middle-class blacks being called "nigger" on the street. Instructors may describe experiments where whites and Mexican Americans both apply for residency at the same apartment and the Mexican Americans are rejected. These are real examples of racism, but in many ways they are the least significant. The real racism: the regulation of black women's bodies through welfare restrictions and forced birth control, the public colonization of black male bodies through professional sports and the media, and the ongoing political terrorism against Latino Americans through anti-immigration fervor, are ignored because the tenor of the class is focused on proving racism exists in overt and palpable ways for white people. This is further evidence of how whites' unspoken knowledge limits the discussion and content in the classroom. If this unspoken assumption is that racism does not exist, then it is up to the instructor or other students to use subjugated or insurgent knowledge to contest that claim.

Although this display of quantitative evidence for racism's persistence may help in getting the message across, I usually avoid using this type of evidence in my courses. I have found that focusing on how race creates meaning through hierarchy is a generally effective pedagogical strategy. For instance, in my course on race and ethnicity, I discuss the controlling image of the black male rapist. This requires me to locate the controlling images of white women, black women, and the noticeable absence of an image of white men. Then I can link the oversexualization of black women to similar controlling images of Latinas and Asian American women. After a historical discussion of how these images were used to justify lynching, rape, and other forms of violence, we discuss the role these images still play today in justifying violence against people of color and in influencing public policy decisions.[22] This is one example of how to avoid freezing the curriculum in a debate over statistics on racism—a debate that is grounded in the knowledge base of whites. I always work toward constructing my curriculum from the subjugated knowledge of people of color.

Unspoken knowledges of domination manifest themselves in curricula as invisible standpoints from which the course was created. This means that the white standpoint structures the course for the instructor and the students, regardless of their own individual racial identities. The knowledge constructed in the course is constructed from a white epicenter, where the white gaze is focused on various racial and ethnic groups. Frankenberg's concept of whiteness as a standpoint is useful here.[23] She says that the white standpoint is a place from which white people look at themselves, at others, and at society. In another article, I contend that even students of color can take on the white standpoint.[24] This ensures that all students see the world, and "others," as whites do. This is a fundamental flaw in any course addressing the system of racism.

In race and ethnicity textbooks, themselves, is one of the most compelling examples of the white standpoint. Many of these textbooks read: Chapter One: African Americans, Chapter Two: Mexican Americans, Chapter Three: Asian Americans, and so on. By spending 30–50 pages of white narrative on an entire people, the publishing company and sometimes the instructor feel they have successfully educated their students in the "other." This style of teaching about racism has several limitations. First, it obscures the fundamental problem of racial oppression by naming chapters and topics with racial or ethnic groups instead of forms of domination. This makes it seem as though the individual groups are the problem instead of the various forms of oppression. Dedicating a separate chapter to each racial group makes it seem as if each group has its own unique problems with discrimination unrelated to the experiences of other groups. This format downplays the similarity that many groups share in their experiences with racism. Even a cursory review of leading textbooks on race and ethnicity reveals a predisposition toward organizing chapters by racial group.[25]

Further, these chapters imply that one can "know" about these groups and "their problems" in the time it takes to read the chapter. This format commodifies people of color for easy consumption by whites. These textbooks on race and ethnicity are a part of the problem with teaching from a white standpoint. An alternative textbook organization would be, Chapter One: Racial Domination and the State, Chapter Two: Racist Discourse, Chapter Three: Racial Violence and the Body, and so on. This alternate organization would also allow the author to include gendered analyses of domination and avoid treating men and women of one ethnic group in a monolithic way. Most importantly, textbooks using this alternate organization would refocus the attention on forms of racism, sexism, and so on, and place the emphasis where it should be: on the oppressor. Many textbooks are now organized as if the racial and ethnic groups themselves are the problems needing to be solved.

The deviance of people of color is another common theme in many courses. By focusing on the alleged deviance of people of color, whites' deviant and racist behavior is ignored. Many courses on racial and ethnic inequality focus on issues such as black on black homicide rates, single parent headed households, drug subcultures, and high-school dropout rates. These topics focus on the perceived deviance or pathology of communities of color instead of a larger, more systematic exposure of racism. People of color are often characterized as deviant and pathological with an implied comparison to the "normalness" of whites.[26] This is further evidence of the power of unspoken knowledges of domination. Courses that focus on deviance within communities of color reinforce the idea that communities of color are disorganized, chaotic, violent, and self-destructive. Whites' unspoken knowledge systems create discourses on race and ethnicity that characterize people of color in particular ways and then, by implication and omission, characterize themselves as normal.

The subjugated knowledge of people of color starkly contrasts to whites' unspoken knowledge. Subjugated knowledge is insurgent because it challenges assumptions about reality constructed from white, male hierarchies. The knowledge created from the lived experiences of people of color is often subjugated, and ironically, this is especially true in courses on race and ethnicity.

Issues important to people of color in their struggles against racism are marginalized in our courses on race and ethnicity because they are typically not constructed from the knowledge systems of people of color. This maintains their subjugated status. One example of this is the issue of colorism, or skin color privilege, within communities of color: the systematic elevation of light brown skin and the degradation of dark brown skin. Colorism is a tool of racism to keep people of color divided and to continue white privilege. It is also something people of color deal with on a daily basis.

As a very light-skinned black woman, I have been a keen observer of the color politics that exist both inside and outside of the black community. I have used my own status as light-skinned, and thus privileged on this dimension, to initiate a discussion of colorism in the classroom. I believe that my students are more open to this discussion because I begin by acknowledging the existence of light-skin privilege and the damage it does to all of us, but most particularly to darker-skinned people. I also utilize my intimate knowledge of white culture to explain to my students that whites also make distinctions among people of color by skin color. Colorism is not simply a problem of the black or Mexican American community, but it is a part of our larger and shared racial ideology that values all things approximating whiteness, including phenotype. This discussion of colorism is an example of how my own identity and position, as African American, biracial, and extremely light-skinned, help me facilitate this discussion in my classroom.

However, a course created from the standpoint of whites would not introduce this issue because exposing colorism also exposes white supremacy. Many instructors have an ideological investment in keeping whiteness at the epistemological center of their courses. This investment would be significantly challenged if instructors began to consider issues from the experiences of people of color because these experiences reveal entrenched systems of racial domination, such as colorism.

The debate within many communities of color over naming is another example of subjugated knowledge. For instance, Filipinos debate the colonial implications of "to P or not to P." This debate focuses on whether Filipinos should use a precolonial pronunciation of their name as Pilipino (the "f" sound was introduced by the Spaniards), or whether they should use the colonial pronunciation and use the "f" instead.[27] Mexican Americans debate the usefulness of pan-ethnic identities like Latino, and African Americans debate whether or not we should abandon the term "black" altogether. These debates are largely unknown from the standpoint of whites and these courses often ignore such issues. Consequently, students receive a very limited view of contemporary issues in racial and ethnic relations if these courses are taught from a white standpoint. This reiterates my initial assertion that altering the epistemological assumptions of courses, from a white standpoint to the subjugated knowledge bases of students of color, would enhance the education of both students and faculty.

The white and male standpoints are able to maintain their power in part because they maintain the invisibility of the active white and male subjects in history. Many courses retain the invisibility of whiteness and white privilege by framing inequality as something that "just happens" to people of color instead of something that whites actively participate in. This may be articulated in many ways. For instance, the use of the term "society" is a frequent stand-in for whites, men, or even capitalists. When students or instructors say, "Society doesn't value African styles of beauty," what they really mean is, "White people do not value African styles of beauty." The first sentence that uses the signifier "society" obfuscates the presence of white power and hides it behind a falsely unified notion of society. When we replace "society" with "white people," we then have a clearer image of what the power struggle is about.

The construction of history is another way that the white subject may be absent from classroom discussion. Educators often retell the colonization of the now southwest United States as, "And then the southwest became a part of the United States." The subject of the sentence is avoided when using passive voice.[28] The significance of this history changes drastically if we say instead, "Anglos colonized Mexico and stole from them what we now know as the southwest United States." We create a more honest analysis of what happened in this country and around the world when we put the active white subject back into history. Although it is sometimes difficult for white students to hear, they cannot move forward in their thinking about racism until they acknowledge this history. In addition, whites need to see where they intervened on behalf of people of color or fought next to them throughout history. In order to recognize these roles, whites must have a sense of their presence in history. By making whites accountable for the oppressive actions they took, we can also make visible all the resistance to oppression that they initiated.

There is a similar parallel with the invisible male subject. Many courses describe white people as if they were genderless. In fact, white men and women often had very different racial roles in history. When courses teach about the raping of enslaved black women they often say, "Many black women were raped." Again, there is a missing agent in this sentence. White men must also be visible in history as we rewrite it more accurately to say, "Many white men raped black women." It is important that educators reinsert the male subject in history. This is particularly true because white women's roles in perpetuating racism in the U.S. South, for instance, were very different from men's. The cult of white womanhood (fragility, virginity, and dependence) was developed to both control white women and to elevate their status in relation to black women. Both men and women must be visible actors in the history of racism so that all the different forms of domination can be examined, exposed, and used to change our current conditions.

This is further evidence of the benefit of teaching from the standpoint of women of color. We are better able to expose the actions of whites and men when we ground our thinking in the lived experiences of women of color. We begin our analysis of race from the lives of women of color not because they have a more authentic experience of racism, but because through their lives we are better able to see the contradictions not only of racism, but also of patriarchy, and even capitalism. The daily experiences of women of color include many intersecting dimensions of oppression. By starting from the lives of Mexican, African, Indian, Puerto Rican, Filipino, indigenous, and other women's lives we can see how racism interacts with other forms of domination such as sexism and capitalism. This provides us with a more complex and nuanced analysis of racism that does not use the male experience of racism as a universal experience, but situates it in a context of gendered, economic, and political relationships.

Shifting the Center:
Examining the Subjugated Knowledge
of Students of Color

Students of color differ from whites in their assumptions about racism, and those assumptions also vary by ethnicity and class. Of course not all students of color have the same understandings of race, but as ethnic groups they tend to have different epistemological assumptions of race and racism, than do white students. From my teaching experiences, I have identified three overarching racial epistemologies that different students of color utilize: the black/white racial paradigm, the colonial framework, and the immigrant framework. I will describe these three epistemologies and the student groups whom I think tend to identify with each of them most often.

Many African American students understand the world through a black/white racial paradigm. Many are already familiar with a racial paradigm of power relations, an important concept in most courses on racial inequality. Whether they have personally experienced discrimination or not, African American students often have a collective consciousness about racism. Commonly, African American students do not require convincing that racism still exists with charts and statistics because it is already a part of their worldview, if not part of their immediate experience. This means that spending a large amount of time convincing students that racism actually exists is not only unnecessary for many students, but it is also a waste of their intellectual energy and time. Much more time can be focused on unearthing the more significant meanings of race and racism in our society when the students already accept the persistence of racism as a current reality. This would allow students and teachers to explore issues such as: the political campaign against women of color through the "welfare reform" movement, the relationship between colonialism and the globalization of capital, or the effects of a restructured U.S. economy on third-world immigrants.

The identity for African Americans as the "most authentic victims of racism" is another aspect of African American attitudes created in the black/white racial paradigm. Many black students, and black people in general, feel they have a monopoly the identity as "oppressed." Because of the history of African slavery in the United States, and subsequent U.S. definition of race and racism focused on African Americans, the quintessential experience of racial oppression is represented as American chattel slavery. Therefore, many black students understand themselves to be the only group who has suffered seriously from racism.

Additionally, many other students of color have internalized this very same paradigm. They also think that blacks are the only truly oppressed group and that their own experiences of racial discrimination are not as significant. For example, I have had Mexican American first generation college students say that they have never experienced any racial discrimination. These students have not learned to question why their entire neighborhood is Latino, why they only considered attending an underfunded California State University instead of Harvard, or why they are prohibited from speaking Spanish at school or work. Much of this is because racism is seen as something that only blacks experience. The term racism or racial discrimination is not used to describe the oppressive situations that many other racial and ethnic groups endure. Latinos and Asian Americans often do not use a racial lens when examining their own experiences.

The practice of only naming certain experiences as "racial" is an important point and can be used as a "teachable moment." When we teach from the standpoint of students of color, we can identify the collective hesitation to name racism and work to uncover the reasons for this hesitation. This will allow us to deal with the tendency for students to try to rank order groups by perceived levels of oppression. By discussing openly who feels they have and have not experienced racism in their lives, we can expose the more subtle and taken for granted forms of racism such as residential segregation, language use, and sense of ownership and entitlement to the nation's educational resources. Open discussion of these issues is often difficult because they are personal and emotional subjects that affect students' sense of identity and community. Therefore, it is imperative that, as educators, we think about how we manage the emotional exchanges in our classrooms.[29]

Managing emotions is an important part of any instructor's job in the classroom. There have been instances in my own classroom where African American students challenged Latino students on the authenticity or severity of their experiences with racism. At moments like these, I gently, but firmly, remind the class that different groups experience racism differently and no one group can claim the ultimate and worst experience with racism. No one wins the "oppression sweepstakes."[30] In the beginning of each semester the students create an "identity list" where they list their social identities (race, gender, class, sexual orientation, and so on) and then list whether each identity is generally oppressed or privileged.[31] I always point out that identities they did not list are often categories where they experience privilege: such as able bodied, or heterosexual, or native English speaker. This is another lesson in the invisibility of privilege. The exercise shows that each student has some privileged categories and some oppressed categories and that no one can claim authentic victimhood. In instances where students do challenge someone else's level of oppression, I always refer back to the identity list exercise as a reminder of this lesson.

As a biracial woman, I have a unique racial status in the classroom that I use to my advantage in the negotiation of emotions. I have found that both the white students and the students of color in my classes feel as if we share certain experiences. I think that white students feel a closeness to me because of shared physical characteristics (I could probably pass as white if I chose to). I think my physical appearance also makes it easier for white students to "forget" that I am not (only) white and, therefore, to feel less threatened by me than someone darker-skinned. Similarly, many students of color also feel that we share similar experiences, for instance, as members of the African American community. Also, because of the small number of professors of color on most campuses, students tend to be particularly grateful for our presence at the university and our influence on course syllabi, departmental politics, and student life. These are all ways that my own unique identity helps me to make connections with many different types of students.

Another strategy that I use to help manage emotions and build community in my classroom is to make a consistent effort to use the term "people of color" and "women of color" in my courses. I use these terms to show the similarities of experience with racism across groups. My intention here is to reduce the feelings of hostility between communities of color and help them see each other as allies and not enemies. I also think this helps promote solidarity among communities of color, something we have had much trouble achieving here in Los Angeles.

Perhaps one of my most important tools for negotiating emotions in my race and ethnicity course is the tool of self-critique.[32] I have often used examples about myself, real or created, to help teach a concept in the course and to reduce student anxiety about doing or saying the wrong thing. For instance, when I teach about multiracial identity and our society's general discomfort with racially-ambiguous-looking people, I give an example about my own behavior. I tell the class that when I meet a person whose racial identity is not apparent, I know it is not acceptable to ask them about that identity in order to categorize them. This is something that I have found very objectifying over my lifetime. However, I "confess" to the class that even though I know better, I find myself consumed with figuring out his or her background. This "confession" on my part serves a few purposes. First, it allows the students to avoid feeling defensive about their own behavior and to know that I am not judging them, even as I criticize the "need to know." This is especially important when I am the teacher because my own racial identity is often unclear. Students may hesitate to admit to a racially-ambiguous-looking person their strong need to racially identify people. By admitting that I have that same misguided need, students know that I will not judge them and that they can be open about this issue. With their defenses down, we can then have a discussion about why "we" feel the need to racially categorize all people, what we get out of it, and what it says about the meaning of race in everyday life.

The strategy of self-critique also helps maintain the notion that as teacher and students we are in this process of transformation together, and that we all have work to do to reduce our internalization of racism. These examples all support the premise that in order to best manage our students' emotions in the classroom, particularly around issues of race, we must be familiar with the knowledge bases of students of color. As teachers, we must be aware of potential assumptions and fears about racism in order to best negotiate the emotions and learning experience in the classroom. I intend my discussion of these epistemological frameworks to help us all better understand the knowledge bases of our students.

In contrast to the black/white racial paradigm is what I call "the colonial framework." Some students of color utilize this colonial framework to understand racism. This framework is often adopted by people from colonized lands. Many first- and second-generation Mexican American, Central American, Native American, and Filipino American students (as well as others) are familiar with a colonial framework of the world. They are aware of Spain's takeover of Mexico, the Americas, and the Philippines, and they are aware of how many people have internalized racism as a result of European colonialism. This kind of knowledge base is unique and quite different from the U.S. black/white racial paradigm. Students who see race relations through a colonial framework are often aware of a precolonial identity from which they may often gain pride (Aztec culture, Visayan culture, or Algonquin culture, for example).

Students who come to the classroom with this framework will have unique forms of knowledge about race and racism. For instance, many Latino students are aware of cultural norms that prefer light skin to dark skin, an effect of centuries of European domination. When this issue is raised in my courses, students who have a racial epistemology based on colonialism can immediately see the effects of a European presence in their home countries. They are often better able to understand the relationship between a history of colonialism and present day racism. These students can be catalysts for the understanding of other students.

This knowledge of colonialism and its effects creates a unique knowledge base for some students of color. Because European colonialism sets the stage for most racism in the world today, students who have an understanding of the power of that history are better equipped to understand today's race relations, especially in the United States. The way that European values and aesthetics have insidiously seeped into our own value systems is only evident when you have a sense of a precolonial identity. Precolonial identities are usually forged in struggle to resist internalized racism and assimilation. Precolonial identities are identities based in aspects of a culture before it was subject to European domination. These identities tend to value group pride and solidarity, as well as resistance to Americanization or assimilation. This can be useful knowledge in the classroom because those students who identify with cultures before they were colonized by Europe can help other students see connections between European colonization and current European and American hegemony.

More and more university students today are immigrants or children of immigrants. I believe that this group of students tends to use what I call an "immigrant framework" to understand U.S. racial inequality. Students who are either immigrants, or children of immigrants, often possess specific kinds of knowledge about immigration. They usually do not subscribe to the common stereotype that immigrants are lazy. In fact, they generally know the opposite to be true as they witness many hardworking family members and neighbors sacrificing to improve their lives in a new country. This subjugated knowledge provides them with a rich understanding of the politics of immigration, assimilation issues, and racial nativist rhetoric. Linking discrimination against immigrants to racial discrimination is usually an avenue to introduce the topic of racism to students of color who might not initially label their experiences as racial. Reviewing the history of racist/nativist propaganda in the United States is an easy connection to the histories of discrimination that many immigrant groups, such as Asians and Latinos, have suffered.

Students with an immigrant framework are also more likely to see race as a social construction, a difficult lesson to teach, because they are aware of different racial definitions somewhere else. Latino students may make a connection between how the *Indio* identity is disparaged in their home countries and the degradation of racial minority groups in the United States, despite different racial/ethnic compositions. Also, Latino students are generally more familiar with fluid racial category systems. Asian students who have familiarity with home countries or cultures may also be critical of the grouping "Asian American" as a pan-ethnic group. They are likely to see the grouping as unnatural, and purely political. This helps to teach the concept that race is a social construction.

The immigrant framework, like all epistemologies, creates certain commonsense assumptions. One of these assumptions is that even though inequality exists, that inequality can be overcome with hard work. It is also often assumed that assimilation toward the dominant group is the best way to overcome any discrimination. Assimilation is often taken for granted as desirable and something to be achieved as soon as possible. This is a commonsense assumption of the immigrant framework of race relations, and stands in contrast to the black/white paradigm of race relations that tends to see racial inequality as a more permanent feature of the United States and assimilation as something generally undesirable.

This contrast in orientations to assimilation often manifests itself in the classroom as disagreements between students. This disagreement is usually about what the appropriate response should be to racism. Students who adopt the immigrant framework tend to minimize the force of white supremacy and believe that the best remedy to discrimination is simply to "work hard." In contrast, students who use the black/white racial paradigm or the colonial framework see simply "working harder" as assimilation, and assimilation as part of the problem. I make an effort to respect the ideologies of many of my students and their parents by acknowledging how important hard work and high achievement are for people of color, and acknowledging that our best chance for economic mobility is still education. However, with that caveat, I am extremely critical of the assimilationist project in the United States. I teach my students the concepts of hegemony and discourse to help structure my critique of the enormous push to become white, to adopt a culture of domination, and to degrade one's own culture. I rely on the work of scholars such as Paula Gunn Allen to help make this point.[33] For that matter, one of my primary goals in writing this chapter is to resist assimilation. I challenge white epistemologies and implore educators to rely on the subjugated and insurgent knowledge bases of students of color, and women of color particularly, that challenge assimilation at its very root.

The previous three racial epistemologies do not constitute an exhaustive list of possible ways of understanding racial inequality. These frameworks also do not include all students of color and are not limited to certain groups for each framework. Instead, this discussion outlines what I have identified as some common ways of understanding race among different groups of students of color. This description serves as a starting point as we try to build new epistemologies into our curricula.

Insurgent Knowledges:
Decentering the White and Male Standpoint
in the Antiracist Classroom

The three previously described racial epistemologies: the black/white racial paradigm, the colonial framework, and the immigrant framework all construct knowledge of race and racism slightly differently. I have described these examples of subjugated knowledge to highlight how they differ from the unspoken knowledge of whites. Subjugated knowledge is also insurgent knowledge because it contests white and male understandings of reality. Courses on racial and ethnic inequality must begin incorporating insurgent knowledge of men and women of color into the curricula. The following are suggestions for beginning curricular transformation.

1. Decentering the White Standpoint

We must avoid spending too much time convincing students that racism really does exist. When we do that, we avoid talking more deeply about racial issues in our society. When we spend time proving that racism is real, we also keep the dialogue focused on what white students are comfortable with. This maintains whiteness as the center of our courses. By forging ahead into more threatening and fundamental areas of racial inequality, especially those mined from the racial epistemologies of students of color, the class is taught from the perspective of people of color. The organization of the class is part of the lesson. Decentering whiteness can be a very uncomfortable process for whites and people of color alike, but it can be an excellent learning experience for all involved. Students may want to hear from "the other side" or they may want a more "objective" analysis. Often students want to hear from more white authors because they give authority to whites that they do not give to people of color. Nonetheless, the organization of the course is part of the lesson and therefore the course must delve into deeper topics in racial and ethnic studies if it is to be effective.

Decentering whiteness is particularly important at predominantly white institutions. It is up to the instructor to provide an experience for white students where their own understanding of the world is not a taken for granted epistemological foundation of the course. Using the knowledge of students of color to create a course is not just for the benefit of students of color. In fact, it is arguable that white students may benefit even more from a decentering of whiteness because they have even less experience understanding the dynamics of racism. Decentering whiteness pushes white students to move beyond the superficial concerns with race, and toward the fundamental issues of racial domination that they may feel more comfortable ignoring.

2. Dismantling the Invisibility of Whiteness

It is imperative that we begin to dismantle the invisibility of whiteness in our curricula.[34] Whites and men must be active subjects of history and, consequently, agents of their own racism and sexism. We can no longer teach courses that say, "African Americans were enslaved" or "Many early Chinese immigrant women were forced into prostitution." We must rewrite white people and men back into history and say, "White people enslaved African Americans" and "White and Chinese men forced Chinese women to work as prostitutes." This rearticulation of history makes white people and white privilege, as well as men and male privilege, visible. By providing a more honest and straightforward discussion of racism and sexism we create a dialogue with active subjects. All students need to know what different groups and individuals did throughout history. This also helps them understand how things have changed over time.

As we create active white subjects, we need to expose white identity as a valid racial identity. Too many white students see themselves as "just regular" or "just American." Maintaining the invisibility of whiteness perpetuates its power. The growth of critical white studies, as well as the work already done by many scholars of color, can help us expose whiteness for what it really is: a structural and symbolic standpoint of power. Therefore, when we list which groups our courses on race and ethnicity will cover, such as African Americans, Native Americans, and so on, we must also list whites.

White identity is crucial to the creation of the identities of people of color. Lipsitz argues that part of the possessive investment in whiteness in the United States involved making blackness synonymous with slavery and whiteness synonymous with freedom.[35] This is an example of how the two identities rely upon each other for their relational meanings. Another example of this is the creation of the Latino and Asian identities as "foreigner" and the complementary identity of whites as "natives." These contrasting images illustrate how identities are relational and how they depend on each other to derive meaning. To be white is not to be black/enslaved, but to be free. To be white is not to be a foreigner, but to be a native. This type of identity formation must be made known to students as they learn about the history of racial domination.

3. Providing Alternative Models of Whiteness

When we create active white subjects, we can then discuss how whites have resisted racism throughout history. Many whites have had active roles in antiracist movements: the abolitionist movement, the modern Civil Rights movement, and so on. Highlighting the roles of whites, when they fought with and for their brothers and sisters of color, is important for two reasons. First, it provides white students an alternate role to identify with in courses on racial inequality. White students generally see themselves solely in the role of oppressor (for good historical reason), but this offers them no alternative. If white students can see members of their own group occasionally doing the right thing, this provides them a model for their own behavior. The second important reason for this is that students of color will not see all whites exclusively as the enemy. Showing white people resisting racism also shows students of color that there are some white people with whom we can build coalitions and movements.

4. Women of Color as Subjects of History

We must characterize people of color as active agents of their own history. Just as it is important for us to allow whites to be agents of their own racism and resistance, people of color must also be agents in history. We can talk about resistance through social movements and coalition building with other groups in our courses. Wherever there is domination there is also resistance. It is important for students of color to see their own people resisting and changing what often seems like a concretized system of power relations. This can then become an area where women of color are visible. Many social movements in the United States and around the world have been organized by women and they demonstrate the long history of resistance to domination by women of color.[36]

Further, it is important for white students to see people of color, not only as victims, but also as wielders of power and active changers of history. It can be useful to build into a syllabus examples of organized or everyday resistance to the domination of racism. For instance, when we teach about the epidemic of lynching in the South as a form of social control, we can also talk about the fearless activism against lynching of Fannie Lou Hamer and Ida B. Wells-Barnett.

5. Gendering our Analysis of Race

As teachers of race and ethnicity, we must begin to include an analysis of gender in our courses. We should include information from the standpoint of women of color, not just to reveal additional topics, but also to provide a gendered analysis of racism.[37] Typically issues of racism are discussed as if they exist outside of gendered bodies and experiences. The most thorough discussions of race incorporate gender analyses. We are almost always talking about a gendered experience when we talk about racism, and it is usually a male experience masquerading as a universal experience for both men and women. The ways that women and men experience racism are different and it is time for our curricula to reflect women's experiences with racism also and not leave that for the Women's Studies departments to take up.

For instance, the forced sterilization of thousands of Puerto Rican women as presented in *La Operación*[38] is a common Women's Studies topic. However, this is also a racial issue and should be addressed in courses on racial inequality. Differences in educational attainment and income vary significantly by gender within and across racial categories. These statistics need more than racial analyses. They also require gendered explanations.

6. Incorporating Insurgent Knowledge into the Curriculum

We must take the standpoint of students of color and utilize the subjugated knowledge from their many perspectives including the black/white racial paradigm, the colonial framework, and the immigrant framework. These frameworks of knowledge must still be interrogated however, because they each have their own set of assumptions that may be challenged such as the black/white racial paradigm's tendency to view blacks as the most oppressed group, or the immigrant framework's assumption that assimilation is the key to economic mobility. I am not suggesting that we blindly replace white epistemologies with those of people of color. Instead, I am suggesting that we use the knowledge bases of people of color as a place to begin our interrogation of racial domination in this country. The assumptions of the three paradigms I have outlined are still subject to intellectual debate, but by starting from these insurgent knowledges we will expose more topics of investigation and deeper layers of analysis of racial inequality. These knowledge bases are insurgent because they challenge white, hegemonic views of race and racism at their very core.

By starting from the knowledge bases of people of color we will include topics such as sexism within communities of color, inter-ethnic prejudice and discrimination, and internalized racism. Discussing many of these issues is considered "airing dirty laundry," but we will never make progress on that laundry if we cannot talk about it in an academic setting. Many white students will be surprised to learn aspects of racism they never knew about and many students of color will feel catharsis at being able to talk publicly and theorize about important racial issues that are usually personalized or ignored in our communities. Many male students will realize that their experiences with racism are gender specific, and women of color may see commonalities among their experiences. We must begin to construct our courses from insurgent knowledge bases that challenge white and male hegemonic notions of race and racism.

This short list of suggested revisions in our teaching is only intended as a starting point for early action in our classrooms and increased dialogue on the subject. I have tried to initiate some concrete solutions to fundamental problems with the organization of knowledge around race and ethnicity. This chapter can only initiate the beginning forms of change for our courses on race and ethnicity. The dominance of white voices and knowledge throughout higher education for so many centuries will only be slowly dismantled. I hope to show through this chapter that simply offering more courses on racial and ethnic relations in our universities is not enough to reverse the effects of racism. Similarly, only teaching about racism through the eyes of men is inadequate. The knowledge bases of people of color, especially women of color, are key in informing more challenging and radical courses in our universities. We have to be vigilant about how we are teaching these courses on race and ethnicity and what the epistemological assumptions behind those courses are. The privileging of the unspoken knowledge of whites and men and then its complete obfuscation is business as usual in U.S. higher education. We can change this. As we continue to examine and reflect on how our courses are created, for whom, and to what end, we will begin to rebuild curricula and knowledge bases that reflect the insurgent knowledge of race and racism. With the slow transformation of how we teach through the ideological critique of our courses, we can begin to change the seemingly intransigent nature of racial domination in this country. Although in times of desperation it is easy to think that teaching does not change society at all, the hope that it does is what keeps most of us returning to our feminist classrooms everyday.

Notes

1. Marc Chun, Susan Christopher, and Patricia Gumport, "Multiculturalism and the Academic Organization of Knowledge," in *Multicultural Curriculum: New Directions for Social Theory, Practice, and Policy,* eds. Ram Mahalingam and Cameron McCarthy (New York: Routledge, 2000), 229.
2. My identity as a biracial person is central to my involvement in Racial and Ethnic Studies, Women's Studies, and my pedagogy. I have witnessed race through the eyes of my parents, as well as through my own racially splintered eyes. My own racial experiences and identities are complicated by the fact that I am very light-skinned and often mistaken for white (only). My own identity perfectly illustrates the shifting nature of race. I will refer to myself as biracial, African American, black, and as a woman of color throughout this essay. As we have learned from scholars of multiracial identity development, there is no inconsistency in these multiple labels (for more on this see Maria P. P. Root, "A Bill of Rights for Racially Mixed People," in *The Multiracial Experience: Racial Borders as the New Frontier,* ed. Maria P. P. Root

(Thousand Oaks, Calif.: Sage, 1996). Racial and ethnic identities are situational and constantly reconstructed. This is true for all people, but particularly noticeable in multiracial people.

3. Patricia Hill Collins, *Black Feminist Thought* (New York: Routledge, 1991).

4. This issue is well documented in the feminist literature by authors such as Patricia Hill Collins, *Black Feminist Thought* (New York: Routledge, 1991); Theresa Martinez, "Toward a Chicana Feminist Epistemological Standpoint," *Race, Gender, and Class* 3.3 (1996): 107–28; bell hooks, *Feminist Theory: From Margin to Center,* (Boston, Mass.: South End Press, 1984); Emma Pérez, "Speaking from the Margin: Uninvited Discourse on Sexuality and Power," in *Building With Our Hands: New Directions in Chicana Studies,* eds. Adela de la Torre and Beatríz Pesquera (Berkeley: University of California Press, 1993); Chandra Talpade Mohanty, "On Race and Voice: Challenges for Liberal Education in the 1990s," in *Between Borders: Pedagogy and the Politics of Cultural Studies,* eds. Henry A. Giroux and Peter McLaren (New York: Routledge, 1994). Although we are witnessing the slow introduction of courses such as "Race, Class, and Gender," in some academic departments, for the most part, universities still maintain a "monist" approach to stratification studies. For more on the "monist" approach see Deborah King, "Multiple Jeopardy Multiple Consciousness: The Context of a Black Feminist Ideology," *Signs* 14.1 (1988 Autumn): 42–72.

5. Winona LaDuke, *All Our Relations: Native Struggles for Land and Life* (Cambridge, Mass.: South End Press, 1999).

6. Chandra Talpade Mohanty, "Introduction: Cartographies of Struggle, Third World Women and the Politics of Feminism," in *Third World Women and the Politics of Feminism,* eds. Chandra Mohanty, Ann Russo, and Lourdes Torres (Bloomington: Indiana University Press, 1991) 4.

7. For more on this idea see Chandra Talpade Mohanty, "On Race and Voice: Challenges for Liberal Education in the 1990s," in *Between Borders: Pedagogy and the Politics of Cultural Studies,* eds. Henry A. Giroux and Peter McLaren (New York: Routledge, 1994).

8. Henry Giroux, "Living Dangerously: Identity Politics and the New Cultural Racism," in *Between Borders: Pedagogy and the Politics of Cultural Studies,* eds. Henry A. Giroux and Peter McLaren (New York: Routledge, 1994); Peter McLaren, Zeus Leonardo, and Ricky Lee Allen, "Epistemologies of Whiteness: Transgressing and Transforming Pedagogical Knowledge," *Multicultural Curriculum: New Directions for Social Theory, Practice, and Policy,* eds. Ram Mahalingam and Cameron McCarthy (New York: Routledge, 2000); Ruth Frankenberg, *The Social Construction of Whiteness: White Women, Race Matters* (Minneapolis: University of Minnesota Press, 1993); Michelle Fine, "Witnessing Whiteness," *Off White: Readings on Race, Power, and Society,* eds. Michelle Fine, Lois Weis, Linda Powell, and L. Mun Wong (New York: Routledge, 1997).

9. Toni Morrison, *Playing in the Dark: Whiteness and the Literary Imagination* (New York: Vintage Press, 1992); David Roediger, *Towards the Abolition of*

Whiteness: Essays on Race, Politics, and Working Class History (New York: Verso, 1994); Theodore Allen, *The Invention of the White Race* (New York: Verso, 1994); Martha Mahoney, "The Social Construction of Whiteness," in *Critical White Studies: Looking Behind the Mirror,* eds. Richard Delgado and Jean Stefancic (Philadelphia: Temple University Press, 1997).

10. I have reviewed many syllabi for introductory courses in race and ethnic relations from campuses in southern California. Most of those syllabi do not take up what it means to be white at all. The courses that do investigate whiteness usually do so from the perspective of whites as ethnics, consequently avoiding the identity of whites as a dominant group.

11. Toni Morrison, *Playing in the Dark: Whiteness and the Literary Imagination,* (New York: Vintage Press, 1992), 5.

12. Toni Morrison, *Playing in the Dark,* 6.

13. Mary F. Belenky, Blythe M. Clinchy, Nancy R. Goldberger, Jill M. Tarule, *Women's Ways of Knowing: The Development of Self, Voice, and Mind* (New York: Basic Books, 1986); Bonnie Thornton Dill, "The Dialectics of Black Womanhood," in *Feminism and Methodology,* ed. Sandra Harding (Bloomington: Indiana University Press, 1987); Sandra Harding, *Whose Science? Whose Knowledge? Thinking From Women's Lives* (Ithaca, NY: Cornell University Press, 1991); Carol Gilligan, *In A Different Voice: Psychological Theory and Women's Development* (Cambridge, Mass.: Harvard University Press, 1982); Dorothy Smith, *The Everyday World as Problematic: A Feminist Sociology* (Boston: Northeastern University Press, 1987).

14. For a list of textbooks that ignore such topics, please see endnote 25.

15. Dorothy Smith, "Women's Perspective as a Radical Critique of Sociology," in *Feminism and Methodology,* ed. Sandra Harding (Bloomington: Indiana University Press, 1987) 87.

16. For examples of textbooks that are constructed from the standpoint of whites and men, see endnote 25.

17. Paulo Freire, *Pedagogy of the Oppressed* (New York: Continuum, 1970).

18. Paulo Freire, *Pedagogy of the Oppressed,* 74.

19. Kimberlé Crenshaw, "Color-blind Dreams and Racial Nightmares: Reconfiguring Racism in the Post Civil Rights Era," in *Birth of a Nation 'hood: Gaze Script and Spectacle in the O.J. Simpson Case,* eds. Toni Morrison and Claudia Brodsky Lacour (New York: Pantheon, 1997).

20. Proposition 209 was passed by California voters in 1995. The proposition ended all Affirmative Action programs in state-run agencies and universities.

21. Crenshaw.

22. For more on the relationship between controlling images and public policy see, K. Sue. Jewell, *From Mammy to Miss America and Beyond: Cultural Images and the Shaping of U.S. Social Policy* (New York: Routledge, 1993).

23. Ruth Frankenberg, *The Social Construction of Whiteness: White Women, Race Matters.*

24. For a more full discussion of this phenomenon see Margaret Hunter and Kimberly Nettles, "What About the White Women? Racial Politics in a Women's Studies Classroom," *Teaching Sociology* 27.4 (1999 October): 385–97.

25. I have included examples of some leading textbooks that use this very framework for organization. Although several of these books offer chapters on various basic concepts and theories in the field, all of these textbooks revert back to individual chapters per ethnic group. Adalberto Aguirre and Jonathan Turner, *American Ethnicity: The Dynamics and Consequences of Discrimination*, 3rd ed. (New York: McGraw Hill, 2000); Anthony Dworkin and Rosalind Dworkin, *The Minority Report: An Introduction to Racial, Ethnic, and Gender Relations*, 3rd ed. (Fort Worth: Harcourt Brace and Co., 1999); Harry Kitano, *Race Relations* (New Jersey: Prentice Hall, 1997); Martin Marger, *Race and Ethnic Relations: American and Global Perspectives*, 5th ed. (Belmont, California: Wadsworth, 2000); Vincent Parrillo, *Strangers to These Shores: Race and Ethnic Relations in the United States*, 6th ed. (Boston, Mass.: Allyn and Bacon, 2000); Richard T. Schaefer, *Racial and Ethnic Groups*, 8th ed. (New Jersey: Prentice Hall, 2000).

26. Peggy McIntosh, "White Privilege and Male Privilege: A Personal Account of Coming to See Correspondences through Work in Women's Studies," in *Critical White Studies: Looking Behind the Mirror*, eds. Richard Delgado and Jean Stefancic (Philadelphia: Temple University Press, 1997); Michael Omi and Howard Winant, *Racial Formation in the United States* (New York: Routledge, 1994); Pearl M. Rosenberg, "Underground Discourses: Exploring Whiteness in Teacher Education," in *Off White: Readings on Race, Power, and Society*, eds. Michelle Fine, Lois Weis, Linda Powell, and L. Mun Wong (New York: Routledge, 1997); Christine Sleeter, "How White Teachers Construct Race," in *Race, Identity, and Representation in Education*, ed. Cameron McCarthy and Warren Crichlow (New York: Routledge, 1993); Stephanie Wildman, *White Privilege* (New York: New York University Press, 1996).

27. Linda Revilla, "Filipino American Identity: Transcending the Crisis." In *Filipino Americans: Transformation and Identity*, ed. Maria P. P. Root (Thousand Oaks, Calif.: Sage, 1997).

28. Robert B. Moore, "Racist Stereotyping in the English Language." In *Racism and Sexism: An Integrated Study*, ed. Paula S. Rothenberg (New York: St. Martin's Press, 1988).

29. Arlie Hochschild, *The Managed Heart: Commercialization of Human Feeling* (Berkeley: University of California Press, 1983).

30. Walter Allen introduced this term to me in a graduate seminar at UCLA.

31. This is a modified version of an exercise my colleague Kimberly Nettles introduced to me.

32. For more on this pedagogical strategy and theory see bell hooks, *Teaching to Transgress: Education as the Practice of Freedom* (New York: Routledge, 1994).

33. I have used Paula Gunn Allen's work to help make this point. I find the following essay particularly powerful. Paula Gunn Allen, "Who is Your

Mother? Red Roots of White Feminism," in *Social Theory: The Multicultural and Classic Readings*, ed. Charles Lemert (Boulder: Westview Press, 1999).

34. Henry Giroux, *Teachers as Intellectuals* (New York: Bergin and Garvey, 1988); Chandra Talpade Mohanty, "Dangerous Territories: Territorial Power and Education," in *Dangerous Territories: Struggles over Difference and Equality in Education*, eds. Leslie Roman and Linda Eyre (New York: Routledge, 1997); Linda Roman, "White is a Color! White Defensiveness, Postmodernism, and Anti-racist Pedagogy," in *Race, Identity, and Representation in Education*, eds. Cameron McCarthy and Warren Crichlow (New York: Routledge, 1993).

35. George Lipsitz, *The Possessive Investment in Whiteness* (Philadelphia: Temple University Press, 1998).

36. Some examples of these movements include The Black Women's Club Movement, the Mothers of the Plaza De Mayo, Iroquois women's organized resistance to war, African American and Latina mothers' resistance to prison violence in Los Angeles, the anti-lynching campaign led by Ida B. Wells-Barnett and others, and the rural, South Asian women's recent organizing for seats in the government.

37. Deborah King, "Multiple Jeopardy Multiple Consciousness: The Context of a Black Feminist Ideology," *Signs* 14.1 (1988 Autumn): 42–72.

38. *La Operación*, Director, Producer, Ana María García, Latin American Film Project and Skylight Pictures (New York: Cinema Guild, 1982).

Works Cited

Aguirre, Adalberto and Jonathan Turner. *American Ethnicity: The Dynamics and Consequences of Discrimination, Third Edition.* New York: McGraw Hill, 2000.

Allen, Paula Gunn. "Who is Your Mother? Red Roots of White Feminism." *Social Theory: The Multicultural and Classic Readings.* Ed. Charles Lemert. Boulder, CO: Westview Press, 1999.

Allen, Theodore. *The Invention of the White Race.* New York: Verso, 1994.

Belenky, Mary F., Blythe M. Clinchy, Nancy R. Goldberger, Jill M. Tarule. *Women's Ways of Knowing: The Development of Self, Voice, and Mind.* New York: Basic Books, 1986.

Chun, Marc, Susan Christopher, and Patricia Gumport. "Multiculturalism and the Academic Organization of Knowledge." *Multicultural Curriculum: New Directions for Social Theory, Practice, and Policy.* Eds. Ram Mahalingam and Cameron McCarthy. New York: Routledge, 2000.

Collins, Patricia Hill. *Black Feminist Thought.* New York: Routledge, 1991.

Crenshaw, Kimberlé. "Color-blind Dreams and Racial Nightmares: Reconfiguring Racism in the Post Civil Rights Era." *Birth of a Nation 'hood: Gaze Script and Spectacle in the O.J. Simpson Case.* Eds. Toni Morrison and Claudia Brodsky Lacour. New York: Pantheon, 1997.

Dill, Bonnie Thornton. "The Dialectics of Black Womanhood." *Feminism and Methodology.* Ed. Sandra Harding. Bloomington: Indiana University Press, 1987.

Dworkin, Anthony and Rosalind Dworkin. *The Minority Report: An Introduction to Racial, Ethnic, and Gender Relations,* 3rd Ed. Fort Worth, IN: Harcourt Brace and Co., 1999.

Fine, Michelle. "Witnessing Whiteness." *Off White: Readings on Race, Power, and Society.* Eds. Michelle Fine, Lois Weis, Linda Powell, and L. Mun Wong. New York: Routledge, 1997.

Frankenberg, Ruth. *The Social Construction of Whiteness: White Women, Race Matters.* Minneapolis: University of Minnesota Press, 1993.

Freire, Paulo. *Pedagogy of the Oppressed.* New York: Continuum, 1970.

Gilligan, Carol. *In A Different Voice: Psychological Theory and Women's Development.* Cambridge, Mass.: Harvard University Press, 1982.

Giroux, Henry. *Teachers as Intellectuals.* New York: Bergin and Garvey, 1988.

————. "Living Dangerously: Identity Politics and the New Cultural Racism." *Between Borders: Pedagogy and the Politics of Cultural Studies.* Eds. Henry A. Giroux and Peter McLaren. New York: Routledge, 1994.

Harding, Sandra. *Whose Science? Whose Knowledge? Thinking From Women's Lives.* Ithaca, NY: Cornell University Press, 1991.

Hochschild, Arlie. *The Managed Heart: Commercialization of Human Feeling.* Berkeley: University of California Press, 1983.

hooks, bell. *Feminist Theory: From Margin to Center.* Boston, Mass.: South End Press, 1984.

————. *Teaching to Transgress: Education as the Practice of Freedom.* New York: Routledge, 1994.

Hunter, Margaret and Kimberly Nettles. "What About the White Women? Racial Politics in a Women's Studies Classroom." *Teaching Sociology* 27.4 (1999 October): 385–97.

Jewell, K. Sue. *From Mammy to Miss America and Beyond: Cultural Images and the Shaping of U.S. Social Policy.* New York: Routledge, 1993.

King, Deborah. "Multiple Jeopardy Multiple Consciousness: The Context of a Black Feminist Ideology." *Signs* 14.1 (1988 Autumn): 42–72.

Kitano, Harry. *Race Relations.* New Jersey: Prentice Hall, 1997.

LaDuke, Winona. *All Our Relations: Native Struggles for Land and Life.* Cambridge, Mass.: South End Press, 1999.

La Operación. Director, Producer, Ana María García. Latin American Film Project and Skylight Pictures. New York: Cinema Guild, 1982.

Lipsitz, George. *The Possessive Investment in Whiteness.* Philadelphia: Temple University Press, 1998.

Mahoney, Martha. "The Social Construction of Whiteness." *Critical White Studies: Looking Behind the Mirror.* Eds. Richard Delgado and Jean Stefancic. Philadelphia: Temple University Press, 1997.

Marger, Martin. *Race and Ethnic Relations: American and Global Perspectives.* 5th Ed. Belmont, California: Wadsworth, 2000.

Martinez, Theresa. "Toward a Chicana Feminist Epistemological Standpoint." *Race, Gender, and Class* 3.3 (1996): 107–28.

McIntosh, Peggy. "White Privilege and Male Privilege: A Personal Account of Coming to See Correspondences through Work in Women's Studies." *Critical White Studies: Looking Behind the Mirror.* Eds. Richard Delgado and Jean Stefancic. Philadelphia: Temple University Press, 1997.

McLaren, Peter, Zeus Leonardo, and Ricky Lee Allen. "Epistemologies of Whiteness: Transgressing and Transforming Pedagogical Knowledge." *Multicultural Curriculum: New Directions for Social Theory, Practice, and Policy.* Eds. Ram Mahalingam and Cameron McCarthy. New York: Routledge, 2000.

Mohanty, Chandra Talpade. "Introduction: Cartographies of Struggle, Third World Women and the Politics of Feminism." *Third World Women and the Politics of Feminism.* Eds. Chandra Mohanty, Ann Russo, and Lourdes Torres. Bloomington: Indiana University Press, 1991.

———. "On Race and Voice: Challenges for Liberal Education in the 1990s." *Between Borders: Pedagogy and the Politics of Cultural Studies.* Eds. Henry A. Giroux and Peter McLaren. New York: Routledge, 1994.

———. "Dangerous Territories: Territorial Power and Education." *Dangerous Territories: Struggles over Difference and Equality in Education.* Eds. Leslie Roman and Linda Eyre. New York: Routledge, 1997.

Moore, Robert B. "Racist Stereotyping in the English Language." *Racism and Sexism: An Integrated Study.* Ed. Paula S. Rothenberg. New York: St. Martin's Press, 1988.

Morrison, Toni. *Playing in the Dark: Whiteness and the Literary Imagination.* New York: Vintage Press, 1992.

Omi, Michael and Howard Winant. *Racial Formation in the United States.* New York: Routledge, 1994.

Parrillo, Vincent. *Strangers to These Shores: Race and Ethnic Relations in the United States,* 6th Ed. Boston, Mass.: Allyn and Bacon, 2000.

Pérez, Emma. "Speaking from the Margin: Uninvited Discourse on Sexuality and Power." *Building With Our Hands: New Directions in Chicana Studies.* Eds. Adela de la Torre and Beatríz Pesquera. Berkeley: University of California Press, 1993.

Revilla, Linda. "Filipino American Identity: Transcending the Crisis." *Filipino Americans: Transformation and Identity.* Ed. Maria P. P. Root. Thousand Oaks, California: Sage, 1997.

Roediger, David. *Towards the Abolition of Whiteness: Essays on Race, Politics, and Working Class History.* New York: Verso, 1994.

Roman, Linda. "White is a Color! White Defensiveness, Postmodernism, and Antiracist Pedagogy." *Race, Identity, and Representation in Education.* Eds. Cameron McCarthy and Warren Crichlow. New York: Routledge, 1993.

Root, Maria P. P. "A Bill of Rights for Racially Mixed People." *The Multiracial Experience: Racial Borders as the New Frontier.* Ed. Maria P. P. Root. Thousand Oaks, California: Sage, 1996.

Rosenberg, Pearl M. "Underground Discourses: Exploring Whiteness in Teacher Education." *Off White: Readings on Race, Power, and Society.* Eds. Michelle Fine, Lois Weis, Linda Powell, and L. Mun Wong. New York: Routledge, 1997.

Schaefer, Richard T. *Racial and Ethnic Groups.* 8th Ed. New Jersey: Prentice Hall, 2000.

Sleeter, Christine. "How White Teachers Construct Race." *Race, Identity, and Representation in Education.* Eds. Cameron McCarthy and Warren Crichlow. New York: Routledge, 1993.

Wildman, Stephanie. *White Privilege.* New York: New York University Press, 1996.

Smith, Dorothy. *The Everyday World as Problematic: A Feminist Sociology.* Boston: Northeastern University Press, 1987.

————. "Women's Perspective as a Radical Critique of Sociology." *Feminism and Methodology.* Ed. Sandra Harding. Bloomington: Indiana University Press, 1987.

CHAPTER ELEVEN

REPRESENTATION, ENTITLEMENT, AND VOYEURISM

Teaching Across Difference

Melanie Kaye/Kantrowitz

Sisterhood Seems Simple

For my generation, Women's Studies did not exist; we had to create it. My point of entry was University of California-Berkeley, as my sister graduate students came together during campus mobilization against the war in Vietnam. Together we founded the Comparative Literature Women's Caucus, raised our consciousness about sexism in the world, the movement, and the department; and we mentored each other through orals and dissertation prospectuses. Our lasting legacy was a departmental course on women and literature and the power to pick who would teach it. I was the first, and at the first class—this was 1972—we pooled the names of every woman writer we could think of. The list fit on one page.

That class (and I suspect many of the early, ecstatic, openly politicized Women's Studies classes) was distinguished by a near-leveling of power between students and teacher because of our mutual vast ignorance and passionate inquiry: students and teacher, at least at this elite state university where many students could devote full time to their studies, put so many hours into extra meetings, projects, and readings that concepts like credits and grades seemed bizarre. The class was of necessity interdisciplinary—the texts were literary, but our discussions of them demanded forays into territories nothing in graduate school had prepared me for—and it emphasized the commonality of women's experience. From a twenty-first century perspective, we—at least I and my students—seem to have rampaged through the texts seeking reflections of victimization, resistance, and female solidarity, and bypassing whatever fell outside that mold. Second Wave feminism is often ridiculed for this glib notion of monolithic sisterhood. In reality, radical white women in that intensely political moment certainly knew that all women were not white middle-class housewives longing to work outside the home. But differences in experience were muted, and complicating issues of location and privilege likewise.

If that first phase of Women's Studies might be characterized as "add women and stir"—*women and politics, women and literature, women and whatever,* huge topics because there was so little written—the next phase, initiated by the challenge of identity politics, asked: add WHICH women and stir? Who does the stirring? Yet identity politics generated its own distortions, an ever-lengthening list of seemingly equated identities ("I am a white Norwegian thirty-something able-bodied s/m lesbian vegetarian Virgo from the suburbs"), while the "politics" aspect shriveled in the Reagan-Bush years. From mass movement to small (-er and smaller) groups to self-help: not an inspiring trajectory.

The current phase of Women's Studies splits between two possibilities. One is stuck in the gridlock logic of identity politics, offering courses on this or that group of women. The other steps back to consider structural subordination of all kinds from a transnational perspective. Such a perspective seems to me essential in the light of globalization: the migration of capital across national borders, the power of the U.S. dollar, the World Bank, the International Monetary Fund pushing relentlessly for privatization; and the movements of people—refugees and workers—across national borders, driven by economic and political changes, and by forces set in motion by colonization. This phase emerges as we dislodge the United States (or "the West," or "the North") from its imaginary position at center stage and in the vanguard of feminist progress, as we disrupt the assumption that "we" are advanced and women in other nations will pass through identical stages if they're lucky. Included in this phase is a reformulation of identity and community in diaspora. As we in the United States witness essentials like shelter, food, health care, and education transformed from a hardwon category of human rights to a private store of goodies for those who can afford them, with women and children disproportionately affected (I almost wrote "afflicted"), a transnational perspective encourages us to investigate how human rights are imagined in other parts of the world. This means a shift from conceiving of Women's Studies as an annex or ladies room for the traditional disciplines, to envisioning Women's Studies as a site of shifting boundaries and at least a little insurrection—a perspective that unsettles traditional disciplines and academic frameworks and examines the ways in which structures of oppression and privilege inflect one another.

Why, then, "Women's" Studies? A good question. I am not for discarding the name—even the new fashion of "Gender Studies" makes me nervous, dangling as it does the possibility that men will once again wind up occupying center stage. But as an unregenerate Second Wave feminist, I recall the power of Women's Liberation, linked to the searing critiques of race, class, and imperialism launched by the radical movements of the 1960s. Thus I resonate to the suggestion offered by Vivien Ng, of SUNY-Albany, that we should be yoking Women's Studies together with the other "others," Ethnic Studies, Jewish Studies, Queer Studies, and Postcolonial Studies under the rubric of Liberation Studies: a suggestion that reminds us of the point. And at this millennially-hyped moment of resurgent fundamentalisms and capitalist triumphalism, we need to remember the point.

Polishing a Multiple Lens

How do we move past a longer list to make visible the connections among various structures of subordination? How do we teach students to look for pockets of resistance, to understand how resistance is strengthened or undermined? What might a course from this juncture of postcolonial and feminist perspectives look like?

In 1995, I joined the Hamilton College faculty as the Jane Watson Irwin Visiting Professor of Women's Studies, a position that has been occupied by such shaping influences as M. Jacqui Alexander, Chandra Talpade Mohanty, Ama Ata Aidoo, and Papusa Molina. I was handed the course title "Gender/Race/Class/Nation" with some general goals, which I interpreted thus: to teach students to see through a multiple lens, and to understand that gender is inherently a multiple lens; to destabilize whiteness; to refocus so that where we are—in this case in the United States at a small elite liberal arts college—is not construed as the epicenter of the universe; to heighten awareness of economic class and the shift of resources from public to private that typifies contemporary social policy.

Remember the first day of that class in Berkeley in 1972, the one-page list? These days the stacks of books are daunting. Instead of excavating basic texts, we need to make sense—at least to make questions—of complex and seemingly infinite information. In this class I use a range of materials and disciplines, but the daily news remains central. I want students to see gender, race, class, and nation in practice not as problems in addition or multiplication (double jeopardy? triple jeopardy?), but as complex and interlocking systems of subordination that require complex and interlocking strategies of resistance.

At the first class I divide the students into small groups, hand each group a different *New York Times* article, and give them 20 minutes to read and discuss the relationship of the constructs in the course title to the events in the article. On any given day, the *Times* will have at least five or six highly appropriate articles, treating, for example, childcare for workfare mothers; ethnic Chinese, "the Jews of Asia"; English-only legislation garners support; *maquiladoras* along the Mexican border and sweatshops in New York's Chinatown; statistics on AIDS among heterosexuals; high incidence of domestic violence reported by police wives; gay adoption tears town apart; clemency for Puerto Rican political prisoners. . . .

Students are encouraged to tease out the various threads: What has workfare to do with organized labor? How does scapegoating serve the status quo? Why are sweatshops always perceived as located "out there"? What has happened to the public discourse on AIDS as the epidemic's perceived center shifts? Is there a relationship between racist police brutality and domestic violence? Why is homosexuality threatening? How do claims of national liberation and women's liberation relate?

Also on the first day I discuss objectivity and bias; centrality and margins; and state very clearly (though I will have to repeat this many times throughout the semester) "I am not saying it's not ok to be who you are, white, middle class, christian, male, straight, whatever; I am saying, you have to notice it and where it places you." Because my own perspective and biases are sharp and explicit, I need to stress again and again (and model, through behavior in class) that students need not agree with me. Even so, I expect each semester at least one virulent accusation of favoritism or bias. I have learned the best defense will emerge from all the students who feel respected despite differences in values and opinions. But it is worth mentioning that I, an itinerant academic, am not constrained by possibilities of tenure—I often have nothing to lose. And as a white woman in middle age, I no longer have to fight to establish my authority, as I did when I was young. At Hamilton, my colleagues of color face privileged white students who may have never had experience with people of color in positions of equality, never mind authority. Women professors of color, especially, are often perceived by such students as inherently unauthoritative, unkind if at all critical, and vulnerable to attack. All of which argues for white women tackling these hard issues in our classes.[1]

For our opening readings I establish a postcolonial feminist perspective with Chandra Mohanty's "Under Western Eyes" and Edward Said's "Reflections on Exile"; and challenge the myth of objectivity with Maia Ettinger's witty "The Pocahontas Paradigm, or Will the Subaltern Please Shut Up?"[2] I also establish a format: we begin each series of new readings with written questions (my own, or drawn from their questions about the readings), to be answered in small groups of three or four); questions such as:

1. Ettinger describes a Person Lacking an Agenda—a PLA. What does she mean? Is there such a thing as a PLA? What might another name be?
2. Drawing on Said's essay, what relationship do you see between exile and national identity? Between nation and nationalism?
3. What connections do you see among the three articles?
4. What is Mohanty's criticism of Western feminist scholarship? Is she saying third-world women aren't oppressed as women? Summarize in your own words her concerns. What is the "third-world difference"?)

Dividing into small groups with focused questions gets quieter students talking, and makes each student responsible to the others for completing course readings on time.

More recently, teaching a similar class at Brooklyn College of the City University of New York, I've added to the class "openers" Jamaica Kincaid's "Mariah,"[3] a brilliant story that weaves together the four strands of gender, race, class, and nation; and African American feminist legal scholar Kimberlé Williams Crenshaw's "Beyond Racism and Misogyny: Black Feminism and 2 Live Crew,"[4] which provides a conceptual framework of intersectionality, and challenges students to grapple simultaneously with racism and with violence against women. And I close with Ghanaian Ama Ata Aidoo's *Our Sister Killjoy, or, Reflections of a Black Eyed Squint,*[5] a lyrical novel that revisits the themes articulated in Kincaid's "Mariah" with a more explicitly political focus.

Such a course demands tricky footwork. Students with very sophisticated gender and race politics are learning alongside of those whose understanding is rudimentary. For traditional age students, often most interested in the self, the course's emphasis on situating the self in the context that makes said self possible can feel like a guilt trip. Adept and complex as the instructor and materials may be, some students nevertheless freeze in the stance of victim, thereby shunning responsibility. Others jump on the attack bandwagon.[6] Where there are only one or two students in any of the minority categories, there's a danger of voyeurism, or of one or two people pressed into service, or appointing themselves, as spokespeople. At Hamilton, the few people of color were usually so surrounded by an overwhelming white majority that individuals among them had little space in which to individuate distinct experience (e.g., Bronx-born Puerto Rican, Brazilian immigrant, Japanese foreign student, California-born Filipina, Trinidadian, African American), much less examine complex concepts like authenticity, passing, race vs. ethnicity, or ownership of history.

At Brooklyn College, my students were working adults singled out for high ability, who had already studied together for three semesters, creating a fierce and joyful bonding.[7] The class had more women than men but the skew was far less than in a Women's Studies class, and the racial, class, and national diversity disrupted the centrality of gender and demanded a true multiple focus. While my bias and perspective were explicit, there was significant political range in the class, as well as a willingness to challenge received wisdom. There was not a topic we investigated that did not have at least two or three partisans, plus a Canadian to interrogate privatized health care, an ex-con to rehumanize the category of "inmate," many union members, a number of Caribbean folks of different ages and class origin, a French-born Israeli-raised orthodox Jewish woman, a Brooklyn-born woman of Syrian descent, a man whose mother is Ojibwe. It is in this educational opportunity that I see most dazzlingly the gifts of a diverse student body. Conversations about identity and authenticity, for example, were remarkable. The man whose mother is Native American (call him Jim) came to talk to me about his term paper. Jim was not taught about his heritage and moves through his life essentially passing as a white man. He wanted to focus on his identity, but was not sure he had the "right" to do so, a self-conscious uncertainty that characterizes the post-immigrant generation in many diasporic communities.[8] Earlier that week another student, an African American woman (call her Lisa), had spoken in class about growing up as an army brat taught nothing about her own identity and culture. It was easy for me to ask Jim if he thought anyone would challenge Lisa's "right" to explore her roots. Why not? Because Lisa's African descent shows? In that moment I could see Jim deepen his sense of entitlement to his own past. His project revealed a growing recognition that identity is not a fixed commodity but a process in which he participates, consciously or not, a recognition with far-ranging implications for diaspora studies.

Negotiating Bigotry?

As a teacher it's different—I started to write easier, but the truth is it's sometimes easier, sometimes harder, but usually *different*—for me to confront, point to, examine bigotry around categories of oppression that I share. For example: I am always out as a lesbian. In the Brooklyn College class, three or four students were also out. When we were learning about heterosexism, several students volunteered that, according to their religion, homosexuality is a sin. The freewheeling discussion that followed was fantastic. I did not tell them they were wrong. Perhaps because I am an out lesbian I felt able to catch and handle whatever they threw, and could frame again and again what they were saying in terms of their beliefs. And I felt confident that the gay and lesbian students would not feel exposed or undermined.

Important too that at the point in the discussion where most students were sort of longing for liberal resolution—the students in this class were close and no one wanted to hurt anyone else or even really to acknowledge the deep disagreement—at that point I explained the difference between calling someone a homophobe (or a sexist or a racist) and *naming a given practice or statement* as homophobic. Encircling the behavior or language allows for change; no one *has* to repeat the offensive act. But, I go on, recycling the words of the sin-invoking students, thinking it's better to be heterosexual *is* homophobic. Refusing to attend a homosexual wedding because it's homosexual *is* homophobic.

And then we sit there, together, liking each other immensely, with the knowledge of our differences. It's not comfortable, but why should it be?

On the other hand, I have noticed that, as a white/Jewish woman dealing with race, I'm much more likely to run interference, especially if the classroom is heavily white; much more apt to cut off racist statements and to try to contain a weird kind of curiosity that seems to manifest when white students get the opportunity to interrogate an actual person of color (suddenly metamorphosed into cultural ambassador) about everything they've ever wanted to know about. . . . In these situations I am not always sure how much to control and deflect. I have to monitor my impulse to protect, which may or may not be appropriate as either a teacher or a white ally on these issues. The difference, I think, is as a queer (a woman, a Jew, a person with working-class roots) I have considerable faith in my own radar. As a teacher openly asserting my identities, I create some sense of protection around those identities. Students are likely to assume, even if I allow bigotry temporary airtime, that I do not share it. With identities that I don't share, on the other hand, students have no such guarantee, no such sense of protection; thus I feel obliged to provide it. But there are no rules with which to determine when to step forward or back off. A teacher has to develop instincts, which means, being willing to make mistakes. I hone my instincts by checking out later with students with whom I have strong rapport and can ask freely, should I have, did you wish, did that feel, what did you wish I would do?

Negotiating bigotry is especially difficult when the class makeup itself is very skewed. Teaching about racism to an all or nearly all-white class is painful and stiff. At SUNY-New Paltz, in an impossibly compressed summer-school version of this course, once again under the Women's Studies banner, students were all women, almost all white (one Puertorriqueña), and mostly young (two over 40). Predictably, discussions on race were unsatisfying and formulaic, ranging from the stereotype to the anecdotal exception. This is delicate, because recognizing diversity of experience is one form of challenging bigotry; only in this way can individuality emerge. On the other hand, the dialectical counterpart: we need to grasp how shared categories of structural oppression often suppress and override individuality; only in this way can we confront oppression. To make this point I often pull out Pat Parker's wise poem, "For the white person who wants to know how to be my friend," which opens:

> The first thing you do is to forget that I'm Black.
> Second, you must never forget that I'm Black.[9]

Balancing between themes of individual and collective identity and experience is a task for the feminist/progressive[10] educator. Next time I confront a mostly-white class I will tap the college's speakers budget or my friendship network to bring to class a guest panel of women of color activists, and I will ask white students to focus sharply on white people's relationship to racism.

The truth is, in the social justice classroom the students' attitudes and experience are part of our texts. This is rewarding and complicated. When issues of sexism, racism, class, or other experiences of oppression are discussed, students get angry, at the issues and at other students' attitudes. At Hamilton, a white woman, eyes brimming with tears, relates how Elsie, the African American housekeeper who raised her, was really family, and a Latina counters, "Who was raising Elsie's children?" A white man blurts out, "Why do we need pigeonholes, why can't you see me as a person?" "You make us feel guilty for being straight," two sorority sisters accuse the in-your-face class queers. At Brooklyn College, an African American woman cuts through vapid generalizations about welfare: *I've been on public assistance,* she says, and a white businessman begins to interrogate her about her experience until finally she says, *I don't want to be the welfare poster child.* At this point, I—risking that mistake I mentioned earlier—choose to comment on the businessman's sense of entitlement in seeking to gratify his curiosity. For the instructor, finding the delicate balance between supporting the anger while keeping the classroom a safe place takes skill, tact, time, and attention to group process, including figuring out when students need to meet in small groups and divided according to what logic.

This is more elaborate than it sounds. When we focus on gender, groups divide into women and men. On sexuality, I ask them to self-identify (a tactic that could only work in explicitly tolerant settings; otherwise I'd problematize the issue, explaining why I'm *not* asking people to self-identify). Given the usual paucity of out queer students, I group them together, and the straight students likewise—though I think for traditional age students, at least, it would be wise to create a group for exploring students unwilling or unable to pin themselves down. On race, it depends on numbers: where possible, I create one group for students of color, one for white/Christian students, and one for Jews[11]—a problematic compromise that would be disrupted (in a very educational way!) by the presence of Jews who are also people of color,[12] and of Muslims, Hindus, Sikhs, and others who are neither Christian nor Jewish.

Class origin is most convoluted. I ask each student to complete a form that elicits concrete data about class status, and then I use these forms to divide students into groups of similar class backgrounds. Students are often angry about these forms, perceiving them as intrusive, a reaction that makes for fascinating discussion. Student difficulty in determining their own class background, and their resistance to divulging it, also become part of our text. Why don't parents (which parents?) talk to their children about income and assets? Why is it more acceptable in our culture(s) to ask people how often they have sex than to ask how much money they earn?

I have not yet divided students into small groups for our discussion of nation, a point which occurs to me only as I write this article; I think division around family history and current immigration and citizenship status would reveal new perspectives and new layers of meaning. The mix-and-match format for small groups works well to create multiple bonds, though a small "why can't we just be people?" contingent never quite abandons a preference for discreet silence.

"We're All Middle Class, Right"?

At Hamilton the topic of economic class had enormous power. Class background groups were hugely important for the poor and working-class students, serving to strengthen their (few) collective and individual voices. There is always electricity in the room when I explain—an obvious point that rarely gets made—that while differences in gender, race, and so on, do not inherently dictate inequality, class structure cannot exist without inequality because class *is* inequality. In this section of the class I try to make capitalism as a system visible. I talk about the traditional Marxist definition of surplus value, and suggest expanding the concept of surplus value to include the gap between what a professional woman might earn and what she pays another woman to perform her reproductive labor (housekeeping, cooking, childcare, and even, at the current historical moment, actual pregnancy). I include materials on increasing income disparity, and on welfare rights and workfare.

Some of the most provocative and engaging student projects have centered on class. At Hamilton, one focused on how students perceived and treated housekeeping and janitorial staff at the college. (This project also included an analysis of dynamics between the student coauthors, an Asian-Pacific woman whose mother is a housekeeper and an upper-class European man.) Another project organized a cost-sharing experiment; drawing on the work of Felice Yeskel,[13] this student elicited class identity from a group of friends at the college, and through open discussion of this information, facilitated the group's allocation of the cost of eating dinner at a restaurant in a way that "felt fair" to all of them, thus breaking through the silence around money that often pervades even close friendships, and modeling an approach not strictly based on private property.

Even at Brooklyn College, where students were relatively sophisticated about class (mostly working- and lower-middle-class origin, with several—all women of color—who'd grown up on or had themselves received public assistance), discussion was still charged with a sense of discovery. When a white woman in her fifties who identified very strongly as working class described herself at one moment as a nice white middle class woman, I could point to what she'd just said and, together, we could investigate the mechanism whereby she'd momentarily "forgotten" her class because it conflicted with her sense of normality: when she wanted to emphasize her privilege (white and heterosexual and presumably not poor, not dependent) the language available to her was "middle class."

At SUNY-New Paltz, in a crammed summer session with no time for students to fill out class background sheets, I let the students talk me into convening random class groups. Mistake! I should know by now that students, at least in the United States, almost always resist breaking up into small groups, especially by category, and the results were startlingly predictable. One small group reported back to the class that they were "pretty much the same background." When I reminded them that in earlier discussions one of these women had volunteered that she'd grown up on public assistance and another, that her family was upper middle class, they mumbled, "that was growing up, we were talking about *now*." Without the opportunity to share experience with folks of similar class background, these mostly young women had missed the significance of background, and had performed that ultimate bourgeois housekeeping chore of conferring sameness. The poor and working-class students had not found their voices in this exercise, and I was the main learner: sometimes you can't skip steps. Much as I would like to hurry students through the time-consuming labyrinths of group process, learning sometimes takes time.

Reverse Racism?

In Women's Studies classes, I find that there is usually a core of students who will parrot basic truths, including some that could use examination by a fresh eye. The question, for example, can people of color be racist? long answered with, *No, only white people can be racist because racism is power + prejudice and people of color lack power.* . . . I have come to believe that this formulation rests on an assumption that race divides into stark opposites, white and black, and fails to acknowledge the unequal power and relationship of different communities of color to white supremacy and to class structure. I try to challenge the knee-jerk response in two ways. First by posing examples that break apart the easy binaries.

> Well then, poor whites—do they have power?
> *Relative to people of color, yes.*
> A white woman on Aid to Families with Dependent Children (AFDC) and a Pakistani male surgeon?

Women's Studies students, often generous about granting victim status to everyone except white men or even rich white Christian heterosexual men, may end up in the untenable position of asserting that only a very few have any power at all. . . .

And everyone else? Does anything they do have any impact?

Without measuring white skin privilege vs. class privilege vs. gender privilege, as if any of these privileges had legs and could themselves enter the ring and duke it out, I usually try to lead students to at least recognize that someone can be privileged along one axis and subordinated along another. Even with regard to a single axis—say, racism—the question isn't really, *who can and can't be racist?* Rather it's *did X or Y commit an act that objectively speaking strengthens racism?*—thus forcing students to contextualize whatever *any* individual does inside a system of white supremacy. This formulation helps us distinguish between, say, can a Pakistani male surgeon inflict racist practices upon a Haitian woman (his practices could strengthen racism), or, likewise, an African American woman gynecologist upon a Vietnamese woman (ditto); vs. can any person of color inflict racist practices upon anyone white? The larger context of white racism suggests that reverse racism is a nonsense phrase, yet contexts shift. A middle-class Mexican woman may be white in Mexico and "Hispanic" north of the border; a Ukrainian Jew is a Jew in Ukraine but "becomes" white when she arrives in the United States. Pointing to immigration is the easiest way to stress context, but I try also to explain context as an historical narrative. I lead students through a relatively uncharged paradigm, my own position as a woman professor. I'm not a CEO, I say, but in this classroom, I grade you, I can write you letters of reference, I can praise or embarrass you. Minor power, granted: but can I be sexist against male students? Usually our well-trained Women's Studies students respond, No, I can't. I try to shift the question from *can I be* (never mind, *would I be*) to *what would happen if I were?*

At this point I back up to trace the path of ascent to this position. How did I get here? I ask them, and then get very specific. I had to graduate from college and go through years of graduate school, where virtually all of my professors were men. What would have happened if, as a student, I had exhibited bias against men? Would I have received good grades; earned my degree; garnered positive letters of reference, fellowships, and so on? But that was then, I continue. Suppose I hid my bias or only recently developed it. What about now? Suppose I discriminated now? I talk about complaints to the chair or dean, common against Women's Studies professors and professors of color. How simple it is for men or for white people to assume they are being discriminated against; how super-fair feminists and people of color need to be, to protect against such accusations; how vulnerable people in subordinated groups are to charges of bias. Thus I press students to consider the larger world context in which a classroom or doctor's office or personnel regulation is situated, once again trying to teach the balancing act between an individual act—which can be infinitely eccentric—and the social pattern.

Violence Against Women / Against People of Color

In addition to the topic of economic class, the topic of violence against women always has great power—no surprise: at Hamilton College, for example, young women were raped at fraternity parties on an average of one a weekend. In class, connections between hate of all varieties was easy to draw, and when a lesbian student received an obscene threatening letter, I was proud that it was students from this class who leapt into action, covering the campus with graffiti and hundreds of copies of the hate letter, transformed by their comments.

We also try to integrate the sexism and racism that shape the historical and contemporary para-military aspect of women's oppression. Through the work of Kimberlé Crenshaw[14] and Angela Davis,[15] we wrestle with decentering the experience of (white) women and (male) blacks. Through my own work on violence and resistance, we explore the magnitude of violence against women, and the significance of women's frequent reluctance to even consider self-defense.[16] One of our most provocative discussions in the Brooklyn College class came from a woman who questioned why she would not hesitate to use violence to protect her children but could not imagine using violence on her own behalf.

In spring of 1999, as I was teaching this class, I was also one of the more than 1,200 people who engaged in civil disobedience and were arrested—many of them for the first time—to protest the police murder of Amadou Diallo[17] in particular, and police brutality and harassment in general. Planning lessons about violence against women while dealing on a daily basis with organizing against police brutality underscored for me the interconnectedness of the various systems of power and domination. Looking—side by side—at violence against women and police violence, battering and brutality, sexual harassment and police harassment, it was hard to miss the connection: random individualized violence where the victim is blamed and the perpetrators seem to be acting both as out of control "rogues" and as conspirators in some vast unspoken plot, the goal of which is to humiliate and degrade a whole people, to terrorize, to restrict freedom of movement, of expression, even (if you consider how fear can obsess and control) to restrict freedom of thought: ultimately to shrink and diminish a people's capacities. We examined the instability of the categories: how police brutality is often sexual brutality, the rape of Abner Louima[18] providing an especially vicious example; how violence against women often includes sexual brutality and may also be police brutality (note the high rate of wife-battering by police officers).

Finally we consider the point of stretching across the boundaries into which categories sometimes constrict our brains: the point is not only intellectual mastery but political strategy. If we understand how to see simultaneously, we increase our ability to organize our constituencies together, beyond the smallness of identity politics toward the mass movements that solution requires. In a guest class at Brooklyn College, and again this summer at SUNY-New Paltz, long-time New York City organizer Leslie Cagan raised the possibility of a Take Back the Night mobilization that would target both sets of violence, and we spent some time discussing what such an effort would demand, and what obstacles stand in the way.

Beyond the Self

Students are predictably most detached from the "nation" unit, even at Brooklyn College where nearly half were immigrants. I found films and guest speakers invaluable for embodying abstractions like *sweatshops* or *International Monetary Fund*, and for teasing out the relationship between the United States and these concepts (foreign aid, sweatshops at home as well as abroad, union busting, and so on). Speakers have included Saraswati Sunindyo on feminism and militarism in Indonesia, JoAnn Lum on organizing women sweatshop workers in New York's Chinatown, international health worker Chris Fung on globalization and development, Charlotte Bunch on international women's rights/human rights, and Moustafa Bayoumi on postcolonial theory. Films on Nike plants and on the School of the Americas are also useful, as is the fast-paced and witty *Black Nations/Queer Nation* (which yokes together race, sexuality, and postcolonial thought in interesting and provocative ways).

Initially I focused on U.S. power wielded in the world, and on exposing the normative construction of West=modern vs. the global postcolonial perspectives of Mohanty and Amrita Basu.[19] More recently, Anne McClintock's "'No Longer in a Future Heaven': Gender, Race, and Nationalism,"[20] helped me and at least some of the students grasp the critical category of citizenship as entitlement, though the article's convoluted language led one student to explode bravely, "You're torturing me, I'm being tortured" (followed by substantial concurrence). This exploration of citizenship as privilege decodes the contemporary shift in progressive discourse from civil rights to human rights. This section of the class would be especially useful to students preparing to study or work abroad, especially if paired with some kind of framework for return-decompression.

What changes would I introduce to this course? As noted above, there are no shortcuts through personal experience. The theoretical articles on their own do not grab students, and the combination of first-person narratives and experiential-based small group discussion is essential. In addition, because— let's face it—things are pretty bad, this class can feel overwhelming and depressing. What militates against depression are the stories of resistance: for example, Palestinian American poet Naomi Shihab Nye's "Banned Poem,"[21] interviews with Israeli peace activist Veronika Cohen[22] and with labor organizer Katie Quan, working with Chinese immigrant women;[23] films like *Salt of the Earth* and *Ballot Measure 9*; guests like the Urban Justice Center's Heidi Dorow, organizing workfare workers. From now on, I would consciously include with each topic some information about resistance.

Finally, I plan to add a unit on religious hegemony. I think we—feminists and progressives—have regularly underestimated the role played by religion in demonizing various groups and thus justifying oppression, from anti-Semitic scapegoating of Jews for the evils of capitalism,[24] to Calvinist assumptions that poverty is a sign of damnation, wealth a sign of divine blessing, assumptions that so readily translate into "the undeserving and immoral poor." I think, too, the relationship between Christianity and colonialism, and Christianity and whiteness has barely been explored. The anti-Western, anticolonialist edge of fundamentalist practice needs to be understood, in order for us, in the West, to understand the struggles of women around the world against the range of fundamentalisms. Attention to Christian hegemony in the United States seems critical: to counter media hyperemphasis on Muslim fundamentalism, and to investigate possibilities of alliance among religious and sexual minorities confronting a rising and virulent Christianity. At the same time, students need to attend to the complexity of "Christianities": the liberatory power of the African American churches in the struggle for black liberation and of Latino liberation theology in the quest for social and economic justice. And, on a third hand, students need to understand that most religious institutions constrict the options of women and deny the holiness of queer sexuality. The documentary *Ballot Measure 9*, about organizing against the homophobic ballot measure in Oregon, is extremely useful not only for modeling resistance, as mentioned above, but also for recognizing how other subordinated groups responded contextually to a danger they recognized as also their own: in Oregon, where the Klan was organizing early in this century, Jewish organizations and institutions unanimously opposed the measure, and Catholics voted significantly against it. Discussions can be built around comparing these facts with, for example, church response to the multicultural Rainbow Curriculum in New York City in the early nineties: most church groups—including black and Latino churches—opposed the curriculum because it included gays and lesbians in the Rainbow.

I have come to believe that the appropriate place for this class is as an all-college requirement. I think this is the direction in which Women's Studies needs to press: we need some minimal level of integration into the college curriculum. Instead, Women's Studies, especially at public institutions, is under attack by the same forces that savage affirmative action and public assistance, trash immigrants, defend courses that depict happy slaves, and relentlessly pump out misinformation to keep all of us at each other's throats. Witness a recent report that "many educators are beginning to think boys should get more attention," pitting the educational needs of girls against boys, and, more insidiously, against students of color—as if such concerns are mutually exclusive.[25] The intersections of gender, race, class and nation are not abstract. What's needed is a post-postmodernism to move beyond fragmented identities, to rebuild the bridges between theoretical and practical work that characterized the best of early Women's Studies. And, as also characterized that time, the struggles to create and sustain the courses, programs, and curricula we seek, are part of our learning curve feminist educators can share with our students.

Notes

Portions of this essay appeared, in earlier versions as "Liberation Studies Now?" in *Women's Review of Books* (1999) and "When Did Politically Correct Become a Dirty Word? Theory and Practice for the Social Justice Classroom" in *Transformations* (Fall 1999).

1. As a product of 1960s radical education movements strongly tied to the Civil Rights and student rights movements, I've always had my students call me by my first name, as I call them by theirs. And though I continue this practice, I'm less comfortable in the light of information from women of color colleagues that they are much more likely to use their full titles to assert authority with white students, whose only experience with women of color may well be as nannies and other service workers in their family homes.

2. Chandra Mohanty, "Under Western Eyes," in *Third World Women and the Politics of Feminism,* eds., Mohanty, Russo, and Torres (Bloomington: Indiana University Press, 1991); Edward Said, "Reflections on Exile," *Granta*

(Autumn 1984), 13; Maia Ettinger, "The Pocahontas Paradigm, or Will the Subaltern Please Shut Up?" in *Tilting the Tower*, ed., Linda Garber (New York and London: Routledge, 1994.)

3. Jamaica Kincaid, "Mariah," *Lucy* (New York: Penguin, 1991).

4. Kimberlé Williams Crenshaw, "Beyond Racism and Misogyny: Black Feminism and 2 Live Crew," in *Women Transforming Politics*, eds., Cohen, Jones, and Tronto (New York & London: New York University Press, 1997).

5. Ama Ata Aidoo, *Our Sister Killjoy* (Essex, England: Longman, 1988).

6. See my discussion of the Good White Knight, who positions her/himself as the only white "good" on racism, which s/he demonstrates by attacking and shaming other whites ("Anti-Semitism, Homophobia, and the Good White Knight," *off our backs* [May 1982]). The "Good _____ Knight" can manifest among any dominant group.

7. The Special Baccalaureate program, in the Adult Degree Programs.

8. Diaspora as applied to indigenous people is a complicated concept, since diaspora means, literally, dispersal, scattering, exactly the opposite of (in the United States) concentrating people onto reservations. In addition, diaspora, implying as it does "immigration," seems to run counter to the meaning of indigenous. However, in the United States national borders are not congruent with the borders of tribal lands. Most indigenous people in the United States (i.e., that small percentage who survived Manifest Destiny) were driven from their ancestral lands. Furthermore, the shift in population center of the majority of Native Americans from reservations to urban centers qualifies in my mind as a diaspora of major proportions.

9. In *Movement in Black* (Ithaca, New York: Firebrand Press, 1990; 1st pub. 1978).

10. It breaks my heart to yield the word "radical," my first impulse; but with the increasing yoking of radical to right, one can't any longer use radical unmodified to signify "left." Progressive, though more wishy-washy (I think of it as fifties code for left), at least points in a particular direction: forward.

11. I ask them to answer the following questions: 1. Describe your growing-up family and your race/ethnic/class/cultural/religious background. 2. What other peoples were around in your growing-up neighborhood(s)? What were your/your family's relationships to them? 3. What are your earliest memories of color other than your own? What information were you given to deal with these differences? 4. What are your relationships with people across lines of color now?

12. For a full-fledged exploration of the question of Jews and whiteness, see Melanie Kaye/Kantrowitz, "Jews, Class, Color, and the Cost of Whiteness," in *The Issue Is Power: Essays on Women, Jews, Violence, and Resistance* (San Francisco: Aunt Lute, 1992); and "Jews in the U.S.: The Rising Costs of Whiteness," in *Names We Call Home: Autobiography on Racial Identity*, eds. Becky Thompson and Sangeeta Tyagi (New York and London: Routledge, 1996).

13. "Coming Out About Money: Cost Sharing Across Class Lines," in *Bridges: A Journal for Jewish Feminists and our Friends* (Vol. 3, No.1).

14. See note 4 above.
15. "Rape, Racism, and the Myth of the Black Rapist," in *Women, Race, and Class* (New York: Random House, 1981).
16. Melanie Kaye/Kantrowitz, "Women, Violence, and Resistance: Naming it War," in *The Issue Is Power: Essays on Women, Jews, Violence, and Resistance* (San Francisco: Aunt Lute, 1992).
17. An unarmed Guyanan immigrant standing in the lobby of his own Bronx apartment building, Diallo was shot by four un-uniformed police officers who fired 41 bullets; 19 of these hit Diallo.
18. A Haitian immigrant taken into police custody in the Flatbush section of Brooklyn, Louima was tortured and raped with a broomstick at police headquarters.
19. For Mohanty, see note 2, above. Amrita Basu, ed., *The Challenge of Local Feminisms: Women's Movements in Global Perspective* (Boulder, Colorado: Westview, Press, 1995).
20. Anne McClintock, in *Dangerous Liaisons: Gender, Nation and Postcolonial Perspectives*, eds. McClintock, Mufti, and Shohat (Minneapolis: University of Minnesota, 1997).
21. From *Never In a Hurry: Essays on People and Places* (Columbia: University. of South Carolina Press, 1996), and the banned poem itself, "For the 500th Dead Palestinian, Ibtisam Bozieh," *Red Suitcase* (Brockport, New York: BOA Editions, 1994).
22. In *Visionary Voices: Women on Power,* Interviews by Penny Rosenwasser (San Francisco: Aunt Lute, 1992).
23. Ruth Milkman, "Organizing Immigrant Women in New York's Chinatown: An Interview with Katie Quan," in *Women's Lives: Multicultural Perspectives,* eds., Kirk and Okazawa-Rey (Mountainview, California: Mayfield, 1998).
24. German Socialist August Bebel dubbed anti-Semitism "the socialism of fools."
25. Tamar Lewin, "How Boys Lost Out to Girl Power," *NY Times Week-In-Review* (Dec. 13, 1998), p. 3.

Works Cited

Aidoo, Ama Ata. *Our Sister Killjoy.* Essex, England: Longman, 1988.

Basu, Amrita, ed. *The Challenge of Local Feminisms: Women's Movements in Global Perspective.* Boulder, Colorado: Westview Press, 1995.

Crenshaw, Kimberlé Williams. "Beyond Racism and Misogyny: Black Feminism and 2 Live Crew." *Women Transforming Politics.* Eds., Cohen, Jones, and Tronto. New York and London: New York University Press, 1997.

Davis, Angela. "Rape, Racism, and the Myth of the Black Rapist." *Women, Race, and Class.* New York: Random House, 1981.

Ettinger, Maia. "The Pocahontas Paradigm, or Will the Subaltern Please Shut Up?" *Tilting the Tower.* Ed. Linda Garber. New York and London: Routledge, 1994.

Kaye/Kantrowitz, Melanie. "Anti-Semitism, Homophobia, and the Good White Knight." *off our backs* (May 1982).

————. "Jews, Class, Color, and the Cost of Whiteness." *The Issue Is Power: Essays on Women, Jews, Violence, and Resistance.* San Francisco: Aunt Lute, 1992.

————. "Jews in the U.S.: The Rising Costs of Whiteness." *Names We Call Home: Autobiography on Racial Identity.* Eds. Becky Thompson and Sangeeta Tyagi. New York and London: Routledge, 1996.

————. "Women, Violence, and Resistance: Naming it War." *The Issue Is Power: Essays on Women, Jews, Violence, and Resistance.* San Francisco: Aunt Lute, 1992.

Kincaid, Jamaica. "Mariah." *Lucy.* New York: Penguin, 1991.

Lewin, Tamar. "How Boys Lost Out to Girl Power." *NY Times Week-In-Review* (Dec. 13, 1998).

McClintock, Anne. "'No Longer in a Future Heaven': Gender, Race, and Nationalism." *Dangerous Liaisons: Gender, Nation and Postcolonial Perspectives.* Eds. McClintock, Mufti, and Shohat. Minneapolis: University of Minnesota, 1997.

Milkman, Ruth. "Organizing Immigrant Women in New York's Chinatown: An Interview with Katie Quan." *Women's Lives: Multicultural Perspectives.* Eds., Kirk and Okazawa-Rey. Mountainview, California: Mayfield, 1998.

Mohanty, Chandra Talpade. "Under Western Eyes." *Third World Women and the Politics of Feminism.* Eds., Mohanty, Russo, and Torres. Bloomington: Indiana Univ. Press, 1991.

Nye, Naomi Shihab. "Banned Poem." *Never In a Hurry: Essays on People and Places.* Columbia: Univ. of South Carolina Press, 1996.

————. "For the 500th Dead Palestinian, Ibtisam Bozieh." *Red Suitcase.* Brockport, NY: BOA Editions, 1994.

Parker, Pat. *Movement in Black.* Ithaca, NY: Firebrand Press, 1990; 1st pub. 1978.

Rosenwasser, Penny. *Visionary Voices: Women on Power.* San Francisco: Aunt Lute, 1992.

Said, Edward. "Reflections on Exile." *Granta* (Autumn 1984).

Yeskel, Felice. "Coming Out About Money: Cost Sharing Across Class Lines." *Bridges: A Journal for Jewish Feminists and Our Friends.* Vol. 3, No.1.

CONTRIBUTORS

BAT-AMI BAR ON teaches Philosophy and Women's Studies at Binghamton University (SUNY). Her primary theoretical and activist interests are in violence, though she escapes them (often?) by pursuing other themes. She is the author of *The Subject of Violence: Arendtean Exercises in Understanding* (Lanham: Rowman and Littlefield, 2002) and the editor of *Jewish Locations: Traversing Racialized Landscapes* with Lisa Tessman (Lanham: Rowman and Littlefield, 2001); *Daring to be Good: Essays in Feminist Ethico-Politics* with Ann Ferguson, (New York: Routledge, 1998); *Women and Violence: a special issue of Hypatia* (Fall 1996); *Engendering Origins: Critical Feminist Readings of Plato and Aristotle;* and *Modern Engenderings: Critical Feminist Readings in the History of Modern Western Philosophy* (both, Albany: State University of New York, 1994).

ALLISON DORSEY is an assistant professor of History at Swarthmore College, where she teaches several courses in African American history including "Black Women in the Civil Rights Movement" and "Black Communities, 1800–2000." She is the author of *To Build Our Lives Together: Community Formation in Black Atlanta, 1875–1906,* forthcoming from the University of Georgia Press. She is currently at work on a history of black migrants and white migrant aid committees in New York.

MICHIKO HASE is an assistant professor of Women's Studies at the University of Colorado at Boulder. Her research interests include historical and contemporary relations between African Americans and Japanese, and globalization and sports with a focus on race and gender.

MARGARET HUNTER is an assistant professor of sociology at Loyola Marymount University in Los Angeles. Her areas of specialization include skin-color stratification, intersections of race, class, and gender, race and pedagogy, and feminist theory. Most of her research focuses on issues of skin color and beauty for African American and Mexican American women. She has published several articles in these areas including, "'If You're Light You're Alright': Light Skin Color as Social Capital for Women of Color" in *Gender*

& Society, April 2002; "What About the White Women? Racial Politics in a Women's Studies Classroom" with Kimberly Nettles in *Teaching Sociology* 27.4, October 1999, and "Colorstruck: Skin Color Stratification in the Lives of African American Women" in *Sociological Inquiry* 68.4, Fall 1998.

MELANIE KAYE/KANTROWITZ is a writer, scholar, teacher, and activist, born in Brooklyn and educated in the New York City public school system. She earned her Ph.D. in Comparative Literature from the University of California, Berkeley, where she taught the department's first course in Women's Studies. She has taught writing, Women's Studies, Jewish Studies, and race theory all over the United States, including as the Jane Watson Irwin Distinguished Professor of Women's Studies at Hamilton College, and the Belle Zeller Distinguished Professor of Public Policy at Brooklyn College-CUNY. She is currently the Director of the Queens College-CUNY Worker Education Extension Center in Manhattan. Dr. Kaye/Kantrowitz's work is widely published and anthologized in the feminist, gay and lesbian, and progressive Jewish press, and she is the author of several books, including *The Issue Is Power: Essays on Women, Jews, Violence, and Resistance; My Jewish Face & Other Stories;* and *Diaspora: A Novel.* She coedited *The Tribe of Dina: A Jewish Women's Anthology,* which, along with *The Issue Is Power* is widely taught in Women's Studies and philosophy classes. An activist since the early 1960s, she is the founding director of Jews for Racial and Economic Justice in New York City, and continues to serve as the organization's co-chair.

AMIE A. MACDONALD is an assistant professor of Philosophy at John Jay College/City University of New York, where she teaches courses in political philosophy, multicultural feminism, and the philosophy of law. She has published essays on the impact of nationalism, feminism, and racial identity in higher education.

ERIN MCKENNA is an associate professor of Philosophy at Pacific Lutheran University. Chair of Philosophy and former chair of Women's Studies, she specializes in feminist theory and American Pragmatism, focusing on issues of social and political philosophy. Her book, *The Task of Utopia: A Pragmatist and Feminist Perspective* (Rowman and Littlefield, 2001) focuses on the work of John Dewey. Some of her articles include "Women, Power, and Meat," "Feminism and Vegetarianism," "The Occupied West Bank," and "Some Reflections Concerning Feminist Pedagogy." Along with courses in feminism, pragmatism, and ape-language research, she teaches a service-learning course in ethics.

NANCY SORKIN RABINOWITZ teaches Comparative Literature at Hamilton College. Her research focuses on women in ancient Greece (*Anxiety Veiled:*

Euripides and the Traffic in Women [1993]; *Feminist Theory and the Classics,* coedited with Amy Richlin [1993]; *Women on the Edge: Four Plays by Euripides;* translated and edited *Alcestis* [1998]; *Among Women: From the Homosocial to the Homoerotic in Antiquity* [2002]). Her courses include feminist criticism, feminist theory, and most recently, "The Straight Story?: Revising the Romance." A lifelong advocate for social justice, Rabinowitz is the director of a multicultural feminist project at Hamilton, The Kirkland Project for the Study of Gender, Society, and Culture.

SUSAN SÁNCHEZ-CASAL is an associate professor of Latino and Women's Studies at Hamilton College in Clinton, New York, where she teaches courses on U.S. Latino/a literatures, Latin American women writers, and gender studies. Her research and scholarship focus on U.S. Latino/a literatures, women's testimonial literature in Latin America, and antiracist feminist theory and pedagogy.

BETTY SASAKI is an associate professor and chair of the Spanish Department at Colby College. Her teaching and research interests include early modern Spanish literature, U.S. Latina literature, critical pedagogy, and feminisms of color.

MARIA EVA VALLE received her Ph.D. in sociology from University California, San Diego in 1996, and is an assistant professor of Chicana/o Studies at the California State University, Dominguez Hills. She teaches courses on Latina/o political protest, Chicana/os in education, popular culture, gender, immigration, and community engagement. She writes on Chicana/o ethnic identity, transnational immigrant communities, Chicanas/Latinas, and Chicana/o intellectual traditions. She is currently working on a manuscript that analyzes differences between Chicana/o students of the 1970s and the contemporary generation, exploring how race and gender influences the complex process of identity formation, and changing patterns of activism.

TAMARA WILLIAMS is associate professor of Spanish at Pacific Lutheran University in Tacoma, Washington, where she teaches courses in Spanish Language, Latin American Literature, and Latino Studies. She is the author of several articles on contemporary Latin American poetry with a focus on historical narrative texts, poetry of resistance, and women poets of the *posmodernismo* era. She is also project coordinator of the bilingual edition of Nicaraguan poet Ernesto Cardenal's *The Doubtful Strait/ El estrecho dudoso* published by Indiana University Press in 1995. At PLU, she has held the position of chair of the Global Studies Program and of special assistant to the Provost for International Education.

Index